ANTHO

1989

Supervision of the Offender

Supervision of the Offender

Harold B. Trester

Former Probation Officer
Colorado Springs Municipal Court
Colorado Springs, Colorado

Prentice-Hall, Inc., Englewood Cliffs, New Jersey 07632

Library of Congress Cataloging in Publication Data

Trester, Harold B
    Supervision of the offender.

    (Prentice-Hall series in criminal justice)
    Includes index.
    1. Probation—United States. 2. Parole—United
States. I. Title.
HV9304.T72   364.6 '3 '0973   80-17257
ISBN 0-13-876938-9

Prentice-Hall Series in Criminal Justice
James D. Stinchcomb, Editor

Editorial production/supervision and interior design by *Natalie Krivanek.*
Cover design by: *Mirian Recio*
Manufacturing buyer: *Gordon Osbourne*

Printed in the United States of America

10 9 8 7 6 5 4 3 2 1

Prentice-Hall International, Inc., *London*
Prentice-Hall of Australia Pty. Limited, *Sydney*
Prentice-Hall of Canada, Ltd., *Toronto*
Prentice-Hall of India Private Limited, *New Delhi*
Prentice-Hall of Japan, Inc., *Tokyo*
Prentice-Hall of Southeast Asia Pte. Ltd., *Singapore*
Whitehall Books Limited, *Wellington, New Zealand*

To the Honorable Donald E. Campbell
and the Honorable Matt M. Railey
for their social consciousness.

To my family
for their patience and endurance.

To many others
for their encouragement and assistance.

Contents

Preface

Speaking from a general point of view, it might be said that books serve two very basic purposes—enjoyment and enlightenment. Most of us indulge in literature with these goals in mind—to relax and enjoy or to study and learn. The mark of a classical author is the ability to repeatedly combine these qualities without loss of purpose or loss of readers.

This book attempts to integrate these qualities. It encompasses the historical and legal growth of the professions but it is not intended to burden the reader with theoretical and statistical presentation as this would only serve to limit its appeal. There should be a little bit of something for everyone contained in these pages.

Even though probation/parole is not classically considered a cornerstone in the social services complex, it cannot be denied that it is people working with people in a helping situation. Those of us who have worked in this capacity are well aware of the sickness and the sadness, the mirth and the madness that characterize this endeavor. In an effort to give the reader a vivid and realistic portrayal, some of these elements must be a part of the contents, as a garnish so to speak.

There is nothing hypocritical about a professional criticizing his profession as long as he does so constructively. A book of this nature, in order to be reasonably objective, must look at the correctional field as the house in which we live and perform, for whatever satisfactions we hope to achieve, and with whatever frustrations we may encounter.

It is hoped that the reader may come to appreciate the function of this aspect of corrections. It is indeed unfortunate that our society today is so outspoken in regard to the legal system. The paradox seems to be that the system is good if it protects us and that it is bad if it prosecutes us. Perhaps this reaction may be attributed, in part, to a general lack of knowledge of the professions to be examined here. It is my hope that this particular link in the chain of the criminal justice system will be better understood after reading this book.

Supervision of the Offender

1

Probation and Parole —Misconceived and Misunderstood

If we stop to consider the meanings implied in the phrase "contemporary social issues," a variety of subjects may well pass on parade in our mind's eye. And, like a parade, which always includes some very basic groups, it is also true that certain social problems will always be present in the world. Conditions such as pestilence and plagues, wars and crimes, are but some of the social maladies that have held a consistent place throughout history. But the ability of these social maladies to persevere and to exist is not half as noteworthy as is our inability to understand and to control them.

CRIME

Of the four social problems mentioned above, there is little doubt that crime is the most consistent in its ability to survive. It is simply big business, and there is always a ready and receptive market for its existence. Countless theories have been advanced for the growth of crime,[1] but the simple matter is that it represents a profitable venture in the hands of the criminally inclined despite the risks and liabilities involved. Just how big a business it really is, when measured from a monetary standpoint, can only be speculated upon, although in a recent syndicated newscast a figure of $60 billion was suggested in cost alone to the citizens of the United States. This is very prob-

[1]James Q. Wilson, *Thinking About Crime* (New York: Basic Books, Inc., Publishers, 1975), chap. 3.

1

ably a conservative figure, and there are too many variables to accurately gauge its authenticity. Like viewing the size of an iceberg floating in arctic waters, we may be able to account for and measure the density of its visible parts, but we know that the magnitude hidden below can be as much as nine times larger than what is visible above. In a similar manner, we can only guess about the total cost of crime.

Many well-conceived and well-intended reports such as the Federal Bureau of Investigation *Uniform Crime Reports* may be compared to our iceberg. What remains obscured are the crimes that go unreported, including the inability to effectively gauge the emotional as well as the physical losses of the victims, not only the price paid by the family of the offender but that paid to maintain his family in social service dollars upon his incarceration, the financial input crime syndicates must invest in the maintenance of their levels of functioning and organizations, and perhaps most difficult of all to measure, the "grey area" of crime—meaning those acts that are of a moral nature rather than of a legal nature.

Leonard Savitz stresses that a large number of illegal acts committed require many man-hours on the part of law enforcement officers as well as of the courts, but these acts do not really constitute criminal activities.[2] In his book *Dilemmas in Criminology,* Savitz wonders about what might be called "nuisance responses" required of the police and how, if at all, these statistics are accounted for in the *Uniform Crime Reports.*[3]

For example, there are many offenses that could result in the arrest of the offender, and these might well be categorized by this author as being as much immoral acts as illegal ones, recognizing that morality is the midwife of our legal system and its countless laws and ordinances. I refer to what was previously described as the "grey area" of crime. This category would include gambling, prostitution, and the indulgence in hard-core sexual literature and related sexual paraphernelia as well as certain self-inflicted drug and alcohol abuses. Statistical reports such as the *Uniform Crime Reports* account for a small number of these crimes, even when there is reason to believe that their existence is related to organized criminal activities. As another example, consider the housewife who acts in a sexually promiscuous manner. She may technically not be guilty of criminal behavior. She may be merely acting out of boredom or some unmet/undefined psychological need(s) rather than for economic gratification. Thus, there exist no scientific measuring tools to gauge this level of existence, one in which such activities are indulged in by "noncriminal" citizens.

Crime is certainly a contemporary issue. Rare, for example, is the politi-

[2]Leonard Savitz, *Dilemmas in Criminology* (New York: McGraw-Hill Book Company, 1967), pp. 31–33.

[3]Ibid., p. 32.

cian who does not have a plank somewhere in his preelection platform that does not deal with crime and/or justice in some manner. The citizenry can readily relate to this stand, since we as victims, taxpayers, or acquaintances are going to be—directly or indirectly—exposed to some act of crime in our lifetime even if it be petty in nature. Crime and justice are also very broad and general issues, as is the public's conception of them.

UNAWARENESS THROUGH NONASSOCIATION

Superficiality, a term used here to denote the lack of insight, is a human characteristic that regretfully seems to be forever present in certain aspects of our lives. There is a plethora of reasons why we tend to see things in certain perspectives. This may be due to the fact that we are never quite ready to acknowledge things as they really are. We tend to comfortably tuck ourselves into a warm fantasy world because it is uncomfortable to look at the cold facts of reality. This tendency to be superficial might have something to do with our selfish and personal self-concepts, concepts that are more acceptable to us when we call them "vested interests." More direct, but perhaps no less distasteful in critical self-evaluation, is the fact of our lack of awareness or misunderstanding, which may be bluntly referred to as an *ignorance* of the complexities and dynamics of crime and criminal behavior.

Ignorance and apathy should be accorded the privilege of joining slothfulness and lust on the eternal list of no-no's. There are many people today who would support the theory that not knowing and caring less are both sins of the greatest magnitude, sins that undoubtedly contribute to contemporary problems. Obviously, concern by itself about crime is not sufficient to serve as a deterrent. The real worry is that we are not masters of our own destiny because we cannot control or regulate our fate beyond a certain unknown point. We may practice abstinence as regards our own participation in criminal behavior, but we cannot offer up much more than a fervent prayer that we will not be the victim of such activity. We can only hope that as we contribute our governmental tithes, a portion of them will be used in an attempt to combat and to contain crime.

There remains a vital need for a message to be brought forth on behalf of corrections in general, and on behalf of probation and parole in particular. Despite the fact that probation and parole are indispensable elements in the criminal justice system, up to now little formal attention has been given to either of these services in correctional literature, past or contemporary. However, the National Advisory Commission on Criminal Justice Standards and Goals in its 1973 report entitled *Corrections* states that "probation is viewed as the brightest hope for corrections" and implies that this same service is the main hope for the handling of offenders who do not need to be institutionalized.[4] The same study also states that "parole is the predominent mode of release from prisons for inmates today and it is likely to become even more so."[5]

When such a well-conceived and researched document as *Corrections* places such a high priority on probation and parole services, why, then, is there not more emphasis on the true nature of the functions of these services? It is believed that there are two basic explanations for the general lack of published information and public knowledge. First, it must be initially acknowledged that these are anything but glamorous professions. The clients are neither desirous of the services offered nor are they the most pleasant to work with. The target individual—the offender—is even less likely to recommend these services as being instrumental in his change than he is to advertise the fact that he is an ex-con/offender. Another related factor is that probation and parole officers are not often accorded any professional recognition outside their immediate ranks, and the public conceives of them, if at all, as way stations within the criminal justice system, a checkpoint on the correctional assembly line.

Second, a more readily acceptable explanation for the lack of knowledge by the public is the "remoteness" of these professions. If the reader accepts the truism that experience is a good teacher, then it becomes apparent why probation and parole are abstract professions to the lay person. To most of us, there is little opportunity to know or perhaps to even care what happens behind that ominous steel door once it clangs shut on the offender. We have never been subjected to this experience, and too often we can only relate to what we may have read, heard, or seen on television as being a true picture of the process. The association is not present at a physical level, and perhaps because of fear of the unknown, it is also conceivable that the public may not want to relate to parole or probation even on a mental level.

A more explicit way of portraying this would be to consider the process of what we know to be called "growing up." Human nature, or some other unexplainable influence, seems to dictate that periodically we try to test the limits of our immediate setting to determine just what we can and cannot get away with. Who among us has not run a stop sign or exceeded the speed limit when driving and has perhaps smirked to himself because he was able to do so without being apprehended? Who has not as a child taken a piece of candy from a store when the clerk was not looking, or who as an adult has not had the urge to strangle his/her spouse for his/her inopportune acts? The basic difference between us, as citizens in good standing or as offenders, is quite simple: (1) As good citizens we have realized the futility of our acts readily and the possible consequences if we could not set some

[4]National Advisory Commission on Criminal Justice Standards and Goals, *Corrections* (Washington, D.C.: U.S. Government Printing Office, 1973), p. 311.

[5]Ibid., p. 389.

self-controls to prevent recurrences, and (2) as offenders we have never been apprehended in the act.

Unless actively and habitually involved by virtue of occupation, association, or even having been an offender who has repeatedly been processed through the criminal justice system, there is little opportunity—or even desire—for the lay person to identify with that system. It is hoped that the average citizen frequents the courts more as a spectator than as a participant. Should he, for example, be the victim of an unjust traffic ticket, he may grumble and gripe but not in such a manner as to get himself into further difficulty by doing so. His day in court may be characterized by a plea of guilty, a payment of a small fine, and a quick glance around the courtroom to assure himself that there is no one present who would recognize him. This experience would then be followed chronologically by a visible, if not audible, sigh of relief and a quick exit out the door without so much as a backward glance.

Much of the work of the court goes unseen, unnoticed and, more often than not, without much public comprehension. The legal jargon, obscured as to meaning in Latin derivatives, is as incomprehensible as a physician's explanation of a disease or his handwriting on the prescription for the cure. The observer in court has little understanding of what happens to the offender once guilt has been established, and especially when the disposition is not a visible one in the sense that the culprit can be seen paying his price. If the offender is whisked from sight by an officer of the court to have his sentence implemented, John Q. Public has now lost total contact and he can only experience a sense of uneasiness, a sense that is magnified many times over in the mind of the offender.

TO BETTER UNDERSTAND PROBATION AND PAROLE

The percentage of the public who appear before the court and who meet their obligations through the payment of a monetary fine are far greater in number than those who are placed under some form of supervision through a court probation department. In fact, most courts do not bother with probation services at the misdemeanant level. A more comprehensible fact would be that most misdemeanant courts do not have probation departments except in the larger metropolitan areas where the docket and the nature of the cases are proportionally larger.

> In many areas probation is available only to convicted felons and is provided by the state. County misdemeanant probation programs can offer a valuable alternative to the courts that may both reduce the jail population and far more effectively treat the early offender.[6]

[6]James Coughlin, "Counties Can Lead Community-Based Corrections," *The American Country,* 37, no. 10 (November 1972), 13-14.

The use of probation departments is going to be dependent on the size of the area the court must serve, on the criteria of the judges and prosecutors, and lastly, if not most importantly, on the ability of a probation department to meet the respective needs of the court, the offender, and the community.

Probation is and always must be an *intervention process.* There should be no discrimination or denial of probationary services irrespective of the level of jurisdiction or of the type of offender who appears in front of that particular court. Probation, at the misdemeanant level, may be viewed by the public as a questionable venture at best; at worst it will be looked upon as nit-picking and of no appreciable value. The taxpayer may well feel that there are more appropriate ways of investing his tax dollars than on the petty offender. But remember the saying: "Tall oaks from little acorns grow."

In considering the habitual offender, two concerns are frequently mentioned: (1) that the habitual offender may be seemingly too set in his life style to change his pattern of behavior; or (2) that he is too chronic to be rehabilitated. There is, of course, no easy answer, unless the public can be made aware that the cost of incarceration is considerably higher and that it is far cheaper to work with the offender outside the walls than to deal with him once he is on the inside.

At the informal level, parole might be spoken of as *transitory supervision* of the offender, that is, working with him during his transition from the prison system back into society. The parole officer's task is very demanding because his client has not only been through the court system and a multitude of community service functions, but he has also spent a certain amount of time in a penal institution of some nature. The parolee is now quite sophisticated in his ability to give the correct answers demanded, in being shrewd in his representation of himself and his acts, and he has become conditioned to the criminal subculture of the penal institution, which will certainly affect his attitude of outward compliance but inward rebelliousness toward his parole agent. The use of the word *transition* should not be overlooked because the offender has been out of public circulation for some time, and both his social reentry and his mental outlook must be closely monitored so that his adjustment may be made as smoothly as possible.

Probation is a form of legal supervision given in lieu of a commitment to a penal institution such as a prison. Parole is recognized to be legal supervision of the offender following his release from prison. Not long ago, I received a newsletter from a professional organization, one that is well respected in its field. The primary function of that agency is the treatment and study of alcoholism as well as the education of the general public about the problems of that disease. In the publication was a cartoon of a man enjoying a mug of beer and talking with an amused and interested bartender. Our imbiber is captioned as saying, "That probation officer of mine is a real card. He says that alcoholism is a disease and that he will revoke my parole if I get sick.'' A better example of the semantic problem regarding the misunderstanding of the separate roles of probation and parole is difficult to conceive.

The point is that not only is the difference between probation and parole obviously lost to the author of the cartoon, but it is equally lost to the public as well. The distinction is further confused not only by individual agency policies but also by areas of governmental jurisdiction. At the federal level, probationers and parolees are still handled mutually by one agency and/or officer. This is true despite the fact that at the federal level of government, probation and parole are jurisdictionally the property of two separate divisions; i.e., probation is under the federal court system, and parole is under the Department of Justice.[7] What is unlikely (as depicted in the cartoon cited above) is that an offender would have his parole revoked for having violated his probation. This is bound to stretch the imagination of practitioners, to say nothing of the devastating effect on the less well informed. It is also unlikely, in view of the large caseloads, that any agency wants to become involved in the duplication of services. If there should be dual jurisdiction, it is customary to have supervision waived to the original agency of authority. A situation of concurrent jurisdiction allows the manipulative offender to try to work one agency or one officer against the other for his own personal gain, and should be avoided. In the case of "sick" offenders, the duplication of services only serves to bind tighter the knots that already are contributing to the discomfort and dysfunctioning of these individuals.

Within the city of the author's agency, there are three distinct and separate probation departments, two separate parole departments, and one federal agency that serves both probationers and parolees. It has been found that many requests for information that were initially directed to the Municipal Probation Department were actually intended for one of these other agencies. The public cannot seem to differentiate between probation and parole. All the public seems to be able to grasp is that these functions are somehow related, that both do about the same thing, and that both are supervising people who have run afoul of the law.

Perhaps, in part, making this distinction—between probation and parole—is what this book is really about. It is hoped that the time the reader spends with this text will be of value in his gaining a more comprehensive picture about probation and parole. This book is intended to fill a void in the literature for the individual who is now studying in this field. It wishes to present a picture of reality rather than brief case studies, statistics on recidivism, and flow charts, all of which occupy too much of the too few works available to the public at this time. Lastly, it should help to uncover

[7]H. Richmond Fisher, "Probation and Parole Revocation: The Anomaly of Divergent Procedures," *Federal Probation*, 38, no. 3 (September 1974), 23-29.

the true roles of the professions of probation and parole, roles that too long have been hidden in the dark and sometimes misunderstood criminal justice system. After all, a little light shed on the dark shadows can dispel many misconceived thoughts about what really lurks there.

SUGGESTED READINGS

SCHUR, EDWIN M., *Our Criminal Society.* Englewood Cliffs, N.J.: Prentice-Hall, Inc., 1969.

MANGRUN, CHARLES T., "The Humanity of Probation Officers," *Federal Probation,* 36, no. 2 (June 1972), 47–50.

2

The Criminal
Justice System

Ideally, all court dispositions should be the personification of justice. From a definitional standpoint, justice should encompass qualities such as fairness, equality, compassion, impartiality, and an overall general appropriateness. However, when viewed from a functional standpoint, the complexion of justice becomes somewhat altered, especially if one considers the vested interests and the personalities of the individuals involved.

In the eyes of the offender, justice is equated with an acquittal; whereas in the eyes of the prosecution, conviction would be considered a symbol of justice. The law enforcement officer would hope that a conviction would serve as a deterrent to others who might be inclined to foster and pursue antisocial activities. The citizen wants and longs for the restoration of peace and order in his neighborhood, as well as the right to live his life unmolested and undisturbed. Society wants its standards upheld so that the image will be perpetuated of a morally correct and principally sound social structure, even though this structure has been so conceived because of the legal enforcement of those laws. One rightly wonders if justice can hope to fulfill all these duties and to do so to the mutual satisfaction of all who may be affected by such disposition. Quite frankly, this is an illogical premise—to even hope that justice can assume all these roles.

THE STRUCTURE OF THE CRIMINAL JUSTICE SYSTEM

The use of the phrase "criminal justice system" is an attempt to define the methodology of processing the offender from the time of apprehension through the various levels and methods of treating his case. Generally

speaking, this is a correct definition, with perhaps one notable exception—
the jurisdictionally defined roles of the courts. Although perhaps a
somewhat elementary point, the court system has two very basic roles,
depending on whether the case is classified as criminal or civil in nature.
Confusion often centers on the inability of the general public to grasp the
property of certain courts.

For purposes of clarification, the reader should be aware that criminal
acts are specifically defined here, as well as by law, as those matters that,
upon conviction, may result in the offender being placed in a prison or
reformatory as a possible disposition of his case. Civil courts also handle offenders and deal primarily with cases of lesser degrees of severity, even
though the disposition of these cases can provide for the offender being incarcerated. Such forms of incarceration are for shorter periods of time and
are generally served at the local level, specifically within a municipal or
county jail.

The justice system can be and often is a confusing operation. In all probability, the process should not be oversimplified, for there exist varying
degrees of jurisdictional power as well as various types of cases tried before
those different powers. Most cases in the lower level courts do not involve
anything resembling criminal behavior, and although it is true that incarceration is a definite possibility upon conviction, most offenders at the
lower level court will never get near a detention facility, either while
awaiting trial or upon conviction. The clanging door, the steel bars, the
smell of sweat and disinfectant, the loss of rights and privileges are all
usually remote and cast few threatening shadows at the misdemeanant
court level.

There is, perhaps, a tendency to forget that the backbone of the court
system is the lower level court. The advancement of justice is based on the
primary levels of association, and this lower rung in the judicial system is
more apt to be frequented and used by the public than the courts of a higher
level of jurisdiction. This chapter attempts to focus on the roles and duties
of the court and its related services as the multifaceted process for which it
is intended. It is contended that the courts are intervening agents, designed
to institute social change, and that this is perhaps the least recognized but
yet their true and most noble function.

The accompanying diagram, Figure 2-1, albeit an oversimplification, will
be used to follow the legal course of the courts and those alternatives that
are both part and parcel of the process. Although the pertinence of this
diagram is not limited to this chapter alone, it is viewed to advantage here as
this text moves from the general to the specific. This exhibit has two distinct
purposes: (1) to trace the functioning levels of the system and its related services, and (2) to recognize some of the pitfalls that may not be obviously apparent in the schematic plan but which tend, at times, to taint the justice
process.

THE CRIMINAL JUSTICE SYSTEM

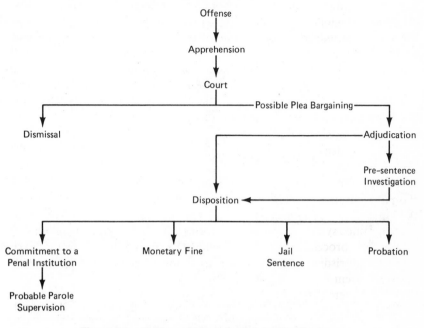

Figure 2.1 *Outline of the Criminal Justice System*

It is conceivable that a combined punishment of monetary fine, jail sentence, and probation could constitute one sentence. However, quite often part of the fine and/or jail sentence may be suspended to assure conformity by the offender to probationary demands. A large suspended sentence or fine becomes the proverbial carrot in front of the offender's nose. He is aware that his nonconformity to probationary demands can be sufficient cause for the court to reinstate the suspended punishments, and that this may cause him financial hardship, loss of freedom, or both.

The criminal justice system is cursorily conceived of as consisting of four main elements: the offender, the law enforcement personnel, the courts, and the correctional system to which the adjudicated offender is banished and wherein he will hopefully be taught a lesson for having defied the laws of the land. These four distinct groupings interact and relate but also function somewhat independently of each other. Without a doubt, there is a good and just reason for the separation of these respective units, despite a sort of grudging interdependence upon one another. It is almost as if four islands existed within an archipelago, somewhat autonomous in nature as individual units but with their total functioning ability being related to their capacities to coexist in some sort of an understanding of each other and their respective roles and relationships.

It seems inappropriate at this point to delve deeply into the role of the offender other than to note that he is the subject and center of attention of the system. Countless volumes have been written about the characteristics of criminal behavior going back many years in time. Such noteworthy social theorists as Durkheim, Morel, Lombroso, Sutherland, Weber, and Merton, to name but a few, have contributed much material concerning crime, criminals, and causes. Little can be added here that would be unique and revolutionary except as penned under a new name. Although it is conceded that the offender sets the wheels of the system in motion, we shall concern ourselves here with the momentum rather than with the catalyst.

THE ROLE OF LAW ENFORCEMENT PERSONNEL

The need for the suppression of criminal activities is constantly voiced in the public cry for greater and better law enforcement agencies. Although the impassioned pleas are made in a rather general way, it is acknowledged that the request takes one of two forms: (1) more police personnel and (2) tougher court decisions. In a recent article, Alexander Smith and Harriet Pollack challenge the fallacy of increased police personnel and courts as an answer.

> More police means more reported crime, not less. As the number of police increases, and as their efficiency and productivity improve, more crime will be detected and more arrests made. Crime rates, which are simply the ratio of reported crime to population, will go up, not down. As crime rates go up, public unrest and demands for protection will increase, creating more pressure to hire more police, thus repeating the cycle.[1]

The theory given here does not suggest any equilibrium between law enforcement and the courts. Rather, it refers to one of several vicious circles of crime involvement. The public's demand is not necessarily for more courts, but for more punitive action by the existing courts. Unfortunately, the invisible ingredients are not accounted for, i.e., more prosecutors, more probation services, more custodial detention facilities. Again the apathy toward corrections in general raises its ugly head. Although this topic will be dealt with in chapter depth at a later point, we point out here that the basic causes of prison riots are related to overcrowding of those facilities along with a lack of meaningful programs for inmates. More police, more convictions, more commitments—all of this is somewhat akin to sweeping dirt under the carpet for it does not cleanse; it merely displaces.

Both the courts and the law enforcement agencies are limited as to their designated functions, but it is the police who have shown the more innovativeness of the two. The history of the court system is both dull and unspectacular. It has been the cases before the courts that have caused

---

[1]Alexander B. Smith and Harriet Pollack, "Less, Not More: Police, Courts, Prisons," *Federal Probation*, 36, no. 3 (September 1972), 13.

notoriety or public interest rather than the judicial method of handling those cases. Perhaps that is why judges continue to wear black robes, for little is colorful about the courts.

The Evolution of Law Enforcement

The growth of law enforcement has far outdistanced any appreciable/comparable gains made by the court system. Protection, detection, and apprehension as true functions of the law enforcement officer were initially private services and were available only to those who could afford to pay for them. Little authority was vested in the night watchman who was the forerunner of our modern lawman. His original role was a monitor of the night who called the hour and watched for fires rather than for fugitives. Initially, the public was fearful of investing any authority in this type of individual, for to do so was to border upon, in the thinking of those times, a military state where favors could be purchased for a price and the honest but poor citizen could easily become a scapegoat to be blamed for the crimes of the more affluent. Therefore, it was not until the late 1820s that law enforcement officers in England were recognized as municipal employees and were subsidized by governmental funding. The efforts of Sir Robert Peel in that country marked the transition into professional police work.[2]

Unlike Old England, most law enforcement agencies in the United States have tended to function and operate along militaristic lines. Emphasis has been on a high degree of discipline, professional pride, and generalized impersonal relationships with the public. The table of organization for any large police department of today tends to parallel military levels of functioning even to the point of job titles and rank accorded its members. Most members of the law enforcement profession, especially within the larger communities, represent a subculture within themselves. Few outsiders intrude within either the professional or the social structure of law enforcement departments unless there is a need to accept "outsiders" as a matter of convenience in the mutual discharge of their respective duties.

The Service Model

One of the most noteworthy and current changes in police work is that of the service model. A very probable basis for the change of emphasis is that the militaristic model has demonstrated certain inadequacies. At least three areas of shortcomings in the perpetuation of the old style are noted: (1) in crowd or group control, (2) in working with minority members of the community, and (3) in preventive work, especially with juveniles. The new service approach is generally characterized by an attempt to promote good will

[2]Daniel Glaser, "From Revenge to Resocialization: Changing Perspectives in Combating Crime," *The American Scholar,* 40, no. 4 (Autumn 1971), 660.

and to change the police image so that the department will receive more public cooperation, based on the general assumption that many police calls are in response to family disputes and problems in community interpersonal relationships. It must be remembered that law enforcement personnel are the only services available to the public twenty-four hours a day, seven days a week. Although this was not intended to be their primary function, no other community agency besides the police is available to be on the scene at one o'clock in the morning to handle a domestic squabble.

Certainly some of these services that the police provide should be the primary role of other agencies, perhaps even of the court if the latter is designed and staffed to perform these functions. Yet smaller communities have few counseling services beyond the utilization of clergy and perhaps physicians. Every community does have police personnel of various sorts and sizes, and intervention in social problems may well become the lot of the police officer for a lack of any other primary source of assistance.

It must be recognized that when society allocates the power of arrest to a law enforcement officer, it also permits him to make judgments in the execution of his duties. An unanswered question is, Just what is the officer relating to at the time of an arrest—the letter or the spirit of the law? This is a very crucial question, and upon its answer depends the degree of success of the professional reaction to the officer's conception of his job; and it is equally crucial in the way and manner the public reacts to the means and degree of efficiency that the officer displays in the fulfillment of his duties.

The Police and the Courts

The interrelationship of the police and the courts is a very good example of the analogy given earlier about dependence and independence. Even though the law enforcement officer is generally one of the worst critics of the inadequacies and the ineffectiveness of the courts, the latter do provide the officer with some degree of protection. If there is probable cause for the police officer to make an arrest, he does so. He has, at this point, acted upon his own judgment, which will eventually be sanctioned by or rejected by the court. If a conviction is rendered, the officer has been legally correct in his act. However, any acquittal by the court should not be viewed by the arresting officer as a personal defeat. Rather, it should be utilized as a possible form of a constructive criticism from which the officer may repair his own weaknesses, weaknesses that may have led to the court's disposition of the case. Cases that are "lost" often reflect poor preparation or procedure by the officer at the investigative level. The role of the court is, then, perhaps to judge not only the offense and the offender, but to correct apparent legal deficiencies that may have been neglected by the arresting officer at the time of apprehension. Since the evidence presented by the officer makes the case, the court, in turn, has the responsibility to assist the officer by imparting knowledge that will facilitate proper processing of future cases.

One factor that has tended to widen the gap between the court system and the police has been the friction between prosecutors and police officers. Primarily, this friction has resulted and has been furthered by a lack of professional courtesy, usually on the part of the prosecutor. The failure of the prosecutor to extend the decency of notification of court continuances on cases, his indifference to facts when plea bargaining, and his assumption of superiority based on higher education and pay—all of these elements tend to widen the gap and to reduce the possibility of prosecutors and officers working together in an effective manner.

The role of the police cannot be underestimated. In addition to the classical functions expected of them, the quality of the work that they produce is most instrumental in facilitating the work of the court. The heart and soul of any case in attempting to secure a conviction are not the legal technicalities as much as the sheer evidence that can be given only by an efficient law enforcement officer. Without sufficient evidence, without probable cause, without the establishment of venue, the court personnel must be dependent on assumptions to establish a case. An officer who is poorly prepared for court, who is insufficiently explicit in his affidavit, or who becomes emotionally involved can offer little but his presence to the trial.

The conception of the law enforcement officer as being one who has a strong back but a weak mind is no longer applicable. Most officers today are not only involved in a continuing program of training, but many are highly educated people who are socially concerned and may be expected to execute their duties with finesse and fairness as opposed to muscle and might.

THE FUNCTION OF THE COURTS

The primary function of the court system is the administration of justice through the hearing of the facts related to the case, an evaluation of the evidence at hand, and a proper and appropriate disposition to the matter if guilt is established. To assume that the existence of well-trained and conscientious court personnel is sufficient to assure that these functions will be carried out is to deceive ourselves. The very fact that our courts operate on what is known as an *adversary system* is both an asset and a liability. This legal contest attempts to assure a degree of fairness, but it also serves to complicate the effectiveness of the courts by slowing down the process of justice by countless continuances of cases for researching the legal arguments presented both pro and con. It is theorized here that although the objectivity of the court is a rather basic factor, the consistency of the courts does leave a lot to be desired.

The principle of the adversary system is a relatively sound one in theory. It is predicated on the legal arguments of the prosecution and the counter-arguments of the attorney for the accused with the understanding that the best presented, researched, and documented arguments will be sufficient to enable the judge to effect a finding in that particular case. However, the adversary system is grossly slanted in favor of the prosecutor if the offender does not have good legal representation of his own. The accused may be acting in totally good faith and honesty, but his failure either to understand the intricacies of the adversary procedure or to be legally self-prepared often can be sufficient grounds to lose his case—simply due to his inability to cope with the system.

A second weakness of the adversary system is noted in cases where much technical evidence is presented that is predicated on findings of other courts. It is inconceivable that the judges of today, in light of their crowded dockets, can be expected to reasonably keep abreast of anything other than major court decisions, let alone factually relate to obscure cases, without the opportunity for major research and study—a time element not in keeping with the court demands. A judge may ask for the presentation of briefs to evaluate the evidence offered by other court decisions, but such a practice only slows down the disposition of the case under consideration and further complicates and delays the opportunity to attack the backlog of other cases. The interpretation of laws is based on precedents as much as on the wording of the ordinance upon which the matter is being tried. Therefore, laws are rarely stabilized except in theory and principle, and precedents are the loopholes wherein the Achilles' heel may be attacked.

One of the reasons for the existence of the court system is to protect the public from the libelous accusations of others, even if those "others" be law enforcement personnel. The exalted theory is that all are to be considered innocent until proven guilty, a theory that is contradictory in content and nature. The burden of proof of guilt is supposedly to be provided by the prosecutor, and the offender does not have to testify in any way if he does not see fit to do so. Yet, unless the offender offers contradictory evidence to substantiate his case, his chances of gaining an acquittal are nil. As Karl Menninger addresses in his classical work, *The Crime of Punishment,* the court system is only concerned with what is legal, not necessarily with what is proper and appropriate.[3] If, in fact, the offender is not willing, or is in some way unable to offer a contradictory argument with legal merit and basis, there remains the distinct possibility that his silence will be used to his disadvantage. It would appear that the offender, especially the offender without the benefit of legal representation, is damned if he does testify on his own behalf and likewise damned if he doesn't.

---

[3]Karl Menninger, *The Crime of Punishment* (New York: The Viking Press, 1966), p. 16.

It is also suggested that the somewhat ethereal qualities of the court tend to foster an atmosphere that defies understanding by the public. The court occupies a position in our society like motherhood and apple pie. To challenge the mysticism that surrounds some of the qualities of the court is unthinkable, undesirable, and un-American. Many exhibitions of symbolism exist and are flaunted before the public. The magic number in a jury, the black robe of the judge, the fact that the term "His Honor" is a lifelong and accepted method of addressing the judge, the rising of the audience when the judge enters and leaves the courtroom, all promote and propagate the aura that exists. It is small wonder that the public is wary of the significance of these acts, let alone the complexities of the hearing itself. *Honor* may imply respect, but *awe* retains an element of uneasiness and perhaps fear.

LEGAL SERVICES FOR OFFENDERS

Certain animosities are voiced against the court system even though the role of the court is to ensure the legal protection of the rights of the public. The ironic basis for some of these hostilities is that the court's role is directly aimed at the protection of legal rights. The Constitution of the United States guarantees the accused the right of a trial to prove his innocence or to establish his guilt. In keeping with this, the accused has the right to demand that society prove its case against him and also that society provide him with legal counsel upon demand and upon meeting some basic qualifications. The accused may ask that the cost of counsel be borne by the court at no expense whatsoever to him. Even though there may be every reason to suspect that the offender has previously bitten the hand of the public, he may now ask that the public provide him with these designated services. The origin of ambivalence toward the court becomes more understandable when the public is placed in the position of having to protect the offender who has wronged it (the public) in the first place by his antisocial behavior.

The right to have legal counsel provided for the accused, although assured by the law, is both an abused and inconsistent privilege. This service is not universally provided for at all court levels. Many misdemeanant courts are not blessed with the financial ability to provide for such a service. The old justice of the peace courts and magistrate courts (magistrates who have been appointed to their posts although they have no formal legal background)—and there are many of these "courts" still in existence—cannot comply with this requirement. Legal aid services are rarely found outside of metropolitan areas, and like money at Christmas time, there is never enough to go around. The waiting period to get an appointment is often too long, and the accused becomes discouraged. Because of the volume of demands made on these agencies, the criteria for the acceptance of clients (even those who are indigent) are very selective. It would appear that indigency is often secondary to the level of the offense brought against the accused. Not only is legal representation sometimes denied, but the legal giving of advice is also limited. Little but sympathy can be offered to those offenders who do not qualify or who live in areas where such services are not available.

The right of legal counsel on behalf of past convicted offenders—especially probationers and parolees—and the need for the courts to provide legal services have only recently been acted upon by the Supreme Court.[4,5] An in-depth discussion of these rights as well as the other rights accorded to this specific grouping will be covered in a later chapter.

At the risk of being repetitious, we state again that the ignorance and apathy of the accused denote somewhat of a blight on the American judicial process. The ramifications of a conviction, and hence a police record or entry, are often not fully understood by the offender. For some unknown reason, many offenders will not even consider a not guilty plea, let alone a jury trial, unless they have an attorney to represent them; yet this is their right. The author can recall innumerable cases where guilty pleas have been entered for the sake of expediency, to merely "get it over with." It is certainly the legal privilege of offenders to enter whatever plea they desire, but they often fail to recognize the legal and sometimes the social ramifications of pleas inappropriately entered. Employment that demands security clearances and the bonding of employees required in conjunction with a job are two specific instances where applicants with a record may be rejected because of the improvident entrance of guilty pleas to even minor (misdemeanant) offenses.

PLEA BARGAINING

One of the biggest criticisms of the courts—both from within as well as from without—is the use of plea bargaining. Simply stated, plea bargaining is a pact or understanding reached between the court and the offender or his attorney either as to the handling of a plea or as to the disposition of a case. Usually such agreements are secured outside the formal confines of the courtroom and often without the initial knowledge of the judge since the agreements are usually negotiated for the court by the prosecutor. The court often enters into this legal triad only when a "disposition has been reached," and the legal sanction of the court is now required.

The arguments about the use of plea bargaining abound. Powerful

[4]Morrissey v. Brewer, 408 U.S. 471, 33 L. Ed. 484, 92 S. Ct. 2593.
[5]Gagnon v. Scarpelli, 411 U.S. 778, 36 L. Ed. 656, 93 S. Ct. 1756.

authorities have commented on the subject from both sides of the proverbial fence.

> The disposition of criminal charges by agreement between the prosecutor and the accused, sometimes loosely called "plea bargaining," is an essential component of the administration of justice. Properly administered, it is to be encouraged.[6]

> As soon as possible, but in no event later than 1978, negotiations between prosecutors and defendants—either personally or through their attorneys—concerning concessions to be made in return for guilty pleas should be prohibited. . . . Until plea negotiations are eliminated as recommended in this standard, such negotiations and the entry of pleas pursuant to the resulting agreements should be permitted only under a procedure embodying the safeguards contained in the remaining standards in this chapter.[7]

If the Supreme Court of the United States indirectly advocates the continuing use of plea bargaining, but the National Advisory Commission on Criminal Justice Standards and Goals recommends the complete and immediate abolition of such a practice, to whom, then, do the courts owe allegiance? Obviously there is no easy answer to this dilemma, but the assets and liabilities are easily examined as they relate to the use of this process.

Before weighing the alternatives, there needs to be a brief examination as to what forms or disguises plea bargaining may take. The most widely used form is probably the *reduction of the original charge* to a lesser offense. Clarification of this issue to the general public is difficult. For example, how can one determine what value there would be in changing a plea of "not guilty on burglary" to one of "guilty on criminal trespassing"? Again honor still exists among thieves, and the distinction is a very real one to the accused. The issue here is not so much another entry on the police record as the difference between freedom and incarceration.

Two other practices common in plea bargaining are the use of *deferred sentencing* (sometimes referred to as *deferred judgment*) and *deferred prosecution*. The legal difference between these two is merely the entrance of a plea and/or a finding by the court. In deferred sentencing/judgment, a finding of guilty has been made or a guilty plea has been accepted, but there is no disposition of the case made at that point. On deferred prosecution, no finding has been made, and it is conceivable no plea has been entered, but usually this agreement has been prefaced by the entrance of a not guilty plea. Both deferred sentencing/judgment and deferred prosecution are continued for a specified period of time, often with court-imposed contingencies being a condition of the deferment. An eventual dismissal of the case is the desired goal following a successful period of deferment.

---

[6]Santebello v. New York, 404 U.S. 257, 30 L. Ed. 427, 92 S. Ct. 495.

[7]National Advisory Commission on Criminal Standards and Goals, *Courts* (Washington, D.C., 1973), p. 46.

The Case for Plea Bargaining

The plea bargaining process has advantages for both the accused and the court system. When such a process benefits both parties, it becomes apparent why the justice system is reluctant to relinquish its hold on the practice. Originally it was thought that the use of the deferred practice was intended for juveniles.[8] The justice system has long been concerned with its juvenile offenders and "the age of reason." This phrase implies that, up to a certain chronological age, juveniles are not considered emotionally mature enough to be held legally responsible for their delinquent acts. Rather than burden them with a record at a very early age, it was felt that it would be more benevolent to give them the opportunity to either redeem themselves or to determine if they are prone to continue their pattern of delinquent activities. It was therefore hoped that a favor would be returned (discontinuation of delinquent behavior) for a favor given (not being adjudicated).

Plea bargaining, on behalf of adults, becomes quite common under specific circumstances. Many states have a law pertaining to what, with varying titles, it called the "habitual criminal act." According to this law, chronic offenders, especially those with felony charges of many entries and types, are subject to commitment to a penal institution, based as much, if not more, on the length of their record as on the last actual case upon which a conviction was made. Any offender, when facing the possibility of commitment, would thus promise the court and society to behave (plea bargain) if he is but given another chance. If he can "cop to a lesser plea," it may mean the difference between incarceration in a penitentiary and a lesser punishment. Certainly it is to his advantage to seek to have his charge reduced so as to eliminate the possibility of a prolonged stretch behind bars.

Another case for plea bargaining would be instances where, upon conviction, an offender could be punished more than once for his offense. Reference is made here to traffic offenses as a prime example. First, the subject is obligated either to pay a fine over the counter for this violation or to go to court where he may face the possibility of both a fine and a jail sentence. Then, if he is the resident of a state that assesses points on his driver's license, he may sooner or later lose his driving privileges because of the accumulation of points based on traffic offenses. Next, he faces the distinct possibility that his insurance rates will increase. Finally, he may lose his employment if part of his job involves driving for his employer. Certainly it is to the advantage of this offender to seek a deferred status from the court.

Plea bargaining works on behalf of the court system as well. It is sug-

---

[8]James M. Dean, "Deferred Prosecution and Due Process in the Southern District of New York," *Federal Probation,* 39, no. 3 (September 1975), 23.

gested here that plea bargaining is often used because a guilty plea can be processed in a smaller fraction of time than that required for a formal trial. Jury trials are long, tedious, and expensive for the public. It is suspected that no one knows this better than the attorney for the defense. Although it would not be ethically correct to assume that the defense requests a jury trial on behalf of his client as a means of gaining consideration for plea bargaining, neither can it be assumed that this is not one of the defense lawyer's ulterior motives.

Furthermore, courtroom time accounts for only a small part of the expenses borne by the taxpayer in jury trials. The time spent in the preparation of a case by the prosecutor, the subpoena process of securing witnesses and the time and cost for the officers of the court to serve same, the fees paid for jury members as well as the feeding and housing of them if they are to be sequestered for any prolonged period of time, the work of the court recorders, the time spent by clerical staff in processing the paper work, the overtime paid to the police officer who must appear in court, all are rarely measured, and the cost of man-hours alone in this area is staggering. When such costs are combined with a growing caseload, along with the problem of insufficient personnel and services to handle those cases, it is obvious why the courts look to plea bargaining for some form of judicial relief. Indeed, it is difficult to see how the courts could maintain their workload without the use of plea bargaining irrespective of the form it may take.

The Case against Plea Bargaining

One of the major criticisms of plea bargaining is that it often takes place in a rather clandestine manner. If plea bargaining is to be used, there is no reason why it should not be made available to everyone. However, unless the public is unusually attentive and possesses some degree of legal insight, it is probably unaware that plea bargaining is a right that it can exercise. The secrecy of the process has been perpetuated because the courts, as a part of their advisement of rights, do not make it known that they will entertain a negotiation process with any and all defendants. It is obvious why they fail to advertise, for to do so would only serve to swamp the courts with requests of this nature. This has become a skeleton in the dark corner of the closet, one that the courts prefer to keep hidden from public view. It is contended here that if the right for plea bargaining is available, then it should be offered to all.

Most plea bargaining is not initiated by the accused; rather, it is done on his behalf by an attorney. Again, legal ethics could become suspect, for it might be deduced that the chances of plea bargaining are lessened for those offenders who do not have or cannot afford the price of legal counsel. One would question, if this premise has some merit and element of truth, whether there is the possibility of some legal discrimination on the part of the courts. To imply that the court system is not above suspicion is to make a very dangerous accusation, but the possibility for and the grounds to make such an assumption are not without cause. If the courts do not like the accusation, then they should not put themselves in the position where fertile seeds of doubt can sprout. It is also reasonable to predict that even were the courts to divulge such information regarding plea bargaining, it is highly probable that the preponderant number of cases actually granted this opportunity would be those where legal counsel was present.

Another point against plea bargaining is that it is quite probable that offenders who become involved in plea bargaining for lesser charges may be sacrificing some very basic legal rights. For example, if the accused was in fact innocent of the charges, but the evidence of his being suspect was so overwhelming that his chance for an acquittal was remote, then he may be incriminating himself by pleading to a lesser charge. If our Constitution provides that the accused need not testify against himself—that this is his legal right to exercise if he so chooses—is he not, then, losing those rights by plea bargaining to a lesser charge? Perhaps the courts do not want to consider this possibility since the use of plea bargaining is generally to their mutual advantage.

Furthermore, the concept of being innocent until proven guilty is not applicable where plea bargaining is concerned. The accused is persuaded to enter to a lesser charge on the theory that he will establish his innocence if he can but uphold the contingencies of the deferment. He may be winning a battle but losing a war. In short, he is involving himself in an agreement that voluntarily precludes his exercising his legal rights to go to trial, in exchange for some crumbs from the table of the court.

Plea bargaining also does not endear the court to law enforcement personnel. Smith and Pollack term it "revolving door justice."[9] Their contention is that plea bargining takes justice out of the hands of the judges and places the authority to dispose of a case in the hands of the prosecutor. Instead of the hoped-for deterrent effect, the police are seeing the offender back out on the streets with a chance that he may go completely untouched by a legal disposition. In turn, the law enforcement personnel may harbor the feeling that the courts are not supportive of their efforts, and the gap of distrust becomes wider and wider.

A further argument against plea bargaining is that the courts, as a representative of the public, are becoming independent of public scrutiny. If plea bargaining is to persist, and there is little doubt that it will, it must become an open process. At present there is the tendency for the illusion to be conveyed that the courts will regulate and administer their own shortcomings without public intervention because plea bargaining is largely

[9]Smith and Pollack, "Less, Not More," p. 14.

clandestine. The public thus feels it is losing control over the courts as implements to serve society.

Perhaps James Dean, who argues as strongly as any one man can in his crusade to eliminate plea bargaining, best states the arguments against this process in the following brief but comprehensive summary.[10]

1. The public loses in the plea bargaining process for their protection from serious crime is hampered by the clogging of the criminal system.
2. The defendant loses because he may be branded with a conviction as a result of his self-conviction.
3. The law is poorly served because it has to severely compromise its ideals to cope with the practical problems presented by a huge number of cases.
4. The legislature [loses] since it does not feel the pressure it should to redefine the scope of the criminal law within more realistic bounds so that it can once again serve the needs of society for protection.

WEAKNESSES IN THE SENTENCING PROCESS

Many judges, in relatively unguarded moments, have expressed legitimate concern about the sentencing process. There appears to be little academic or professional training in schools of law to prepare a judge-to-be. Legal precedents are offered to assist in the interpretation of cases and points of law, but at the time of sentencing most judges are on their own. The only *legal* framework they have as a guideline may be a time-reference frame where a sentence may be identified by law as being worth a certain number of years on a specific offense. The reader should note the emphasis on the word *legal*, for it points to the lack of the social aspects that should be considered at the time the sentence is imposed.

By far, one of the weakest links in the criminal justice system is the sentencing process and the lack of adequate sentencing alternatives. If the premise may be even partially correct, that our courts are—or should be— agencies of social concern, then it should follow that the judiciary should also view the offender as a social creature at the point of sentencing. The shotgun approach to sentencing—defined as "leveling a blast in a general direction"—seems to prevail for many reasons, none of which is logical, but most of which have long since been accepted as traditional and commonplace.

The Role of Fines

An indirect function of many courts is to act as a source of revenue for the municipality or district that they serve. Although it would be grossly unfair to even suggest that justice is secondary to the income derived, it is a relatively honest fact that at the level of the justice of the peace and

[10]James M. Dean, "The Illegitimacy of Plea Bargaining," *Federal Probation,* 38, no. 2 (September 1974), 21.

magistrate courts, little else but dollars—and infrequently jail—are considered as a disposition.

Furthermore, in an affluent society, it is often easy for some to pay a fine. Even when monetary dispositions create financial hardships, many citizens would much prefer to dispose of their cases in this manner rather than to have to appear before the court and to exercise their legal rights to have their case heard. Thus, for those municipalities that have inadequate tax revenues, court fines may well provide a convenient source of income. Although the reaction may be that such a judicial byproduct has a negative reflection on the system, we must remind ourselves that in our colonial days, punishment often took the form of either labor performed on behalf of the betterment of the community or some other contribution made toward the general welfare of the residents of that locality.

However, if the only disposition to be imposed by a court is of a monetary nature, then this may be highly discriminatory against the indigent offender. Even though pauper prisons are illegal, it is suspected that there still are individuals "doing their time" in jails across the country due to their inability to pay a fine. Despite any intent and desire to pay, financial circumstances may often dictate that the offender cannot do so at the time it is demanded of him. And incarceration will not only be disruptive to the individual and his family, but it will possibly cost the offender his employment and righteous role within his family and within the community. One social ill, then, is satisfied, but several others are created to take its place.

The Overload of Cases

Another factor contributing to the weakness of the system is that many of the lower courts are burdened with "junk" items on their dockets. By this it is meant that many of the cases that appear before the courts really do not belong there. For example, issues centering around interpersonal relationships such as domestic squabbles and neighborhood complaints reach the courts largely by default—there is no other place for them to go. Such matters tend to clog the lower court system and to thereby decrease its effectiveness. The wife beater, the "your kids versus my kids," the noisy neighbor, the dog that barks all night—all of these and many more such cases have become legal issues for our courts to handle. Judgments rendered upon these trivial matters—trivial from a legal standpoint—achieve little when the lack of sentencing alternatives is considered. The court is capable of making a legal value judgment, but there is no social cleansing of the issues at hand. It is suspected that both the defendant and the complainant may be equally guilty, but it cannot be expected that both parties will be dealt with equally; i.e., there will be only *one* finding despite the fact that historically it requires at least two parties to constitute a fight.

There are several reasons for the overloading of the courts with these kinds of cases. First of all, as mentioned earlier, law enforcement departments are the only social agencies that operate twenty-four hours a day, seven days a week. More importantly, these services are free. And, if the citizen, when contacted, wishes to make a formal complaint in the hopes of the immediate alleviation of a problem, the officer may have no other choice but to accept the complaint because he cannot intercede in any other effective way. Then by virtue of the acceptance of the complaint, the matter is automatically brought to the attention of the court and is subsequently docketed for a hearing or a trial.

Furthermore, at times of stress, anger, and fear, it may be quite difficult for the citizenry to isolate causative factors. If dad drinks because his wife nags, and the wife gripes because they are behind on their bills, and dad is frustrated because he can't find a job, and dad drinks to relieve his frustrations and inadequacies—who can isolate and determine what came first or who begot what? Quite often the patterns of behavior are so complex and so interrelated that crises intervention can only take the form of getting—in this case—dad out of the house and probably taking him to jail until all cools down. But to get dad in jail an arrest is required, and then there must be some legal intervention by the court. The right of the public to seek the intervention of the court is a natural one and one that is certain to be exercised. Hence many cases that may not rightfully belong on the docket are there for reasons such as this.

Suffice it to say, legal decisions have little lasting effect in these types of cases. Because these participants are held in low esteem by some judges, little consideration is accorded them at the time of disposition. It is suggested here that the disposition of the court, unless it attempts to deal with the source of the problem, will make little by way of a lasting impression either on the offender or on the offended. It is highly possible that legal intervention without social insight and concern may only serve to fan more brightly the coals that smolder and to reignite the flames of combat that have never really been extinguished.

Disparity in sentencing is also indirectly encouraged through a lack of any concentrated effort by the judicial system to change itself and to communicate. Frederic Kellogg laments the total disorganization beginning at the very top—within the federal system.

> Management by objective has never made much of an impact on the administration of criminal justice. This is most likely because there is so little agreement as to the "objectives" of criminal justice, the purpose of punishment, and the most appropriate strategy to reduce crime.[11]

[11]Frederic R. Kellogg, "Organizing the Criminal Justice System: A Look at 'Operative' Objectives," *Federal Probation,* 40, no. 2 (June 1976), 50.

132, 231

Additional Reasons for Weaknesses
in the Sentencing Process

In addition to the general weaknesses as discussed above, there are other factors that interfere with the proper application of justice, as listed below.

Varying Levels of Jurisdiction. Different types of cases at different court levels are not conducive to either blanket legislation or general policy. Although it is possible to set a minimum/maximum sentence for certain offenses, it is not practical to attempt to do so in an all-encompassing manner for all courts. For example, there are certain instances where felony cases are less severe and less aggravated than some misdemeanor cases. Thus the concept of punishment to fit the crime is not always applicable when jurisdictional levels are crossed in certain cases.

Court Services and Philosophy. Especially pertinent to this book is how any court sees itself and its function. If the emphasis is strictly on the legal process and the social duties of the court are ignored, the court's efficiency will be greatly reduced. On the other hand, even the most socially concerned and treatment-orientated judge will fall short of his commitments if he lacks the services to implement the needs he sees.

A Lack of Cooperation and Communication. With few exceptions—the state of Oregon, for example, stands out—there have been few concentrated efforts by trial judges to work together setting standards and being concerned with consistency in their *total* judicial efforts. Failure to do this promotes a lack of consistency in standards for the courts and may likewise result in an undermining of efficiency.

A Lack of Legislative Intervention. Even though the policies of the courts may be decided upon within their own structure, each level of court is responsible to, as well as being at the direction of, legislative bodies governing that jurisdiction. Unless there is administrative guidance from the top permeating down through the courts, little chance exists that any change to correct sentencing disparities will be effected by the courts themselves. It appears, however, that the extent of legislative involvement and input is largely restricted to the development and enactment of laws and a sentencing frame of reference for those laws. Thus it would seem that these governing bodies are more willing to pass the buck to the judicial system and to thereby avoid the responsibility of assuring that the spirit as well as the letter of the law is upheld than they are to enact corrective legislation.

Personal Characteristics of the Judiciary. Two specific factors appear to affect the quality of the judiciary. First of all, despite attempts to alter the system, judgeships long have been—and some still are—political plums to be plucked or to be granted as favors. Up to now we have failed to find a better system, but it is obvious that the association with a particular political party does nothing to reflect the qualifications of an individual to be a judge. It is unfortunate that judgeships are assigned to individuals solely on the basis of their political affiliations.

A second factor is that few judges have the inner strength to go through prolonged periods of service without being touched either by the demands of the position or by the futility caused by a lack of meaningful alternatives to the present sentencing process. There is the tendency to either become callous or to "burn out" and thereby lose objectivity. At the lower court levels, it becomes commonplace for judges to see the same old and now familiar faces standing in front of the bench with great regularity. Both the judge and the offender have not only become well known to each other but they also have come to realize the ineffectualness of past and probable future attempts to avoid further appearances.

The term *burnt out* is used specifically here in association with the sentencing procedure. Although to be dealt with in detail later, relative to sentencing alternatives, a discussion of *burnt out* is previewed here in the context and sense that pressures on the judiciary, contributing to the so-called mortality rate of judgeships, are not so much an indirect result associated with the legal aspects as the direct result of social implications at the point of sentencing. The feeling of futility most commonly associated with judgeships is primarily caused by not being able to find meaningful dispositions rather than worrying about relating cases to legal precedents. The failure to find "legal cures" may well become internalized and may reflect both professionally and psychologically on those judges who cannot resign themselves to the hazards associated with their positions. Until and unless they recognize that their personal limitations are not necessarily to be associated with personal failure, the judicial "burn out" rate will continue to be commonplace.

There are a few judges who will become obsessed with the power that their position carries. This change often is marked by feelings of omnipotence. The author served his apprenticeship under a very well-known and respected judge. Years later, after the judge had retired from the court system, we chanced to meet and His Honor inquired about the usual amenities of life, and then asked a question that I believe exemplifies one who has spent too much time in the saddle. He inquired as to what I was doing, and upon ascertaining that I was still in the same old business, asked what court I was with and who my judge was. Upon being given this information, he asked the significant question, "Does he know me?"

Possible Improvements of the Sentencing Process

Several things should be changed, then, if the judicial system is to keep up with the demands made upon it. First, there is a need to expand the curriculum in law schools so as to include courses that will train students for possible judgeships. A special emphasis should be put on the social/legal obligations of the position. Second, there is a need for the court system to provide alternatives to eliminate unnecessary or inappropriate cases from the docket. Third, a check and balance system should be introduced and implemented to provide for ongoing training for judges as well as to find an honorable way of easing out of service those judges who, for one reason or another, are incapable of fulfilling the needs of their position. Last—and most important from the standpoint of the theory behind this book—is the need to provide better sentencing alternatives.

THE NEED FOR BETTER SENTENCING ALTERNATIVES

The correctional process, no matter how elaborately contrived, cannot function effectively if the offender does not receive the sentence that most suitably fits the needs and concerns in that particular case. Inappropriate and/or poorly planned sentences do not protect the community, do not assist the violator, disorganize the process, and destroy the credibility that must be maintained in a nation's justice system.[12]

The key to effective sentencing is the inclusion of both the social and the legal factors and the assurance that the disposition will reflect appropriateness, effectiveness, and awareness. Although the first two qualities are often considered in any discourse on sentencing, awareness of the social implication is somewhat more unique and is often overlooked by many judges. Sentencing has three basic and apparent purposes:

1. To protect society by the removal of the offender from the community;
2. To provide a deterrent effect on the offender by instilling within him the fact that his antisocial behavior cannot and will not be tolerated, and by using him as an example (as a deterrent) to other would-be offenders.
3. To reeducate the offender—whenever possible or appropriate—through his forced involvement in a specified program for rehabilitative purposes.

Weaknesses in the Correctional Process

There is a very definite break or demarcation point in the justice system at the time of sentencing and when commitment to some type of a penal institution is ordered. Few judges seem to know anything about the jails, reformatories, or penitentiaries to which they assign offenders—except from a remote standpoint. A preliminary supposition is that they maintain no contacts either with the institution or with those offenders they have committed because of the assumption that they no longer have any legal or social obligations to the case. They are satisfied that their role has been

---

[12]Walter Evans and Frank Gilbert, Jr., "The Sentencing Process: Better Methods Are Available," *Federal Probation*, 39, no. 4 (December 1975), 35.

fulfilled in its entirety and that there exists no further need for their involvement.

The legislatures, too, are at fault in not providing adequate direction to the courts. An example of the shortcomings and paltry involvement of the legislatures would be their legal sanctioning of blanket sentencing acts. The most specific example of such legal behavior would be the indeterminate sentence. Although such a sentence may or may not call for a minimum/maximum sentence, it provides for a discretionary release from penal custody earlier than the maximum allowable sentence. The use of the word *indeterminate* may not have been meant to designate a "vague" sentence, but *vague* and *indeterminate* are synonymous in meaning. The indeterminate sentence is used at the discretion of the parole board in conjunction with prison officials when in their joint estimation the offender should be, or is considered ready to be, released back into society.

The indeterminate sentence also allows for a legal "cop-out" by the judiciary. In effect it states that the courts recognize that something should be done with the offender, but just how much of that "something" he should have to do in terms of actual time served is not of particular concern to the court. Thus, it shows that the judiciary is really dependent on other sectors of the correctional system (prisons/parole boards, etc.) to determine when the sentence has been effectively served.

It is somewhat of a paradox that although the court retains both jurisdiction and interest if the offender is placed on a probationary status, the commitment of an individual to a reformatory or penitentiary terminates any further judicial involvement. This seems wrong if for no other reason than it fosters the lack of awareness and interest on the part of judges as to both the appropriateness and effectiveness of the sentencing process.

Suggestions for Improving
Jurisdictional Involvement

Consideration should be given to the possibility of further court intervention and for legal action to be taken against the offender when the latter does not conform to the penal system. Such action could take one of two forms:

1. The court of commitment could retain jurisdiction and only relinquish that jurisdiction when either the sentence has been served in full or when the offender is released on a parole status. In conjunction with this the court should have and should exercise the authority to resentence inmates to a longer term when the inmate fails to try to adjust to the correctional system.
2. In lieu of the above, there could be vested within the penal institution the authority to have a further hearing at the jurisdictional court level to provide for resentencing of the habitual troublemaker and nonconformist.

The premise behind such a theory of continued jurisdictional involvement would insure the involvement and working agreement that do not now exist between the court and the institution. This might also prevent the courts from using the prison system as a dumping grounds for certain cases upon which they (the courts) may have failed to act appropriately.

Continued jurisdictional involvement would also hold the imprisoned offender more responsible for his institutional behavior while in custody as well as punish him for any nonconformity. Such an inmate now may only lose early parole consideration or may merely have to serve his full sentence. He is, in effect, serving his punishment for the act that resulted in his commitment, but he is not being held responsible for further acts of violence while institutionalized. If the inmate could be convicted of additional criminal acts committed in prison, then such a proposal would be comparable to a habitual criminal status, and the institution could conceivably resentence an inmate, for example, who is on a five- to ten-year rap, to a ten- to twenty-year sentence if he persists in fighting the system.

In summary, the court system must learn to use *selective sentencing*. Although it may be feasible to terminate some cases with routine dispositions such as certain traffic violations, sentencing must never become wholly routine. It is acknowledged that punishment must fit the crime, but the key is to tailor the sentencing to fit the particular needs of the offender whenever possible.

Appropriate sentencing demands that the following ingredients be blended well if the recipe is to be successful.

Recognition of Social Causative Factors Peculiar to the Offense.   Lower court judges are inclined to give little consideration to the causes behind "nuisance" cases on the docket. The traffic accident where the vehicle had "an odor or alcohol throughout" might be more than sufficient grounds to believe either the driver or his passengers have been drinking. Unless the judge pursues the case by asking pertinent questions or unless he reviews the past arrest record of the defendant and notes that there have been prior arrests for drunk and other alcohol-related cases, he is in no position to determine a cause, let alone a possible cure. Good doctors diagnose from symptoms, and good judges should likewise learn to practice that art.

A Thorough Understanding of Sentencing Alternatives.   Despite the fact that the role of the court is the protection of society, judges must constantly review cases at the time of sentencing to mentally evaluate whether or not incarceration is better than probation in view of the offense as well as in view of the particular offender. Although the offense may be of great aggravation, it may be the first time before the court for this offender. The accused may be of otherwise good character, and the disposition may very well tip the scales in how he will react to both the judicial system and authority in the future if his personal social attributes are not taken into account. Appropriate sentencing must be a composite of what is good for all—society and the offender—and if there is any way of providing satisfaction with deterrence, it is the role of the judge to explore all such possibilities at the time of sentencing.

Positive Use of Community Resources. Judges often feel that legal matters should be handled in a legal context within the court system. Their frequent failure to recognize that resources exist to assist them within the community might be termed "blind sentencing." Judges in small communities where mental health or counseling services of a classical nature are not available often feel that if the community cannot tolerate the offender, neither can they. Yet the smallest of hamlets can offer the services of clergy, physicians, and educators, any of whom may be able to offer counseling assistance or suggestions as alternatives to penal commitments.

The Development of Court Services. Although sounding like a commercial for the balance of this book, we would like to suggest that the court is making futile gestures if it demands adherence of the offender without being able to monitor his progress. We acknowledge that there are some offenders without a social conscience and who have no regrets about what they have done other than the fact they were caught. However, this text addresses itself to the hopefully repentant offender who has genuine regrets about what he has done and would like to not only make amends but would like some assistance in assuring himself and the court that he can do so.

It is this type of assistance that probation and parole try to provide. The court cannot unto itself correct the actions of all offenders, nor can the time spent in prison assure even the offender that he may not reoffend upon release. It is only by trying with assistance and guidance from parole and probation officers that the offender can find out if he's been worth the efforts of the justice system to make him into a better citizen.

SUGGESTED READINGS

ADAMS, THOMAS F., *Introduction to the Administration of Justice: An Overview of the Justice System and Its Components.* Englewood Cliffs, N.J.: Prentice-Hall, Inc., 1975.

American Bar Association Project on Standards for Criminal Justice, *Standards Relating to Sentencing Alternatives and Procedures.* New York: Office of Criminal Justice Project, Institute of Judicial Administration, 1968.

BESHAROV, DOUGLAS J., *Juvenile Justice Advocacy: Practice in a Unique Court.* New York: The Practicing Law Institute, 1974.

CARTER, LIEF H., *The Limits of Order*. Lexington, Mass.: D.C. Heath & Company, 1974.

Chamber of Commerce of the United States, *Modernizing Criminal Justice Through Citizen Power,* College Park, Md., 1973.

CLARK, RAMSEY, *Crime in America.* New York: Simon & Schuster, 1970.

COFFEY, ALAN, EDWARD ELDEFONSO, AND WALTER HARTINGER, *An Introduction to the Criminal Justice System and Its Components.* Englewood Cliffs, N.J.: Prentice-Hall, Inc., 1974.

COFFEY, ALAN, AND VERNON E. RENNER, eds., *Criminal Justice as a System: Readings.* Englewood Cliffs, N.J.: Prentice-Hall, Inc., 1975.

FOGEL, DAVID, *We Are the Living Proof: The Justice Model for Corrections.* Cincinnati: W. H. Anderson Company, 1975.

FRANKEL, HON. MARVIN E., "Lawlessness in Sentencing," *Cincinnati Law Review,* no. 1 (1972).

GARDINER, JOHN A., AND MICHAEL MULKEY, eds., *Crime and Criminal Justice.* Lexington, Mass.: D. C. Heath & Company, 1975.

HIRSCH, ANDREW VON, *Doing Justice: The Choice of Punishment.* New York: Hill & Wang, 1976.

HOGRATH, JOHN, *Sentencing as a Human Process.* Toronto: University of Toronto Press, 1971.

MATHER, LYNN M., *Plea Bargaining or Trial?* Lexington, Mass.: D. C. Heath & Company, 1976.

National Advisory Commission on Criminal Justice Standards and Goals, *Criminal Justice System.* Washington, D.C., 1973.

PRASSEL, FRANK R., *Introduction to American Criminal Justice.* New York: Harper & Row Publishers, Inc., 1975.

3

Probation and Parole: Historical Overview

In all of the history of literature, there has never been assembled a more bizarre group of creatures than can be found in mythology. Were it possible to bring but a handful of them to life, it might be expected that they would be quite comfortable as trick-or-treaters on Halloween or in supporting roles on the horror shows that appear on late night television.

The ultimate examples of probation and parole officers might well resemble some of these mythological creatures. To be totally effective in their respective roles, these officers would have to be almost as physically grotesque as anything in ancient Greek mythology. They would have to be of tremendous stature to command the fearful respect of some of the offenders they must supervise. Each of them would also have to be possessed of an unusually large head to house the vast knowledge needed to portray a father or mother surrogate, a junior psychiatrist, a magician, and an exorcist, all in addition to the normal human qualities. The head would be encircled by many eyes, enabling the individual to be totally and visually aware of everything that is going on everywhere at all times.

The mouth would contain two tongues—one coated with a caustic substance and the other saturated with the sweetest of condiments; and both such organs would operate independently of each other. The heart would be replaced by a computer, and the body would be graced by multiple arms—one to beckon and invite, one with which to strike and reject, a third to manipulate the paper work involved, and a fourth to protect the posterior. The ability to leap buildings at a single bound and to travel faster than a speeding bullet would be nice but not mandatory.

Although it is acknowledged that mythology and reality are antipodal in nature, so for that matter are some of the conflicting roles that must be assumed by probation and parole officers in the course of the fulfillment of their duties. Likewise there has been a divergence over the years from the historical conception of these roles to the stereotyped supposition accorded them today—albeit from different perspectives—by offenders and the lay public, as to the intent and functions of probation and parole. The basic purpose of this chapter is to trace the rise of these professions and their growth into current models of practice. When viewed from the standpoint of professional recognition, these are relatively young fields of endeavor. Their basis of origin, however, is deeply entrenched in the annals of history, law, and the social concern among people one for another.

One of the prefatory assumptions for this type of a book has been that there seems to be a general lack of understanding about probation and parole as a whole, as well as seemingly undistinguishable differences between the two professions when scrutinized by the unknowing. Perhaps this is because the functional differences are not apparent since quite often the methods, roles, and clients dealt with by probation and parole are similar. Both professions are dealing with offenders, who are sometimes unwilling recipients of the process and are there out of necessity, rather than by choice.

For introductory purposes, a probation officer works with offenders prior to, or in lieu of, the latter being sent to a penal institution, whereas the parole officer supervises offenders after they have been released from a penitentiary or reformatory setting. In short, one provides guidance and control before the fact of incarceration, the other after the fact.

HISTORY OF THE JUSTIFICATION OF PUNISHMENT

Direct Influences of Christian Teachings

It first must be accepted that the legal laws of today are the outgrowths of moral laws. When Moses returned from the mountain top bearing the tablets of stone, it is doubtful if even his prophetic vision would have enabled him to foresee the fruits of his labor in shaping the social and legal standards as our society knows them today. Biblical history, especially as taken from the Book of Exodus, relates the prescribed punishment for certain acts as committed against one's brother or neighbor. Although the text does not state in so many words who was to impose these penalties—for this was long before the sophistication of our correctional processes of today—certainly a precedent by chronicle was set forth. Little by way of theory has changed today. The basic difference of note is that provisions have since been made for not only the establishment of guilt but for an appropriate—if not always humane—manner of the implementation of some form of legal action for punishing the offender.

Somewhat like statistics, the Bible is often used to support arguments and to document or to disprove almost any topic, with each interpretation being shaped by the particular needs of those who used it. If, however, one accepts the written words of the Bible at face value, there is little doubt as to the reflections upon evil, justice, and punishment. Although not the best of literary practices, the quoting of excerpts, without documentation and out of context, is often used to prove a point. From the use of such Biblical verses as "An eye for an eye, a tooth for a tooth" and "Because sentence against an evil work is not executed speedily, therefore the heart of the sons of men is fully set in them to do evil," one can readily conclude that when men dropped from the favor of God, that the further verse, "Vengeance is mine saith the Lord" became a precedent that has since been assimilated by our judicial system today.

It might be concluded that some of the elements of Christianity called for retribution as well as a no-nonsense attitude toward those factors that might contribute to the perpetuation of immoral/illegal acts. We must then accept the fact that moral values have had a very specific place within not only the framework of the law but within corrections, for hundreds of years. The Calvinistic influence represents a melding of elements of both Christianity and a rudimentary approach to corrections as a deterrent to further unacceptable acts. The phrase "An idle mind breeds mischief" is not necessarily attributable to Calvin, but it can be assumed that had it been a popular saying in his time, Calvin would have had it engraved and hung in a very prominent place for all to see!

Calvin advocated that good hard work was beneficial not only to the body but also to the soul and mind of man. Labor had two intrinsic values: (1) It promoted a product that served a useful function to others; and (2) it promoted a matter of pride within man through a sense of legitimate achievement. The word *legitimate* is a meaningful key, for it connotes the idea of gain through the efforts of one's own doing, in contrast to *illegitimacy,* which bears the implication of achieving without earning, often the mark of certain offenders who plunder others for gain.

The influence of the teachings of Calvin has been apparent throughout the years. The early workhouses that played such a prominent history in colonial America were a carryover in both theory and practice from England. Rather than mere punishment, work was used as a form of atonement and retribution to a society that had been wronged by the act of the offender. Not only was it hoped that the forced labor would have a benign effect on the offender, but it was a means to help him become cognizant of the fact that there is value in doing good for others by making a meaningful contribution through the fruits of his own labor. The workhouses, theoretically like the sentencing procedures of today, attempted to match the act and the ability of the offender to his punishment. The adult male offender, for example, had to cut and stack wood for the community fires, whereas the adult female or youthful offender was given a less physically demanding job commensurate with her/his ability to produce.

The old chain gangs of the South and western parts of the United States were not that far removed from Calvinistic theories. Even though much of the labor of offenders committed to penitentiaries and reformatories is designed for a diversionary and management purpose—remember the saying "Idle minds breed mischief"—it was also thought that hard work would have the tendency to break the spirit of the individual. To belittle and to reduce was not unlike the breaking of a wild bronco, so that once broken, the individual would become manageable and serve a useful function.

Perhaps Calvin had, as his frame of reference, chapters 21 and 22 from the Book of Exodus. These chapters concern themselves primarily with what could be called—in the terminology of today—acts of violence and appropriate methods of restitution and retribution. There may well be some correlation between this terminology and that of the courts today. It is noted that most court forms use the basic terminology of *the people of the State of* or *of the City of* to designate that this is a crime or an offense against not merely an individual victim but against society; hence the use of the term *the people.* The association between the concepts of Calvin and our current times is quite apparent.

The relationship between *crime* and *sin* is but a further extension of the principles of Christianity. A sinful person was more often than not recognized by the way in which he behaved—that is, he acted in a manner that was not in keeping with, and was in opposition to, the moral values of society. To act in a sinful manner or to engage in evil acts was generally an indication that such persons were possessed of the Devil. *Possessed* was interpreted to mean that the Devil actually inhabited the body and controlled the mind of those individuals, and only by casting out these evil spirits could the individual return to and fulfill the role of a decent and law-abiding citizen. If all acts of the holy men failed in their efforts to dislodge the evil spirits, it then sometimes became necessary to destroy the individual in order to likewise destroy the Devil that existed within him. Christianity provides not only this explanation of the individual's sinful behavior but, as David Dressler suggests in a discussion of the doctrine of sin, Christianity included the idea of punishment for various and sundry transgressions as a means of making amends.[1] By having to suffer or to pay a physical price, the sinner thus atoned for his transgressions.

Perhaps one of the most vivid portrayals of the attempt to exorcise evil

---

[1]David Dressler, *Practice and Theory of Probation and Parole* (New York: Columbia University Press, 1969), p. 3.

spirits from the bodies of "possessed" individuals is exemplified by the witch hunts of early New England. Witchcraft is interpreted here to mean the art of controlling or manipulating natural forces by power(s) that were attributable to or obtained from the Devil. Supposedly the possessors of such powers had gained this ability by having entered into a pact with the Devil for the possession of their bodies and souls. Although the nature of "witchly" acts was ill-defined, one form of punishment was customarily prescribed for those individuals who were judged to be so possessed—that is, death. The execution usually took the form of burning at the stake, and it was done in full view of the whole community. In fact, it was demanded that the town turn out in force to watch this happening so not only might the people have the assurance that the evil had been overcome, but also the punishment was deemed to act as a deterrent to anyone who might be tempted to take over the art and practice of the deceased.

It might be assumed that many individuals labeled as "witches" were mentally ill or retarded individuals who acted in peculiar ways because of their special afflictions. It was characteristic to view such people as having been punished by God for a sin that they had committed and to see their mental state as representative of this chastisement. It was not illogical for our colonial forefathers to assume that when a person dropped out of favor with God, he then might align himself with the Devil as the only other source that could provide him with favor.

Witches were deemed evil people for two specific reasons. First of all, no one patronized a witch unless he wanted a curse or other ghastly act to be directed at an enemy or at someone who had wronged him. Since it was wrong to retaliate against one's brother, the witch became the colonial predecessor of today's "hit man," and he (she) was "employed" to punish or create hardship for a designated person. Considered equally wrong, and reflective of the times, was the fact that witches did not involve them-selves in gainful labor, and they were thus able to gain some form of profit—their fee for a curse rendered—through a means other than the results of righteous toil.

Indirect Influences of Christianity

During the late eighteenth and early nineteenth centuries, philosophers who adhered to the principles of the Englightenment began to seek an ex-planation that would sever the relationship between sin and crime. The argument of this period was that offenders were not to be considered as possessed by evil spirits but rather they should be thought of as being possessed of the desire for criminal involvement for personal gain. It became understandable that the offender preferred to pluck the apples from the trees of another rather than to cultivate an orchard of his own. The theorists surmised that involvement in a criminal act was a deliberate choice and could only be offset or deterred if the pain that was inflicted at the time of apprehension was sufficiently strong so as to offset the pleasure or profit that was to be gained through the illicit activity.

Perhaps two other indirect Christian contributions should be referred to at this point. The word *indirect* is used here to denote the concepts of certain Christian groups that were applied with some degree of success in working with offenders. One such Christian group that left a rather indelible mark on corrections in general, and especially on penal institutions, was the Quakers of Philadelphia. The other contribution was the monastic concept as practiced in the Auburn prison system in New York State. Both are discussed below.

In the late 1700s, the Quakers working with offenders who were housed in the Walnut Street jail in Philadelphia advanced the idea that prisoners should be forced to meditate upon their behavior, to reflect upon their shortcomings, and to think and dwell upon their acts of evil. The hope was that through self-examination, the futility of their ways would be revealed to them and that such offenders would be self-launched into a program of rehabilitation. Such self-scrutiny could be related to two words not uncommon to the teachings of Christianity—*penance* and *penitent*. The Quakers were especially fond of the use of the idea of being penitent, and they felt that offenders who could use this quality would be capable of effecting changes within themselves so as to become more socially acceptable. What is even more significant, perhaps, is the relationship between the words *penitent* and *penitentiary*, a fact that does not leave much to the imagination as to the hoped-for function of the early penal institutions. Suffice it to say, the derivative remains with us. The companion penal institution for lesser offenders is still called, in most states, *the reformatory,* another derivative springing forth from still another hoped for byproduct—the ability to reform or to change one's ways.

The second indirect Christian contribution came from the Auburn prison system of New York. The Auburn system, as it is referred to in correctional circles, borrowed a page from Christian concepts and probably was not even aware of having done so at the time. In many monasteries, today as in times past, only the most basic needs of the monks are provided for, including the small cubicles in which they live. These cubicles are painfully barren by intent. The lack of any personal embellishments is supposedly conducive to thought and meditation because all worldy distractions are removed. Living a simple, barren, and sterile life will then enable the individual to focus on the immediate task at hand. The Auburn prison apparently used some of these monastic concepts, for it was one of the first penal institutions to provide single cells for inmates. Further, it is said that about the only thing that was furnished, in addition to a place to sleep and provision of the basic personal needs of the inmates, was a Bible.

Few correctional administrators within the penal system would readily correlate the use of cells with Christian concepts. Although the primary desire of such administrators would be for the repentance or the reform of their wards, the general consensus of most wardens and other such administrators would be that it is insufficient to expect that isolation alone, even with the aid of a Bible, would be adequate by itself to effect the rehabilitation of most offenders. Reality tells us that individual cells, if our prison population could allow for the luxury of them, are used primarily for purposes of control and management as well as for protecting the inmate from being either the perpetrator or the victim of violence.

PROBATION

Probation might best be described as a trial period during which time an individual is expected to prove his worth and ability to meet certain required standards. The same definition applies to an offender, a person in a new job or an applicant to a social organization. Each case requires an examination of the individual's qualities. In the case of an offender, he hopes to be able to prove himself—or at least to be found worthy of—a second chance before being locked up in a penal institution.

Probation is a legal tool of the court and is granted, with certain legal exceptions, by a formal order of a judge as a disposition of the case at hand. The probation officer is a legally empowered officer of the court who has the authority to uphold any demands of a reasonable nature imposed upon the client as well as to take the appropriate action necessary to enforce conformity to those demands. Generally, probation officers have the power of arrest and the ability to detain and to bring their client back before the court to determine a further legal course of action—if the offender has not conformed to the standards set for him.

The notable legal exceptions referred to above are pertinent primarily in matters concerning juveniles. There is a growing trend today to use diversionary-type programs where juveniles are concerned. Such programs offer alternatives to law enforcement officials in processing juvenile matters. The officials initiate probable legal action by arresting the child and placing him in custody. This action may necessitate court involvement and result in a police record. The alternative is referring the juvenile to a youth service bureau where emphasis is on providing service rather than punishment. Such cases may never be exposed to a court system, and the desire is to act on a preventive basis on the behalf of the offender while he or she is yet young enough to be successfully turned around in a socially acceptable direction.

Part of the rationale for the growth of programs of this nature is based on a socio-legal principle relating to juveniles, called the "age of reason."

The implications are that somewhere along the lines of a developing mental and chronological age a moral conscience develops. It is suggested that very young offenders probably are not so much "immoral' as they are "amoral" in nature.

The theory behind the age of reason concept is that there is a point in time, although not obviously the same for each individual, where a juvenile can be held socially and legally accountable for his own actions and delinquent behavior. Prior to this somewhat nebulous socio-psycho-legal point in time and maturation, it is theoretically questionable if a child really understands the ramifications of his behavior, even though his act may be a totally volitional one, for which he receives some degree of pleasure or excitement. For example, the small child of five years of age who steals a piece of candy in a grocery store may recognize some wrongness in his act, but he certainly cannot be expected to recognize the moral implications of such an act.

Even among courts, it is difficult to reach any degree of conformity in defining a level of jurisdiction based on age. A legal determination of a juvenile varies and may extend from 16 to 21 years of age, depending on different local statutes. Certain institutions and jurisdictions, notably at the federal level, think of *youth* rather than of *juveniles* in the designating of confinement facilities. To complicate matters even more, some jurisdictions gauge the offense and the degree of its severity in determining the type of penal institution to which an offender may be sentenced.

Some jurisdictions still archaically demand that a child be adjudicated in order to grant a probationary status of a formal nature. *Adjudication* is a legal declaration that simply means that little Johnny is now the possessor of a record, that he has been determined to be a bona fide juvenile delinquent, and that he is so declared because he has been found guilty of the act for which he was apprehended; in short, he has been declared a junior criminal of sorts. He now is possessed of what is popularly called *a police record,* an entry of legal note on the court file. Although there exists a means of expunging or deleting this record at the legal time of entrance into adulthood, this rap sheet meanwhile may be used against the juvenile if for no other reason than from that of social expectation, i.e., that he is a troublemaker who can be expected to reoffend and he is therefore not to be trusted.

Moral and social standards demand a more equitable handling of juvenile matters, and therefore a close scrutiny is needed for probation intervention. Many injustices to juveniles still exist within the court system, primarily because of a lack of meaningful alternatives as well as because of traditional responses to certain circumstances. The child who is a habitual truant from school is a good example of this. His truancy may be related to his intellectual inability to cope with his academic obligations, and he faces certain frustrations and failures when he does attend as required. He may be truant because of cultural reasons or simply because his family does not place any value in a formalized education. Due to compulsory education laws and a truancy record, this child may be brought before a court and declared a delinquent child, one who without any social accounting for his behavior by society could conceivably be committed to an institution for delinquents. Thus, unless the specific needs of the juvenile offender are recognized and a specialized placement effected based on those perceived needs, it is conceivable that the child may experience more adverse affects than if no diversionary tactics were attempted whatsoever. Status offenders—those cases involving runaways and habitual truants—should be isolated from juveniles who are placed in programs based largely on their delinquent, criminal-type forms of behavior.

Part of the blame must be given to the courts—for improper and poor judgment, as well as for a lack of meaningful and appropriate sentencing alternatives. The blame, however, should also be on the shoulders of society, for the law is based on social demand. A faint echo seems to be present from times of old when there existed only two alternatives available to an individual—gainful involvement in an activity of social merit, or a predestined career in antisocial activities.

The Growth of Probation

Although many of the concepts for corrections in the United States were borrowed from the English system, the literature relating the history of criminology from the Continent is very limited regarding the use of probationary functions. Mention is made briefly here of the efforts of a Matthew Davenport Hill (date of birth 1792), who was an advocate for the use of probation services in England, but the evolution and practice of the program as we know it today were largely unheard of in Europe. It might be safe to assume, then, that the extensive growth and use of probationary practices are the stepchildren of our own American correctional practices.

Perhaps the most common functions akin to probation, used by the English as well as by the American colonial court system, were the practices of judicial reprieve and recognizance.[2] Although often used independently of each other, these practices were remarkably similar and may have eventually resulted in their becoming consecutive acts—recognizance following judicial reprieve—as a possible predecessor to probation. *Judicial reprieve* constituted no sentence by the court. Although guilt was acknowledged, no punishment was prescribed nor disposition made—as we conceive of it today. *Recognizance*, used in conjunction with, or more often than not in lieu of,

---

[2]Barbara A. Kay and Clyde B. Vedder, *Probation and Parole* (Springfield, Ill.: Charles C Thomas, Publisher, 1963), pp. 4–9.

judicial reprieve, was the release of an offender on the basis of his word or honor that he had no further intentions of reoffending.

Probation in the United States goes back about one hundred years, although it began considerably earlier than that on an informal basis. Its nonlegally sanctioned beginning was with what we popularly call today a *volunteer probation officer.* A Boston shoemaker by the name of John Augustus in the 1840s was appalled by the number of offenders who were appearing before the local magistrate on charges of being drunk in public. Even more appalling perhaps to the shoemaker was the fact that the same sick and weary faces were before the court over and over, only to be punished again and again without much hope for any change in their behavior. Mustering up what must have been a tremendous amount of courage, Augustus asked for the opportunity to have an offender released to his custody so that he might attempt to help the sodden unfortunate. The magistrate, probably somewhat surprised but having no real alternatives, released the offender to Augustus, and a new era in court dispositions was conceived.[3]

History does not reflect how extensively John Augustus's help was used, nor the level of success he achieved. It is suspected that his presence and intent caused some feelings of ambivalence among the judiciary of those times. Quite probably, the judges may have been reluctant to utilize unknown "outsiders" and may also have viewed Augustus as a meddler in the affairs of the court. On the other hand, there is reason to believe that judicial frustrations arising out of a lack of effective alternatives were no different then than they are today. One thing is certain, however, the one-to-one relationship of a caring individual for another can and often does work wonders.

Legislation initially provided for probation only at the municipal level. Even so, there existed some real controversies as to the legality of this function. Boston, which provided for the advent of this service in 1878, first had to question the feasibility of suspending a sentence as a method of a court disposition. The legal ramifications were studied and argued about for some fifteen years before the legality of this action was upheld. Today the *suspended sentence*—suspended in full or in part—is both an accepted and common practice when probation is granted.

During this same period of time, probation supervision was the function of the police rather than of an officer of the court. It was not until 1890, again in the state of Massachusetts, that probation became a recognized and sanctioned function of the courts at other than the municipal level. The first probation officers were approved by legislative act, and probation became a specifically paid profession. Even so, probation was conceived of initially as

---

[3]Charles P. May, *Probation* (New York: Hawthorne Books, Inc., 1974), p. 5.

being a service for juveniles only, and it was not until several years later that adults became bona fide clients of this service as well.

Probation Justified

There are many logical arguments for the use of probation services by the court system and on behalf of both society and the offender. One of the more basic causes is predicated on sheer economics. Although the costs will vary among penal institutions, and although the extent of the services they offer will also vary, the Federal Bureau of Prisons states the cost of confinement per inmate per day in 1975 was $20.34, or approximately $7,425.00 per inmate per year.[4] Based on the fact that probation officers are rarely able to devote more than an average of one hour per week to their clients in routine supervision, and based on an estimated starting salary for probation officers of $900 per month, this means that the cost of working with a probationer comes out to approximately $5.00 per week. This is, of course, on the assumption that intensive services are not included as part of the rehabilitative process and that general investigative work and court time have now been completed. It might be argued that not only is service delivery cost less, but that the offender can continue to support himself and his family. Therefore, it is much more economical to use probation rather than prison.

Some courts have been able to diminish their costs for probation services by assessing what is known as *probationary fees* to be paid for by the client. Although these monetary contributions may serve to hold down costs below the figure given, the probationer may feel that he has been ethically "had" by having to pay these fees. Many probationers, although it might be recognized as a rationalization process, object to these probationary fees, contending that they are being "charged" twice, if not more than that, for the privilege of being under probationary supervision. They argue that they had a fine to pay, that they must now pay costs, and that conceivably they are also paying in another way when they have to miss work to report in as scheduled—all this for a service they do not want and feel they do not need.

It is obvious, then, that the offender who is allowed to remain in the community while under the supervision of a probation officer will certainly be less of a tax burden—both in regard to himself and in regard to his family. This must be qualified by stating that this can only be true if there is sufficient control and motivation for him not to reoffend. His failure to conform and to learn from his experience will obviously only serve to raise the total costs to society. A further amount would have to be added to the taxpayer's tab—the amount it would cost to process a new charge, not to men-

---

[4]United States Department of Justice, *Federal Bureau of Prisons, 1975* (Marion, Ill.: Federal Penitentiary. Printed by Federal Prison Industries, Inc., 1975).

tion the cost to the community and to the victim of the new offense. Probation must assume a high portion of the responsibility to assure this does not
happen, but more selective sentencing by the court will also assure a greater
chance of success with probationers.

There are some equally important but rather controversial reasons for
trying to work with certain offenders while retaining them in the community.
A major question is often raised in the literature of corrections—or in
criticism of corrections—as to whether too much emphasis is being placed
on treatment, and even more significant, whether there really exists such a
thing as a "sick" offender.[5,6] Although this subject will be dealt with in
detail in a later chapter, it may be assumed—for the sake of discussion
here—that some offenses are characteristically "sick" in content and
nature. Reference is made here to sexual crimes and perhaps certain acts of
arson. Without going into detail on the pathology of such offenses, we must
acknowledge that treatment is more likely to be available to the suspected
"sick" offender who is living in the community than will be available to
him during his period of incarceration. At times of economic stress, the
budgetary cutbacks in penal institutions almost always touch first on treatment resources. Most prisons are more inclined, if for no other reason than
social pressures from the outside community, to hire two new guards rather
than one caseworker or one psychologist. This is true even when there is no
appreciable monetary difference between one professional or two nonprofessional positions. Despite the attempts of correctional administrators
to provide treatment programs within the walls, security will almost always
be given priority over such programs. It must be acknowledged, however,
that most inmates want no part of treatment programs anyway; their main
concern is to get their time over with and to get out.

The courts face a problem when they have to choose an appropriate
sentence for the mentally disturbed/dysfunctional offender. The alternatives seem to be three in nature: (1) the classical penal institution, (2) a
mental hospital, or (3) probation. Quite often, these are not even practical
choices, for the penal facility lacks treatment services, the mental hospital
lacks security facilities, and probation cannot effectively deal with control,
treatment, and community resentment at the same time. In most cases, it
might be facetiously said that the court usually reaches a decision by attempting to grease the wheel that is squeaking the loudest and contents itself
by passing its own responsibility off onto another.

It is recommended here that certain disturbed offenders should be treated
within the community whenever it is feasible to do so. Not only are there

⁵Judith Wilks and Robert Martinson, "Is the Treatment of Criminal Offenders Really
Necessary?" *Federal Probation,* 40, no. 1 (March 1976), 3–9.

⁶Frank Dell'Apa, et al., "Advocacy, Brokerage, Community: The ABC's of Probation and
Parole," *Federal Probation,* 40, no. 4 (December 1976), 3–8.

usually more therapy resources available that can be brought to bear on the offender, but treatment in the community is more likely to be a total treatment. Total therapy/treatment implies working not only with the offender but with the offender's family as well. It becomes an attempt to therapeutically manipulate the offender and to manipulate his environment also. For example, most therapists recognize that counseling, especially marital counseling, is a relatively futile process unless both partners participate willingly and openly. Such a therapeutic process allows for confrontation and mutual decision making. A program of total therapy of this nature, within the prison structure, is not at all practical due to a lack of both professional staff and time as well as the fact that limited accessibility to the penal institution precludes the participation of the offender's family in the therapy program.

Closely related to this theory of the manipulation of the environment is the argument that prisons represent an artificial environment and are therefore not conducive to the solution of problems that may have been contributing factors in the offender finding his way there in the first place. The fact that an individual "ripped off" a bank to get money to feed his family because he could not find sufficient work cannot, of course, be socially justified. But there is not much justification in attempting to work with the same offender in some type of budgetary counseling or instructing him in the art of how to find a better job if he still has to do fifteen years before he can put his newly found knowledge into practice.

Penal institutions are conditioning situations. The basic learning process assimilated by the inmates has little to do with the subject of repentance; rather the inmates are concentrating their attention on how to manipulate their way out and on how not to get caught the next time if they decide to continue their criminal habits on the outside. The conditioning or programming process may merely convince the offender that he lacked the necessary expertise or luck to pull off a job and not get caught, rather than teaching him how to face temptation and overcome it by seeking more socially appropriate alternatives.

Probationary services cannot be expected to provide a total solution to the problem of continued criminal behavior. The weakness of the court system has been stated to be the lack of ability to gauge the potential of an offender and to be able to determine whether or not he is a good prospect for rehabilitation. Probation is and always will remain a service of limited potential; it is not a panacea. Its degree of effectiveness must be based on the recognition of not only its own weaknesses but also the weaknesses of the clients with whom it must deal. A wit once said that the epitome of failure is a pregnant prostitute. Failure in the probation profession is epitomized by indiscriminate referrals from court to an otherwise adequate probationary staff. To deny that there are other factors that contribute to probationary failure is to whistle in the dark.

PAROLE

If probation can be conceived of as an elementary level of schooling in an attempt to straighten out the offender before he is committed to a penal institution, then it logically follows that parole supervision is postgraduate work. Parole may be defined as the supervision of an offender following his release from a prison or reformatory and during the period of time that he is being reintegrated into society. Parole is a privilege rather than a right and may be said to be earned rather than be routinely given. Its uniqueness is that it is applicable only to those individuals who have been granted an early release rather than having to serve the full sentence that was imposed on them by the court at the time of sentencing.

Parole should not be confused with a pardon. The latter is an act of clemency wherein a sentence may be terminated by executive order. If the offender is in a state institution, the pardon would be granted by order of the governor; whereas it would take the order of the president to release an offender from a federal penal facility.

Parole eligibility is determined by an appointed or designated board that functions specifically for this purpose. The board is usually comprised of from three to seven full-time professionals, who work closely in conjunction with prison officials and the parole personnel serving the offender's community of residence or the proposed community to which he will return upon being released.

The Origins of Parole

Many Americans who take pride in their family tree might well be appalled to know that some of their colonial forefathers may have been convicts released from English prisons to come to America. The fact that many of those ancestors were pardoned rather than paroled would do little to appease the dignity of those few citizens who are more concerned that the blood should be running blue rather than red in their veins. Yet this is one of England's historical contributions to the colonization of America—the deportation of criminals.

England, prior to the Revolutionary War, was caught up in a rather severe economic depression. The colonies, on the other hand, although not rich, had more than adequate resources to provide for their needs, but they were experiencing an insufficient labor force. The colonists had only one real choice and that was to appeal to their mother country for assistance. England, however, could find only an insignificant number of volunteers who were willing to be uprooted from their country to go to a vast, unknown, and savage wilderness. The English government also did not want to part with any of its skilled tradesmen for fear that the loss would be a permanent one. Further, it is speculated that even at that time the English rulers had an uneasy feeling about the eventual and inevitable independence of the colonies, so they were unwilling to grant any loans because they might never be repaid. Therefore, to achieve a mutual need without jeopardizing its own interests, the mother country began to cast an eye at its bulging prison population, and English prisoners began being transferred to the colonies in the early seventeenth century.

Around 1617 the Privy Council permitted individuals convicted of robbery and who appeared physically capable of heavy work to be "pardoned" to the American colonies. There their services were sold on a bid basis, and they were then acknowledged in this capacity to be "indentured servants." This procedure was eventually extended to convicted felons other than those classified as dangerous criminals. Offenders, to be eligible, were required to meet certain standards. Their initial sentence to prison had to exceed seven years but could not exceed ten. Those who met this initial requirement were eligible after four years in custody but not after six years. The English government also established some other requirements along the following lines.[7]

1. The power of revoking or altering the license of a convict could be used in the case of his misconduct.
2. If the offender wished to retain the privileges accorded him, he had to prove himself continuingly worthy of the clemency that was granted by the Queen.
3. The offender, in order to retain the privileges, had to exhibit good work habits and refrain from associating with characters of ill repute. Evidence of his failure to conform required that he be returned to prison to complete the terms of his original sentence.

It should be noted that England did not retain legal custody over the offenders released to America, although it was expected that the colonists would uphold the conditions of the agreement and would take the necessary legal action to implement the suspended sentence if the offender failed to uphold the conditions of his pardon. Following a successful period of adjustment, a "ticket of leave" was provided for the offender. This was a declaration signed by the colonial governor that excused the convict of any further obligations and then permittd him to live an independent life. Although the release of English prisoners to the colonies represented more of a pardon than a parole, the seeds were now sown for a type of parole that was in keeping with this form of release as we know it today.

In the 1830s, Alexander Maconchie, who was later to become the governor of Norfolk Island, made the personal observation that the prisoners confined at Norfolk were little more than slaves of the system and that their

[7]Charles L. Newman, *The Work of the Probation and After-Care Officer* (Atlantic Highlands, N.J.: Humanities Press, Inc., 1967), pp. 25–26.

"state of depravity" was attributable to their general treatment. In an effort to upgrade their mental state, Maconchie came up with the idea of granting marks, which were designed to serve as a form of wages. At his suggestion, the duration of an offender's sentence came to be measured by units of labor accomplished and accounted for on a daily basis. It is unfortunate, however, that Maconchie's stay at Norfolk was limited to about a four-year duration. Even so, the ideas he advanced were noted to be full of promise and seemed relatively successful in reaching some of his desired goals during his short tenure there.

When Sir William Crofton became the head of the Irish prison system in 1854, he borrowed some of the concepts of Maconchie. He began by instituting a system whereby the classification of offenders was governed by marks given for good conduct as well as for individual achievements. Crofton felt that prisons should be more than mere facilities for the safekeeping of offenders and that the dual role of these institutions should include a reward system to be considered in the form of tickets-of-leave for achieving inmates. Under Crofton's leadership, offenders coming out of prisons were subjected to a strict reporting system quite comparable to the parole standards of today. In rural areas of Ireland, "ticket-of-leave men" came under the supervision of the local police. In Dublin, there was created a position manned by a civilian with the title of "inspector of released prisoners." He maintained supervision of his charges and attempted to find them employment as well as helped ease their general transition into the community.[8]

After the Revolutionary War, when England no longer sent prisoners to America, the continent of Australia was established as a penal colony for British subjects. Contrary to the procedure used with the American colonies, the prisoners who were sent to Australia were not pardoned but served their full time, unless their behavior was so outstanding that they were rewarded by an early release. It was a rather ironic situation, however, because the released prisoners had no place to go unless they had unusual means that allowed them to return to England. Instead of being prisoners of walls, these men were prisoners of waters, waters that prevented them from being reunited with their families. The best they could hope for was to either have their family provide a financial way for their return, or to find gainful employment and, in turn, send for their family to join them in Australia.

The use of formal parole in America for its citizens goes back to the Elmira Reformatory in New York, which opened its doors in 1876. There, under the leadership of Superintendent Z. E. Brockway, a provision was made for what were called "good time laws." These laws provided for the early release of prisoners in exchange for good behavior. This system

---

[8]Charles L. Newman, *Sourcebook on Probation, Parole and Pardons* (Springfield, Ill.: Charles C Thomas, Publisher, 1958), p. 31.

represented a reward to the inmates that was eagerly sought for, but there was also a practical side of the matter, a solution to the overcrowding of the prisons. The "good time act" allowed a day and a half credit for every day served if the inmate was a model prisoner. As such, the prisoner could cut his time in half if he was willing to conform to the standards imposed on him. Brockway is also given credit for conceiving of the idea of an indeterminate sentence and advocating its use by the courts of that time.[9]

The "good time act" was not a pardon. The early release was granted on the stipulation that the offender had to report back to his local police department on a monthly basis until such time as he was originally sentenced for was completed. The police departments were used because there was no provision yet for a parole officer and because it was felt that the police were the only existing agency capable of exercising the needed legal authority, as well as the fact that they would have some knowledge of the whereabouts of the offender and his activities.

Parole was created by legislation in Massachusetts in about 1837.[10] In all likelihood it grew out of both social and legal needs. It may be surmised that the police, who were initially responsible for the supervision of parolees, felt that they had more important things to do than to "babysit" for ex-offenders, a task that was undoubtedly unpalatable to them.

We can only speculate, then, as is the case today, that there existed a percentage of parolees that could not or would not relate to supervision by the police. We can assume, then as now, that this grouping represented those offenders who were more likely than not to reoffend or at least to go through the balance of their lives with a chip on their shoulders and thinly disguised resentment toward society. The resentment has always been mutual. The offender, using typical defense mechanisms, blames everyone and everything—especially the police—for being committed to prison in the first place. And the police take a rather general reaction that implies "once a con, always a con." Their trust in the parolee is minimal and singular; he will reoffend at the slightest provocation and opportunity.

The police generally have not been interested in the parolee as anything other than a suspect. The social needs of parolees must be considered, but most police are not versed in the fine art of counseling skills. The social problems of the parolee reentering society are great, but this is not a role that the police can assume, even if they have the interest to do so. What the police can provide, however, is the deterrent effect to stimulate some motivation for the parolee to try and succeed in "making it" on the outside.

[9]Ibid., p. 33.

[10]Robert M. Carter, Richard A. McGee, and E. Kim Nelson, *Corrections in America* (Philadelphia: J. B. Lippincott Company, 1975), p. 201.

The Social Concern for Parole

In recent years, there has been a great deal of discussion centering on the future of parole. There appear to be two distinct trends of thought, which are characterized not only by a stand pro or con, but also by whether the opinion emanates from within or from without the correctional field. It would appear that a majority of the public who want the discontinuation of parole are those who are not professionally affiliated with the field of corrections and who objectively fail to see the possible consequences that would result from the curtailment of this privilege. Yet these cries for abolition are mixed with ambivalent sounds indicating the desire to have the cake and eat it too.

Society has long had difficulty in accepting the return of the prodigal son unless he comes with a money-back guarantee. The public wants neither inferior products nor inferior citizens without some possible recourse if something goes wrong. To many people, the convicted offender is representative of inferior quality. To illustrate this point, take the two perspectives, that of the public and that of the offender, when considering the individual who has "done time" in a penal institution. The offender will generally refer to himself as an *ex-con*, whereas the public tends to drop the prefix *ex* when making a similar reference. The offender prefers to think that all this is behind him, but the public refuses to make this distinction.

This example serves to illustrate part of the ambivalence found in the public cry to discontinue parole. Although Christian ethics may tell us to turn the other cheek, we add our own addendum in saying, "I will, but if he strikes too hard . . ." The public is most comfortable when it is least threatened, and opening the prison doors early is a decided threat to many. We demand some assurance that the parolee is changed, that he is ready, that he has been restored and is now complete. We feel that if he is let off too easily, he has gained nothing other than the tolerance needed to wait out a part of his sentence and to be able to play the necessary role until this opportunity is accorded him. The public reacts to the offender as if he were a bottle of wine who will become more mellow if he has the opportunity to age by spending time in the cooler before he is set out before the public eye. The real premise is, however, that the public habitually harbors the image that the offender has only suppressed his criminal tendencies and that he will forever remain a potential threat—hence the demand that the offender pay his price in full and with interest if necessary.

The perceptive public should realize that prisons cannot continue to absorb new offenders without the need to disgorge some of the old ones. The unexpressed hope is not for the discontinuation of parole, but for better parole services with more stringent controls placed on returning offenders. What is implied here is that the public grudgingly recognizes that sooner or later the offender must be considered for release, so what is needed is a bigger and better group of watchdogs to monitor these individuals. If concessions have to be made, let the public be protected through the use of vigilant parole agents who will not stand for the backsliding of their wards.

The general thinking from within correctional circles would seem to be that parole should be retained as an absolute necessity within the overall program.[11,12,13] Although criminologists and administrators of correctional agencies do periodically take a semiserious look at the functions of parole, they do so more out of necessity than because of any overwhelming desire to replace the program. There would seem to be at least three basic reasons why parole should not be discarded: management purposes, client responsibility, and public protection.

Mention has been made about the conditioning effects of penal institutions. The convict doing his time in a prison soon learns that there is little by way of a middle ground in the choice of roles he can assume; he is forced to fall on one side of the proverbial fence or on the other. He can fight the system and thereby win a solid place among his peers in the prison pecking order, or he can give an outward show of conformity that may or may not serve to fool staff, peers, and himself. For all practical purposes, the proposed abolishment of parole would do away with the need for conformity. Short of a pardon or some type of clemency, the offender would realize that there is no reward for him until his time is actually served in full. The possibility of an early out via parole is a management tool that is used by penal administrators to elicit acceptable inmate behavior. The prison snitch or stool pigeon is not giving information to the guards and administration because he is in opposition to a plan his peers have conceived such as an escape plot; the snitch is merely looking for a chance to feather his own nest and perhaps to get an early-out consideration because of his contribution.

When an incentive system is removed or taken away from either an individual or a group, there remains little motivation to seek recognition for good behavior since it will merely go unrecognized. Parole represents a sanction that offenders desperately want, and one that prison administrators can use to the advantage of management. Feedback of either a positive or a negative nature to parole board members from prison staff members may very well carry sufficient weight to confirm or to deny parole. To deprive or to remove sanctions such as parole will merely contribute to more unrest and more acting out behavior among the inmates.

The reintegration of the offender back into society is a difficult task. For many years, as an example, it was demanded that a parole candidate be able

[11]Daniel Glaser, *The Effectiveness of a Prison and Parole System* (New York: The Bobbs-Merrill Co. Inc., 1969), pp. 264–271.

[12]Reed K. Clegg, *Probation and Parole: Principles and Practices* (Springfield, Ill.: Charles C Thomas, Publisher, 1964), p. 31.

[13]Maurice H. Sigler, "Abolish Parole?" *Federal Probation,* 34, no. 2 (June 1975), 42–48.

to show proof of having gainful employment waiting for him at the time of his proposed release. Assuming that the offender did seven-years time, it is highly unlikely that he could produce any current letters of reference, show any marketable skills, or be current in his knowledge of contemporary changes and methods of doing a specific job, let alone be able to solicit work—because of such factors as a lack of a chance for a formal interview, an unknown date to be available for employment, and no opportunity for a firsthand view and study of the labor market. Preparole planning can assist in this matter, and a major part of such planning must be the responsibility of the parole officer.

Many crises can come and go while an offender is in custody, crises that may affect his very life but ones that he can do nothing about. His wife may have found a new boyfriend, his house may have been repossessed, his unmarried daughter may now be pregnant, and so on ad infinitum. The hopelessness and the despair the offender feels must be dealt with in an objective manner. Although he may initially feel that he can take care of these problems when he is released, his method of dealing with them may only serve to get him into more difficulty. Planning should commence on his own and his family's behalf before parole, not after. The assistance that can be given him by preparole planning may not only help strengthen the relationship with his family when he is released, but may also help solidify the relationship he will need with the parole agent.

Reentry into society for the convict is almost as difficult as the reentry into the earth's atmosphere for the astronaut; both require a lot of planning and a lot of assistance. Often potential employers are more concerned with the offenses than with the offender and his ability to hold and to produce on a job. And the fearful wife may wonder what kind of monster the prison has made of her husband and if he will be worse, not better, than when he was committed. Only through parole planning can some of the natural fears of the community and of the family be resolved.

Lastly, the public is only going to be willing to tolerate the parolee if it has adequate assurance that the ex-offender is being monitored during his adjustment period. This is one of the most probable reasons why parole will not be discontinued—the need to offer assurance to the public that controls will be maintained. One of the key characteristics of most offenders, which tends to go unnoticed in the search for more dynamic reasons for their activities, is the trait of irresponsibility. Holding the parolee, or for that matter the probationer, responsible for certain elementary demands is a very definite way of underscoring the fact that supervision exists. Although neither parole nor probation should be based on sheer intimidation, the fact that standards *are* imposed is sufficient to demand that they should be upheld.

Parole is the most common form of release from prisons and probably will continue to be so unless some innovative plan is devised to better gauge release methods. In 1970, it was estimated that approximately 70% of all felon offenders who were released from prison were released on a parole status.[14] It remains unclear whether the national crime rate is climbing as is often popularly acclaimed or whether the apprehension and conviction of offenders are greater than in the past. Suffice it to say, the overcrowding problems that face our penal institutions are reflective of an increasingly large number of penal commitments by the courts. Prisons are faced with the distinct possibility of having to replace at least one steel door with a revolving one because of the high commitment rate and the overtaxed space within the institutions. Bigger prisons are not the answer, but then neither is what facetiously might be called *indiscriminate parole*. This type of release is being necessitated, however, because of the high commitment rate. The Federal Bureau of Prisons, in its 1975 report, indicated that it is experiencing a 5.5% above operational capacity population, which could be even higher had the Bureau not contracted for services from community-based operations such as halfway houses or other facilities of a private nature.[15]

The use of parole as a management factor again becomes apparent. The necessity of having to place three to four prisoners in a cell designed initially for only two illustrates the lack of humane treatment for which prisons are sometimes criticized. Although it is recognized that inmates are always going to find fault with the penal system, overcrowding lends merit to their arguments. The lack of privacy, with the corresponding lack of opportunity to "back off and think," will only serve to foster violent acts arising out of problems in interpersonal relationships among inmates.

A further management problem is the provision of meaningful activities—be they vocational or of a leisure-time nature—as a means of keeping inmates gainfully involved in some type of productive enterprise. There may be grounds to feel that the use of the terms *meaningful/productive activities* are misnomers, but these terms are used here in the very real sense of actively involving the inmates in some type of time-consuming behavior not so much for the mere sake of learning or producing but for the advantage of the administration. The warden dwells under the correctional assumption that an idle inmate often uses his time for negative purposes, and such purposes are contradictory to the rationale behind prisoner control and the peaceful administration thereof.

The study of the history of probation and parole reveals two rather pertinent factors. First, despite Christian contributions to and influences on the origin of corrections, it has become apparent that although we may have

---

[14]National Advisory Commission on Criminal Justice Standards and Goals, *Corrections* (Washington, D.C.: U.S. Government Printing Office, 1973), p. 389.

[15]*Federal Bureau of Prisons, 1975*, p. 6.

adopted the principles for our own use, we have failed to likewise adopt the related ethics. Society, as related to its view of corrections, is caught in a quandary, a quandary characterized on one hand by tradition and on the other by empiricism. Because crime involvement is viewed as a choice to be individually decided upon by the offender, it remains difficult for the public to assume the role of its brother's keeper. We operate on the premise that certain forms of social misery are a product of chance, whereas others such as crime are a product of choice. We may show sympathy and sadness for the adolescent who becomes addicted to drugs at a very early age, but for the middle-aged problem drinker who has become addicted to alcohol, we feel little but disgust and contempt. We are fickle forgivers.

A second factor is that quite probably some of the public negativism that is directed toward corrections in general is an outgrowth of a seeming lack of innovative programs that are supposed to work in the rehabilitative process of turning the offender around. In conjunction with this, it is interesting to note that one of the most innovative and best publicized programs in the last decade has been the rebirth and revitalization of the volunteer counselor under the able leadership of the Honorable Keith Leenhouts of Royal Oak, Michigan. This now national association—Volunteers in Probation—has taken the concepts of John Augustus utilized some one hundred thirty years ago and has provided for the establishment of an "I care" approach in helping offenders to help themselves. Because many successful programs of today are directly based on old concepts, one may infer that nothing new or worthwhile is to be found in corrections.

Corrections, generally—aside from the above example—seem to have become somewhat stagnant. Research in the field is at a low ebb, and instead of new ideas, we are renovating old ones. Corrections are constantly faced with serving two masters—the offender and the public. Neither is the easiest master to get along with, and the only thing they both seem to have in common is expectations. Making satisfying as well as meaningful inroads is a difficult chore. Although a mason may be able to stand back at the end of a day's work and visibly account for how much he has accomplished, tangible effects are not as readily available to the human eye when working with individuals. Whether you call them *offenders, clients,* or *patients,* there is no readily available measuring device. History may never be able to record the event(s) in corrections that will mark the turning point in the cessation of crime, and the best efforts of the probation and parole officer may likewise seem futile. The fable of the race between the hare and the tortoise was based on a mismatch, but the correlation between that contest and the role of probation and parole should be obvious: "'Tis better to go slow and steady than it is to go fast and nowhere."

SUGGESTED READINGS

ABADINSKY, HOWARD, *Probation and Parole: Theory and Practice.* Englewood Cliffs, N.J.: Prentice-Hall, Inc., 1977.

CARTER, ROBERT M., RICHARD A. MCGEE, AND E. KIM NELSON, *Corrections in America.* Philadelphia: J. B. Lippincott Co., 1975.

CLARE, PAUL K, AND JOHN H. KRAMER, *Introduction to American Corrections.* Boston: Holbrook Press, 1976.

FOX, VERNON, *Introduction to Corrections.* Englewood Cliffs, N.J.: Prentice-Hall, Inc., 1972.

HAMER, JOHN, "Criminal Release System." Washington D.C.: Editorial Research Reports, 1976 (pamphlet).

KILLINGER, GEORGE C., HAZEL B. KERPER, AND PAUL F. CROMWELL, JR., *Probation and Parole in the Criminal Justice System.* St. Paul, Minn.: West Publishing Company, 1976.

KNUDTEN, RICHARD D., *Crime in a Complex Society: An Introduction to Criminology.* Homewood, Ill.: Dorsey Press, 1970.

MAY, CHARLES PAUL, *Probation.* New York: Hawthorn Books, Inc., 1974.

PARKER, WILLIAM, *Parole: Origins, Development, Current Practices and Statutes.* College Park, Md.: American Correctional Association, 1972.

STANLEY, DAVID T., *Prisoners among Us: The Problem of Parole.* Washington, D.C.: The Brookings Institution, 1976.

4

Professional Growth and Training

The attempt to determine the intrinsic properties of a "professional" is not without its problems. The classical definition tries to distinguish the professional from the amateur on the basis of the degree of self-involvement for the expressed purpose of earning a livelihood. There are, however, other implied qualifications as perceived by the public that alter and enlarge on the perception of the individual under consideration. One such qualification is the educational and/or skill-training demands for the role to be assumed.

Most "professionals" are perceived to be in the same category as doctors and lawyers who have not only achieved the benefits of a college education but have also had to undergo postgraduate work. In addition to such formalized training, it is required that these professionals achieve a form of certification or license based on demonstrated knowledge as well as practical skills before they are allowed to advertise their wares as bona fide members of their professional brotherhood.

In keeping with the relationship between professionals and their respective training backgrounds, the area as well as the institution of study may go a long way toward fostering the perceived level of the abilities of a practitioner. For years, as an example, a graduate of any of the Ivy League schools such as Yale, Harvard, or Princeton was viewed with awe and a somewhat holy respect. The reputation of such universities was such that their alumni were once reasonably assured of opportunities not readily accorded graduates from other less publicized schools. Today, however, it is acknowledged that although many universities have excellent programs, certain academic institutions are renowned as having departments or "schools" of special emphasis that take precedence over similar disciplines in other institutions, even in the Ivy League institutions.

Skills and training are key factors in the growth of a professional person, but the ability to remain near the top in one's profession is also directly related to a more subtle quality, that of ethics. We want our physician not only to have good medical skills, but also to have an equally good bedside manner. Although we may not always care to listen to the truth as regards our medical condition, if the truth is known, it can be better tolerated than a sugar-coated placebo. Ethics, then, is the upholding of the dignity of the profession and treating the client to be served in a conscientious and scrupulous manner.

Both probation and parole involve professional people offering their services to clients. It is the basic purpose of this chapter to review the contributing qualities and conditions necessary to achieve as well as to maintain professionalism in the duties of probation and parole, both of which are needed vocations and important links within the criminal (and noncriminal) justice system.

AGENCY EXPECTATIONS

First of all, it is acknowledged that the expectations of any agency (including those of probation and parole) are going to be strongly characterized by the theme or philosophy of that particular agency. There are two other important factors that will strongly influence the method of overall operations for probation and parole personnel, and these are the age and the type of client that the various personnel will be working with. All of these factors, in turn, will be influenced by public expectations and levels of tolerance. For example, it can generally be expected that the treatment approach to the juvenile delinquent will differ greatly from that used with the chronic adult offender. And although the primary roles of probation and parole officers do not appear to differ appreciably in content and means, there will be certain differences due to societal demands that will reflect the degree of permissiveness and flexibility that these professions may use in the discharge of their respective duties.

The procurement of staff members for probation/parole agencies will be characterized by the perceived concept that the agency has of itself and its function. It is suggested that there are multiroles to be assumed by staff members, but it would be idealistic to think that selective assignments to caseloads can be routinely practiced. Most agencies are neither prosperous enough or even uniform enough among their staff philosophies to be totally committed to one central treatment approach—if, indeed, all such agencies are treatment-oriented. It would be even more idealistic to think that all clients would avail themselves of probation/parole services because they recognize that they need such therapy services. Rather, the average parole/probation officer will have a caseload made diverse by age, past record, attitude, and individual needs of his clients.

There are four criteria peculiar to probation/parole agencies that influence the recruitment of new staff members for these agencies. These traits are—the client's age, his degree of criminal sophistication, the level of his motivation to focus on his problems, and the level of the agency's jurisdiction. While these criteria are self-evident, the third criterion may cause concern. Reference is made to agency/institutions that deal with the disturbed offender whose mental state would prevent entering into a normal problem-solving relationship without the services of professional and clinical resources.

Many agencies that serve juveniles exclusively seek to recruit younger staff members. The premise for this is quite simply to deal with and to hopefully overcome what has popularly been called the *generation gap*. Every adolescent, sooner or later, must go through a soul-searching process in the alignment of his value system. What may be thought of—under terminology peculiar to his or her age and peer group level—as being in vogue and acceptable for the youngster, may be abhorred and condemned by the adolescent's parents. Therefore, it is often felt that a younger probation/parole officer can relate better to this type of youthful offender who may be acting out his conflicts in a delinquently characteristic manner. A more youthful-appearing officer may be easier to identify with because of a lesser chronological age difference from that of the offender. The older officer may become symbolic, in the eyes of the juvenile, of the parent, who is the object of his immediate hate and rejection, because of the age similarity between the officer and the parent. This youngster cannot and probably will not relate to this type of perceived authority figure despite the latter's intent and abilities.

There will still remain a definite need for a few older and perhaps grayer heads to be found within juvenile probation and parole agencies, based on some very substantial reasons relating to interpersonal relationships, as discussed below.

1. *Many youthful offenders are truly in need of a relationship with a mother or father figure.* Countless studies have made reference to the fact that an often-found characteristic in the lives of delinquent offenders is that they are products of a one-parent home. Many such children have no real concept of the socially expected and socially desired roles of an adult, especially an adult who can show an equal mixture of acceptance as well as discipline and control. The juveniles who need this type of attention may not readily make the immediate association, but its value cannot be

overestimated, and such a relationship may well be their first prolonged one with an effective adult figure.

2. *Younger probation/parole officers are more apt to have their authority questioned.* It is a natural and inbred instinct for many juvenile deliquents to try and challenge the system and especially their supervisor as a representative of that system. If the officer—irrespective of his or her capabilities—appears young and perhaps naive to the offender, there may be the tendency by some juveniles to challenge the authority of that officer, making him/her work doubly hard to prove his/her capabilities. Any alert supervisor should readily be able to perceive and to handle this challenge, and the immediate establishment of controls and the consistent enforcement of them are mandatory if the supervisor is to avoid placing himself in a defensive role.

3. *Parents of delinquents are less apt to respond to younger officers.* Many parents of delinquent children resist the advice given by younger officers, and they resist entering into a working relationship with them. One explanation for this attitude is that some parents perpetuate the delinquent activities of their children because they practice similar behavioral traits as a part of their routine life style. They therefore attach no negative significance to such behavior. Other parents have guilt feelings about their child's delinquent activities and tend to associate such behavior with their own inadequacies or guilt. Rather than deal with these feelings, these parents may throw up a multitude of defense mechanisms designed to derail the officer who is working on the case. One of the most classic mechanisms used especially against the younger officer begins as follows: "How many children have you of your own and don't you agree that all children do things like this?" Such parents are operating under the assumption that young officers do not yet have children of an age where possible conflicts could occur, so they feel that these parole/probation officers lack the experience needed to handle the situation.

One of the key characteristics sought, then, in the recruitment of probation/parole officers is an ability to establish and to maintain rapport with the delinquents. However, empathy and sympathy are not enough by themselves; a good counseling relationship must also be built on mutual respect and understanding between the officer and his client. This relationship should extend over into working with the offender's family and the community agencies as well. The very fact that an officer is unmarried, or has not raised any children, should not disqualify him from working with a juvenile and his family. The ability to establish needed rapport as well as the art of recognizing and dealing with defense mechanisms, is a much more important qualification than the officer's marital status or age.

It is desirable to seek sexual diversity and to have both male and female staff members working together in probation and parole agencies. Although many studies have confirmed the benefits of heterosexual therapeutic relationships in the mental health field, there has been little attention given to men working with women and the reverse roles in the corrections field. Mention was made earlier of the need for mother and father figures for younger juvenile offenders, but this is only a limited application. Many of the smaller agencies have found it necessary from a staffing standpoint for a male officer to supervise female offenders or for a female officer to supervise male offenders, but already some puritanical concerns have been expressed about such relationships. There seems to be little feeling one way or another within correctional circles; rather, most such criticism comes from the public. It is for this reason—the public's unfounded fear of sexual contamination—that most agencies seek a sexually mixed staff of officers. Men classically work with men, and women with women, and rarely is there a crossing of the sexual boundaries. Actually, it is frequently easier for a female offender to discuss problems peculiar to that gender with a female counterpart than it is for her to talk to a male officer on the same subject matter.

By necessity, parole agencies must demand mature and well-seasoned individuals on their staff, perhaps being even more selective in recruitment qualifications than probation departments would be. It would be analogous to throwing a Christian into the lion's den if a neophyte of any less than usual qualities was placed in a position of supervising the habitual chronic offender/parolee as part of his/her initial job assignment. After all, the ex-offender has survived his prison experience by learning how to "look good" and by giving the desired answers to his supervisors while incarcerated. If this conditioned response has carried him through his prison term relatively unscathed, and the giving of correct answers has allowed him to win his parole, there is a very good possibility that he will continue to use this technique following his release and in his relations with his parole officer.

It is on this assumption that the parole officer who is assigned an adult caseload has hopefully received his/her baptism earlier in client exposure. Some parole agencies tend to season and mature their staff by assigning them to juvenile parole agencies to gain initial experience. If this is neither feasible not possible, parole officers may be recruited from potential candidates who have had law enforcement backgrounds or other correctional employment experiences to complement their native abilities in working within this type of a setting. Experience, then, is often acquired through past associations with offenders and thereby eases the transition of parole officers into their new roles.

One further comment needs to be touched on in the discussion of agency expectations. Reference is hereby made to the failure to set high standards, as regards agency as well as client goals, because of heavy work demands. It is acknowledged that there always will be administrative chores and mountains of paper work in governmental agencies, paper work that sooner or later must be dealt with. Some agencies are also guilty of spending too much time in staff meetings, so that they must relegate client time to what is left over after their own problem-solving processes. All agencies—whether probation, parole, mental health, or whatever—must adhere to the recognition that their first obligation is to their clients. Probation and parole agencies sometimes are at fault in making their clients wait too long before honoring their appointments with them. Often such a wait is rationalized by saying that those clients must pay by waiting, as part of their price for offending. In the next breath, the officer then wonders why he cannot establish rapport with an individual for whom he is responsible.

FORMAL TRAINING FOR PROBATION AND PAROLE

Most probation and parole agencies demand that applicants for employment have a college degree at the bachelor's level. Although there remains some grounds for consideration for individuals who can show a combination of education and practical experience, their chances for being selected as immediate employees are apt to be relegated to a role that is becoming known as the *paraprofessional*. Although this functional position will be discussed in greater depth further along in this book, it can be said here that the paraprofessional presently represents neither fish nor fowl within the correctional system, this in spite of a crucial need for more and better manpower in parole and probation services.

Although there is a general consensus of thinking among probation and parole agencies as to the level of education needed by their employees, there remain questions as to the best areas of study required of graduate as well as undergraduate students. Whereas the study of criminal justice is the most desirable academic background for probation/parole officers, the combination of other disciplines in the social science areas are being discussed. It is obviously desirable and effective to have employees with graduate training for the enhancement of agency status as well as for more experience in handling client rehabilitation.

Most agencies are seeking individuals who hold degrees—at the bachelor's level—in those areas of studies comprising the social sciences—commonly including sociology, psychology, and presocial work. This does not preclude other areas of study, however, and this author has known many effective probation and parole officers over the years who have received their academic training in a wide range of subject matter extending from English literature to environmental sanitation. It is not, therefore, the clothes that make the man but the reverse order of fact. Even in the holy triad of social science disciplines mentioned above, it is unfortunately true that undergraduate training in these areas is inadequate and sometimes inappropriate for probation/parole training. The most benevolent statement that can be made is that the social science program at the bachelor's level of study offers a good solid background for its participants in preparation for graduate work. It is recognized that the strengths and weaknesses of the various social science disciplines will vary from institution to institution, and the students will be at the mercy of their department heads as to the extensiveness and thoroughness of their educational process.

For many undergraduate students, the social science major represents merely a prelude until the students are more decided in their choice of a career. Any of the human services occupations are pertinent to and use the students of the social science disciplines. Few other academic disciplines represent the "catchall" that uncommitted students can relate to on a general basis. A teacher is a teacher; there is no question about that. But a social scientist is somewhat of an unknown until he can find his way around in the academic shadows and can plot his own course of endeavor. At the extreme risk of being derogatory, the choice of a "general" social science area of study is likened unto being hungry and entering a restaurant without any knowledge of what you will order once seated. Not until you have had a chance to study the bill of fare—be it of physical or mental substance—do you have any idea of the choice of alternatives available to you.

It is not the student nor the academic institution alone that may be at fault. The author recalls one penal institution that could not satisfy itself as to the academic descriptions and qualifications for a position known as a "correctional counselor." By way of explanation, the choice was between a probation or a parole officer who would operate within the walls of the institution. This specific facility would first affiliate and flirt with one discipline, actively recruiting its graduates, and then would suddenly switch to another. Whether or not it ever made an ultimate and lasting decision is not known, but the search seemed eternal at the time.

The adequacy of specific academic training must be obtained at the graduate level of study. We can make the analogy of comparing a cut and polished stone with one that has merely been hewn out of its original element. The accomplished professional in his specific field of endeavor is the polished stone. Any of the social science disciplines must go from the general to the specific in the training and preparation of its students, resulting in a finesse that marks them as a step beyond merely being capable. It is, however, at this point of demarcation that the correctional system loses recruitment glamour. The monetary rewards for individuals who have received a master's degree are greater in private practice and/or industry than in governmental employment, under whose authority probation and parole are to be found. Furthermore, in its material on training for probation work, the National Advisory Commission on Criminal Justice Standards and Goals notes that individuals sent to graduate schools of social work, for example, often leave the agency as soon as their commitments are fulfilled, and the commission relates this to personal frustrations over inabilities to utilize their knowledge and skills.[1]

The weaknesses of undergraduate programs of study in the social sciences area are many in nature. Although these programs offer a broad and varied composite of material, this very factor can contribute to their downfall in providing adequate student preparation in a specific skill. Such courses are so generalized and loaded with theory—often to the exclusion of anything else—that there is little opportunity either for practical application or for meaningful experience.

A realistic part of the problem of education at the undergraduate level, with perhaps the exception of student teachers, is that there exist few opportunities to see both sides of the chosen vocational coin—the good and the bad, the glamorous and the routine, all are unknowns that remain hidden from the student's view until he has committed himself to taking his position in a chosen career. For example, a field trip to a mental hospital for a class in modern social problems or psychology will only be as revealing as the public relations representative for the hospital will allow it to be. An anthropology class may study relics in a museum and thereby glean some knowledge from their observations. What remains hidden behind the scene are the hours of drudgery, of exhausting research, of perhaps luck, as well as the hard work that went into the finding and display of these objects.

It is granted that most colleges and universities cannot offer comprehensive programs for every profession. What could and should be considered, however, are programs of individualized study that allow students the opportunity to pursue areas of interest not available in standard course content. The selective use of visual aids, while initially expensive to a school, can also represent better than average substitutes if all else fails. For example, the student studying oceanography in Iowa may not get the practical viewpoint he needs while on campus, but with some departmental imagination, reasonable alternatives can be explored and developed.

The blight in any area of our academic institutions that hurts students more than anything else is the area of professional jealousy among the various disciplines. Each department has become somewhat of a world unto itself and has thereby deliberately chosen to ignore the existence of its academic counterparts. It has become popular to ignore overlapping areas where each department could make contributions, and to thereby become selfish to the point that each is deluding itself—and quite often its students—into believing that no other god but one can exist and that this god has taken up residential alignment with that particular department.

Too often this myth is perpetuated by the institution itself. The more

---

[1]National Advisory Committee on Criminal Justice Standards and Goals, *Corrections* (Washington, D.C., 1973), p. 316.

research the discipline faculty can account for, the more professional articles in learned journals, the more books published, all bring public acclaim and hopefully more funds from the alumni to keep the program going. But quite often the student is assigned academic obligations that do not meet his particular needs, although his efforts may qualify him as a builder of walls to screen out another department of lesser imagination. Quite obviously, the need implied is for the return of institutions of higher learning to their basic purpose, that is, to prepare students to succeed in their fields of academic endeavor for their own cause, not the cause of the school.

Each of the three disciplines mentioned—sociology, psychology, and social work—have strengths as well as weaknesses, contributions as well as distractions in the formalized training of probation and parole personnel-to-be. Our immediate concern is to evaluate the respective assets and liabilities here as these are pertinent to the professions of probation and parole.

Sociology

Sociology offers an understanding in many areas that can be of inestimable value to probation and parole officers. For example, there are frequent statements in recent publications indicating that a high percentage of our prison populations are comprised of minority groups. Various authors and researchers have attempted to correlate certain offenses with ethnic groups in the understanding of crime rates. The rudimentary conclusion to be made is that there exists some relationship between these two factors. Without attempting to pass judgment on this possibility, we remain well aware that cultural factors and mores may account for a large part of the entries on police records even though these are misdemeanor offenses.

In Old Mexico, for example, a young man growing up was expected to have his fling, so to speak, in his mid to late teens. The cultural theory that attempts to account for this behavior states that the male needed to act in this manner so as to get his rowdiness out of his system and to do so completely before taking a wife. If this behavior entailed a period of brawling and boozing, it was generally accepted and absorbed by his particular culture. He was then supposedly relieved of this desire, and it was assumed that such behavior would not be likely to arise again therafter and cause domestic problems once he had married. By venting this behavior where it was both accepted and absorbed by cultural standards, it was understood that the individual was now ready to settle down and assume the responsibility of a husband and father of sound moral turpitude.

This may well have been an acceptable cultural form of behavior south of the border. If, however, a second-generation Mexican attempted to carry on in this particular customary fashion—even while residing in a Mexican-

American part of, say, San Antonio, Texas—there would be a strong and very distinct possibility that such behavior would result in his being arrested. Although his degree of rowdiness may have only been severe enough to rank him as a misdemeanant offender, it nevertheless would be an entry on a police blotter, one that could legally be used to his disadvantage at a later time.

A function of an adequate sociology department might be to contribute the needed insight into cultural-legal sources of conflict. Each cultural and ethnic group has standards that are peculiar to that group, standards that are accepted as commonplace within that specific group. The social conflicts that contribute to ethnic misunderstanding are usually not so much related to inferior practices or norms as they are founded on inferior thinking about the nature of those norms.

We spoke of rapport as being an essential ingredient in the probation/ parole relationship with a client. Yet one of the biggest stumbling blocks in correctional work is the gap of understanding that exists between officers and clients of different ethnic backgrounds.[2] Blacks, for example, have been heard to rightfully complain about the "white man's laws." Such an ethnic reference is not without a degree of truth. Because of his own cultural background, the Anglo probation/parole officer may try to unconsciously impose the standards of a white, middle-class society and to enforce their adherence on a black offender from the most blighted of slum areas. Were such an offender even remotely accepting of these demands, he might find that both he and his community could not for long tolerate them, for such standards could well be incompatible with his particular life cycle. It is even conceivable that his failure to adhere might be construed as a failure to respond to supervision demands, and the individual could then be subject— erroneously, of course—to further legal action.

The discipline of sociology should be of greatest assistance in helping students to understand these implications. The contribution of this particular field of study can help to focus, then, on cultural factors and possible conflicts relating to probation/parole supervision or correctional rehabilitation. Sociology should also be able to shed some light on peer and group pressure value structures and how these may reflect on the offender's manner of relating to social demands.

We have agreed that our laws are a direct product of our social value system, although we will not try to determine here why such laws fail to provide for adequate representation of all citizens regardless of color or background. One of the weaknesses of sociology is that it merely attempts to offer explanations for causes, but it offers little by way of making any

[2]William M. Breer, "Probation Supervision of the Black Offender," *Federal Probation,* 36, no. 2 (June 1972), 31–35.

meaningful contribution to the alteration of these underlying factors. A sociologist is a mathematician who can set up the problem on the black-board but who cannot solve it because the formula escapes his memory. He is cognizant that a problem exists, and he can explain the nature of the problem; but alas, he has no solution to it that has practical application.

Sociology departments have long harbored well-meaning people. The role of the faculty seems to have been relegated to the reporting of facts and to let the student decide what the solutions to the problems may be. Sociology is a study of theories and documented suppositions about social facts, but the discipline has terminated the extensiveness of its studies prematurely. Like the mice who wanted to put a bell on the cat so they could be warned of its whereabouts, the issue had been defined but the implementation of the solution remains to be reckoned with.

Psychology

Psychology also can provide some sound background for the training of probation and parole personnel. Whereas sociology looks at the individual as a product of the group and at the relationship between his behavior and his cultural background, psychology concerns itself with the personal dynamics of the individual. This discipline concentrates on the individual mannerisms of adjustment and the various methods of coping or failing to cope with given situations. Other facets of psychological study are devoted to research techniques, the use of psychometric tools, and a multitude of other specialized disciplines, all of which enable the student to decide if he wants to invest further time in becoming a candidate for a master's degree. The implication being made here is that often the material comprising the bachelor's level of psychology is but a prelude to preparing the student for more specialized work to be taken at a later time.

The strong point of psychology as a training vehicle is that the practitioner at the undergraduate level is gaining the ability to recognize areas of dysfunctioning and to understand the rationale for such behavior. The key use of psychological techniques is to help understand the problems of individuals through the use of clinical interviews on a primary level. The author has deliberately avoided the use of the term *diagnosis* since this is little more than skillful labeling and/or pigeon-holing for classification purposes. For absolute certainty in understanding the problems of a client, more than one diagnostic tool is needed. The concept of categorizing clients often becomes a frantic effort to find an appropriate receptacle for purposes of clinical classification. The best categorical receptacle might well be the garbage can, for not all offenders can be termed a "sociopath," "psycopath," "Character disorder," etc., and neither is such labeling necessary for treatment purposes.

A second favorable feature of psychology is that it provides the foundation for good mental health principles. Many well-intended counselors fall far short because they either fail to recognize the severity of a client's illness or they are obsessed with the assumption that meaningful intentions are sufficient to effect a cure. The ability to assess the needs of the client and to effect appropriate referrals should be a trait provided for by even elementary training in psychology.

Psychology differs little from sociology in its obvious weaknesses for students at the undergraduate level. It endeavors to offer its disciples a little bit of knowledge about a lot of different things without really providing anything tangible or much that may be efffectively used without additional study demanding further time and application of theory. It provides a fertile ground for thought and for provoking new ideas, but the ability to use those ideas remains, at this level, virtually nonexistent. Neither sociology nor psychology fulfills a basic training need at the undergraduate level of study.

Social Work

Social work has, whether deliberately or not is unknown, hidden its true meaning behind a veil of obscurity. Undergraduate social work programs retain very little by way of comparison with graduate level material. The lay public is readily confused as to the difference between social work and casework, and as in the case of probation and parole, it tends to use the terms interchangeably. Undergraduate social work is fittingly placed on the same level as psychology and sociology since it is steeped in theory and only provides the preparation needed for graduate training.

Since little positive has been said up to this point about undergraduate levels of study in these three disciplines—social work, psychology, and sociology—perhaps the logical step would be to examine what changes are wrought by virtue of graduate study and training. Before doing so, however, it must be said that the benefits from a master's degree in sociology represent very little in the way of specific vocational preparation for a career in parole or probation—except for some self-study programs, research, and the preparation of a thesis.

The advantages of graduate study in psychology and social work—the latter term being used to denote the comprehensive program as distinguished from special areas of study—are skill preparation and theory application. Both disciplines now begin to prepare their students in areas of their choice. Psychology may focus on providing extensive training in any of several areas such as clinical counseling, psychometrics, research, and industrial relationships and does so with even further distinctions within these categories. Social work provides for specialized work in casework, group work, community organization, and school social work, to name but a few.

Practicums—in both psychology and social work—are offered in field work experiences, progressing from general to more specific field placements in areas of study emphasis and interest. The opportunity to utilize learned techniques in reality situations and with competent guidance through evaluation and feedback suddenly transforms the perceived into reality. The beauty of practicums is twofold: (1) The student can begin to utilize his learning experiences and hopefully make a determination as to whether or not his choice has been a good one either in terms of the tools he is using or in deciding whether he wants to continue in the position as a career; and (2) practicums allow the use of professional practitioners to supervise and to impart their knowledge of the discipline to the student, which takes him out of the realm of mere theory.

Graduate training provides psychologists and graduates of social work schools with a professional status and a method of certification and/or licensing. Private practice, especially for the psychologist, usually entails meeting certain standards as prescribed by state board levels. To advertise their wares as certified practitioners, both the psychologist and the social worker will find it to their advantage to be licensed to practice, and the graduation from accredited schools with appropriate experience is an assurance of being granted this sanction.

Of the two disciplines of training, the social work degree would seem to hold more potential and promise for training in the areas of probation and parole. David Dressler holds that probation and parole should be regarded as social work,[3] and other literature has also reflected this thinking. The case for or against social work as a generic discipline is contingent, however, on the perspective taken in the methodology of offender rehabilitation. One may logically argue the case from both points: (1) that offenders are "sick" people or at least people with adjustment problems who need the benefit of specialized treatment services; or (2) that offenders are products of free will and choice, and treatment disciplines should be focused on those individuals whose social malignancy is not of their own volition. In short, it is futile to waste professional time and training on offenders who have no desire to change their life style.

Public treatment or therapy services within the mental health context are most often provided by professional social workers. Although no figures for purposes of documentation are offered here, there is every reason to believe that this is a true and valid statement. Contrary to popular belief, the psychiatrist (M.D.) and the clinical psychologist (Ph.D) are not the dominant figures in community-type mental health clinics for two specific reasons: (1) because there are insufficient numbers of qualified personnel to fulfill the demands of treatment teams, and (2) because the cost of maintaining the number needed for specific treatment purposes rather than in

---

[3]David Dressler, *Practice and Theory of Probation and Parole* (New York: Columbia University Press, 1969), p. 102.

consultant roles would be prohibitive. Social workers, then, represent the most common and readily accessible form of mental health services to the general public.

It would appear that if the philosophy of the probation/parole agency is treatment-orientated in nature, then the most likely job applicant to be recruited would be one with graduate training in social work regardless of his generic area of study. Although different institutions of higher learning may lean toward specific schools of treatment, there is no need for concern if the officer-to-be is flexible in his thinking and in his treatment approach to clients. Treatment, irrespective of the doctrine of academic training, contains some very basic elements and will always focus on exploration, isolation, confrontation, and recognition of symptomatic behavior. Basic and core treatment at this level should not be concerned with effecting a total cure; the mere ability to learn to adjust through understanding and behavioral substitutions is generally sufficient to allow individuals to cope with their problems.

If social work has any weaknesses, these are more often than not internal rather than obvious in nature. Graduate training programs over the last twenty years have come a long way in overcoming these internal problems. However, there are still some external weaknesses that the public belabors, and one of the most prominent is the stereotyped image of what social workers are. A few years ago, a social worker was conceived of as a dour and humorless individual who still dressed in basic black and wore high-button shoes. This misconception was furthered by the image that the only role social workers assumed was the doling out of unpalatable items and institutional type clothing to the poor to sustain them during particularly hard times. The concept of the social worker as a specialist with a crucial role to play is even today not accepted by many because they have not had the occasion to understand either the extent nor the expertise of the service offered.

The important internal problem with social work in general is its inability to embrace—or to be embraced by—the correctional field. If the premise is accepted that an offender needs some professional assistance in his "adjustment patterns" and that treatment is needed in order to determine if he can benefit from a comparable program along these lines, probation/parole agencies, if unable to provide staff service for this treatment, will refer the offender to a community agency. Most such community agencies are staffed with a high percentage of social workers, and the psychologists and psychiatrists are left to focus on crisis intervention and to fulfill consultant roles. Based on these facts, we can assume that the social worker in the community agency will probably be the key figure in the treatment of the offender.

For one reason or another, casework services to the offender—or for that matter, services of any form of social work—have not been particularly successful. There are several possible reasons for this situation. First of all, the worker may well be dealing with a new breed of client. Although times change and programs change in conjunction with time, this author has never heard of a program with a generic area of forensic social work as a specialty. Therefore, most such workers "back into" corrections due to agency and community necessity.

Complicating the process is the attitude of the offender/client. Most offenders will enter into treatment only under duress. The individual offender is sent there by order of the court or his/her probation/parole officer. He/she is not particularly desirous of the treatment; in fact he/she may not now or ever conceive that there is anything wrong with him/her that necessitates therapy. Also, quite frankly, many of these offenders may be referred for treatment purposes because probation and parole officers cannot discover a handle for working with them and are looking for a pocket panacea. Furthermore, such offenders may be there merely to seek a reward for attending, and are not trying to effect any personal change other than to keep their supervisor off their back. The reward sought probably will be for some leniency—such as an early release from supervision—in return for playing along with the treatment role.

Thus, many treatment agencies and social workers find themselves caught in the middle of a shoving match. The offender is desperately trying to convince his therapist that he has made a remarkable recovery and that the therapist should advise the former's officer that therapy is no longer needed. The correctional agency, on the other hand, recognizes that the offender has been able to manipulate his way through most of his natural life and that he is now trying to manipulate the treatment agency to terminate treatment. One faction is pushing to keep treatment going, and the other is pushing to get out of therapy. Therefore, the therapist, along with his frustration in discovering that normal treatment modalities are not productive, is finding it extremely difficult to justify anything to anyone, including himself.

Criminal Justice Administration Programs

There has recently been noted a growth in the number of academic programs that might be grouped generically under the category of *public administration*. From a broad point of view, public administration programs represent a comprehensive study of governmental systems and the correlation between the various structural levels as they operate independently as well as being connecting cogs in the overall system. A common component—although often an independent program in and of itself—contained in this area of study is the study of the criminal justice administration/system. Simply put, criminal justice studies focus—especially within the generic program of public administration—on the duties and functions of the criminal justice system, giving a general overview, largely but not exclusively, from an administrative perspective.

Listed below are some of the reasons why few line personnel attempt to take advantage of advanced educational opportunities in criminal justice training programs.

1. The incentive system is often weak in civil service positions, and change is often accomplished only by virtue of a lateral or sideways movement rather than by an upward one.

2. Course material is often either theoretical or philosophical in content. Although such an approach may allow for speculation and animated discussions of course content, the opportunity to use the material presented is limited, and the information is usually "warehoused" until a later time and place.

3. Most governmental budgetary allocations—especially in the areas of probation and parole—are minimal and are designated for basic operational functions only. Thus the chance to be innovative or to do research is limited because of the nature of the primary demands made on the staff and because of insufficient subsidization.

4. There exists an insufficient number of curriculum/major areas of study readily available to the average line probation/parole officer. It is believed, however, that as this specific discipline becomes more refined, there will be sufficient professional enlargements and distribution, thereby making graduate programs more commonplace and more readily accessible. Until this becomes commonplace, however, few line officers can be released from the growing demands of agency expectations to further their education.

5. Graduates from criminal justice programs often find little available to them where their learning experiences can be utilized. Mention was made earlier in this chapter that trained social workers at the graduate level often leave their parent agency at the first opportunity due to frustration from the inability to utilize their learning experiences within their parent agency. If such individuals have agency commitments to honor in exchange for academic leave and/or subsidization, their frustration/bitterness may well interfere with the effective discharge of their duties.

6. Lack of opportunities to use specific training within the parent agency usually results in staff mobility and turnover. To change positions means the loss of seniority in a job, perhaps a complete relocation to another community, and other personal sacrifices that always accompany such movement.

7. Governmental agencies that utilize criminal justice specialists are quite often bureaucratic "pressure cookers" and operate under strong political tones if not commitments. Therefore, quite often, funding for such agencies is uncertain for prolonged periods of time, and the future status of the agency as well as that of its employees is forever dwelling under a dark cloud of precariousness.

8. Lastly, individuals who make the transition from line positions may now find themselves more concerned with working with budgets rather than directly with clients, a position in contradiction to their philosophy for going into this particular service in the first place.

For a more qualified and comprehensive understanding of these programs, the reader is directed to an article by Richard Myren in the June 1975 issue of *Federal Probation.*[4]

There remains little incentive, then, for the line probation/parole officer to seek a graduate degree in an area of study—especially since it will not alter his workload, will not provide new abilities, or will not allow for a promotion or a reward for his completion of such a program. The chief administrator of probation/parole agencies, once entrenched in his position, becomes an unchallengeable incumbent. Although it is correct that good administrators should have this protection, one can understand the futility that line personnel feel about seeking advanced training if they must wait a prolonged period of time to put such knowledge to any practical use.

The criticism to be made here is not so much of these academic programs, their philosophies and their objectives, as it is of the system into which the graduates are fed. Probation/parole agencies with differing philosophies and established pecking orders are not ready to accept new arrivals with new ideas, despite their excellent credentials and abilities. The archaic concepts of seniority tend to thwart challenges from neophytes until they have been established for some time within the agency. Potential skills of new employees are often treated like children, i.e., "to be seen and not heard."

A rapidly growing area where little recognition is given is the programs at the junior college level that are providing associate degrees in areas of corrections in general, and in other related fields. The role of the paraprofessional in probation/parole has been slow to develop and even slower to be accorded the recognition it deserves. Perhaps one of the most underestimated yet significant features of the academic programs at this level is the fact that junior college students are not conditioned to adhere to and to believe in any one of the traditional social science disciplines. Thus they are entering the field with a firm foundation in correctional fundamentals without being contaminated by dogma and theory other than that pertinent to their immediate area of study. It is equally pertinent that these students can later choose a specific discipline for further study based on the philosophy of their parent agency as well as by personal choice.

The Interdisciplinary Approach

When the time comes that a formalized training program is effected for the potential probation/parole officer, this program never should be the property of any one area of study or discipline. The interdisciplinary approach should be a mandatory one since most of us in this business must, at

[4]Richard A. Myren, "Education for Correctional Careers," *Federal Probation,* 39, no. 2 (June 1975), 51–58.

one time or another, wear a variety of hats in the discharge or our roles. Whether or not such a program is feasible is seemingly dependent on four very basic factors: (1) the size and ability of the faculty at a given university, (2) the perceived needs of the students and their ability to voice their training concerns, (3) the concerns of the correctional professions about staff preparation and qualifications, and (4) the ability of our universities to overcome professional jealousies within departmental and disciplinary ranks.

The majority of our colleges and universities are still firmly behind the idea that a good liberal arts education must contain many elements and that the student must be exposed to a variety of teaching, disciplines, and ideas if his education is to be a well-rounded one. However, too many elements can constitute a wasteful situation. The point is not that all excess fat should be trimmed away, but rather that the need for prerequisites should be disposed of early in the academic program, instead of having them sprinkled indiscriminately throughout the four years.

It is, perhaps, at this point that the author may leave his element and risk the wrath of professional educators by advocating some new ideas about a college degree program. Although a faint heart supposedly never won a fair lady, neither have changes evolved from an unknown genesis without some means to maintain momentum. After some fifteen odd years in the area of corrections, the author believes he has some knowledge regarding the weaknesses of programs for the professional preparation of parole and probation. With this in mind as a building point rather than as an apology, the following elements are submitted here as basic and needed factors in a formalized training program.

It is first proposed that our universities should consider a new and perhaps unique approach to the education and preparation of certain individuals prior to the granting of a diploma and a degree. It is herein advocated that a five-year academic program be considered to allow for both the generalization and specialization of studies, including practicums in certain areas of study. Not only would this provide a more diversified and specialized form of study, it would assist in the creation of programs where certain would-be professionals could seek and obtain either a certification or licensing without the necessity of graduate school at least not immediately and not at the risk of continuing financial hardship. This proposal represents a compromise whereby those supposedly necessary prerequisites could still be maintained but not to the point of sacrificing other equally important courses in pursuit of a given choice of a career subject.

It is supposed that there could be a variety of arguments for certification in almost any field of endeavor. The public accountant is certified as well as the law enforcement officer who receives some specialized training to further his skills and his career. The teacher must be licensed to utilize her skills, and although would-be teachers may have a practicum of sorts while student teaching, they could benefit from that extra year of specialized training as well. It is the career probation and parole officers, however, whom we are concerned about here, and the following material will represent an attempt at developing some of the needed skills that ought to be contained within a bachelor's program of study.

Some mention has already been made regarding the strengths and weaknesses of certain disciplines as an asset or liability to professional probation/parole training. At the risk of redundancy, there is a need to elaborate further at this point about the sharpening of skills that some of these disciplines may provide for. The case for sociology and psychology has been made earlier, and these disciplines can provide courses pertinent to the understanding of cultural conditioning effects and methods of behavior. Such courses should be a valuable part of our program proposal to assist in understanding the roles of certain minority groups as they relate to the demands of Anglo-middle-class-socio-legal-authoritarian agencies and to various defense mechanisms and areas of dysfunctioning as might be peculiar either to cultural or socio-emotional problems of clients. Since these courses may be known by a wide variety of titles at different schools, it is senseless to attempt to be specific here. But generally, courses on the following subjects might be included: ethnic awareness, specific socio-psychological problems, principles of mental health, social deviancy, and correctional theory and its related forms—all of which could be the contributions of the sociology and psychology departments.

Whether or not probation/parole services are really forms of social work and its generic areas of specialization is not the issue to be considered here. What is important, for careers in probation and parole, is the appropriate use of counseling skills regardless of the form or vehicle used. Casework services usually imply a one-to-one relationship on an intensive basis, and many offenders are in need of this service; but group counseling or reporting may be more useful where there are large caseloads and where little counseling time is available to the probation/parole practitioner.[5]

The use of counseling skills is not the sole responsibility of social work training, however. The appropriateness of such training is totally dependent on what problems are to be reached through the counseling process. If the practitioner is concerned with the application of good mental health principles, then social work techniques are a "must" within our proposed program of study. Yet there are advantages to the use of psychology and even of other disciplinary contributions in this area. Many educational departments of universities offer most commendable counseling programs under the guise of guidance titles, and the emphasis offered by this particular

---

[5] Herbert Vogt, "An Invitation to Group Counseling," *Federal Probation,* 35, no. 3 (September 1971), 3-7.

discipline may be most appropriate when other areas of counseling are being pursued, such as in planning a career future with the offender.

An even more radical contribution might well be considered in conjunction with counseling skills, that of communication and the possible expertise that this discipline might offer. Intensive counseling, for example, can only be effected once rapport with the client has been established. Establishing good rapport is often the result of being able to communicate one's interest in a client and having the ability to convey to that client that your interest is genuine rather than merely a professional facade. It also should be recognized that the effectiveness of a good counselor is predicated on his or her ability to be a good listener. Many individuals can find a fairly ready solution to their own problems if they have a good sounding board available to them, such as being able to bounce ideas off the "resonant" counselor at hand. Although being a good listener may not be the sole responsibility of a university communication department, there is every reason to believe that communication skills can make a meaningful contribution to the training process we seek.

Probation and parole officers should also have some fundamental exposure to and training in the fundamentals of the law. Probation officers are more apt, perhaps, than parole officers to be working directly with the courts, prosecutors, and attorneys for the offender. However, parole officers, especially those in outlying or rural areas, need training in legal fundamentals too. For example, they may find that the initial responsibility of seeking a revocation hearing on a parolee and the presentation of the facts necessary to initiate this procedure may be their sole responsibility. Certain condensed procedures in the way of legal gymnastics, as are pertinent to the parole/probation officer's exposure to the judicial system, should be made a part of our program. There are several Supreme Court rulings that are pertinent—which will be dicussed in a later chapter—rulings that have a distinct and legal effect on the work of practitioners in the field. Although experience is a most apt teacher, it is even better to have some prior knowledge of the legal ramifications and knowledge of the contributions of the judiciary in the implementation of the probation/parole career.

Certain aspects of the training offered in police science courses as well as in police training academies should also be included in our program. Most probation/parole officers are legally acknowledged to be peace officers and many are likewise deputized, but they function as card and badge-carrying members only. The contributions to be made from these police training programs should contain some very basic instruction, including the principles of interrogation and investigative techniques. Many jurisdictions provide that probation and parole officers may arrest without the benefit of a warrant if there is reason to believe that their probationer or parolee has, in fact, violated any of the conditions of his/her contract with the agency/

officer in charge. Although all probation/parole officers should not attempt to be investigators to the exclusion of any other function, they at least should have their facts correct before attempting to make an arrest. Investigation and interrogation techniques are equally important tools in securing information needed to make objective reports to the courts, institutions, and parole boards relative to the disposition of a pending case.

Lastly, there is the need for some administrative techniques to be made available to program candidates. Although of less initial importance to the beginner in the field, management skills, program development, public relations, and even grant-writing techniques might fall into this category. Since many agencies are field units not geographically accessible to their divisional office, some of the above functions may very well be needed in the general fulfillment of a parole/probation officer's duties.

SELECTIVE CRITERIA
FOR PROBATION/PAROLE OFFICERS

Short of educational expectations, good character references, and some native ability, little use is made of screening techniques in the selection of probation/parole officers. As in the case of any law enforcement personnel, there are obviously certain types of individuals who should automatically be eliminated from consideration for this role, based on either inherent weaknesses or ulterior motives of those specific applicants. The criminal justice system already has enough image problems, problems that are compounded by cases of power-hungry judges, unscrupulous attorneys, brutal prison guards, and the abuse of power by law enforcement personnel when overreacting to the perceived duties of police work. The final kill would be the hiring of unfit representatives of the probation/parole profession.

Most individuals entering the field of human services are inclined to devote their lives to their professions largely out of unselfish reasons. Their hope is to attempt to contribute to the overall betterment of mankind and to be able to make some indentation into this process. At the time of this writing, few probation/parole prospective officers are asked to take any type of polygraph test, let alone be subjected to the use of certain psychometric tools that could divulge the type of characteristics that would be sufficient grounds to rule them out as unfit applicants. As a result of this inadequate screening, some less-than-desirable individuals have been able to sneak through the professional door into these fields of service and have become a few rotten apples that contaminate and infest the other good ones in the barrel.

Undesirable Professional Characteristics

Three basic types—with some variations—are discussed here as being typical of those individuals that should be eliminated at the onset of application to enter any form of law enforcement or criminal justice work. Somewhat facetiously, they are referred to as the Crusader, the Searcher, and the Avenger.

The Crusader. The Crusader is a trait often found among the new and therefore relatively inexperienced probation and parole officers. Even after years of service, there are some among the ranks who will continue to harbor and retain some of these basic identifiable characteristics. Such persons, new or old to the field, seem to be on a continuing and chronic ego trip, which is indicated by the belief that they can—sooner or later—overcome and solve the problems of any client they may deal with. The end product, especially when working with specific types of offenders, is for such officers to be manipulated rather than to manipulate, and therefore they are unable to effect the needed behavioral changes in their wards.

It would seem, at this point, that some explanation should be made in reference to the use of the word *manipulate*. Many bona fide practitioners of the art of therapy will shudder at the use of such terminology. To them, *manipulate* precludes or eliminates the concept of being able to effect meaningful changes, changes that would enable their clients to lead a more wholesome and productive life based on some cognizance of their own problems. The author submits here, however, that *manipulation* is a very appropriate description of working with offenders on the assumption that client offenders are in a therapeutic type of relationship with their supervisors by necessity rather than by choice. Practitioners in probation and parole are usually trying to effect change based not so much on clinical principles as on and through duress for which there is a legal precedent. Used in this context, *manipulation* seems both correct and realistic.

To the Crusader, the panacea to all client problems is just around the corner and but a couple of steps away. Although the hardened professional in corrections may have some grudging respect for the enthusiasm of the practitioner of this approach, the futility of trying to apply such tactics to reconstruct the behavior of many offenders is apparent. The recognized malady of the Crusader is that he or she has not been able to accept the realistic fact that some clients are not amenable to change, either now or later, and any conformity noted may be but a thin veneer for purposes of deceiving their supervisor.

The shock of reality is sometimes a painful experience for these Crusaders. The author has seen many new probation practitioners who initially could not identify a basis for certain offenders being placed under supervision. For example, several years ago, the author had a chance to observe a class of student nurses and probation trainees undergoing a practicum in their training by working in a mental hospital. Several of these students fell into a unhealthy relationship with patients because of a lack of knowledge of pure mental health dynamics. Instead of being able to help and treat these patients, the students were getting the treatment instead. The most important result of the practicum experience was that the students were able to reconcile themselves to the reality of the situation as well as to the pathology of disassociation with their clients.

The Searcher.   The Searcher has good intentions also. Too often, however, he makes his entry into the human services field unconsciously seeking a solution to some of his own problems while working with the problems of others. Some of these individuals are motivated indirectly by guilt feelings and are attempting to overcome these personal shortcomings by doing a sort of penance through service to others. For example, the parent who has lost a child to a drug overdose may suddenly and fervently throw himself into the breach in an attempt to diminish the public's use of all drugs. Although some vested interests are always a conditioning part of our life choices, the rationale for some types of action may be based on a self-inflicted punishment. Many parents blame themselves for their child's delinquent behavior. Although self-reflection is not to be criticized, the danger lies in their attempts to overcompensate for the weaknesses they perceive within themselves.

A related form of this perceived role is the individual who hopes to find a client with a similar problem and thereby find a mutual solution that will benefit both of them. In the search for answers to the client's problems, the problem besetting the counselor may suddenly become minimal or forgotten. His true and total concern, although subconsciously hidden and denied to himself, is for self-gratification through using his client as a means to his own ends.

The Avenger.   The Avenger loves nothing more than authority. The opportunity to dominate others is one of his greatest sources of pleasures. If there is a legal basis for domination, then there is the chance that such sanction will only add momentum to those individuals who employ this particular tactic. A source of sadistic pleasure is gained from the misuse and usurpation of power when it can be twisted and be made to become the basis to rationalize about its use again. It is the relatively few police officers on a force who are unnecessarily abusive in the discharge of their duties who foster the public cries of police brutality. There are certain individuals who will always endeavor to utilize authority either for personal gain or for self-gratification. Their sole weapon is one of force, and they advocate that "might makes right." They utilize the legal sanctions vested in their position of authority to justify their acts and behavior.

There are certainly probation and parole officers who employ this principle to manipulate their clients. Although some clients are conditioned to be able to absorb mistreatment and threats, the ability to do so only serves to allow them to internalize their feelings that society is rotten and that the criminal justice system is even worse. To other clients, this ability serves to bar the release of any true feelings that they might want to divulge and to seek actual help with. The individual who fears that acceptance will be denied him also has reason to reenforce those feelings if he is denied the opportunity to respond except upon demand and to prostrate himself to prove compliance to his supervisor.

There are also some professionals who should be categorized within this order as misplaced vigilantes. These individuals are totally dissatisfied with the criminal justice system or are convinced that no system even exists. Their sole mission is to compensate for this inadequacy as they perceive it. Their role is to attempt to enforce and to interpret the law as they feel it should be and to create on-the-spot enforcement of self-discerned standards. Although a professional in any field should have the ability to improvise to meet an existing need, the need must be one equally recognized by others in an objective manner. The strict enforcement of standards is meaningful only if the standards are realistic. Unless a demand can be ethically substantiated, it remains useless in nature and content.

Other Problems in Career Development

Despite the detailed and devious route taken to make this point—about the proper selection of personnel—the core of the problem is not singular in nature but is cursed by several inadequacies. First of all, if probation and parole personnel are to assume a vital role in corrections, they must be without anything in the way of ulterior motives other than perhaps an altruistic desire. Thus, there is a need for a thorough but simplistic means of making this determination, one that apparently defies the scope of our selective process at this time. With the exception of policy-type personnel, corrections as a profession has maintained a somewhat self-degrading process specifically because of a lack of any formalized screening process of individuals attempting to make this a career field.

Another problem today is that our civil service system appears to operate on the premise that protection of its members is given in exchange for loyalty rather than for quality of services rendered. Despite general incompetency, despite a lack of productivity, despite almost everything, little—except death or gross abuse of agency expectations—will cause any incumbent under civil service to be ousted from his place within the pecking order. It would appear that the door only swings one way—inward—until the incumbent is ready to push it in the other direction. The general inadequacies of the civil service system only serve to detract from its overall function. The field of corrections is, of course, only one such subgroup that suffers from a form of managerial cancer. Certainly this is not the only causative factor, but it is one of many that arouses public criticism for the need to revise our criminal justice system.

PROFESSIONAL ETHICS

Personal integrity and ethics must comprise a cornerstone in the foundation of probation and parole work. No one should be without scruples, but a lack of high standards in the correctional profession may very well hammer the last nail in its coffin. Periodically a scandal is uncovered that rocks and nearly destroys a police department and the faith of the public. If morality for morality's sake is not enough, correctional personnel must not forget that they are public servants and that they are expected to be above approach. The citizen both demands and is entitled to services in return for his tax dollar, and he is certainly justified in raising objections if he feels that he has been shortchanged. The correctional professional who rocks the boat by involving himself in distasteful or illegal acts cannot only expect the worst; he is deserving of it.

There are too many opportunities, when working with offenders, for probation and parole officers to contaminate themselves. The offender who wants to either get into or to retain the good graces of his supervisor may find fertile grounds on which to thrive. Sex, drugs, "hot goods" at a minimal price—if priced at all—are but a few readily obtainable factors that can become available if appropriate hints are made. The transition from scratching each other's backs to cutting each other's throats is but a short step apart. The concept of giving favors for favors rendered is one distinct and peculiar aspect of corrections; it can have both long-reaching legal and social consequences and must be avoided.

If ethics is to have meaning, it must contain respect for our own value system as well as the value systems of others. Vested authority does not allow individuals to become self-righteous to the exclusion of or displacement of others. Ethics has a prominent part in allowing for a reasonably humane approach to any client, whether the latter is coming to us in a voluntary or an involuntary state. The professional in corrections recognizes, as does the client, that he has the legal upper hand, but to abuse the power in an officer-offender relationship is self-defeating. Likewise, as parents, we may find it necessary to punish our children when they have been out of order. The right to punish, however, must not be predicated on the fact that we are parents but on the basis that a learning experience must be conveyed. In probation and parole services, the analogy is equally appropriate.

It is frightening to consider the power that the probation/parole officer has at his disposal. When one has the authority to advocate for the loss of freedom of another, when one possesses intimate psychological/psychiatric knowledge of a client, or when the details of an offense remain confidential only as long as the officer cares to keep them as such, only then do the ramifications become apparent as to the power vested in the position. If innocent slips of the tongue can cause undue difficulty for a client, a deliberate shove of information in the wrong direction is nothing short of a traumatic avalanche as far as the offender is concerned. The failure to respect confidentiality of information is a breach of ethics whether in medicine, mental health, or corrections.

Values are transmitted by example and by association. Although we may think of ourselves as justified in the "do as I say, not as I do" approach because of a legally defined position and the vested power of that position, we cannot expect any consequential positive effect from it. It will not enhance the rehabilitation of offenders if the individual probation or parole officer responsible for their behavior is unethical in his approach to his client as well as in his approach to any other social obligation.

IN-SERVICE TRAINING

In all due respect to the dedicated individuals involved in in-service training, it is rarely an effective or routinely used tool outside of metropolitan areas or large agencies/institutions. To consider in-service training to be an ongoing process is highly speculative. Although most agencies of any consequential size have a training officer, his duties are often dubious and spasmodic. For example, the orientation of new employees usually only covers such routine subjects as the distribution of policy manuals and employee restroom keys, information about the various idiosyncrasies of the judges and the chief supervisor, where to park a car, and other various and sundry advantages and disadvantages of the position.

Ideally, a training officer would find it desirable to present agency staff with new concepts and proposals, to perhaps bring in consultants on a periodic basis for a give-and-take session of information and related questions, to update the staff on new policy and new community services, and perhaps to attempt to elicit employee input for agency/staff changes to enhance the total functioning of both. However, all of this is an ideal function, and ongoing training can only be practiced as time and funding allow, and quite often it is relegated to a rather spasmodic schedule with increasingly longer gaps between meetings when the novelty and subject matter both wear thin.

Many probation and parole agencies are one-person offices that are remote from the judicial level of supervision and also serve a large geographical area of four to six counties. In-service training for such remote stations exists only at the time the employee is inducted into his assignment, and any ongoing program of new information will take the form of written communication, supplemented by periodic visits from the "home office." Policy will dictate in part what these officers are expected to do, but changes will occur from within because the officer will have no immediately available model to study and to use for his program and client needs. Innovative changes are more apt to be dictated and implemented through the use of services not necessarily related to corrections, services such as can be found in the immediate community.

In an attempt to circumvent the lack of ongoing training, professional associations at state or local levels have been developed and enlarged upon. Some of these may have affiliations with national organizations, but many are based strictly on the local needs of the brotherhood who comprise their membership. The percentage of members who can actively participate in national level organizations is minimal, and many of the probation/parole officers who are fortunate enough to be involved are doing so at their own expense and time.

Most local associations are formed around primary interest groups and are based on the area of jurisdiction. Such associations might be organized according to juvenile or adult community agencies working with those clients who are not in an institution, or a third category, which might be either adult or juvenile in orientation, that of the specific penal institution. The membership of such organizations may be increased by including fringe-service agencies, which can assist in a direct manner the work of probation, parole, and penal agencies. The primary purposes of such organizations are as follows.

1. To seek unity and professional status through organizational strength in the attainment of satisfaction of mutual goals.
2. To exchange information about new programs or the acquisition of new services.
3. To bring in the expertise afforded by "outside" professionals not usually available to individual agencies because of location or economic reasons.
4. To publicize the status and goals of corrections as well as to educate the general public about the various functions.
5. To familiarize and to coordinate needs with related individuals such as legislators, judges, district attorneys, and others whose functions directly affect correctional services.
6. To provide a service such as lobbying for better programs and legislation and for subsidization for those programs, as well as for the betterment of the needs of correctional personnel.

Such organizations try to hold at least one main or annual meeting with some mobility as to locations so that local interest will be stimulated and maintained. In addition, several workshops may be held at regional levels throughout the year on a periodic basis. For many professionals, these meetings represent an opportunity to exchange ideas, to hear of new concepts and programs, and perhaps to view the employment market either to seek a new position or to actively recruit new employees for their own agency. Probably the most practical application of such meetings is the unique opportunity of participating in the only ongoing educational and training approach that some personnel will receive because of a lack of their own agency resources.

Despite intent, such associations are often political in nature and are further rendered ineffective by vested interests. Often the same old faces appear regularly in leadership positions, and these individuals maintain a hold on legislative matters as well as on program content and interest. Such offices are actively sought by some to use as stepping stones for their own future plans, rather than having the good of the membership in mind. Gaps often occur based on levels of specific interests, such as between juvenile and adult agency factions. In theory, rehabilitation should be the prime concern, and with the exception of program innovations, there should be little to differ one agency from another as to purpose.

New groups often justify their emergence by the fact that program purpose and content of the mother agency were too general in nature. Although there may be come merit to this argument, the suspected reason for the birth of a new group is that the political structure of the old group was rapidly approaching a dynasty of sorts. Usually, the leadership positions, especially in the long established agencies, are more often than not comprised of agency administrators rather than line officers, or even a combination of the two. The bitterness that becomes apparent is a direct reflection on the domination by a few over many with a lack of input from the mass.

A further schism exists between professionals and nonprofessionals, a comparison based here strictly on what might be called white-collar versus blue-collar workers, i.e., a probation officer versus a reformatory guard. The differences are at a functional level based on a distinction of duties. The "officer" may be possessed with delusions of grandeur since he is "better educated" and higher paid and therefore feels he has nothing in common with the "guard"; but he is misguided in that latter assumption because it's the guard who ends up with the probation officer's failures!

CAREER OPPORTUNITIES

In summary, a brief look needs to be taken at the career possibilities for probation and parole personnel. Although much of our discussion up to this point would indicate that there exists little that would distinguish between probation and parole personnel, Chapters Five and Six will assist in making this distinction. One of the most certain and safe assumptions that can be made about the future of both of these careers is that they will continue to exist. With the crime rate steadily rising not only in the United States, but almost consistently among other nations, it is a relatively safe bet that the practitioners of probation and parole arts are not going to be without a practice and a caseload for more than just a few years to come.

One of the most enticing parts of any job is the benefits, particularly the pay scale. Although the pay scale will vary somewhat within jurisdictions, based on priorities given corrections, the expected qualifications of applicants, the types of offenders being dealt with and the general cost of living index, beginning officers in both parole and probation can expect a starting wage comparable to that of teachers, accountants, and others fresh with a bachelor's degree.

The wage scale remains relatively constant despite the location of the position, i.e., whether behind the walls or within a community. Other benefits may differ slightly. Although much of the work involves collateral contacts within the community as well as with the offender himself, a travel allowance generally is provided. Because some parole officers need to commute to and from state institutions, some states provide vehicles for these individuals. Generally most probation officers use their own vehicles, but they are given a travel allowance based on a flat weekly or monthly rate or computed on a per mile basis. Other expenses may also vary. Some agencies and individual officers feel the necessity of handcuffs and weapons as essential equipment for the position and type of offender for whom they are responsible. These again may be provided for or may have to be at the expense of the officer.

Placement or the location of work also will vary. For simplicity's sake, it is easier to distinguish between community placements and those behind the walls of penal institutions. Probation officers are almost always community-located and may have little contact with the prisons or other detention facilities to which they channel offenders. Most parole agents, on the other hand, have a common working knowledge of penal institutions and make regular and frequent contacts with both the staff and the offenders at the institutions. It is not unusual for one or more parole officers to be assigned to prisons for preparole planning and to actually spend most of their time working within the institution itself.

A further factor might be noted here, one that is peculiar to large metropolitan areas. Frequently, probation and parole officers may work as part of a geographic team. The theory is to assign officers to a particular area, and a subagency is established there. This principle allows the assigned officers to get to know the area, the people, and the services and problems peculiar to that area. Another less common practice is to place officers within other agencies such as public housing projects, community centers, or geographic subdivisions of community agencies such as mental health climincs or even halfway houses. Also some of the larger cities specifically employ probation officers to work the streets or other such areas in an effort to engage in some preventive work with youthful gangs who frequent specific and well-defined territories.

Probation and parole professionals frequently find themselves engaged in a variety of community activities. Many are to be found—either voluntarily or as a representative of their agency and profession—to be serving on various community boards and in advisory capacities. It is gratifying to see that secondary schools are becoming conscious of the roles that these services play in the affairs of the community. Probation/parole officers often find themselves being asked to make speeches, to participate in career days, and to assist in various other functions, all of which is making society more and more aware of the roles and purposes of these professions.

In passing, one further thought needs to be conveyed to potential professionals in this area regarding the nature of the work of probation and parole officers. It should be realized that gratification in the field is not always readily apparent. To those individuals who are estranged from the law and social standards, probation/parole personnel are mere extensions of the police and the courts and are therefore to be viewed in the same manner. It is no profession for the anxious and insecure, for offenders will continually and habitually test their supervisors, much as a child would his parents to evaluate their true intent and motives. There is little comfort to be found inside jails and prisons for the visitor, let alone for those who must work continually inside clanging doors with alien and hostile inmates who may want to use you for their immediate gain and will give little in return. If you feel that you cannot relate to this type of a life, then probation and parole work may not be what you desire.

There are, however, rewards where you least expect them. In conversing with each other, probation and parole officers take pride in success stories. As has been stated, it is difficult to measure success readily in this business. Many cases that may seem lost because of a lack of relationship rather than a new offense may not have been lost at all, although the ability to see immediate progress is not apparent. Sometimes rewards come from out of nowhere and from individual offenders that officers may have felt they never reached. An old client comes out of the thin air to ask advice or to have you meet his wife or just to say "Hello," and suddenly the job isn't all that dreary anymore. Variety, they say, is the spice of life—and probation and parole certainly can offer that element to the individual who wants to have a go at it.

SUGGESTED READINGS

AMOS, WILLIAM E., AND CHARLES L. NEWMAN, eds., *Parole: Legal Issues/ Decision Making/Research.* New York: Federal Legal Publications, Inc., 1975.

JOINT COMMISSION ON CORRECTIONAL MANPOWER AND TRAINING, *A Time to Act.* Washington, D.C.: J-CCMT, 1969.

MANGRUM, CLAUDE T., JR., *The Professional Practitioner in Probation.* Springfield, Ill.: Charles C Thomas, Publisher, 1975.

NATIONAL ACADEMY OF SCIENCES AND SOCIAL SCIENCE RESEARCH COUNCIL, *The Behavioral and Social Sciences: Outlook and Needs.* Englewood Cliffs, N.J.: Prentice-Hall, Inc., 1969.

NATIONAL ADVISORY COMMISSION ON CRIMINAL JUSTICE STANDARDS AND GOALS, *Criminal Justice System.* Washington, D.C., 1973.

NATIONAL COUNCIL ON CRIME AND DELINQUENCY, Criminal Justice Planning, *Criminal Justice Newsletter,* vol. 5, no. 14 (July 15, 1974).

PRESIDENT'S COMMISSION ON LAW ENFORCEMENT AND ADMINISTRATION OF JUSTICE, *Task Force Report: Corrections.* Washington, D.C., 1967.

SECHREST, DALE K., "The Accreditation Movement in Corrections," *Federal Probation,* 40, no. 4 (December 1976), 15–19.

5

Probation: The Functional Aspects

Probation, just as most other human services, may be said to encompass a diversity of duties. Each client that a probation officer faces in the discharge of his duties will represent a different perspective based on individualized problems, unique characteristics, and personalized methods of coping with reality. Some clients will be aggressive, others submissive; some will never talk, others will never cease verbalizing. An attempt to deal effectively and constructively with such clients necessitates a carefully tailored approach based on the specific idiosyncrasies of each case.

Relatively routine tasks would appear to be of a rather elementary nature in their discharge, but the degree of effectiveness and the meeting of realistic goals will be determined primarily by whether the client is treated as a routine case or an an individual possessing genuine feelings. Treatment, or rehabilitation if you will, is contingent on the ability to transmit true concern rather than the mere exhibition of professional interest; and equally important is the use of good therapeutic tools in effecting change. It is on this basis and for this very reason that volunteer counselors have been extremely effective in working with their cases. Their assistance is offered in return for a better product, not a bigger paycheck.

Caseload management in probation services, as in parole, entails a variety of functions. Although some of the duties expected may be cursorily described as being routine in nature, a closer examination of content dynamics would reveal a lack of repetitive behavior if for no other reason than the variety of individuals and situations confronting the individual officer. If it appears that the tasks at hand are little more then ignoble toil, several assumptions can be made: that the individual officer is not mentally or emotionally qualified for the job, that he is burned out because of overexposure, that the agency has failed to cultivate the potentials of its staff, or that the officer has repeatedly failed to challenge the task immediately before him for whatever unknown reasons.

It has been suggested that probation officers, in the course of the discharge of their duties, must wear a myriad of hats. And, there are instances when this is true because of intersecting roles. For simplicity purposes, these roles/functions can generally be isolated and classified into four rather basic categories, three of which will be followed and analyzed throughout the balance of this chapter on probation. These three categories are: (1) investigation, (2) intervention-mediation, and (3) secondary functions. The fourth category—supervision—will be covered in its own chapter—Chapter Nine.

THE PROBATION PRESENTENCE INVESTIGATION

One of the most crucial roles performed by probation departments is the preparation of a case study upon request by the court. Usually the presentence investigation (to be referred to hereafter as *PSI*) is evoked after a determination of guilt has been made by the court. Its specific purpose is to assist the judge in better understanding the offender and his problems and to provide some realistic as well as alternate sentencing options. PSI cases are continued for a specified period of time to allow for as complete and thorough an investigation as possible to be conducted by the probation department. Ideally this period should not extend any longer than a month to six weeks maximum from the time that guilt has been established until the case is returned for sentencing purposes. Justice should be quick to be effective because the offender, who must wait a prolonged period of time for a final disposition, is merely doing "dead time," and any bitterness that may result from this wait will only detract from a hoped-for positive attitude that is needed if a program of rehabilitation is to be adequately effected.

There are, of course, exceptions to the suggested time limits given. Certain cases, specifically those involving "sick" offenders, may be subject to prolonged periods of intensive psychiatric observation of the offender on an in-patient basis. Although some preliminary evaluations may be productive as well as informative through brief projective testing and clinical interviews on an out-patient basis, a small percentage of offenders may require hospitalization in a psychiatric setting for a long period of time before a comprehensive evaluation can be completed and the findings then submitted to the court prior to and in keeping with sentencing considerations.

Judicial Concerns

A PSI may be requested by a judge for a variety of reasons. Some of the more common judicial concerns would include the following situations.

Insufficient Facts about the Incident. Many PSIs may be ordered at the lower (misdemeanor) court level following the entrance of guilty pleas at the time of arraignment. In situations of this nature, judges often lack sufficient knowledge of the circumstances surrounding the case that would normally be exposed during the time of trial by witnesses and arresting law enforcement personnel through their testimony. The chronological series of events and mitigating circumstances leading up to and surrounding the commitment of the offense will probably not be discovered, let alone be documented, because there has been little investigation done and prepared for the court other than the initial statement of the investigating officer at the time the arrest was made or the summons issued. It is probable that the witnesses, arresting officer, victim(s), and perhaps even the family of the offender—all of whom are individuals who could provide some insight—may not even be aware that the offender is in court and that his case is to be perhaps routinely disposed of.

Perceptive and dedicated judges are not apt to be content in accepting guilty pleas without explanations when they are convinced that there may be far more to the case than meets the judicial eye. There are some very obvious clues that they should seize upon which should alert them to the fact that certain offenders are perhaps trying to hide the facts of the case. Usually these clues are provided by the defendant verbally at the time he stands before the bench and following an all too eager plea of guilty. Take the following two examples.

1. *"I just want to get this over with."* Many individuals fail to recognize the ramifications of an improvident plea. When the offense is rather severe or even of a dubious legal nature, judges should rightfully challenge the defendant to ascertain the motivation for his plea of guilty. Although it cannot be presumed that all such pleas entered are done so without some premeditation, judges should be cognizant of the fact that one of their basic roles is to ensure that justice is done, but even more important is the fact that all the evidence should be understood. Obviously not all such pleas that might be construed to be improvident should entail a PSI, but judges should not hesitate to seek assistance of probation or other court personnel to satisfy themselves that the offender is aware of the repercussions of pleas that appear to be inappropriately entered.

2. *"I'm guilty, Your Honor, and I deserve the worst you can give me."* Some offenders are repentant, and they want the punishment to be just and quick. Sometimes, however, such a remark as this is given to beguile and to

deceive the court. The difficulty judges face in establishing a set of criteria for weeding out those offenders who deserve further scrutiny. and whose problems are real rather than feigned is not easily solved. There are certain offenders who are overly cooperative and who present this front as a smoke screen for purposes of distraction and so that the true facts of the case will not be discovered at the risk of further legal action or a more severe punishment.

Inappropriate Behavior or Characteristics of the Offender. Improper and inappropriate affect, irrespective of the initial plea, may induce a judge to request a PSI. Although probation officers, unless possessed of exceptional credentials and skills, should not be placed in the position of diagnosticians, they should be capable of screening such offenders for the purposes of evaluating improper or inappropriate courtroom behavior. For example, stoical silence may represent suppressed hostility or simple resignation, but it also may be used to disguise inadequacies or incompetencies that could not only alter the eventual sentence if guilt is established but could allow the question to be rightfully raised as to whether or not the offender is/was cognizant of the legal procedure brought against him.

Clinicians would agree that no diagnosis should be attempted without an adequate evaluation. Neither should a judge or a probation officer be forced into making a calculated guess about the competency of an offender. The issue before the court at the time of sentencing is not to judge the competency of the offender but rather to try to tailor the disposition to meet the expressed or determined needs of that offender. In those cases where mental incompetency is suspected but where the true nature of the incompetency is obscured, a diagnostic work-up should be made prior to a disposition, if not prior to the completion of the actual trial itself.

Inappropriate behavior that seemingly is not in keeping with the true and known character of the offender may require the assistance of the probation personnel of the court. Many crimes might be viewed, in retrospect, as impulsive in nature and contrary to the social expectations and general behavior of the offender. However, antisocial and abrupt acts of severe intensity may not necessarily represent a psychotic break or even an emergence of long-suppressed hostilities. It is possible that certain forms of behavior of this nature could be attributed to physiological contributing factors as much as to mental imbalances or inadequacies. Again, sentencing appropriateness must be dependent, in part, upon ancillary services, services that can be provided to the courts by well-staffed and trained probationary personnel.

An Attempt to Gauge the Rehabilitative Qualities of the Offender. Presentences are often ordered by the court to answer two basic questions that will condition the disposition or sentencing process: (1) What is the motivational level of the offender to change or to better himself? (2) Is the offender apt to reoffend, i.e., is he a good or a bad risk for rehabilitation purposes?

Many offenders will initially agree to almost anything in an effort to convey compliance and to thereby seek leniency from the courts. Too often, such conformity is evident only for a short period of time—until a disposition is made of the case and the sentence is fulfilled. Then, unless a control and check system is apparent and enforced, there is the tendency to revert back to old patterns of behavior and to be less amenable to change. There exists the attempt to "fake looking good" in the hope that the facade will deceive the court and the subsequent disposition will be less painful and demanding.

Courts are looking for both an intervening agent and an appropriate sentencing alternative when viewing an offender who appears to be developing a pattern or chronicity of arrests. The hypothetical question the judge may have to consider is that if monetary fines and threats of incarceration have been ineffectual in the past in stopping the landslide of offenses, is there any other method short of incarceration that should be tried? Although certain segments of society may look at imprisonment as a victory, to many judges it represents a defeat. At the lower court levels particularly, imprisonment means that normal sentencing alternatives are both inadequate and ineffectual. Some misdemeanant offenses are often not severe enough in nature to warrant incarceration, but unless other alternatives can be suggested, the courts may find it necessary to resort to using jails.

The Need for Supplemental Information and Services. PSIs can be of immeasurable value to judges in advising them as to what services for rehabilitation purposes, if any, have been previously utilized and with what degree of success or failure. If past programs have shown some degree of appropriateness during the time an offender participated in them, consideration might be given to returning him there for further services. It would also be appropriate for alternate treatment plans to be suggested from yet untried community agencies if it appears that such services might be in keeping with the suspected or determined needs of the offender.

Although there is a tendency to associate treatment with mental health services, this should not preclude the use of other community agencies and organizations. Programs such as budget counseling, medical assistance, employment referrals, training programs for new vocations, and AA groups and their auxiliary units are but a few community services that might well meet the needs of certain offenders depending on the problems evidenced. Since the source of criminal behavior cannot be routinely and universally isolated, it can only be hoped that the subjecting of offenders to a multitude of services may, sooner or later, alleviate their antisocial behavior.

Supplemental investigation implies collateral contacts. The offender who appears before the court presents merely the tip of the iceberg that shows above the waterline. To understand him as a total person rather than merely as a violator of the laws of the land, all segments of relevant information should be brought together to present a total picture for the court's understanding. This may necessitate compiling feedback from the offender's family, employer, neighbors, victims, and other individuals and/or agencies, any of whom may have firsthand knowledge of him.

Components of the Presentence Investigation

Presented here is an outline of the PSI form used by the court of the author. Although such reports will differ to a degree depending on the needs and the philosophy of any given agency, it is felt that the model used here will give a fairly comprehensive picture of the types of information routinely requested as part of the investigative duties of the probation officer.

Statistical Information.   Statistical information is relatively routine information that may not seem to be much other than fact-gathering. Several things are pertinent in this category that might, however, go undetected. The entry regarding nicknames and aliases is significant from two standpoints. First, it sometimes is helpful in establishing and maintaining rapport if the offender prefers to be called by a name other than his formal one. Although care must be exercised so that the offender does not try to abuse the relationship because formality has been lessened, the use of informalities can be effective in helping the offender relax and to make the interview more productive.

Second, some offenders have gone by other names either under aliases or under names used prior to a marriage, a divorce, or a legal name change such as by adoption. Also, the offender may have an extensive record under the other name, a fact that may have gone undetected in the current case investigation. It is helpful to be able to ascertain this because arrests under another name may change the whole perspective in considering whether or not the offender is a good risk for probation purposes.

Although not as apparent in this outline, the number of moves and the mobility of the family of the offender as well as those of the offender himself can be revealing. The inability to establish roots and community relationships for any prolonged period of time may have some psychosocial implications pertinent to the understanding of the offender.

Family Constellation.   The Family Constellation category is also deceptive to the untrained eye. The number of siblings in the family and the rank of the offender in relation to the others from a chronological standpoint, along with the sexual ratio of siblings and presence or absence of parents, can be most revealing. For example, if the offender was the last of nine children, there may be questions about whether he was a wanted child, and whether the parents were perhaps too old or too sick or too busy to foster a relationship. The ninth child—in families of few economic resources—may have been the recipient of the castoffs of his siblings, including clothing and parental love. In such cases, this individual may have a lot of negative feelings that have become apparent through antisocial acts.

The author has had cases referred where there was concern about some homosexual or bisexual tendencies of the offender. If the particular offender was the only boy in a family of eight siblings, or if his father was unknown to him, or if he had no real male figure to relate to, any of these factors might well account for his behavior. Another factor that might be pertinent would be the number of marriages and divorces of the parents of the defendant, or the number of children borne by an unmarried female offender.

All of these family constellation factors are related to the ability or the inability of the offender to handle his/her interpersonal relationships, especially at an adult level. For example, one would wonder why a person was unable to make a success of his three marriages and what factors contributed to those failures. Or what might be the feelings of a mother of numerous children conceived and born out of wedlock. What would be her feelings about her own self-worth? What, one might wonder, would be her feelings about men in general and the way she is used by men? A critical survey of the information in this category of the PSI worksheet may be revealing, then, as to possible contributing factors to certain behavioral patterns.

Occupation.   An employment history is also revealing. The individual who cannot hold a job or indicates that he has lost many jobs because, for example, "the boss didn't like him," may be not only having problems in interpersonal relationships. He also may be indirectly telling us about his feelings regarding authority figures. Many volumes dealing with the sources and causes of crime sooner or later focus on poverty as being a possible/probable contributing factor. Our PSI model here has deliberately not gone into the subject of poverty because theory and speculation seem to have the tendency to obliterate facts. Our rationalized stand is that we are not so much concerned with the "why" as we are with a more generalized approach.

One area not included in this particular model is a financial survey of the offender. Some PSIs go into a complete accounting of the assets and the liabilities of the offender as a routine part of the investigative process. Such material, if used appropriately, would be of use in determining the financial needs of the offender for possible use either in a budget counseling program or in helping him learn to provide for himself and for his family's future.

I. STATISTICAL INFORMATION

Name_____ Nickname? Alias used_____

Address_____ Apt/Lot#_____ Telephone_____

Time at this address_____Prior address_____

Length of time in this area_____

Residence prior to living in this area_____

Date of birth_____ Current age_____ Place of birth_____

II. FAMILY CONSTELLATION

Marital Status: Single____ Married____ Divorced____ Separated____ Widowed____

How many times married_____ Dates_____ Time separated/divorced_____

With whom living_____ Relationship_____

Family	Name	Age	Address	Occupation
Father				
Stepfather				
Mother				
Stepmother				
Brother(s)				
Sister(s)				
Spouse				
Children				

Marital history of parents_____

If parents divorced, how old was subject at time_____

General adjustment to family/spouse_____

III. OCCUPATION

Employer _____ Address_____ Telephone_____

How long employed with above_____Position_____

Pay rate_____ Source of income if unemployed_____

Last job held_____ Reason for terminating_____

If on welfare, training program, or other subsidized program of assistance, name of worker, type and amount of grant_____

_____ Social security number_____

IV. EDUCATIONAL BACKGROUND

Highest grade attended in grade/high school_____ Graduate?_____

If terminated before completion, why_____

School attended/attending_____Current grade level_____

General adjustment to school_____

Activities took part in_____

College/trade/military training_____

V. MILITARY RECORD

If subject was in military service what branch_____

Date of enlistment_____ Date discharged/proposed_____

Highest rank held_____Job assignment_____

Current unit of assignment_____ Last rank held_____

Unit/duty telephone_____ Current rank held_____

Company commander_____ First Sgt._____

Adjustment record in service_____

If on active duty, home of record_____

VI. SOCIAL ACTIVITIES

Religious affiliation_____Active church_____

Organizations belonged to_____

Leisure-time activities_____

VII. INSTITUTIONAL HISTORY

Has subject ever been placed outside of home by family/agency_____

Where placed_____ By whom_____ Dates there_____

Basis for placement_____

VIII. COURT HISTORY

Has subject ever been on probation or parole_____

Where supervised_____ Dates_____

Basis for placement_____

Name of probation/parole officer_____

IX. EXPRESSED PLANS OR NEEDS

X. Current charge is_____ Return court date is_____

Original plea was_____ Trial by court/jury_____

Name of attorney_____ Other charges pending_____

Date of hearing/trial pending_____ Where pending_____

XI. EXPLANATION OF CURRENT OFFENSE

XII. COLLATERAL INFORMATION

XIII. PAST RECORD

XIV. IMPRESSIONS OF DEFENDANT

_____Interviewer _____Date of interview

Although there should be no reason for any officer to violate the ethics of his office as well as those of his own personal standards, it is conceivable— and accusations have occasionally been made to this effect—that financial information given is periodically used in determining the amount of fine that could be paid by the offender as a disposition to the case.

Educational Background.   Juveniles who have come to the attention of law enforcement agencies may or may not have a poor track record in school. Collateral information gained from talking with the guidance counselor or the respective dean at the school where the juvenile is enrolled can give a great deal of insight into his/her functioning level. For example, is the student trying? Does he/she have any mental or physical handicaps that prevent him/her from achieving at the proper academic level? Does he/she truant a lot, and how do the parents respond to the concern of the school officials?

Other points in the model used here are equally pertinent. If the individual terminated school prior to completion, the basis for his termination may well be important. Circumstances beyond his control such as a personal handicap or family stress/losses may be understandable, if not altogether acceptable, as reasons for his leaving school. If, on the other hand, the offender states he dropped out of school because he was too far behind in his credits, or he couldn't get along with his teachers, or if he was suspended and never went back, such patterns of behavior may be significant. A perceptive interviewer would want to follow up on these responses in an effort to determine—either directly or indirectly—what was really going on. Of equal importance might be the grades the subject is getting and his level of involvement in school activities. For example, if he has/had low grades and is/was not active in any social or athletic programs, it might be expected that he has/had no desire to identify with the school and the overall academic process. Follow-up again is pertinent in attempting to determine why, for there could be legitimate reasons for this, such as working in addition to attending school full time.

Military Record.   If the agency serves a community with many military personnel—as does the author's agency—or even if it does not, the model used is applicable. Although much of the material contained here may appear to be mere statistical gathering, pertinent questions are asked. The ability or inability to adjust to authority, for example, is pertinent in understanding an offender and his potential for rehabilitation. The individual, whether active or inactive from a military standpoint, who has been court-martialed, or who has been reduced in grade, or who was released from the service earlier than his normal enlistment period called for, poses grounds for further exploration by the interviewer. How does the individual see himself in light of certain military disciplinary actions taken against him, and what does he feel might have been a contributing factor? Was he experiencing marital problems at the time because his wife couldn't adjust to this life style, and are there still marital problems? Was drinking or the use of drugs a contributing factor, etc.?

Social Activities. The material concerning the religious involvement of the offender is pertinent from two standpoints. First of all, although there may be law-abiding atheists as well as confirmed church-goers who are offenders, the religious beliefs and disbeliefs of the offender can be significant. For example, if the life style of an adolescent offender is in contradiction to that of an overly religious parent, conflicts may arise within the home. If in an effort to escape the religious value system of the parent the adolescent seeks acceptance from the street culture, he may either find himself in conflict with the law because of the activities of his newly found group, or he may find internal conflicts because he values the parental relationship in other areas.

Second, in many small communities, a minister may be a treatment ally for probation/parole agencies. The ability to refer to an agency or to an individual where the offender may already have some positive relationships is an asset to be utilized. A common knowledge of each other, for example, between a minister and a member of his congregation, should allow for a relatively smooth transition into a therapeutic relationship. In small or rural communities, the clergy may be one of the few resources that can provide understanding and assistance to an offender from a counseling standpoint.

The way an individual uses his leisure time can also tell an astute observer much about him. Can he engage himself in activities that are constructive? Does he have to be part of a crowd to be comfortable? Does he—if married—share his experiences with his spouse, or does he still continue to go out with the boys and possibly create marital conflicts?

Our model was used in a special way in regard to the leisure-time activities of the offender. It became pertinent material when we were trying to match a volunteer counselor with an offender. The offender was naturally suspicious of the ulterior motives of the volunteer and the latter was skeptical of how he would establish rapport. In the course of the experimental matching process, we found that any common denominator between the two was a good cornerstone on which to build a relationship. The activity level and interest area of both parties became a basic ingredient that we were able to use to match the two. Thus the responses often proved effective more times than not in allowing for initial overtures to develop.

Institutional History. Our model was concerned about possible placements outside the home, including a detention facility other than a jail, i.e., a reformatory, penitentiary, or training school that might have housed the offender at one time or another. A foster home situation or other type of a group placement generally indicates family problems or personal disorganization. The placement in a mental hospital or other treatment facility can give clues as to the adjustment or other problems of the offender that might contribute either to his general life style or to his involvement in criminal activities.

In addition to the advantage of having this information conveniently at hand, a great deal of evaluation time can be saved if information possessed by other agencies who have worked with the offender is available to our agency. Reference is made here specifically to noncorrective types of agencies as opposed to penal institutions, because it can generally be assumed that those individuals who have been previously incarcerated (in penal institutions) will have to be dealt with by the court in a more punitive manner than first-time offenders, since the second-time offenders' experiences in having been incarcerated did not act as a deterrent to their reoffending.

Court History.   Our model contains the category of Court History for several reasons. First of all, it clarifies if there have been other community correctional contacts such as other probation departments. This provides not only for a sharing of information between two probation departments, but it also prevents duplication of services should the offender be under the supervision of another comparable agency. Second, it represents a check and balance system, for if the offender should divulge that he is on parole but at the same time claims he has never been in a penal institution, then he is certainly falsifying statements made to the interviewer. Third, the honesty of the offender can be gauged when comparing his responses to the questions in this category against his prior arrest record as provided by the other law enforcement agencies.

Expressed Plans or Needs.   The category of Expressed Plans or Needs has been used in several different ways by our agency. First, it allows the probation officer to work with the client for realistic goal setting to achieve the latter's hoped-for plans. Second, it may enable the interviewer to determine how realistic the offender may be, and in some cases how honest he is when measuring the distance and probability of "getting from where he is to where he wants to be." Third, it allows for the offender to express some of his concerns about himself either in conjunction with or devoid of the offense for which he is now awaiting disposition. It gives him an opportunity to talk about his problems and what, if anything, he would like to do about them. On the reverse side of the coin, it also is an indicator of how much and how well he practices self-denial.

Other Categories in Our Model.   Less emphasis and less explanation need be given for the balance of the categories in our model. The Explanation of Current Offense allows for the offering of mitigating circumstances and for an explanation of the events leading up to the act itself, the latter an aspect that courts often overlook unless they are concerned with the showing of intent. The Collateral Information merely provides a convenient entry space within the intake form for documentation and acknowledgements of outside information relative to the case. The Past Record Category is used to itemize the past arrest record of the offender and also serves as a further check of honesty because the police "rap sheet" can be used to verify or to document those offenses. This category may also be pertinent in trying to establish a pattern of offenses for reference purposes.

The space under Impressions of Defendant is used in this model to record the behavior of the offender during the course of the interview. Traits such as nervousness, belligerence, evasiveness, and perhaps general mental state are common characteristics that should be noted and might be used as a treatment reference point at a later time. This may be especially applicable if the probation department will eventually have to assume a supervisory role with the offender.

Additional Factors Not Included in Model. In retrospect, perhaps two other areas of information might be appropriate to the PSI form, although these were not shown in our model. These are: (1) the general state of health and related medical problems of the offender and (2) the use of references. How medical information could best be used would be dependent on the purpose of the PSI. A very real concern would be to know just how the medical problems of the offender affect his level of functioning and how he handles them emotionally. Would ongoing treatment of the malady be a problem if incarceration is to be considered? Could either the illness or the form of treatment/medication be a mitigating factor that might have contributed to the offense itself? For example, the author recalls more than one arrest of suspicious individuals who failed to respond to verbal directives of law enforcement officers. The reasons for their nonconformity were later acknowledged to be due to a variety of causes ranging from deafness to medication that dulled the senses and reflexes of the individual, although of course none of these were known to be contributing factors at the time.

The use of references and the material gained from their use can be a sensitive area. Our model does not contain this grouping for a very particular reason, that is, the questionable validity of some of the responses. Experience has indicated that such references often may constitute a "stacked deck." Unless specifically structured, the names given are often those of peers who have been instructed to give "correct and positive" answers. Some references have actually been from members of the individual offender's own family who have portrayed themselves to be someone else. It can be reasonably ascertained that the responses given by these individuals will be less than objective in nature.

If there is any basis for the assumption that the poverty level of an individual might be a contributing factor to his involvement with crime, then it might also be assumed that members of the lower socio-economic class might not be able to provide any socially meaningful references outside their own immediate grouping. This assumption is predicated on the fact that quite often the contacts of such offenders are limited outside their immediate neighborhood, employment, and social relationships. A very similar situation exists when the focus of a PSI is a juvenile. References on behalf of juveniles are difficult to evaluate and hard to find. Quite often the only adult relationships they may have outside their immediate families are limited to teachers, sometimes to the clergy, and if they are fortunate enough to have a job, to their employer.

The model used here has substituted the category of Collateral Information in lieu of a specified reference request. There is reason to believe that if the offender is worthy of the respect of others, that this positive feeling will sooner or later come to the fore as a voluntary expression of fact from these contacts. An observant interviewer should be able to pick up readily those feelings of individuals about the offender without direct questioning, and should be able to note an overall pattern of responses that will give insight into the general adjustment and behavior patterns of the individual being investigated.

The Presentence Report

A PSI report should combine brevity along with comprehensiveness. If this sounds somewhat contradictory, it is not meant to be so. What is suggested is a condensation of the investigative report—a short form that can be readily scanned by a judge while on the bench, one that will not occupy too much time nor provide too much detail for fear the true purpose may be lost. The following model is used by the court of the author. Although it is recognized that certain cases demand a more detailed accounting, this form has been found to generally suffice for the bulk of our cases.

This summarized model can be contained, and hopefully can be ably presented, on one sheet of legal-size paper. Copies are reproduced for the prosecuting and defense attorneys. With perhaps two notable exceptions, all the material is shared with the prosecuting and defending attorneys. The first exception is that the case is also discussed with the judge prior to court convening so that questions can be answered and alternatives discussed. This allows the judge to familiarize himself with the case so that the original details and perhaps his original concern for ordering the PSI are not lost. It also gives the prosecution and defense counsel the opportunity to be aware of both the findings and the recommendation and to raise any appropriate issues prior to sentence being passed. The second exception deals with the psychiatric/psychological impressions interpreted by the clinician who administered the test. It will be discussed in the chronological order of the PSI report contents below.

```
Name_____ Age_____ Marital status_____
Address_____City_____Telephone_____
Employment_____ Position/rank_____
Length of time in present job_____
Offense and date of same_____
Prior court date_____ Original plea_____
Name of attorney_____
Defendant's statement:



Impressions:



Collateral information:



Psychological summary:



New offenses pending since original court appearance:



Recommendation:




_____
Probation officer


_____
Date of report
```

The background statistical information requested in the form is used largely to refresh the memory of the judge about the case. It represents a brief summary of the initial status as to the plea, attorney, and other relevant information that may contribute to the court's recall of the case.

The Defendant's Statement allows for interpretation by the defendant, from a social rather than from a legal standpoint, of the facts of the incident resulting in his arrest. It further allows for the presentation of mitigating circumstances and events that may have led up to or resulted in his apprehension and subsequent conviction. It is found, for some offenders, that this is an opportunity to express themselves in a way not provided for in court or during the formalized proceedings of the trial. Although the case may have been adequately presented, this may have been done completely by the defending attorney, and the defendant's statements and general presentation may well have been tailored for him in advance. Therefore, the defendant may have been a participant in a proceeding that is alien to him and that he may not have totally understood. Social facts are not always acceptable during the course of the trial for fear that the weaknesses presented may represent an acknowledgment of guilt or a propensity for this type of behavior. Social facts by the defense only become apparent when adjudication and a guilty finding have been made, and then their only role seems to be as an attempt to request leniency.

The category relating to Impressions may seem merely one of casual observation. It is important to a judge, however, to be able to utilize whatever clues are provided him for this purpose. Repressed defiance is more characteristic in the court room than one would suspect, because a show of feelings may not only be inappropriate, it may also be construed as grounds for incurrng the wrath of the court. These feelings often become apparent during the course of the PSI interview. Feelings can be construed and interpreted in several significant ways. For example: They may reveal the true attitude of the offender toward authority, they may give a clue as to his ability to respond and to use his anger in an appropriate way, and/or they may clear the air so that he becomes easier to talk to and deal with by having vented his emotions.

Collateral Information is factual material that the court was lacking at the time of trial, and it may shed a totally different light on the offender as a social creature rather than as a violator of the law. Such information may not be legally pertinent during the course of a trial, and it may represent hearsay evidence that is not admissible as part of the proceedings *at that time*. What is to be reiterated here is that a trial has two basic components—the legal and the social facts. Like daylight and dark, the consideration of one must follow the appearance of the other, for both cannot share center stage at the same time. In many cases, it is far more difficult to establish an appropriate disposition based on the knowledge of the offender than it is to determine his guilt or innocence.

Collateral information should assist the judge in determining the true character of the offender. For example, is there sufficient information to label the defendant as a relatively harmless individual, one who is not apt to reoffend, or is the general consensus of opinion that this is a habitual offender who has difficulties in adjusting to any number of given situations? Also included in this category is a history of the individual's past record of offenses. This history may be a critical factor—if the offender has a prior record of similar offenses and/or behavior—in determining his potential to reoffend or to be rehabilitated through the use of appropriate programs of service. This arrest record can also be used to confront the offender's honesty. The author has never ceased to be amazed at the number of offenders who cannot—conveniently so—remember their past arrest record until it is placed before them.

Reference was made earlier about two exceptions to sharing in full the information of the PSI with the prosecution and defense attorneys. One of these exceptions has been discussed, and the second should be considered specifically here in relation to the next category, the Psychological Summary. Many defense attorneys share all the information, including letting the offender read the PSI report personally, with their client. The procedure with our model is to incorporate the recommendations of our consultant with the PSI report, but to avoid the presentation of the complete psychological findings to anyone other than the judge.

The rationale behind this restriction is simple. We feel that the sharing of psychological findings about the offender, devoid of interpretation by anyone other than a qualified clinician, is both unethical and inappropriate. With the possible exception of the judge, neither the defense attorney nor the prosecutor should be concerned with a diagnosis other than for the possible consideration to determine the competency of the offender. Any clinically detailed information should be used for purposes of program referrals only, in an attempt to treat the specific needs of the offender. Diagnosis and the psychodynamics of the offender are generally more pertinent after the fact of trial than before, unless the competency of the offender to stand trial is in question.

The Recommendation of the PSI report should incorporate findings related to the overall prognosis of the offender, including the recommendation of appropriate disposition by the court tailored to the needs of the offender. Although some PSI reports may suggest a specific fine or sentence, this is a function that the judge is more than capable of doing himself, and it is therefore only a partial solution to the needs of the court. What the judge should be concerned with and what he wants to know is not just the needs of the offender, but how best to meet those needs. Further, is the offender willing to work on his own behalf, or does he need some motivation to involve himself? And what type of a motivational factor would be required to assure conformity? Probation is but a hollow term if it assumes its function to be no more than a screening process for the courts. What probation must do to fulfill the function of the court is to provide a cornerstone on which to build a program for the rehabilitation of the offender. It is for this reason that probation many times is predicated on a suspended sentence, to serve as a carrot in front of the nose of the offender and to thereby enforce his involvement in a therapeutic program.

Most probation departments feel that one of their vital functions is preprobation investigations and the evaluation of offenders who have made application for probation. Any PSI report worth the paper on which it is written should weigh the pros and cons of probation as a possible disposition to any case and should defend, from a summary standpoint, the rationale for either advocating or rejecting the idea of probation as a disposition alternative. However, some courts *routinely* entertain probation applications from offenders and/or their legal counsel, and this is what we object to here. The application for probation submitted voluntarily should be reviewed, and there would appear to be no need to treat this application any differently than one would respond to a normal PSI; the same basic information would be needed to arrive at a possible recommendation. The need does exist, however, to subject the applicant for a self-requested probation status to a cursory examination to determine his rationale for such a request. Without attempting to blow this feature out of proportion, the real motivational factor should be explored. What, for example, is the applicant's understanding of probation, and what does he expect to gain from it? How does he want to use it? What goals might he be ready to set for himself? And are these goals at all realistic? These questions properly asked and analyzed can provide some revealing insight and perhaps isolate the true nature of his request.

INTERVENTION-MEDIATION IN PROBATION

Both probation and parole have been unjustly accused of protecting the offender and of being too easy on him when society is demanding that more punitive methods be applied. It should be recognized, however, that often there has been enough pressure put on the offender by himself and by his immediate environment. Society, then, instead of assuming a helping role, only serves to increase the pressure on the offender when it demands a tougher approach. If society chooses to turn the cold shoulder on the offender, it must assume part of the blame if the offender repeats his act.

One of the most difficult cases this author ever personally encountered was the matter of a juvenile whose father was a psychiatrist. If any professional person should have had cognizance of the need to communicate and to understand the acting-out behavior of an adolescent, this gentleman should have had. Instead of trying to alleviate the problem, our professional repeatedly attempted to alter the issue and tried to put the officer on the defensive through the tactics of psyco-intellectual arguments. It was little wonder that his son was in difficulty, for the needed fulcrum point in his life had been adeptly kicked out from under him.

Perhaps the use of the descriptive phrase *intervention-mediation* should be replaced by the dual concepts of advocation and community manipulation. This book has and will repeatedly express the thought that the adjudication of an offender is not merely a judicial act, but that the offender will be judged time and time again by society and even within his primary relationships. If the reader can accept the concept of internalization, then the results will support the need to intervene in probationary cases from time to time.

Probation intervention-mediation is generally focused on three targets that are crucial in the maintenance of the offender. These are: (1) the family, (2) the community service agencies, and (3) society as a whole.

Family intervention and counseling assistance are probably most pertinent in cases involving juveniles. Although the causative factors for delinquency are many, often the lack of consistency of approach is a contributing agent. If a child has gotten to the point that he is controlling his parents rather than being controlled, a definite role of the probation officer is to help the family establish a solid and consistent approach with the juvenile. The juvenile who can manipulate one parent against the other is going to utilize, to the utmost, his ability to do so to his own advantage. Limit setting, to be effective, has to be unified, and responsibility has to be taught through consistent demands that are to be consistently enforced. The roles the parents assume—or neglect—can have an adverse effect on the child as well as grant the child the license to make his own choices irrespective of parental thinking. Control can only be exerted when it becomes both meaningful and regular in its application.

Conflicts must be dealt with immediately. These conflicts may be natural or artificial. Natural conflict is defined as "inappropriate expectations" and characterized by excessive demands. Artificial conflict is defined as "manipulation," achieved by threat of punishment if conformity is not achieved. It may well fall the lot of the probation officer to coordinate and to establish a realignment of the value structure, so that such conflicts may be resolved. The lack of communication and excessive demands on the part of parents, the labeling by schools arising out of their expectations of offenders within their programs, or the unrealistic thinking of the delinquent himself in the process of goal setting can all only accelerate the confusion, and conflicts will grow unless change can be evoked. The social branding of juveniles serves to isolate them, rather than allowing them to be integrated into society's mainstream.

Intervention may also assume the role of having to acknowledge that the environment can no longer be manipulated and that a definite change must take place, a change usually in the form of an outside placement. Although an extreme change might involve commitment to a penal institution, normally the change of a community, or perhaps a change within the community of residency or schools, might be considered. Society expects probation officers to continually bird-dog the offender and to pounce immediately and revoke his probationary status at the first sign of weakness. Therefore, probation officers may sometimes find it necessary to protect the offender from society rather than protect society from the offender. If trust is to be gained, trust must be granted. Any therapeutic relationship demands mutual understanding and input, but more important, it also demands a degree of flexibility. If an offender is just that because of association, it may be well to remove him from such association.

To intervene on behalf of the offender may require the mobilization of other community resources. Placement of a juvenile delinquent at other than a penal institution may need the subsidization of a department of social services or other child-care programs. Although the resentment of the youthful offender and his family may be great, it can be dealt with routinely and with a greater degree of effectiveness after the placement has been made.

Individualized vocational and training intervention may have to be made with the help of the institution. The limited juvenile may continue to act out his frustrations in response to the academic demands of a normal school program. One has to consider that the desire to avoid repeated failure is a common human need we all possess, and to subject anyone deliberately to a situation where failure is imminent is nothing short of cruel and inhuman punishment. Working with school authorities to provide a more appropriate academic program or to seek some vocational training—be it for adults or juveniles—is a routine duty that the probation officer should be prepared to perform.

Specialized programs that can be of immeasurable value are often overlooked. Two programs that the author has been associated with come to mind, both of which had some rather dramatic and unexpected results. One such program was for a group of tough, intercity delinquent girls who were subjected to a class in modeling. The contents of the course included the tailoring of appropriate clothing for each particular figure, the proper use of makeup, personal hygiene, and proper posture. The transformation was more than physical in nature. The girls began to take some pride in themselves, and they were able to find satisfaction in things that they could legally accomplish, with a change of perspective that was readily apparent.

In another program, the author worked with an older female offender whose self-image was quite poor. She hung around bars because she felt that normal and wholesome social outlets would not accept her. As a result of her habits, she was invariably getting drunk, into fights, and into poor relationships with men who marked her as an easy prey. We convinced her to enroll in a Dale Carnegie course, which was subsidized by a local philanthropic organization. One of the most memorable things that became apparent following the completion of the program was the color of her eyes. This is not to imply that the color changed, but in all the years I knew her, this was the first time she ever looked me straight in the face so that I could tell what color her eyes were. Her outlook on the world was not only different, it was more direct. Although this may not sound like a major rehabilitative accomplishment, to her it was a major one because her self-image had improved, and she could find some good things about herself.

Intervention involves the use of a highly skilled imagination as much as it requires anything else. Probation officers should be acquainted with their communities as well as have cognizance of the specific needs of their clients. Success sometimes is merely a matter of matching up the two forces and sitting back to await results. Although the two examples given above may be the exception rather than the rule, one can always surmise what might have happened if such experiments had not been tried.

Probation has to be people working with people to be effective. It cannot be suggested that this is an easy task, for such a relationship generally has its beginning in the form of an armed truce. Once, however, an understanding is reached and some mutual goal setting can be determined, then the possibility of positive movement becomes a reality. The key is the use of the word *mutual*. Mere restrictions and rules are not sufficient to get the job done. Control is necessary, but the exertion of control can take many forms, forms that can be either distasteful or meaningful in nature. The key is *agreed upon and acceptable goals*, goals that will alter the individual and make him want to change because *he* sees the need to do so; it should be a choice of his rather than the demands of another.

SECONDARY PROBATIONARY DUTIES

There are often duties demanded of probation personnel that might not initially appear to be the true functions of such a service to provide. Reference is made here to investigations for personnel recognizance bonds and, quite often, the investigation to determine the eligibility of offenders for court-appointed attorneys. Since the probation department generally represents the investigative arm of the court system, perhaps we should satisfy ourselves that these functions are not totally alien to the primary role of the department.

Personal Recognizance Bonds (PR Bonds)

Personal recognizance bonds are granted by the court to offenders who are awaiting trial, in lieu of posting cash or a surety bond (bail posted by a professional) to assure the attendance of the individual in court. Probation officers are involved here as a natural part of their role as investigators; but of equal importance is their ability to conduct a meaningful interview, and this is one of the basic skills demanded of the profession. Various elaborate systems have been set up to ascertain if the word of an individual is sufficient to ensure his attendance for trial.

One of the most common methods for determining eligibility for PR bonds is a rating form where specific weights are used to denote positive or negative factors. Various social and economic factors are weighed and graded on the basis of assets and liabilities determined. Let us assume that we demand a total of 75 points of a positive nature before a PR bond could be recommended to the judge, who must eventually sanction or deny the request. The following factors would have to be considered as part of the investigation and rating system.

1. *Length of residence in the community.* For every year the offender has lived continuously in the community, points can be credited at the rate of 5 per year. Four years in the community and simple arithmetic tells us the offender has 20 points toward his needed 75 for PR bond consideration.

2. *Employment.* The inability to hold a job consistently tells much about the offender and his ability or inability to accept supervision and to perform competitively. Five points a month, for example, might be credited for each month on the same job.

3. *Marital status.* The married individual, although not always more trustworthy by virtue of his marital status, is generally acknowledged to have started to develop some responsible roots and to have assumed some responsibility for his family. Points might well be credited for each year of continuous marriage during which the offender has lived with his/her spouse without separation or divorce. A second assmption here is that it is far easier for single individuals to be mobile and to feel less compunction about suddenly moving or changing jobs than it is for married persons.

4. *Credit rating.* A PR bond is a contract of sorts to be either honored or defaulted by the offender. His ability to show some proof of past obligations of a contractual nature having been met would be grounds for the crediting of positive points for PR consideration.

5. *Character references.* For each positive—and suffice it to say, meaningful—reference that can be documented, points should be credited to the positive side of his ledger. The statements of employers, of reputable associates, or community-involved individuals such as clergy, etc., would be considered as pertinent.

6. *Police record.* If the subject has no prior record, positive or plus points could be accorded him. If, however, he has a prior arrest record, then a system can be devised to deduct points from his total. Points would be subtracted for prior offenses, for offenses especially of the same nature as he is now awaiting trial for, and/or for his failure to honor his legal obligations as noted by the indication of a warrant or other instrument demanding his arrest.

7. *New convictions.* New offenses taking place during the time the subject is awaiting trial and out on PR bond may necessitate the forfeiture of his present bond or the retabulation of points to determine his continuing eligibility.

All of the above information results in a rather comprehensive report on the applicant. Probation officers may embellish their report to the judges to include a recommendation along with the tabulation and may suggest some contingencies to be demanded of the offender if the PR bond is granted. Such contingencies may include asking the offender to report in regularly, either in person or by telephone, during the time preceding the trial, or demanding that he participate in a specific program of treatment during this time. However, the legality of forcing the offender into a specified program as a condition of the PR bond does pose some very pertinent questions, not the least of which is related to prejudging the offender on the assumption of guilt.

Eligibility for Court-Appointed Attorneys

Most courts located within metropolitan areas and having a docket of any consequential size have arrangements for the consideration of court-appointed attorneys for individuals who are indigent. To determine eligibility for this service, further investigation and interviewing may be required as a role of probation personnel. The investigative procedure takes the form of a detailed accounting of the financial status of the offender and the giving of the necessary information by the offender to facilitate the investigation. It is not unusual to place the subject under oath at the time of this process to assure that the true facts are given. The investigators compile the assets and liabilities, with documentation required whenever possible and verification made as can be feasibly done. The findings, in keeping with specified standards for eligibility, are then made available to the court, and a judge must then rule in favor of appointing an attorney or deny the applicant legal counsel. Attorneys appointed on behalf of indigent individuals are paid for out of court funds, although some courts demand that the offender pay a portion of this amount.

Other Functions of Probation Personnel

Probation personnel may also be called upon from time to time to provide services to law enforcement personnel, usually on the behalf of an offender. Individuals in custody whose behavior is inappropriate or who have some very real problems complicated by incarceration are often the subject of unofficial referrals to probation departments for help. Conscientious police officers will sometimes go a step beyond the normal execution of their duties, recognizing that routine matters and dispositions are insufficient to resolve the problems at hand, and will request special assistance from probation personnel. Few municipal or county jails are in the position of being able to retain the full-time services of nonpolice personnel who function as social ombudsmen of sorts for the personal problems of prisoners. Usually such requests for services are directed—if they cannot be handled internally—to probation departments for investigation and the necessary assistance to resolve those problems.

The law enforcement officer with a social conscience and empathy may often make "unofficial" referrals to probation departments. If, in the course of his investigation, the officer determines that the problem is greater than the immediate crisis, he may make a suggestion that he will desist from giving a ticket or making an arrest on the condition that the family or the individual offender will contact the probation department to seek specific help in resolving the perceived problem. The officer then alerts the probation department. If this suggestion is followed through by the offender, the officer will be satisfied that he has exercised his options in a correct and socially redeemable manner by offering a constructive alternative. If the offender fails to show or to respond, feedback is given the officer, who can still initiate the summons or make the required arrest.

This chapter has discussed three of the four functions of probation work—investigation, intervention-mediation, and secondary functions. Supervision, the fourth function, will be dealt with in Chapter Nine, as previously noted.

SUGGESTED READINGS

AMERICAN BAR ASSOCIATION, *Standards Relating to Probation.* Chicago: American Bar Association, 1970.

CHUTE, C. L., AND M. BELL, *Crime, Courts, and Probation.* New York: Macmillan Publishing Co., Inc., 1956.

KAY, BARBARA A., AND CLYDE B. VEDDER, *Probation and Parole.* Springfield, Ill.: Charles C Thomas, Publisher, 1963, pp. 28–52.

McCORMICK, MONA, *Probation: What the Literature Reveals.* LaJolla, Calif.: Western Behavioral Sciences Institute, 1973.

MACPHERSON, D. P., "Probation and Corrections in the Seventies, *Federal Probation* (1971), pp. 14–17.

NATIONAL ADVISORY COMMISSION ON CRIMINAL JUSTICE STANDARDS AND GOALS, *Community Crime Prevention.* Washington, D.C., 1973. Pp. 116–130.

NATIONAL ADVISORY COMMISSION ON CRIMINAL JUSTICE STANDARDS AND GOALS, *Corrections.* Washington, D.C., 1973. Pp. 184–189.

NATIONAL INSTITUTE OF LAW ENFORCEMENT ASSISTANCE ADMINISTRATION, *The Bronx Sentencing Project of the Vera Institute of Justice.* Washington, D.C.: U.S. Government Printing Office, 1972.

ROBISON, J., et al., *The San Francisco Project.* University of California, School of Criminology. Berkeley: University of California Press, 1969.

WILKINS, L. T., *Evaluation of Penal Measures*. New York: Random House, Inc., 1969.

WOLFGANG, M. E., L. SAVITZ, AND N. JOHNSON, *The Sociology of Crime and Delinquency*. New York: John Wiley & Sons, Inc., 1970.

6

Parole:
The
Functional Aspects

There appear to be two basic differences between probation and parole. One is the degree of flexibility of operation. The other is the type of client. Although both probation and parole are held accountable for their own level of functioning, parole agents might be described as being somewhat more autonomous in the discharge of their duties than are their counterparts in probation. This illusion of semi-independence is fostered by the fact that parole personnel rarely perform directly under the immediate gaze of their parent governing body. Whereas probation departments are usually found housed either in the same building or adjacent to the system because of their close working relationship with one another, parole officers normally work out of strategically placed district offices.

Theoretically speaking, there should be no appreciable difference in the relationship roles of probation and parole officers in relation to their respective clients. The duties of investigation, intervention-mediation, and supervision remain relatively constant as primary functions of both agencies. It can be expected that some of the problems of the parolee will be magnified by the change in his environment—from a contained environment to a relatively free one.

One of the complexities of parole duties is the fact that parole officers must deal with an unknown quality. Probation personnel can procure a relatively objective reading of the offender in relation to his natural habitat, but this opportunity is not available to parole services. Most offenders coming out of a penal institution have been living in a relatively artificial environment for a period of time ranging anywhere from a few months to several years. The opportunity for those offenders to make meaningful personal decisions has been very limited, and the chance to exercise what is commonly referred to as "free will" has been equally restricted. The special needs of these offenders can best be viewed in relation to a description of how parole officers attempt to meet those needs in the normal fulfillment of their duties, as discussed in the following sections.

PREPAROLE PLANNING

Irrespective of the level of jurisdiction—state or federal—sentencing laws provide that after a specified period of time, parole may be considered. These variations are provided for in a specific relationship to the nature of the crime committed, i.e., there would be a time difference between a Class III and a Class I felony before parole eligibility would be considered. Although it is safe to assume that every offender in penal institutions is well aware of his or her earliest possible parole date, it can also be assumed that only the most exemplary prisoner would be considered for parole at the first eligible date.

Requests for parole consideration may be initiated from two basic sources—(1) from the institutional officials, or (2) from the inmate himself. At this point in the parole administrative process, the governing or review board may or may not officially see the offender for preliminary screening to determine eligibility. More often than not, the case is reviewed on paper as an initial screening process. Parole denial is made known to the inmate as soon as is humanly possible, either by a member of the parole board or by an institutional official, with an explanation of the reason for the denial. The criteria for decision making are initiated from within the institution proper, and contributing information may take the form of various reports to include the discipline record of the inmate, a briefing from his work supervisor, sometimes input from the prison classification committee, and data from the resident parole officer or counselor of the inmate. At this point, parole services from outside the walls are usually not involved.

In some of the more progressive penal institutions, "honor" cell blocks or preparole centers exist to begin to polish the offender for his subsequent release. In addition to specific planning, furloughs of short duration may be granted, and these may be increased in duration depending on the ability of the offender to handle them. Although prerelease programs may vary in content, it is at this point that the investigative duties of the parole officer begin in earnest on behalf of release planning.

Preliminary screening for parole planning is a dual effort. The inmate's residential counselor/parole officer will begin to compile general information and will then initiate the referral for assistance in the completion of the

Preparole Investigation Report

Name_____Date of birth_____

Institution & Case Number_____ Proposed Parole Board Date_____

I. PROPOSED PLACEMENT

Address_____ City_____ Telephone_____

To Live with_____ Relationship_____

Residence Is House_____ Apartment_____ Other as Indicated_____

Residence is Located in Area That is Urban_____ Commercial_____ Rural_____

Housekeeping Standards are Good_____ Adequate_____ Poor_____

Furnishings & Privacy are Good_____ Adequate_____ Poor_____

Residence is Owned_____ Being Rented_____ Rent/Option_____ Other_____

Length of Time at This Particular Address_____

Length of Time in Present Community_____

Last Prior Address_____ City if Different_____

II. FAMILY STRUCTURE

Is Family Presently Intact? Yes_____ No_____ If Answer is No, Explain_____

_____

Dominant Figure in Family is Father_____ Mother_____ Other_____

Primary Source of Family Income Is_____

Estimated Annual Income of Family Is_____

Financial Status of Family is Good_____ Average_____ Poor_____

Number of Persons in Immediate Family, Ages, and Relationship:

Family Involvement in the Community:

III. FAMILY ATTITUDES

General Attitude About Release is Positive_____ Accepting_____ Negative_____

Expressed Concerns About Release If Any_____

_____

General Attitude Toward Law Enforcement/Correctional Programs At This Time Is Positive_____ Accepting_____ Negative_____. Perceived Concerns/Feelings If Any_____

_____

Family's Plans for Parolee:

Family's Attitude Toward Proposed Parole Plan:

114

IV. COMMUNITY RESOURCES

    Possible Work/Employment Evaluation:

    Possible School/Training Evaluation:

    Possible Placement Evaluation:

    Possible Supplemental Resources:

V. PERCEIVED NEEDS OF PAROLEE:

VI. SUMMARY/COMMENTS

VII. RECOMMENDATION:

_____

Parole Officer

_____

Date of Report

investigation from his community counterpart. The latter may or may not have the opportunity to solicit firsthand information from the inmate as to his proposed plans and needs, if for no other reason than that of the geographical distance between the penal institution and the community of probable placement. Some of the expressed desires of the offender as to his outside living arrangements and job prospects or abilities may offer a starting point for the parole officer to begin his investigation. The following model will be our guideline for understanding some of the general areas of concern of the particular investigation and material needed.

The reader will note that this model tries to fulfill several basic functions. First of all, it can be used for both juvenile and adult offenders, and it can also serve as a guideline for final parole and/or for home visits of furloughs from penal institutions. It should be recognized, however, that certain sub-groupings of the model are more pertinent to juvenile offenders perhaps than they would be to their adult counterparts; but since some jurisdictions provide that one agency must service both juvenile and adult parolees, our model attempts to do away with a separate form for each of the two categories.

In analyzing the information required, it will be noted that the emphasis differs somewhat from that sought on the presentence investigation form shown in Chapter Five. The preparole report is far more personal in content and in the nature of the information sought. Perhaps one of the reasons that may account for the "intimate" details is a carryover from the premise that poverty and generally poor standards of living contribute to criminal behavior. Although it has often been advanced that our prisons contain more lower socio-economic and minority ethnic group members than they do middle-class or upper-class Anglos, this does not necessarily mean that there is more crime among the lower class or minority levels. What it may mean is that fewer members of the lower grouping can afford the luxury of capable and expensive defense attorneys, and hence more convictions result. Nevertheless, most parole summary sheets continue to contain similar statistics without any attempt being made to explain the rationale for such statistics.

A more socially practical explanation for these statistics concerns the theory of criminal behavior being related to association. The old socio-logical theory of cocentric circles relating city patterns of growth, mobility, and deterioration would seem to be a more appropriate basis for understand-ing the concern of the relationship between poor neighborhoods and poor behavior. Although crime is not the occupant of blighted areas only, it is easy for desperate individuals, who may be such by virtue of any number of reasons, to seize on desperate measures to satisfy their own basic or perceived needs. Deteriorating neighborhoods have the tendency to become somewhat clannish in population, and any outsider who is nonrepresentative of that neighborhood—whether law enforcement or not—is automatically denied information, common courtesies, or cooperation. One basic reason that correctional methods have fallen short of society's expectations is that although such methods may be able to manipulate the individual, it remains virtually impossible to manipulate the environment.

A lot may be said about pride. Many people still are subjected to life in poor neighborhoods, but the basic difference between them as law-abiding citizens and as criminals is a matter of pride and personal values. A person does not have to be rich to be clean. A dirty $200 suit can look more inap-propriate on a person than a pair of clean but oft-patched jeans. Some of the categories noted in the above model are designed to evaluate personal family pride and the desire to make the most of what one legally has. We have, then, come back to the concept of internalization, which was discussed and referred to in a preceding chapter, and its effects on individuals as they perceive themselves.

A further theme that has been stated on numerous instances within these pages is that the one notable trait of offenders is their irresponsibility. However, this does not mean that an individual who has a tastefully furnished home and landscaped yard will be unlikely to offend. Crime knows no boundaries and makes no exceptions based on income, color lines, or any other criteria. Irresponsibility of individuals, however, may reflect their approach to life and their feelings about their obligations to society. A definite lack of responsibility to their own primary interests can certainly be equated with a lack of responsibility to the value structure of their own community. Although initial assumptions can be erroneous, the parole officer who notes a lack of responsibility to basic living standards might well assume that such an indifference may infiltrate other areas.

Category II, Family Structure, in the preceding model, is designed to gauge the amount of family pressure that the parolee will have to contend with on his release, as well as the degree of family organization/disorganization. It is important to know how the family has functioned during the time one of its members has been incarcerated. This category will attempt to examine family strengths and weaknesses and to determine at a subtle level how each family member might work, either at a positive or negative level, on behalf of the returning parolee.

Family disorganization may often be measurable when it has been determined that one or more of its members, especially juvenile members, has been placed outside the home. When such placements have been ascertained, one of several assumptions can be made.

1. If such a placement was effected because of difficulties with the law, it can then be hypothesized that the value structure of the family remains badly out of alignment.
2. If the placement of a juvenile was made to a foster or group-living situation of a nonpenal/correctional emphasis, it might be assumed that parental responsibility is lacking.
3. If a placement became necessary because of various social or economic hardships, it can be assumed that the family could not or would not deal with the problem adequately.
4. If there is a sufficient degree of hostility or a definite lack of communication in the family structure, it can be hypothesized that these factors may have precipitated acts that required the intervention of one or more social agencies.

More obvious and significant indices of disorganization would be noted if one of the parents has abandoned the family or if a separation or a divorce has taken place. In the case of an adult married offender, the status of the spouse may be equally revealing and pertinent. Has he or she filed or received a divorce or contemplated doing so? Has he or she been living with another adult of the opposite sex while the spouse is incarcerated? Has there been an increase in the size of the family such as a married daughter leaving her husband and coming back home with her two children to live? Has the wife of the offender become pregnant or given birth to a child during her husband's absence?

It is obvious that the findings relative to this category on Family Structure are of utmost importance to the parolee's adjustment back into the community. Not only are such factors significant from the standpoint of living standards and housing arrangements, they are equally important to facilitate the needed preparation of the offender to have an awareness of and be able to cope with reality. It is better to be candid with the offender and to appraise him of impending problems rather than to have unknown factors conflict with his transitional adjustment back into society.

Family income and the ability of the family to meet their basic needs at their current economic level should be examined. Again, this category may be more significant when the proposed parolee is a juvenile. If the return of the offender to the parental home is going to cause undue economic hardships, a further or alternate placement should be explored. The offender should not be punished by being denied parole strictly on the basis of an inadequate placement or because of family rejection, let alone because his family cannot financially assimilate him back into the fold.

The author, in conjunction with his employment in a juvenile institution, can remember several cases where home visits or parole were denied because family economic problems were contributing factors. Quite often the family's inability to find transportation and financing to travel several hundred miles to visit was misinterpreted as a lack of interest and concern. Instead of being accorded parole or a furlough when the offender appeared ready and deserving of same, he remained institutionalized longer than was either necessary or appropriate. The end result was the reappearance of acting-out behavior, which resulted in an extended period of incarceration.

Although the subcategory of Family Involvement in the Community might be questioned as to the appropriateness of its placement here, the rationale for such should not remain obscure. Such a heading as placed fulfills a dual purpose: First, it helps to determine the family's motivational level to accept and to utilize community social services in a problem-solving process; and, second, it helps to determine the family's level of identity with the community and its attempt to integrate the family unit into the social value system of that community.

The appropriate use of community resources is another indicator of family motivational levels. How has the family been able to cope with the stress and trauma surrounding the loss of the family member? Two possible reactions may be noted. One of these is *resignation*. Resignation is indicative of those families who wish to assume no responsibility for their contributing role and will not make any preparation for the future. A word of caution should be entered at this point by way of explanation. The family who cries, "Where did I go wrong?" is the family who is trying to lift the load of total responsibility off the shoulders of the offender for the offense he committed. Do not forget, let alone foster, the fact that offenders nearly always bear the trait of irresponsibility within their personality makeup and their manner of meeting basic obligations.

The second reaction is *remorse*. The sign of healthy remorse is one that enables the family members to take inventory of their value structures and especially their method of coping with reality. This, to be positive in content, is done not in mourning but in the act of learning to deal with areas of dysfunctioning whether they be familial or individual in nature. One can never profit from mistakes unless those mistakes become both identifiable and recognizable in nature. The prognosis of the offender is far more hopeful if his family is willing to work in conjunction with him as a supporting unit and in presenting a unified front for the understanding and correction of their specific and mutual needs. The family who has learned how to use specialized services is in a better position to work with the offender in a program of rehabilitation and treatment.

The family who makes an honest attempt to assimilate even a segment of the value system of the community will soon learn to respect and to protect those values. The ability to identify with any social standard somehow initiates a form of transference process, a process that will bear some positive feelings. The hostility that often exists between groups is a hate or fear that is fostered primarily out of a lack of mutual knowledge of one another. The growth of negative feelings is predicated on what we perceive another to be rather than on firsthand knowledge of what the other person may really be like.

Another important area of responses for understanding the needs of the offender is Family Category III on Attitudes. Not only does this category help to assess the needs of the offender, it may reveal some of the problems that can cause friction between the parolee and his family once parole is granted. Is the family accepting of his return? What seems to be the climate, the family atmosphere, regarding parole? In pursuing this aspect of the investigation, a variety of concerns may be uncovered.

One of the most common problems that parole officers must deal with is the family who rejects the offender due to ulterior motives. Families may harbor some very negative feelings about the return of the offender. Unacceptance of the parolee may be based on the shame a family feels because of his conviction and subsequent incarceration. Such an attitude is characterized by the feeling that the family has lost respect in the community and that it may never again regain its place in the social pecking order. The family may also harbor many guilt feelings reflecting its assumed inadequacies in failing as a parent or a spouse. Finally, it may be bitter beyond seeming repair because of an investment that went sour and because the hand it offered to love and to feed was bitten in return.

Another common problem is that of family rejection of the offender based on a fear of the unknown. There are some classical expressed concerns that parole officers must deal with. What kind of a monster can the family expect to see upon the parolee's return? What negative qualities will be exhibited and retained as assimilated in his prison experience? Will his bitterness permeate and affect the functioning level of the family? Will he be as cruel and as abusive a person as he was before he got sent up? What will the family's legal and moral obligations be if he isn't conforming or obeying the conditions of his parole? What protection will be accorded if the family has to turn him in for nonconformity or other abuses? How will such fears be appeased?

The attempt to perceive the attitude of the family toward law enforcement, the courts, and corrections in general is an attempt to determine whether the family will support or will attempt to undermine parole services. If it becomes apparent that the family is bitter and even remotely hostile, it can be deduced that the family may need as much, if not more, help than the offender does in dealing with its feelings. For example, the family may deliberately and regularly attempt to convince the parolee that he has already paid his debt to society many times over on a "bum rap" to begin with, and that he now has no legal obligations to uphold. Both parole and probation officers are well aware that the source of juvenile client troubles is often the parents. The juvenile parolee will undoubtedly feel a stronger obligation to his parents than he will to his supervisor. This conflict of interest illustrates the old proverb about man's inability to serve two masters.

Little explanation seems necessary about the other subcategories in this part of our model. Suffice it to say, it is not that simple a matter for the investigating parole officer to correctly evaluate the family's feelings about the parole. The officer may have a great deal of difficulty in attempting to reconcile the aspects of idealism expressed by the family and with the reality needs of the parolee. Although there are no known statistics to document this premise, it might well be assumed that the return of many parolees to their place of original residence prior to their commitment is to forecast parole failure. On the other hand, families will usually view a parole placement in another setting other than the parolee's own home as no form of parole at all. The perceived perspective is that of a continuing commitment with only the placement being different in nature.

Category IV, Community Resources, is used exclusively for collateral contacts. Although primarily an investigative function, it will be seen later in this chapter that some mediation-intervention functions are also included. Each of the units represented in the model will be explored as is appropriate on behalf of the individual offender. Proposed and/or potential employment situations are contacted. Although confirmation of a job prior to release can rarely be expected, the market can be explored based on the known skills and abilities of the offender, to determine if he can quality for employment opportunities within the community to which he will return. It may be customary to routinely check his last place of employment to determine the interest of that employer in taking the offender back based on his prior work record there.

The subcategory on Possible School/Training Evaluation is especially pertinent to, but not necessarily limited to, juvenile parolees. The juvenile offender whose age mandatorily demands his return to school must conform to legal dictates unless exception is made by jurisdictional decision. The investigative actions of the parole officer would include the determination of the school to be attended. These, in cooperation with school officials, grade level placement and program content would be explored and decided upon. The level of schooling attained in the penal institution should be used to determine the placement and ability level, and this again would depend on the investigation and consequent recommendations of the parole officer.

It is conceivable that not every juvenile of required school age should go into a normal academic program, and alternate vocational training should be considered. There are also adult parolees who should be considered for some specialized training programs. Both the nonschool-oriented juvenile and the hard-core unemployable adult parolee may need the guidance of apprentice programs, on-the-job training, vocational skill programs, and even semi-sheltered workshops to gain new skills designed to make them more employable and more productive and to enhance some personal pride.

The subcategory on Possible Placement Evaluation pertains to the finding of living quarters and subsidization for installing parolees in living situations other than their own residence or that of their own family. This is, at best, a difficult task where juveniles are concerned. Quite often social service agency funding may have been depleted, and subsidization cannot be provided for. The family may be even less able to help, and it could be surmised that the family may not be motivated to do so even if it were financially able to assist. Therefore it sometimes becomes necessary to seek placement of the juvenile with other relatives as an interim step preparatory to further planning.

The placement of adult parolees may be even more difficult to come by. Infrequently a "live-in" job placement may be found where room and board are considered a part of the wages. Very few placement institutions for adults exist. Some agencies designed specifically to assist the offender, including parole services, may be able to pay a week or two of rent at the local YMCA and provide a meal ticket, but the funding for such provisions is usually limited. For example, the U.S. Bureau of Prisons has contracted for some placement services through a halfway house program.[1] Quite often the contracting of services is sought not only for placement purposes but also to include accompanying programs of therapy under the guidance of skilled residential clinicians. Such services are inadequate on the basis that there are an insufficient number to meet the need.

The subcategory on Possible Supplemental Resources is a cataloging of community services that can be used in conjunction with the rehabilitation process of the offender. Although there is no need for the investigating parole officer to specify the potential services, the agencies that are willing to assist might be listed in this section. A wide range of services are provided by some of the following agencies.

1. Local welfare department.
2. The division of vocational rehabilitation.
3. State employment services.
4. Local mental health clinic.
5. Agencies such as Employee Ex, designed specifically to assist offenders.
6. Specialized school or training programs under the auspices of the local school district.
7. Community health services.
8. Various private social service agencies such as those affiliated with a local philanthropic group.
9. The Salvation Army and other similar programs.
10. Private individuals or firms.

It is helpful if the investigator would include the name of a specific contact person within each agency who can facilitate the processing of the parolee with a minimum of notice and effort.

Category V on the Perceived Needs of the Parolee represents a composite examination that can be given routinely here. In passing, it should be noted that this category can represent a composite of needs as the parolee sees them, as the institution sees him, and how he may now be viewed in light of the information gathered as a result of the preparole investigation. Therefore, a preconceived need may become totally altered as a result of the findings noted.

The material offered under category VI on Summary/Comments should be as brief a report as possible, summing up the findings and expressing some of the concerns noted as a result of the investigation. Under special

[1]U.S. Department of Justice, *U.S. Bureau of Prisons, 1975* (Washington, D.C., 1975), p. 12.

circumstances, there might be a request made for classification material, further academic evaluation, and/or psychological testing—in order to arrive at a better plan based on updated material. Lastly, a recommendation is made advocating for or against a parole/furlough, and some documentation for the recommendation is given.

The disposition of this investigative material may be forwarded either to the institutional parole agent/counselor at the penal facility or directly to the parole board itself. The material is incorporated into the overall report and becomes a segmentary but important basis upon which parole is decided and a parole plan is formulated.

SECONDARY INVESTIGATIVE DUTIES

Two related forms of investigation are often performed as secondary duties by parole officers. The first such duty is the monitoring of offenders on furlough/leave from the penal institution, and the second is the investigation of possible parole placements through interstate compacts. With some alterations, the model used in this chapter could be adapted as a guideline in the execution of these specific roles.

A furlough/leave status is more often than not construed to be a pre-parole experiment. Its basic purpose, with the notable exception being emergency situations, is to allow the offender to begin to reestablish primary and community relationships, to perhaps do some job hunting, to generally prepare for his future upon release, and to allow for observation by parole personnel whenever possible in a mini-evaluation to determine how the offender handles himself during this time.

The ability or inability of the offender to attempt to resolve areas of potential conflict—or at least to give them some objective scrutiny—may well be grounds to condition and to temper the subsequent parole plan. If it appears that the conflicts noted are insurmountable, or if the offender chooses to ignore or to contest reality, it may be deemed necessary to seek an alternate placement at the time of parole. Such a decision should not be premature in nature and should not call for completely "scrapping" the initial plan. Instead, the monitoring parole officer should merely report the nature and extent of the conflicts to his counterpart at the institution. This step should not be construed to be a punitive measure; rather, it can serve as an embarkation point for implementing a problem-solving process within the preparole framework, directed specifically at the areas of friction noted.

Correctional authorities may often have reason to believe that alternate placements would be in the best interests of the parolees. All states work together under a compactual agreement whereby complementary supervision may be provided by an agency in another jurisdiction if an out-of-state placement is appropriate. Prior to the placement of the parolee, a formal request for an investigation as well as for complementary supervision is made to the local agency that is geographically situated to administer this service. The investigation, findings, and subsequent recommendations, along with an acknowledgment to supervise, will then be forwarded to the original referring jurisdiction. No basic procedural change in the investigative process is likely since the general information required is relatively universal in content.

Complementary supervision per se should offer no particular problems unless the offender violates a condition of his parole. In this case, the usual procedure would call for the parolee to be extradited to his original state of jurisdiction for legal action. This could conceivably become a lengthy legal process if the parolee decides to contest the matter, especially if he decides to fight against being returned to the state of original jurisdiction for the reinstatement of his sentence. If, however, the parole violation is the result of a new offense, the task becomes somewhat easier for processing. Incarceration may very well be instituted following the new conviction if adjudication is made. Time will then allow for the administration and legal processing to extradite the offender following the completion of this new sentence.

Revocation Proceedings

Parole officers may, and the use of the word *may* must be emphasized, find it necessary to do more detailed investigative work than their probation counterparts relative to revocation proceedings. Although the trend is toward formal court hearings for revocation hearings, in many jurisdictions the parole board assumes a function comparable to that of the court. This quasi-legal function of the parole board has been upheld in the past as sufficiently lawful to determine whether the condition of parole has been violated to such a degree that the balance of the suspended sentence should be reinstated. Not only can a determination be made by the parole board, but the sentence can also be immediately implemented by the board.

In matters such as this, the role of the parole officer is to provide the parole board with sufficient information relative to the conditions and circumstances of the alleged violation so that a legal determination can be made. Although the situation is rare and is rapidly becoming obsolete, there still are cases and jurisdictions where the parole officer serves in a quasi-prosecution capacity. This situation applies only to cases that are predicated on specific conditions of the parole agreement being either ignored or abused by the parolee. Violations of specific ordinances and the subsequent conviction of the parolee for having violated those ordinances usually constitute sufficient grounds to establish a parole violation. Almost all conditions, whether probation or parole, explicitly contain reference to no new violations of the law irrespective of the jurisdiction.

Such duties, when demanded as a part of the parole officer's role, document the need for some legal knowledge and courtroom demeanor, to which reference was made in Chapter Four, "Professional Growth and Training." The reader should be made aware that such hearings do not necessarily take on the coloring of a regular trial and are not comparable with certain actions in small claims courts where attorneys are not only rare but are barred. The revocation hearing then takes place based on the word of the parole officer, with documentation, against the word of the parolee with whatever meaningful defenses he can offer as rebuttal. However, as will be noted in the chapter on legal rights of offenders, the nature of revocation hearings is becoming more formalized because offenders are now being accorded more legal representation and are utilizing such representation to a much greater extent.

In this investigative capacity, the parole officer must prepare a strong and well-documented case. He must wear, then, more than one hat, for his presentation of the case may necessitate some policelike work to detail the events and circumstances surrounding the allegations; and he also must have the ability to know local due process and be able to present an authoritative case at the time of the hearing. If the investigative aspects of the case and the findings are sufficiently strong and substantiated in content, much of the rest of the proceedings will routinely be taken care of with little more than mere formalities.

Essential in the presentation are facts similar to those presented by a law enforcement officer in the course of his investigation and arrest. These facts would include the nature of the violation, how it represents a conflict with the standards demanded by society, what the specific circumstances and facts of the case were, where and when they occurred, whether jurisdiction (venue) can be established, and whether there was evidence beyond a reasonable doubt to uphold the accusations being made. Revocation hearings can have a tremendous impact. The consequences, if the charges are upheld, can be severe, and will undoubtedly mean that the offender will be returned to prison to perhaps serve out his full time, as originally sentenced. The case, for example, of a normal citizen having a gun in his possession may be cause for some minor apprehension, but for a convicted felon and parolee, it becomes an almost sure ticket back to the penal institution to do more time, time that will almost certainly constitute the balance of his suspended sentence without any further consideration for an early release or another chance for parole.

PAROLE INTERVENTION

Intervention and the Parolee

Since society is somewhat reluctant to accept the returning offender from prison, much of the work of the parole officer involves an attempt to intervene on behalf of his client. It is highly probable that such efforts may cause some pronounced feelings of ambivalence on the part of the parolee. He still retains some of his bitterness toward the system that has contained and repressed him for several years and the parole officer represents an extension of that system. On the other hand, the parolee's lack of social contacts forces him to remain dependent initially on the assistance of others for the procurement of even the most common and basic of human needs.

One of the most glaring differences between probation and parole is the lack of the opportunity to observe the parolee's ability to handle freedom and responsibility. With the probationer, little has been altered other than his legal status and the accompanying demands made of him as a contingency of his new role. Life will generally go on in the same manner as before in spite of judicially imposed regulations. These regulations can usually be taken in stride without too much of an interruption of the probationer's daily routine. Not so in the case of the parolee. Not only must he learn new roles in a world that is alien to him in many ways, but he must also show proof of his abilities to himself as well as to others.

Our society has superimposed at least one demand on its citizens, a demand that is accepted as a prerequisite for such qualities as responsibility, honesty, and human worth—that is, gainful employment. The reader should hearken back to the third chapter of this text and recognize the tones of Calvinism woven into our standards of today. Yet one of the most common unmet needs of the parolee, the need that is most difficult for him to attain, is that of gainful employment.[2]

The only skill that most prisons impart to their inmates is the ability to recognize and to adhere to the penal caste system, along with a few forms of finesse that can be used on the outside if the offender finds it either necessary or desirable to return to his old habits of crime. Most work assignments are generally conceded to be merely time fillers, or the utilization of what might otherwise be destructive time if the inmates were left to their own devices.[3] What the parolee brings with him after his prison experience is rarely a desired and marketable product, especially for employment purposes. The mere desire to work is not always sufficient to compensate for a lack of specific job skills.

[2]Rosemary Erickson et al., *Paroled But Not Free* (New York: Behavioral Publications, 1973), pp. 64–73.

[3]Daniel Glaser, *The Effectiveness of a Prison and Parole System* (New York: The Bobbs-Merrill Company, Inc., 1969), Chap. 10, pp. 156–172.

Even when some basic job skills are possessed by the parolee, the stigma that is often attached to him by society will result in many doors being closed not too gently in his face. The parole agent must then assume the role of an intervening agent on behalf of his client. If gainful employment is one of the stipulations of the contract, then to even consider revoking parole is an injustice if there is little opportunity for the offender to find a job. It is universally suspected that recidivism rates are high among parolees because they often have to revert back to their old criminal methods in order to earn a dollar.

Furthermore, the parolee, who during his period of incarceration was largely dependent on others for having his needs met, may now feel the need to become independent and self-sustaining—qualities representative of his new freedom. His pride and desire to achieve may prevent him from seeking the guidance and assistance needed to find employment.

It cannot be said often enough or strongly enough that probation or parole conditions imposed on parolees must be realistic and must be attainable in content. If there is some operational difficulty in the realization of clients meeting imposed contingencies, two possible solutions might be considered: (1) the reduction or total elimination of the impractical features, and/or (2) more assistance from parole supervisors in helping their client offenders to realize those demands. Although the initial intervention role of parole is at the primary involvement level of integration into the community, the probable success or failure of the parolee within society is dependent on transitional and intervention assistance.

Most employers will be more concerned over the possibility of the parolee reoffending, or over his potential to reoffend, rather than whether he possesses adequate work skills. Intervention by a parole officer often is merely the giving of assurance to the employer that some degree of control and supervision will continue to be exercised over the parolee. Such confirmation does not guarantee that the offender will work any harder or be any more productive if hired; it merely allows some employers to use the parole officer as a "whipping boy" to get the employee back in line if his work capacity or habits begin to deteriorate. Although this is not an enviable role, it may be a necessary one, for it can allow the parole officer to keep a finger on the adjustment pulse of his client and to thereby determine how he is coping with this particular responsibility requirement.

Unfortunately, intervention is often viewed as manipulation and even as infringement on the social and personal life of the parolee. He may be willing to acknowledge the need to "go straight" and to avoid any violations of the law as being a reasonable request. But he will resent emphatically any interference with his right to engage in certain social and personal activities that he feels bear little significance to his job or the conditions of his parole. Reference is made here to the parolee's personal methods of coping to achieve perceived needs, needs that have often been thwarted or denied but which must be resolved within the primary structure and relationships of the individual's immediate environment. A. H. Maslow and Charlotte Towle, among others, make strong reference to some of the basic human needs and their ranking in the hierarchy of all individuals.[4,5] The need to belong and the need for recognition may be denied him through normal social channels. Therefore, gratification of these needs may be sought through undesirable channels. The ultimate achievement of these needs is particularly important to the parolee. It is surmised that he will strive even harder than most people to achieve some of them, for his drive to do so is a counterreaction to the lack of privacy and of self-initiative, qualities that were denied to him during his period of incarceration.

Many of these needs would be considered to be normal and/or acceptable when applied to the nonoffender, but are forbidden to the parolee. For example, having too much to drink, gambling, the use of certain drugs such as marijuana, or a promiscuous sexual affair—to name but a few—are all considered "off bounds" to the parolee. Parole officers, although they realize that a certain amount of tolerance must be exercised, are only too well aware that just as it is impossible to be a little bit pregnant, it is equally dangerous to become a little bit addicted to drugs or alcohol or to play around with an attractive member of the opposite sex who is not the offender's spouse. Parolees engaging in such behavior are literally and figuratively setting themselves up, and their degree of involvement may eventually involve them to a point beyond their control.

Parole officers must monitor such behavior to prevent overinvolvement and subsequent conflicts. A hypothetical question might well be raised as to exactly what the parole officer should concern himself with. We might suggest here that intervention is necessary if the current course of behavior borders on illegality, or if the current form of coping would appear to be on a collision course that would eventually lead the parolee to a violation of the law, thereby endangering his continued right to freedom. For example, although public intoxication is rarely an arrestable offense in and of itself, the lowering of inhibitions due to the consumption of alcohol could very well result in the offender acting in an irrational manner that could lead to his subsequent arrests. This becomes a touchy social and legal matter.

It may not be feasible or even possible to provide intervention in some of the areas of friction prior to parole being granted. For example, although the spouse of the offender may express a desire to see the offender return home, the changes that have taken place over the years of absence may

---

[4]A. H. Maslow, *Motivation and Personality* (New York: Harper & Row, Publishers, Inc., 1954).

[5]Charlotte Towle, *Common Human Needs* (Washington, D.C.: Social Security Board, Bureau of Public Assistance, U.S. Government Printing Office, 1945).

make the reconciliation impossible. Changes in life styles, in standards of living and behavior, alterations in needs and goals, realignment of values, all may suddenly be discovered to cause conflicts and may appear to doom the reconciliation once the offender is released.

Intervention does not imply that mediation must necessarily be the role of the parole officer. His primary role is to recognize the problems and to implement a plan to counteract the conflicts noted. The resolving of such conflicts might more appropriately be the role of a community mental health clinic. For example, the parole officer may find it necessary to demand that the offender and the spouse mutually explore the source of their misunderstandings and seek alternative methods of coping with and resolving their conflicts. Intervention, then, may be defined as the recognition of stress-producing situations, situations that could contribute to possible recidivism, and the mobilization of appropriate resources to counteract the possibility that reoffending might become a reality.

Intervention and the Community

Intervention has a dual meaning in regard to the community. The supervising officer must serve both the offender and society. By easing the transition of the offender back into society, the possible sources of friction are mutually reduced on behalf of both concerned factions. With the possible exception of smaller communities, where intimacy may be more pronounced based on limited population density, the parolee's reentrance will probably go unnoticed if he does not call attention to himself through either inappropriate or illegal forms of behavior. Intervention consists, then, at a simplistic level of definition, of preparing the offender for an adequate adjustment in the community as well as offering the community some assurance and degree of peace of mind by maintaining surveillance and accountability of the offender.

In an effort to appease as well as to serve both the offender and society, the supervising parole officer can choose between two possible courses of action. First, the supervision/surveillance factor can be so punitively structured that the parolee is coerced into conformity. We address here a total demand approach, as opposed to a mutual sharing, working together process between the offender and his supervisor. Conformity gained through the fear of consequence for reprisal sake may appear to be an effective measure in holding down recidivism, but it fails to take into account any specific or personal needs of the individual. Although objective control is needed, the parolee who is labeled as needing extensive surveillance probably should not have been paroled in the first place. Such treatment unequally and unfairly applied denotes a lack of trust in the offender and may repress any desire he has to readjust. Frequently he will revert back into a form of behavior that is commensurate with that utilized while in custody, that of compliance without involvement.

The need to build a protective wall between the parolee and the rest of society can be done away with if the community can be assured that this need can be circumvented through other methods. Circumvention can be relatively assured when public involvement can be mobilized through a total planning process, a process that is of mutual benefit to all concerned.

The following is an example of such a total planning process. In early 1977, the Denver-based Gilliam Youth Center for Juvenile Justice proposed a program designed to involve a variety of community services prefatory to a parole plan being formulated for juveniles from that community. The purposes suggested in the syllabus were as follows.[6]

A.   To provide detail information regarding the youth institutional adjust-ment according to the prescribed treatment objectives that support the youth's readiness to be paroled.

B.   To assist in the development of a service delivery plan with established guidelines to be utilized when the youth is released back into the com-munity and to develop a community treatment prescription.

C.   To develop procedures for identifying and filling gaps of services and eliminating duplication of services.

D.   To clarify this district's roles, policies, resources, and limitations.

What is being suggested here is that a pending parole should be acted on at the community level in order to mobilize resources based on the known needs of the parolee. All community agencies should be informed of the in-stitutional history of the offender to determine the need/availability of community services and specific nature of agency offerings, offerings that could be used in complementing the parole treatment plan of the offender. Further, the results of the preparole planning should be made available to the appropriate division, to be incorporated into the parole plan as sup-plemental services and resources to be used.

At least two very basic and important ingredients are visualized in this proposal. First, parole intervention is no longer to be a relatively solitary and somewhat lonesome effort of one individual. Instead, the parole officer would have community resources available, and these would become an in-tegral part of the overall parole plan. Second, a psychological ploy is put to use to counteract some of the resistance that an uninformed community normally might offer. It becomes counterproductive to "put down" something that you are involved with and have a vested interest in. Those darkened corners are suddenly illuminated, and there no longer exists a need to fear what may dwell therein.

Social pressure is readily recognizable in young offenders/parolees. Juveniles, in their search for recognition, will often demonstrate daring acts

[6]"Proposal For Pre-Paroled Staffings" a memorandum to the Department of Institutions, Division of Youth Services, State of Colorado, March 1977.

or the deliberate disregard of expected norms to establish themselves in the peer pecking order. It has been the experience of the author that the school system that must absorb the juvenile offender on his/her return to the community is one of the most skeptical of agencies about the negative effects and attitudes that can be expected of the parolee. Sometimes such feelings are justified, due to the lack of a progressive institutional academic program, resulting in a shortage of credits. Therefore the parolee must often be returned to a grade placement level not in keeping with either his chronological age or his degree of sophistication. His perceived influence, especially on younger peers at his placed grade level, is both anticipated and feared by school officials.

Such a program as Denver has proposed should go a long way in eliminating unneeded fears, regardless of the source. Not only is it perceived that services will be ready and available for the parolee, but such services should be equally available to the family of the offender. By providing a unified front as well as a comprehensive and inclusive program, intervention is now becoming a community responsibility.

Chapter Three suggested that there should be a need, especially on the part of the initial court of jurisdiction and commitment, to retain not only interest but legal involvement with the offender and his future. The task of parole personnel can become a much easier and more efficient task when continuing interests in the offender is maintained at the community level.

SUGGESTED READINGS

BURKHART, WALTER R., "The Great California Parole Experiment," *Federal Probation,* 40, no. 4 (December 1976), 9–14.

HAMER, JOHN, "Criminal Release System." Washington, D.C.: Editorial Research Reports, 1976 (pamphlet).

KEVE, P. W., *Imaginative Programming in Probation and Parole.* Minneapolis: University of Minnesota Press, 1967.

NEITHERCUTT, M. G., "Parole Legislation," *Federal Probation,* 41, no. 1 (March 1977), 22–26.

PEVEN, H., AND A. ALCABES, *A Study of Practice and Theory in Probation and Parole.* Washington, D.C.: Department of Health, Education and Welfare, U.S. Government Printing Office, 1971.

PRUS, ROBERT C., AND JOHN R. STRATTON, "Parole Revocation Decision-Making: Private Typings and Official Designations," *Federal Probation,* 40, no. 1 (March 1976), 48–53.

REED, JOHN P., AND DALE NANCE, "Society Perpetuates the Stigma of a Conviction," *Federal Probation,* 36, no. 2 (June 1972), 17–31.

STERLING, JOANNE AND ROBERT W. HARTY, "An Alternative Model of Community Services for Ex-Offenders and Their Families," *Federal Probation,* 36, no. 3 (September 1972), 31–34.

WEST, D. J., ed., *The Future of Parole.* London: Gerald Duckworth and Company, 1972.

7

The Rights
of Offenders

Not since the era of the Emancipation Proclamation has our country shown as much concern and seen as many activities in the area of civil rights as have been displayed in the period from the late 1950s to the present. Every group has a cause of sorts, most of which are legitimate in nature. Others can no longer be exactly and specifically sure just what their true cause is, for it probably has been obscured by the dust stirred up from the race for equality. The fight for the rights of prisoners is one of the less publicized causes, but progress is being made.

The rights of offenders, especially those who are incarcerated, have long been ignored. Efforts to have prisoners' rights upheld were generally either sought for on an individual basis or through the efforts of legal counsel, because prison officials have looked askance at any attempt by prisoners to organize themselves for a purpose. Such collective behavior was viewed as dangerous and unsettling to the inmate population, to say nothing of the uneasiness it caused prison officials. Although the term *jail house lawyer* is obscure as to its origin, the title was frequently used to describe an inmate who was vocal and who could not or would not learn to quietly accept his fate. More recently this appellation has been applied to any inmate spokesman who advocates changes on behalf of the offender population irrespective of the topic or the cause. Humility and humbleness, qualities described by the Quakers as predecessors to repentance, were used to describe the opposite of qualities found in inmates who were willing to stand up for their rights and to challenge the system, even when the challenge was based on a sound legal premise.

The thrust of this chapter is to examine the evolution of prisoner/offender rights and to appraise the reader of the progress made if any. Although certain subject matter as treated herein will probably remain constant in theory, any discussion of law is complicated by the fact that it changes so frequently. A law may have remained on the books for years, but it is conceivable that within a short span of time it can be overturned by a high court ruling. The reader should bear this in mind as he progresses through the pages because what may be contemporary today may be obsolete tomorrow.

THE HISTORICAL CONCEPTS OF RIGHTS

A capsule statement about the rights of offenders is best characterized by saying that they were deprived of basic rights. Sheer evidence alone was usually sufficient to sustain the guilt or innocence of the accused. While barristers had their place and their roles, the adversary system of today, wherein legal arguments are predicated on legal precedents was largely unknown. In short, the merits of a case were dealt with on the basis of immediate tangibles.

Early Times

Trials prior to the late nineteenth century were based on evidence, to be sure, but only when the evidence was of a strong physical nature. A study of the history of this period would lend credibility to the assumption that without tangible evidence, social factors, more so than legal factors, tended to color and condition the findings of the courts. For example, was the character of the accused in keeping with the nature of the offense? A good character reference was equal to a good legal defense when there was little else on which to predicate a judgment. The wisdom of King Solomon and his method of resolving the true mother of a disputed child substantiates, in part, our point.[1]

While on the subject of the sagacity of King Solomon, the reader would do well to reacquaint himself with some of the judicial wisdom of the Old Testament. Pertinent to our discussion, the role of today's judges is comparable to the role of yesterday's rulers. Kings of the biblical days ruled not as a politician rules a country but more as a father governs his family. The number of laws that King Solomon enacted reached into the hundreds according to biblical scholars. The temper of the law, or its spirit, if this term is more pleasing from a contemporary standpoint, was based on moral

---

[1] 1 Kings 3:16–28.

realism rather than on any quasi-legal nature. The precedent—short of Divine Guidance—was built on the need for the mutual harmony of the subjects rather than on a legal foundation.

Barristers of early times were certainly knowledgeable of the law, but they were equally, if not more so, adept at speaking on behalf of their clients. It can be certain that although their presentations remained within the contextual framework of the law, their chief function was to speak for the accused, a rather interesting phenomenon of semantics. Most definitions of the word *barrister* include not only "one who has knowledge of the law" but also "one who *pleads* (or *advocates*) for his client."[2] The implication is that not all supplications made of the court were predicated on legal issues. It can be deduced that the accused may have sought the services of a barrister for the purpose of expressing character assets as a countermeasure to be used in his behalf. Even today, impassioned pleas may still be heard in courts about the attributes of "a good old family man."

An even more likely reason for legal presentations not being based on judicial precedents prior to the mid-eighteen hundreds was a lack of communication. Not only were methods of carrying the latest judicial words to remote borders of the country severely limited, but it was a painstaking process to prepare a verbatim copy of the decision. The recording, cataloging, and distribution of high court rulings are a relatively contemporary happening. Even at the time of this writing, appellate court rulings at any level short of the state supreme court or the U.S. Supreme Court levels are too complicated for anyone but the most studious and conscientious of lawyers to keep up with.

At this early point in time, the extent of the defined rights of offenders was an unknown entity. It was not so much an issue of gross deprivation of rights as it was a lack of any formal definition of rights. The public was not particularly interested in prisoners' rights since offenders were viewed as moral lepers who were not deserving of assistance. Help, as such, was conceived to be self-initiated, coming from within as a form of contribution, and only then was the offender deemed worthy of anything more than common courtesies and the most basic human needs.

It was not unusual for offenders, at the time of their imprisonment, or shortly following it, to be subjected to the loss of more than just their freedom. Two legal concepts that served to document this state of affairs were known as *civil death* and *attainder*. Attainder, commonly referred to as a *bill of attainder,* was an English act (although there is reason to believe that it was first practiced elsewhere) that provided for the extinction of all civil rights and related capabilities for individuals who committed a high crime, usually one that was punishable by death such as treason. Attainder

    [2]Henry Campbell Black, *Black's Law Dictionary* (St. Paul, Minn.: West Publishing Company, 1968).

provided for the forfeiture of the property of the offender upon his conviction and established what was called the "corruption of blood," i.e., if the offender was a holder of any title of royalty, both he and his family would be stripped of that power forever.

The American colonies, as with so many of the laws of England, adopted the format of attainder initially. However, this act is now no more than a bit of American legal history. The Constitution of the United States has since stated that this act or any comparable ones are forbidden by law.

A somewhat comparable legal condition of an offender was that known as *civil death*.[3] Individuals falling into this category were deprived of all property that would be passed on to their heirs by common law. At one time, in New York State, a person who was sentenced to be imprisoned was routinely declared to be civilly dead under penal law.[4] Today this is a matter of determination based on state statutes. Although there is some variance, the general rule of thumb appears to be that imprisonment alone is insufficient grounds for a declaration of civil death.

THE SUBJECTION OF PROBATIONERS AND PAROLEES

The ability to demand conformity and to keep offenders under supervision has not always been done under the guise of rehabilitation. More often than not, adherence to probation and parole demands was enforced largely out of a fear of the consequences if such conformity was not met. Offenders rarely explored or demanded that their rights be upheld because they were afraid of rocking the boat or of alienating their supervisor. Such offenders tended to remain grim-lipped and tight of mouth, playing the necessary role until their obligations had been fulfilled.

Even today, probation and parole officers are often guilty of making some mentally cruel and next to impossible demands of their clients. Probation officers especially are "bearers of blank checks," so to speak, given by the courts, which allow any number of specialized conditions of probation to be imposed. A judge may stipulate certain expectations that the offender must adhere to during the period of supervision, but he will leave the final details, enlargements, and refinements, as well as the methods of implementation, to the probation officer's individual discretion. Parole contingencies, on the other hand, are more often than not structured and imposed by a parole board. Even so, the flexibility to alter and to revise parole regulations based on a determined need may often be the prerogative of the supervising (parole) officer.

[3]Quick v. Western Ry. of Alabama, 207 Ala. 376, 92 So. 608, 609.

[4]Platner v. Sherwood, 6 Johns. Ch., N.Y., 118; and Troup v. Wood, 4 Johns. Ch., N.Y., 228, 260.

Basic Conditions

Most probation/parole agreements or contracts include some very fundamental demands, as noted below.

1. That there shall be no new violations of the law, whether at the municipal, state, or federal level of jurisdiction.
2. That the offender will report any change of address, telephone number, or place of employment within a specified period of time after such a change has taken place.
3. That the offender shall not leave the jurisdiction for any period of time without first receiving permission from his supervisor to do so.
4. That the offender shall (a) find and retain a position of gainful employment, or (b) shall remain in an academic (school) program as is required by law.
5. That the offender will not associate with any characters of ill repute.
6. That the offender will not own, possess, or have in his possession at any time, a weapon such as firearm, knife, etc.
7. That the offender will adhere to a schedule of reporting as given.

Although these are rather basic demands, there remain some grounds for discussion and argument over the validity of some of these so-called standard conditions. The author as a probation officer has never been directly associated with a contested case over any of these general requirements, but that does not mean that there are not distinct possibilities for their being legally challenged. For example, traffic offenses can involve both municipal and state laws, yet it would obviously be a question of justice to bring a probationer or a parolee up for a revocation hearing if he was convicted of a speeding charge. The reason for this is that traffic violations generally do not constitute criminal law. It would also be unreasonable for a probation officer to revoke his client's parole if the client's job took him outside the jurisdiction for a three-day period. Just how would you treat the offender who cannot find a job or who gets fired from a job or, in the case of a juvenile, gets suspended from school? All of these are incidents not in keeping with the general standards that are outlined above. Take another example. Is a pocketknife a weapon? Certainly, by some municipal ordinances and standards. If the blade length, when opened exceeds a certain length and if it is carried in the pocket and is therefore concealed, the pocketknife can be classified as a weapon and carrying it can constitute a misdemeanor offense. There is no need for exhausting the list further.

Special Conditions

Specialized rules or conditions present equally specialized problems. Quite often, it is not out of order for courts, probation officers, or parole officers to establish conditions that reflect a perceived need of the offender as a part of the contract. Usually such contingencies are predicated either on the basis of the offense or on evidence that was presented in mitigation. Although the variations are limited only by the imagination, two basic types of contingencies are noted: (1) educational programs, and (2) programs involving some type of therapy.

Educational programs may take many different forms. For example, driver-improvement programs are frequently required of chronic traffic offenders. Often in juvenile cases, judges may demand research papers or other studies that relate to the offense and nature of difficulty that brought the juvenile to the attention of the court. Some offenders are "sentenced" to do community-type work because it is felt that this may enhance their respect for the property they have harmed. Such programs, although not legally under attack for the various forms used, are usually associated with juvenile offenders. The juvenile court system was originally conceived and has long been maintained in format and procedure far different than what has been used in other court systems. The theory was that almost anything bearing some social redemptive contents was acceptable in nature.

Therapy programs are more controversial. The initial reaction is to associate therapy with "sick" offenders or "sick" offenses and to utilize classically clinical services such as those provided by psychologists, psychiatrists, and social workers within a mental health framework. This is only one area of treatment that the court may consider or that probation/parole personnel may want to utilize. Even so, the legal ramifications are present, and when pursued by legal counsel on behalf of the offender, such cases may attract a great deal of public attention.

The discussion of pleas in conjunction with sanity hearings is a subject that demands more time and space, both of which will be granted later in this chapter. Pertinent here, however, is the fact that various referrals for treatment—the author wishes to make it clear that there is a distinct difference between *treatment* and *evaluation*—sometimes may be challenged. For example, a driver who has repeatedly been arrested for driving while intoxicated may provide cause for a judge or probation officer to surmise that he is an alcoholic and should be subjected to some form of treatment.

Alcoholism is a unique disease, and there should be little question in the mind of the reader that it is a disease. The issue is what is the nature of the affliction? Is it medical or social in nature? For a judge or probation officer to attempt to make a medical judgment and to require that this type of offender go on a monitored program of Antabuse (a chemical deterrent to drinking) is to make, perhaps, a nonjudicial decision, one that is fraught with legal dangers. Can a nonmedical person, for example, technically impose a sentence or condition that should be a medical function? Similarly, the heroin addict might be forced, as a condition of probation or parole, to undertake a program of Methadone maintenance (a supposedly nonharmful drug-replacement for heroin). Such actions by the court or its representatives can raise questions of both an ethical and legal nature.

Most offenders would not contest the issue and would exercise what *might* be grounds for an infringement of their rights. Probationers or parolees would be sufficiently elated that they were not incarcerated, and they would respond with a degree of conformity and adherence in exchange for the opportunity to remain free. As drowning men may grasp at straws to remain afloat, so will offenders grasp at any opportunity not to be placed in jail or be returned to prison.

Let a word of caution be entered here. The author does not intend to state or to imply that such programs as mentioned here are or are not in violation of the function of any court, or of any probation or parole officer. This is a legal point that if contested or confirmed should be done so only by the appropriate legal agency. The material here is used *only* to portray an example of one of a multitude of possible areas that might be contested.

In keeping with this discussion, there also may be legal grounds for questioning other stipulated conditions of probation and parole. The key issue is what is appropriate to demand as a contingency. This could result in a moral/ethical controversy as well as a legal one. Suffice it to say, contingencies should be relatively feasible without posing any hardships on the offender. Whenever possible, such demands should be devoid of standards that would conflict with religious/cultural values, and above all they should be negotiable if not proven in the best interests of the offender.

Many members of minority groups, for example, seem to feel that certain conditions imposed as a part of the supervision contract represent middle-class values and standards not in keeping with the offenders' life style and cultural mores. There are some elements of truth as well as distortion in such a response as this. The tenth chapter of this book will be dealing with some of the defense mechanisms offenders often use to manipulate their situation and their supervisor. It is acknowledged, however, that often racial and cultural values are used as a means of shutting out an alien or incompatible class that professes another set of social values. Chapter Four has already touched on some of the realities that block understanding and communication between socio-cultural groups.

Countless legal actions have been brought to bear either by or on the behalf of offenders on matters related to cruel and inhumane punishments. To the best of this author's knowledge, there have been few major hallmark cases where probation or parole was construed to be a sentence per se was challenged on this basis alone. Probation is universally viewed as a function of sentencing rather than as a part of the prosecution process, so there cannot be a true deprivation of rights based on this argument.[5] Parole is viewed

[5] Jerold H. Israel and Wayne R. LaFave, *Criminal Procedure in a Nutshell* (St. Paul, Minn.: West Publishing Company, 1971), pp. 363–369.

as a continuation of a previously imposed sentence with variations related to where and how the balance of the sentence is to be fulfilled. The crux of the issue, from a legal standpoint, should be more concerned with the revocation process, a matter to be dealt with later in this chapter.

Probation should be viewed as a privilege, certainly not as a right. There are two explanations for this perspective, one legal and the other of a more social nature. Under federal law, which is the guideline for all state statutes, no offender who has been convicted of a crime punishable either by death or by life imprisonment will be eligible for probation consideration.[6] Although variances in statutes of the different jurisdictions deny the opportunity to present a clear-cut definition, reference is made here to Class I and II felony offenses. Class I covers those crimes for which the offender may be given either the death sentence or life imprisonment; Class II offenses usually allow for a prison term of an extended period. This extended period will vary from roughly 10 to 15 years up to 50 years.

Probation, from the social perspective, must be arranged on the basis of a workable probation plan. Even though the needs of the offender can be reasonably and mutually agreed on, if a plan of treatment or rehabilitation cannot be effected, probation is a waste of professional time under most circumstances. Again, reference must be made to the now familiar—but undefined—term of the "sick" offender. Perhaps we can come closer to a definition at this point than previously, for when we label offenders as such, we are talking about individuals who could more appropriately be handled within a mental institution or a comparable placement for defective individuals rather than routinely sentenced to a correctional institution. Reference is made to those offenders who have been declared as having a psychosis that is of a nonfunctional nature or where progressive mental deterioration is discovered. It is far better to make a social/medical determination of these "sick" offenders to effect treatment immediately rather than waiting until the offenders are totally unmanageable and require custodial care rather than psychiatric or medical treatment.

CIVIL DISABILITIES

Civil disabilities could facetiously be described as a contemporary refinement on civil death. The classification of civil disabilities is not nearly as final, but it sometimes makes the individual involved wish it were. Although civil disabilities are apt to be more applicable to parolees than probationers, this does not ignore the ex-offender who has served his time in full without the benefit or opportunity of parole. Defined, *civil disabilities* refers to the loss or deprivation of certain rights of an offender based primarily upon his

---

[6]*Crime and Criminal Procedure*, U.S. Code, Title 18, Vol. 4, Chapter 231, 1970 Ed.

conviction and subsequent imprisonment. Some of these privations are more subtle than others, but the facts of the matter are not lost on those who are denied these rights.

Restrictions on Employment

One of the most significant and far-reaching restrictions due to the classification of civil disabilities is that an offender cannot obtain a license for employment purposes. Yet it has been established elsewhere in this book that the work ethic is the most consistent demand made of parolees. Although some forms of employment may be found, finding jobs commensurate with the offender's skills or having sufficient monetary rewards to sustain even the most basic of needs of the offender and his family is almost impossible.

The number of employment opportunities denied to offenders because of licensing restrictions is quite extensive. For example, a rather common vocation that requires licensing, and one that is not overly demanding of time for training, is that of barbers and beauticians. Yet it is rather ironic— a better word might be pathetic—that many penal institutions offer training in this particular vocation. Thus it is absurd that having mastered this skill a parolee can gain permission to move to another state 40 miles away only to find that he or she cannot be licensed there to practice their trade. At the other end of the spectrum are those professions that require more formalized training and the acquisition of one or more degrees such as nursing or law. But the opportunity to take the appropriate state boards will usually be denied parolees despite their education and abilities.

In addition to the problem of licensing, there are many employment situations that require security clearances and that the employee be bondable. Even if parolees and ex-offenders were able to clear the most elementary of security demands, which is highly unlikely, bonding requirements and costs of providing surety would still be prohibitive. In an attempt to alleviate some problems relating to bonding demands, the U.S. Department of Labor, Manpower Administration, in 1971 established a federal bonding program that served to counteract the problem of high premiums demanded by the principal. Under this act, state departments of employment have generally assumed the administrative task of supervising this service. Individuals who could not secure bonding in any other way have reaped the benefits of this program, and this may very well have made the difference between being employed or not employed.

Other Deprivations of the Rights of Offenders

The overall concept of civil disabilities may be referred to as an outgrowth of British law popularly utilized in the American colonies in the Revolutionary period. Commonly known as *attainer,* this concept applied to individuals who had committed a treason or felony where the sentence for that crime was death.[7] The outcome was a series of acts allowing for the deprivation of certain rights and generally accepted privileges. For example, the opportunity to enter into certain legally enforceable contracts, to hold public office, to serve as a juror, or to utilize certain pensions and comparable benefits are all denied. Individuals on active duty with the armed forces who commit acts that would be considered felony offenses for nonservicemen are subject to being court-martialed and to subsequently receive a dishonorable discharge from the service. The end result can be the loss of any benefits administered by the Veterans Administration, such as insurance, training benefits, medical care, pension, and others.[8]

Some states provide that imprisonment is sufficient grounds for the spouse of the offender to file for divorce. One of the more brutal acts once practiced was the sterilization of certain offenders who were convicted and subsequently incarcerated for specific offenses. Also, at one time in the not too forgotten past, parolees could not marry without permission; they could not obtain motor vehicle licenses; they were forbidden to work in establishments where in the course of the duties of their employment they had to serve or dispense liquor; and they could not cross a state line without the permission of their parole officer, and the permission of the state to be entered had to be given in advance.

The general restrictions imposed upon prison inmates bear some scrutiny in the discussion of the rights of offenders. While too numerous to detail here, there have been many legal suits filed on behalf of and by prison inmates in direct relationship to prison/jail methods of operation. Whether the inability to have a bath more often than three times a week or the censoring of inmate mail constitutes cruel and inhumane circumstances are matters that face the courts regularly.

Religious freedom has been one of the issues that has been given much examination. The attempt, however, seems not to be to deprive as much as it is to contain. Participation in and the exercise of religious beliefs have been upheld as long as such collective behavior poses no security risk[9] and as long as the content of the belief is neither discriminatory nor detrimental to the welfare of nonmembers of such groups.[10]

There are a multitude of other court rulings that are too numerous to make reference to here that have upheld the basic rights of inmates. The basic criteria utilized as precedents in the overruling of inmate suite for personal rights and freedom, as these can exist behind prison walls, are

[7]Henry Campbell Black, Black's Law Dictionary (St. Paul, Minn.: West Publishing Co., 1968), p. 162.

[8]Veterans' Benefits, U.S. Code, Title 38, Vol. 8, Chapter 53, 1970 Ed., p. 9197.

[9]Sharp v. Sigler (CA2 NY) 293 F2d 233.

[10]Pierce v. La Vallee (CA2 NY) 293 F2d 233.

predicated on two basic matters: (1) whether the rights sought are limited to specific subgroups and are therefore discriminatory against other members of the prison population, and (2) whether the sanctioning of such rights constitutes a threat to the management and security of the prison program. Included in this rather general category are references to discipline, regulation of mail, regulation of access to newspapers and periodicals, regulation of access to the courts, visiting privileges, discrimination and segregation, and medical care.

One of the major criticisms to be made about civil disabilities is the inability to establish when and what constitutes bona fide infringements on personal matters and interference with the private life of the individual. Some legal determinations seem to be predicated on moral and philosophical premises. Several cases can be made to illustrate this point. For example, the prohibition of holding public office as denied under the civil disability category is advanced on the premise that the public must be protected. One does not need to speculate long about the rapidly growing number of cases of white-collar crime to understand the contradiction implied. The rancid taste that Watergate has left in the mouths of many illustrates this point. Is it worse, in the minds of men, to install a crook in public office or to put a man in office and then to discover he is crooked? Preventive medicine is based on anticipation rather than a diagnosis, but treatment is also more effective when an uncertainty becomes a firm and undeniable reality.

Most states recognize and provide for what are called "common law" marriages. The only requirement for such a union to be recognized in the eyes of the law is the time element. A study conducted on parole policies relative to cohabitation reveals an almost even split in thinking as to the legality and acceptability of such behavior.[11] Call it maturation, call it responsibility, call it what becomes it, the opportunity for a wholesome (devoid of moral connotations) and accepting relationship has contributed as much as any other force short of therapy and coercion to change behavioral patterns in a positive manner. Is such an issue legal or moral in content? Quite probably it is based on a moral foundation with a legal facade.

The reader may be concerned at this point for what may appear to be a lack of professional objectivity regarding the immediate discussion of civil disabilities. Nevertheless, there have existed some very strong social concerns about these restrictions and the rationale for their continuing survival. Individuals with strong social consciences may take heart, however, in the fact that during the last two decades many of these restrictions have been lifted. The loss of most civil disabilities is now limited to the time of

[11]Mary C. Schwartz, and Laura Zeisel, "Cohabitation and the Unmarried Parolee—A National Study of Parole Policy," *Crime and Delinquenty,* 22, no. 2 (April 1976), 137–148.

actual imprisonment, and most rights are restored upon release from confinement.[12] However, many jurisdictions still insist that the right to public office is and will be one of the few rights habitually denied ex-offenders.

THE REVOCATION PROCESS
AND OFFENDERS' RIGHTS

It would be natural for the reader to conclude that trials are synonymous with attorneys. Only within the last fifteen years has legal counsel become commonplace in juvenile court hearings and at revocation hearings concerning adult probationers and parolees, especially on behalf of parolees. The image that juvenile courts long fostered was that these proceedings should be of an informal nature uncomplicated by formal, stereotyped legal maneuvering. For that reason, few attorneys were seen in routine delinquency cases. It was the experience of the author that during his apprenticeship in a juvenile court many years ago, the attorneys who were present were unaccustomed to the legal process and were equally uncomfortable in their roles within this specific court context.

Many courts that dealt primarily with juveniles have been referred to as *family* or *domestic* courts, and some still retain the semantical flavor. In exclusively juvenile matters, the judge often assumed a paternal role, that of the wise father surrogate who was concerned with the social as well as the legal facts. The adversary system that prevailed in other courts was as unheard of at this specialized judicial level as were jury trials. Quite often hearings were held in chambers as opposed to being found within a courtroom. Yet the legal rights of the accused juvenile were not neglected.

The recent changes in proceedings in juvenile matters, wherein the visual awareness of more formality has become increasingly apparent, are the probable result of two factors: (1) the need for greater punitive action based on the increasing level of juvenile crime sophistication, and (2) several high court rulings that have had wide-reading implications. Most juvenile codes have recently been overhauled, although this is not to assume that no more work needs to be done. One of the revisions of significance has been an attempt to separate juveniles in need of supervision from those engaged in more socially unacceptable behavior. This cleavage has resulted in the utilization of different legal-social approaches in dealing with the runaway or truant child as contrasted to the juvenile who engages in destructive and harmful acts.

A second revision provides that the cases of more sophisticated and socially defiant juveniles may be waived to a higher court level and may be processed and sentenced as adult offenders. As a result of this change, more

---

[12]Coffee v. Haynes, 124 CAL 561, 57 P42; and Harmon v. Bowers, 78 Kan 135, 96 p51.

attorneys and therefore more test cases have entered the juvenile justice field. The possible severity of the consequences of conviction and subsequent incarceration of such juveniles has raised many real concerns. Although it is acceptable that such juvenile offenders should be dealt with separately, and be segregated from their less active and destructive peers, the ramifications of placement with more sophisticated adult offenders should be questioned.

Sample Juvenile Cases

In keeping with the discussion on the changing perspectives on juveniles and specifically as relating to revocation processes, three cases will be briefly reviewed below. Although it is difficult, at best, to be objectively selective in using legal precedents to illustrate the nature of our contextual concern, the cases used here have had far-reaching implications in both the judicial and correctional fields.

Mempha v. Rhay.   The case of *Mempha v. Rhay* centered around a seventeen-year-old juvenile who had initially entered a plea of guilty to a joy-riding charge.[13] The subject was placed on probation for a two-year period. He was initially sentenced to 30 days in jail in addition to probation, but that sentence was deferred. Within an approximate four-month period following his being granted probation, the subject was brought back before the court on a motion of the Spokane County prosecuting attorney for a revocation hearing. It was alleged that the subject had violated the condition of his probation by being involved in a burglary.

When this matter was returned before the court, the subject appeared with his stepfather. He had no attorney present with him, and no inquiry was directed toward him by the court as to whether he wished to have an attorney appointed on his behalf. During the course of the proceedings, the court inquired of the subject if the charges as stated were true, to which an affirmative response was given. The probation officer present stated that he had information that substantiated the subject's involvement in the burglary, but that the subject had denied his involvement to the probation officer. The presiding judge, upon accepting the testimony, and without any further statements being elicited from the subject, revoked the probation as granted and sentenced the subject to ten years in the penitentiary.

Two arguments centered around the *Mempha* case prior to the final ruling of the Supreme Court. The first contention was that this was merely an extension of the case where sentencing that was imposed, and subsequently deferred at the time that probation was granted, was reinstated. This premise was predicated on the stand that the legal rights of Mempha were

---

[13]Mempha v. Rhay, 389 U.S. 128, 88 S. CE. 254, 19 L. Ed 2d 84 (1966).

probably not infringed upon since this was not a criminal proceeding but merely a reinstatement of a sentence previously imposed and deferred.

The counterargument was that a probation revocation involves the probable loss of liberty. As such, this argument continued, no offender facing this distinct possibility should be deprived of legal counsel. To so deprive him is not to allow him the full protection of due process.

In summary, the ruling of the Supreme Court emphasized the following findings. First, stating that the Sixth Amendment right to counsel is applicable to the sentencing process of a convicted adult offender, the Court concluded that this process is a "critical stage" in the overall criminal proceeding. Second, the Court acknowledged that although in *Mempha* legal counsel might not have altered the eventual outcome of the case, the presence of legal counsel would have at least assured that the rights of the accused would have been upheld. Third, the Court ruled that the right of counsel at the point of sentencing is pertinent to juvenile proceedings as well as to cases involving adult offenders.

Kent v. United States. The case of *Kent v. United States* involved a sixteen-year-old juvenile who was accused of several counts of robbery and rape.[14] Because the subject had failed to respond to past programs set up on his behalf by the juvenile probation department and because he had been clinically diagnosed as suffering from a psychosis, his case was waived over from the juvenile court to the district court. The case there went to trial, and the jury found the subject guilty on the charges of housebreaking and robbery and not guilty by reason of insanity on the rape charges. The court then sentenced him to 30 to 90 years with credit to be given for the time previously spent in a psychiatric hospital.

The grounds for the subsequent appeal of the conviction by Kent were based on the fact that his waiver was effected without an adequate hearing. A further underlying issue was that he had spent considerable time in a psychiatric setting where treatment was not attempted, but that he was apparently there only for purposes of evaluation. The contention was that the waiver was effected, in part, on the contents of the evaluation without any other efforts being made on his behalf. The waiver, in short, was predicated on a rehabilitative assumption with no apparent attempt to do more than a diagnosis. The juvenile court, in acting in the capacity of *parens patriae,* apparently failed to act in the subject's best interests when the case was waived.

The district court overturned the initial appeal. Several issues were cited to uphold the validity and appropriateness of the waiver. First, it was cited that the juvenile court facilities could not meet the established mental needs of the subject. It was felt that the prognosis of Kent was such that the time

---

[14]Kent v. United States, 383 U.S. 541, 86 S. Ct. 1045, 16 L. Ed 2d, 84 (1966).

period of jurisdiction would expire long before maximum treatment could be effected. Second, it was felt that the facilities available for treatment were inadequate to contain such an offender. Kent was viewed to be disturbed and dangerous, and since the juvenile facility was of a nonsecurity nature, it would have been relatively easy for him to escape. Third, because of the potential danger that the subject represented to himself and to others, a civil commitment to a mental hospital was "an inappropriate alternative to waiver in the district court." Further, it was felt that civil commitment was inadequate to provide the protection that society was entitled to since it would be relatively easy for the subject to escape.

It was the ultimate finding of the Supreme Court that the waiver was, in fact, inappropriate. The Court ruled that many of the arguments used to justify the waiver were based on illogical and ill-conceived assumptions. The Court could not, for example, arrive at any conclusions that supported the premise that the treatment facilities available under a civil commitment would be unable to meet the needs of the subject. In fact, it was apparent that there had been no attempt to meet any needs of the subject from a therapeutic standpoint. Although the Court did acknowledge that the mental competency of the subject was questionable, it ruled that it was the duty of the juvenile court to act in the best interests of the child and society rather than "adjudicating criminal conduct."

The Court therefore strongly admonished the lower courts for failing to have the best interests of the subject at heart. One of the major legal criticisms levied was that the social welfare philosophy of the juvenile court was violated. It appeared that treatment had been considered secondary to punishment, and in so acting, the role of *parens patriae* had been overlooked as to its being the primary function of the juvenile court.

In Re Gault. The *Gault* case dealt with a fifteen-year-old who was on probation for accessory to a theft.[15] With approximately six months left on his period of supervision, the subject was taken into custody on a complaint regarding a lewd telephone call. At the time Gault was apprehended, neither parent was available, and no notice of the subject having been placed in detention was given. When the mother found out this information through her own initiative, she went to the detention facility. She was there informed "verbally" of the nature of the charges being brought against her son as well as being advised in the same manner regarding the date and time of hearing. No formal petition was ever served upon the subject or given to the family, although one was filed with the court.

During the course of the hearing on the following day, an informal atmosphere prevailed. The complainant was not present, no one was sworn in for purposes of testimony, and no transcript or recording of the process was

---

[15]In re Gault, 387, U.S. 1, 87 S. Ct. 1428, 18 L Ed 2d, 527 (1967).

made. The apparent nature of the hearing resulted in questions being directed by the judge to Gault; but these, without the benefit of anything other than memory, were not documented. The judge eventually concluded this hearing with the statement that "he wanted to think about it." Gault was then returned to detention.

Within a day or so following the preliminary hearing, the subject was released. On the same date, the subject's mother received a most informal note from the probation officer advising her that a further hearing had been set and giving the date and time. This notice did not represent any type of petition and was not even submitted on any kind of an official court document or stationery. Despite some unclearness and uncertainty of facts during the course of the trial, the subject was sentenced to the state industrial school for the period of his minority (until his twenty-first birthday) unless released earlier by due process of law.

The disposition of the case was apparently predicated on the following legal assumptions.

1. That the subject was on formal probation.
2. That the subject fell within the legal category of being a delinquent child.
3. That the subject had unofficially been "remembered" to have been involved in other delinquent activities, although no formal filings had ever been made.
4. That the subject was committed "after a full hearing and due deliberation. . . ."

The basic issue surrounding the *Gault* case related to due process and whether or not the subject's rights had been protected. There was one other point of interest to be considered. The State of Arizona did not allow for the right of appeal in juvenile cases. Therefore it was suggested that the Juvenile Code of the State of Arizona was invalid since several rights were alleged to have been denied.

The Supreme Court's eventual ruling indicated that several of the constitutional rights of Gault had, in fact, been violated. These included:

1. The right to counsel, or if indigent, to have counsel appointed.
2. The privilege against self-incrimination.
3. The right of formal notice.
4. The right of confrontation of witnesses.

In summary, the High Court's finding was that the basic rights of an offender, juvenile or adult, civil or criminal matter, must be upheld. In effect, the findings of *In re Gault* assured that the proceedings brought against juveniles must provide for basically the same rights that would be accorded an adult offender.

These cases, as presented, should point out some basic facts. First, the philosophy of the juvenile court system is changing. Although there remains no quarrel with its function as a socio-legal force designed to act in the best interests of the child, it is becoming necessary to recognize that the juvenile court's obligations have expanded. Not only must the social needs of juveniles be met, but their legal needs must also be upheld as part of the due process. In this sense, it can be expected that the atmosphere of this court system will continue to become somewhat more formal in nature.

Second, there has been an inequity between adult and juvenile offenders. The lay public may surmise that the courts have the tendency to be easier on the juvenile, but this is not necessarily a logical assumption. In two of the cases used here as illustrations—*Kent* obviously is not applicable—the sentences imposed were far more severe on the juvenile offender than they would have been on an adult offender facing comparable charges at a higher court level.

Third, should there be some question, it would indicate that the courts are not infallible. Although a degree of independence and informality within the juvenile court structure has allowed for creativity and flexibility, this should not permit abuses to occur in the due process procedure. It may not be fashionable and appropriate to conceive of attorneys as being watchdogs over the courts, but one of their primary functions is their obligation to their clients to assure that due process is accorded them and that their rights will not be overlooked or abused by the courts.

Sample Adult Cases

Earlier in this chapter, it was suggested that there often is the tendency of probationers and parolees to remain relatively passive in respect to the conditional demands made of them. Adult offenders especially were expected to "take their lumps" stoically if, by intent or through an irresponsible act, they violated the contingencies as imposed. In contrast to juveniles, the adult offender was supposed to possess the power of appropriate reasoning and was therefore automatically held responsible for his choice unless extreme mitigating circumstances prevailed.

Thus, it has only been in the last fifteen years that offenders facing revocation proceedings have demanded, in force so to speak, that due process be honored as part of their rights. This is not to imply that no concerns were expressed prior to this time about the lack of legal precedence in the revocation process, but it has only been a recent development to seek legal recourse and to demand that the rights of such offenders be specifically determined by higher court rulings. As in the case of the juvenile matters discussed, the issue has been the assurance that all rights as provided for initially under the Fifth Amendment, and later expanded on by the Fourteenth, be upheld. Two cases follow that will serve as illustrations.

Morrissey v. Booher   The case of *Morrissey* v. *Booher* actually involved two Iowa parolees (Morrissey *and* Booher) who, coincidentally, were accused of comparable acts that resulted in the state of Iowa revoking their parole.[16] The offenders filed petitions with the United States District Court of the Southern District of Iowa contesting the action. Their claim was based on the fact that they were denied due process since the revocation was decreed without benefit of any formal hearing. At the initial review of the case, the District Court denied the petition on the grounds that due process did not require a prerevocation hearing; the United States Court of Appeals upheld this finding.

The U.S. Supreme Court, prior to ruling on the case, remanded the matter back for a determination of the exact procedure taken as part of the revocation process. In opposition to some of the juvenile cases discussed earlier in this chapter, some very real issues were used by the Court of Appeals to document its legal position and finding. These premises are certainly worthy of mention here. Although *Mempha, Kent,* and *Gault* preceded the *Morrissey-Booher* case by some five to seven years, the juvenile matters were all based on probationary cases. (For simplicity sake, the two cases of *Morrissey* and *Booher* were consolidated. They later became classically known and referred to, as has been done here, under the name of one petitioner, *Morrissey.*)

The District Court and the United States Court of Appeals based their *Morrissey* decisions on several pertinent assumptions.

1.   A parolee is completing his sentence outside the prison walls. Technically, he is still "in custody" and is therefore not entitled to a full adversary hearing.
2.   Due process merely demands an informal hearing on matters of revocation, and said hearing must be held within a reasonable period of time.
3.   Revocation is not part of the criminal process, and therefore the full gamut of rights due a defendant under normal circumstances is not applicable to a parole revocation hearing.
4.   A parolee's arrest does not demand that his case be heard by a judicial officer. His fate, so to speak, can be determined by a parole board or another parole officer (other than the one who had requested the revocation).
5.   A parolee may be returned to the penal institution and be held without credit for time served pending the final outcome of his case by the parole board or another designated authority.

It should be stated that although there were some legal basis for the findings of the Court of Appeals, a common premise is apparent—that is, the array of rights normally accorded the parolee is but a limited version of the rights of others under due process. Part of this deprivation seems to have

[16]Morrissey v. Booher, 408 U.S. 471, 33, L. Ed., 484, 92 S. CT 2593 (1972).

been based as much on tradition as it was on legal precedence. The reader must bear in mind that five years earlier, the U.S. Supreme Court ruled that the rights of due process, even at the time of consideration of revocation, were to be upheld. The differences of judicial decisions in Morrissey as opposed to the other cases discussed was predicated more on the fact that *Morrissey* was somewhat of a test case for parolees.

In *Morrissey,* the Supreme Court made several significant points, which would serve as a guide for many cases to come. In the Court's ultimate ruling, two stages of the proceedings were arrived at to be followed in future cases.

I. Arrest of Parolee and Preliminary Hearing
    A. Due process requires an immediate recording of the facts alleged in the case. The recording should be done while "the facts are fresh" and may be used for a preliminary hearing to determine probable cause.
    B. The preliminary investigation should be conducted by either a "neutral" or "detached" party who can objectively evaluate the facts.
    C. The parolee should be given proper notice of the hearing, including the facts substantiating the probable cause or alleged events.
    D. The parolee may appear and speak on his own behalf and may submit evidence of relevant information.
    E. Persons who could contribute adverse information may be questioned in the presence of the parolee unless their presence constitutes a threat to the parolee.
    F. The hearing officer must record all events and must then determine whether or not there is probable cause for a hearing by the parole board.
II. The Revocation Hearing
    A. The opportunity for an interim hearing for an evaluation of any contested facts may be granted at the parolee's request.
    B. The revocation hearing must be conducted within a reasonable period of time after the parolee has been taken into custody.
    C. The right to appointed counsel based on factors of indigency is an individual matter for the states to decide upon, but the parolee may retain counsel of his own choosing and at his own expense to represent him if he so chooses.

Gagnon v. Scarpelli   The subject in the case of *Gagnon* v. *Scarpelli* was an adult initially convicted of armed robbery in the State of Wisconsin.[17] Upon his plea of guilty to these charges, he was sentenced to fifteen years in prison. The sentence was then suspended, and he was placed on probation for a seven-year period. Under an interstate compact agreement with the

---

[17]Gagnon v. Scarpelli, 411 U.S. 778, 36 L. Ed., 2d, S. CT. 1756 (1973).

State of Illinois, the subject was authorized to take up residency in the latter state. Shortly after his change of residency, he was arrested for burglary. Almost immediately Wisconsin revoked his probation, and he was incarcerated in prison to serve his fifteen years as his original sentence stated.

In his petition, the subject alleged that the State of Wisconsin revoked his probation without affording him a hearing or granting him legal representation. This, the subject contended, was a denial of his rights under due process. His appeal was subsequently upheld by both the District Court and the Court of Appeals. One of the key contentions was that the subject was deprived of legal counsel, and that under his constitutional rights the State of Wisconsin was obligated to appoint an attorney to represent him.

In ruling on this case, the U.S. Supreme Court based its decision on many of the precedents in both *Morrissey* and *Mempha*. The finding provided that a probationer, during the revocation process, is entitled to both a preliminary and a final revocation hearing as provided for in *Morrissey*. The uniqueness in this case, however, was the discussion of whether or not offenders facing revocation proceedings are entitled to court-appointed legal counsel. The Court decreed that this was not so. Its contention was that the right to court-appointed counsel must be handled on a case-by-case basis, and there was no determination that such a provision to provide counsel was mandatory. Further, the Court stated that revocation hearings are not adversary matters. As such, there is no prosecution other than the testimony and documented facts of the probation/parole officer who initiated the revocation process and the possibility of any witnesses who are able to testify to the adverse circumstances that supported the alleged violation. In either matter, the offender has the right to question all parties bringing evidence against him. It was felt that under this type of proceeding, the accused would be normally capable of defending himself since he was on a comparable ground with his accusers. By this it is meant that he is not subjected to the confrontations of a prosecuting attorney without a similar ally in his corner. Only in those cases where the offender appears totally incapable and incompetent of presenting his own side of the case should the state feel obligated to provide him counsel.

The significance of *Gagnon* and *Morrissey* is the allowance of due process for probationers and parolees facing revocation proceedings. Included is the assurance that several rights will be provided for, rights that may have been denied or ignored in the past. Rather than being at the mercy of a perhaps irate and vindictive probation/parole officer, the offender can have his case dealt with in an objective, impartial, and professional manner. The number of rights that are now available to the offender have greatly increased, and it is important to clarify that the offender need not feel he is being discriminated against because of his past record.

A further point demands clarification. The preceding paragraph makes mention of an "irate, vindictive" probation/parole officer. Although this may sound like a rather melodramatic description, this type of reaction is typical of many probation/parole officers. Many overly sensitive officers view revocations or new offenses as supervision failures. Like the overwrought parent who asks, "Where did I go wrong?" some correctional personnel take it as a personal affront when their clients fail to make it. Yet it has been estimated that in excess of 20,000 adult parole and 108,000 adult probation revocations are processed annually in this country.[18]

INSANITY PLEAS AND RELATED RIGHTS

It is agreed that the courts are responsible to a variety of taskmasters, namely society and the offender, as well as being subject to the spirit and the letter of the law. It also has been acknowledged that it has proven a difficult task for judges to routinely conceive of appropriate sentencing alternatives to even routine cases. And on top of this, it is bad enough to have to be concerned about a countless number of social and legal factors in the daily docket load, but we have not yet discussed the pinnacle of difficulties in legal right complexities, that is, the not guilty plea by reason of insanity.

Neither the court nor forensic psychiatry has really satisfied itself that there are sufficient guidelines to readily implement the processing of insanity pleas. To complicate matters even more, it may fall the lot of a jury of lay people to determine the validity of the evidence presented in such cases. Yet such a plea may not be improvident, and it is well within the rights of the offender or his legal counsel to enter such a plea in given cases. A chapter on the rights of offenders, then, must of necessity touch upon this plea of not guilty by reason of insanity.

Not guilty pleas by reason of insanity are neither common matters nor are they entered, generally speaking, in matters other than in conjunction with uncommon crimes—vicious and seemingly senseless matters—such as murder, rape, and violent offenses of this nature. The term *insanity* is conceived and generally accepted to be a legal term rather than a clinical diagnosis. It implies a mental disorder, subject of course to an evaluation and subsequent diagnosis, which legally characterizes the accused of belonging to one of two categories. First, the accused may be so afflicted that he has not the mental ability to distinguish right from wrong. Or second, the accused, even if he can recognize that an act is wrong, may be incapable of selecting what is right. In short, he is impaired mentally to the point of not being able to exercise self-control, even when he has some ability to recognize consequences that probably will be associated with his behavior.

[18]*The Courts* (1967), President's Commission on Law Enforcement and Administration of Justice, Task Force Report (Washington, D.C.: U.S. Government Printing Office).

This discussion, unfortunately, needs to be complicated and confused even further before any degree of clarity can be recognized. There exists, first, a need to differentiate between insanity and mental deficiency. Perhaps a better way of defining a mentally deficient individual would be to substitute the word *retarded* for *deficient*. We do so here but with the qualification that this definition is applicable only for purposes of clarification. This does not mean that such a statement is clinically correct and appropriate. It is used here strictly for purposes of making a fundamental and rudimentary distinction with no other implications being intended.

The mentally deficient individual is usually afflicted as a part of a congenital condition, although this may not always hold true. Certain accidents where oxygen deprivation, injuries resulting in organicity, or certain accidental afflictions that can affect motor responses may result in such a mental state. With the possible exception of certain forms of organicity such as brain tumors, which are often progressive, mental deficiency is not conceived of as a progressive mental state or an ongoing deterioration of the mental facilities. On the other hand, insanity *might* be considered a progressive state of mental health. For example, it would be highly debatable to declare an infant insane at birth. Although there have been theories advanced that the mental potential for or leading up to a break with reality may be contained in the genes, inappropriate behavior or neurotic acting-out tendencies may represent only a prelude to a psychotic break. The author has quickly interjected the word *psychotic* to clinically define the point in the mental health continuum where an individual might be acknowledged to be legally insane, having now passed that proverbial milestone.

Psychotic individuals, although legally acknowledged to be insane, are not habitually caught up in constant bizarre behavior. There are many points in psychotic behavior patterns where the patient is momentarily oriented with reality and is well aware of his circumstances. This is in contrast to the mentally deficient (congenital) individual who will remain in a constant state with no major variation in behavior other than what can be taught at his intellectual level of functioning. Certain elementary tasks such as self-care habits or limited work skills can be achieved, and this exception should be noted as part of the qualification of our explanation here.

One other area—that of incompetency—should be discussed in relation to the plea of not guilty by reason of insanity. The courts may find it necessary to define a group of individuals as *incompetents*. Again confusion in terminology allows little for the smooth presentation in our discussion. Whether a person is competent—mentally, and in some cases socially— and capable of being brought to or standing trial is not limited to just the accused claiming immunity from guilt under insanity pleas. Mentally deficient individuals certainly could fall into the category of incompetency and readily do so. But three other subdivisions must be considered. The first such subdivision is the juvenile. There has been considerable discussion in this book about "the age of reason" as this applies to juveniles. For example, there may be instances of children who, by virtue of their chronological age level, may be viewed as socially and emotionally incapable of being held legally responsible for their behavior. There could be some very logical questions raised as to the competency of the accused to understand the nature and possibly the severity of the act that brought him to the attention of the court.

The second subdivision is senility. Senility is an area of social concern that has only recently received the attention it deserves. *Senility* might be defined as a socio-medical term that is applied to behavioral deterioration that sometimes is evidenced in conjunction with old age. It would be totally erroneous to state that senile behavior is psychotic behavior, despite an outward manifestation of some similar traits. There are individuals in assorted stages of growing older who may be considered as not competent to either totally manage themselves or their own affairs. It might be questionable if there are not times when they could not or should not be held legally accountable for behavior that has resulted in court action against them.

The third and last subdivision is the individual who is legally insane. However, this plea may differ somewhat from the plea of not guilty by reason of insanity. The plea in this case concerns itself with the mental state of the accused *only at the time* the alleged offense occurred. Therefore, if there is probable reason to believe that the accused was legally sane at the time of the offense but has since crossed the clinical line, the concern is predicated on his ability to stand trial *at this time* rather than the primary relationship of his mental state at the time of the act.

The legal concern for "mentally afflicted" offenders goes back in history to some obscure beginnings in the thirteenth and fourteenth centuries under Anglo-Saxon law. It has been said that in the time of Henry III (1216–1271) it was not uncommon for the king to grant a pardon to offenders of unsound mind who had committed homicide.[19] At the time of Edward III (1326–1377) madness or lunacy had become an accepted defense, and this was extended to cover almost any criminal case.

In the 1840s, a man by the name of Daniel M'Naghten went to trial in England for the killing of another. The case might have attracted less publicity and might have faded into obscurity were it not for the unusual circumstances surrounding it. M'Naghten's apparent target was Sir Robert Peel, the founder of the modern police force as we know it today, and because Peel was the target, this factor greatly increased the intensity of the investigation by the House of Lords. The principal subject in the case,

[19]Rollin M. Perkins, *Perkins on Criminal Law* (Mineola, N.Y.: The Foundation Press, Inc., 1969).

M'Naghten, was found to be "laboring under an insane delusion," and his mental state was a concern that would unknowingly set a legal precedent. The facts of the case and the findings of the court were recorded initially because of the official inquiry into the matter. It was the answers of the judges that set the precedent upon which guidelines were established that continue to exist and to be used in some jurisdictions of the United States at the time of this writing. Two areas of concern were probed in the investigation of the M'Naghten case: (1) the establishment of a defense based on the grounds of insanity, and (2) the establishment of a precedent consisting of an insane delusion.

The M'Naghten test, as it became known, applied only if the following four qualifications existed.

1. If there was a defect of reason from a disease of the mind.
2. If, because of said defect, the subject did not know what he was doing.
3. Even if the subject knew what he was doing, if he did not know his act was wrong because of the defect of reason.
4. If the offender acted under an "insane delusion" (false belief) and he was overcome by an "uncontrollable desire" (which establishes what is called the *irresistible impulse test,* sometimes referred to as the *right-wrong test*).

In 1954, a second rule or legal test was established, which was known either as the New Hampshire Test or the "Product" Rule. In *Durham* v. *United States,* the District of Columbia court ruled that the proper method of handling this type of a case was to discard any tests of insanity.[20] In turn, a jury would:

1. Determine whether the accused was sane or insane at the time of the alleged offense; and
2. If he was insane, whether the act was a "product" of his insanity.

One of the more contemporary tests is the A.L.I. (American Law Institute) ruling on the model penal code. Under its criteria, a person is not responsible for criminal behavior if, at the time of the act, he lacks the capacity to understand the wrongness of his behavior or to restrict his acts so as to remain inside the law, as a result of mental disease or defect. The apparent thrust of the A.L.I. ruling is to attempt to rule on the criminal capacity of the accused based on a concept of reasonableness. Either the individual offender has that reasonable capacity to conform (although it must be acknowledged that some do not choose to do so), or his capacity has been reduced because of disease or defect.

At a cursory glance, the contents of these various tests would initially ap-

---

[20]Durham v. United States, 94 U.S. APP. D. C. 228, 214 F. 2d, 862, (1954).

pear to differ only in the language and standards used. It must be remembered, however, that it has been primarily the role of the jury, or the judge in non-jury cases, rather than the clinician to arrive at the ultimate decision of whether the accused was or was not legally insane at the moment of the offense. The changes in terminology have represented a "boiling down" of concepts designed to make the process more understandable and workable for jury members.

The plea of not guilty by reason of insanity will be accepted by the court only at the time of arraignment. The court may consider, on its own motion, the need to determine the immediate competency of the accused at a point in the trial; but the plea, as entered either by the defendant or by his counsel, must be made within the time segment defined. The court, upon acceptance of such a plea, will remand the defendant for a psychiatric examination for a period of time to be determined within reason. Reports will be filed, upon completion, with the court, the prosecutor, and the defense. Examining personnel will usually be asked to testify in court as to their findings. It is from this presented clinical evidence that the ultimate determination must be made by the judge or the jury, as the case may be, for the upholding or rejection of the plea.

A probable question of offenders' rights may be noted in conjunction with this plea. Because of impaired insight associated with mental disease or defects, many disturbed individuals are totally incapable of seeing themselves as they really are. A plea of this nature made out of concern and on the behalf of the offender, may be entered over the objection of the accused. In a recent Colorado ruling, the Colorado State Supreme Court ruled on the constitutionality of the state law to have such a plea entered despite the demands of the defendant to disallow it as being invalid.[21] The defendant had claimed that any waiver of constitutional rights must be of a voluntary nature and could not be forced upon him or over his objections without depriving him of these rights.

The assumption in the United States is supposedly held that an accused is to be thought of as innocent until proven guilty. In insanity pleas, the assumption of the prosecution usually is that the defendant is sane and that the burden of proof to indicate otherwise must fall upon the defense counsel or the clinical consultants used in the case. A finding of not guilty by reason of insanity is then quickly followed by a civil commitment to the appropriate mental institution. Once the individual is declared to be competent from a treatment standpoint or upon motion of the court, a release hearing may be granted.

As a commitment to a penitentiary results in a loss of rights of the convicted, the same status is attached to individuals committed to a mental

---

[21]Dawn V. Meredith, 561, Colo. S. Ct. P2nd, 1256, (1976).

hospital as being incompetent, insane, or mentally defective. Almost any involuntary commitment as a result of a medical commission finding will automatically result in a loss of rights. Until the subject has been medically restored to reason or competency, he may continue to be deprived legally of his rights despite the fact that he has been discharged from the mental facility. The restoration of even the most basic of rights is not automatic in nature.

MISCELLANEOUS OFFENDER RIGHTS

In closing, there are some other rights that should be mentioned here. Reference has been made of the rights of probationers and parolees to be given formal notice of revocation hearings and the facts alleging the cause. The right to arrest and to detain should also be noted as a function of the supervisor. The probation/parole officer cannot breach the rights of the offender by searching either his person or his premises without reason to believe that there is probable cause to do so and that evidence may be found to substantiate a violation of the conditions of his status. The probation officer does, however, have the right to arrest without the benefit of a warrant based on probable cause. In the cases of parolees, because of a different level of jurisdiction, the parole officer may find it necessary in some jurisdictional areas, to seek authorizations either from administrative personnel or from the parole board/commission itself. In either case, despite the administrative circumstances of the arrest, the offender must be advised of the nature of the charges against him and the right to have a hearing within a reasonable length of time.

Imprisoned offenders should have the right to know when they are eligible for parole. Two jurisdictional factors may determine this eligibility. First, the court of sentencing may specify the time to be served before parole may be considered. Second, at the federal level, parole eligibility may be computed on the length of the sentence imposed. For example, an adult federal prisoner who has been sentenced to a time to exceed 180 days may be considered for parole release after having served one-third of his original sentence.[22]

At the time of this writing, the United States Parole Commission has just revised its actuarial device of salient factor scoring for use in the prediction of parole outcome. Although it remains strictly an administrative tool, this instrument may have some effects on prisoners in regard to their rights. The right to know what is expected, the right to know what must be done to secure parole consideration, and the right to a reasonable chance to make good with reasonable expectations should be offered to all eligible offenders. As the following chapter will indicate, the chance to succeed is cor-

---

[22]*Crimes and Criminal Procedure,* U.S. Code, Title 18, Vol. 4, Chapter 311, 1970 Ed.

related to the opportunity to allow reformation to take place. The revision of the Parole Commission's predictability table was designed not only to better evaluate the chances of the offender, but it also gave him some less biased scoring areas that represent a truer test of his desire to conform. The most inherent right of all imprisoned, for that matter, of all offenders, is the right to have the opportunity to use prison time constructively for rehabilitation purposes.

SUGGESTED READINGS

COHEN, NEIL P., AND DEAN HILL RIVIKEN, "Civil Disabilities: The Forgotten Punishment," *Federal Probation,* 35, no. 2 (June 1971), 19–25.

DAVIS, SAMUEL M., *Rights of Juveniles: The Juvenile Justice System.* New York: Clark Boardman Co., Ltd., 1974.

FISHER, H. RICHMOND, "Probation and Parole Revocation: The Anomaly of Divergent Procedures," *Federal Probation,* 38, no. 3 (September 1974), 23–29.

FOX, SANFORD J. *Modern Juvenile Justice.* St. Paul, Minn.: West Publishing Company, 1972.

GLUECK, SHELDON, *Mental Disorder and the Criminal Law.* Boston: Little, Brown & Company, 1925.

HANDMAN, HERBERT IRA, *The Rights of Convicts.* Dobbs Ferry, N.Y.: Oceana Publications, Inc., 1975.

HERMAN, MICHELE G. AND MARILYN G. HAFT, eds., *Prisoner's Rights Sourcebook: Theory, Litigation, Practice.* New York: Clark Boardman Co., Ltd., 1973.

KERPER, HAZEL B. AND JANEEN KERPER, *Legal Rights of the Convicted.* St. Paul, Minn.: West Publishing Company, 1974.

KRANTZ, SHELDON, *Corrections and Prisoners' Rights.* St. Paul, Minn.: West Publishing Company, 1976.

———, et al., *Model Rules and Regulations on Prisoners' Rights and Responsibilities.* Boston: Center for Criminal Justice, Boston University, School of Law, 1973.

LANDYNSKI, JACOB W. *Search and Seizure and the Supreme Court: A Study in Constitutional Interpretations.* Baltimore: Johns Hopkins Press, 1966.

OVERHOLSER, WINFRED, "Major Principles of Forensic Psychiatry, in *American Handbook of Psychiatry,* Vol. II, ed. Silvano Arieti. New York: Basic Books, Inc., 1959, pp. 1887–1901.

PALMER, JOHN W., *Constitutional Rights of Prisoners.* Cincinnati: W. H. Anderson Company, 1973.

RUBIN, SOL, "The Man with a Record: A Civil Rights Problem," *Federal Probation,* 35, no. 3 (September 1971), 3–7.

SINGER, RICHARD G. AND WILLIAM P. STATSKY, *Rights of the Imprisoned: Cases, Materials and Directions.* Indianapolis: The Bobbs-Merrill Co., Inc., 1974.

8

Prison—The Dubious Alternative

Our world seems to contain many things that seem unnecessary or undesirable. Although the purpose for the existence of some perceived maladies may escape us, there still remain some well-defined and well-established elements that defy general social acceptance without some form of resignation. Death and taxes, for example, are inescapable facts that most of us do not look forward to, but which are inevitable in our lives.

Another necessary evil is the existence of correctional institutions within our society. Prisons, reformatories, training or industrial schools, detention centers, all appear to be necessary. The public demands that offenders be punished and that society be protected from the dangerous acts of criminals, and there exist few acceptable alternatives that would serve as meaningful substitutes. Another reason for describing penal institutions as a form of evil, is that their sole purpose is to contain evil individuals for purposes of punishment, and any other implied function is little more than an administrative guise concealed behind wishful thinking. Furthermore, the methods involved in the process of containment and punishment quite often necessitate harsh—if not evil—means of control, which go beyond the ordinary concept of punishment and which are not, in any way, compatible with rehabilitation.

The simple premise of this chapter is that prisons and most other comparable penal institutions, despite their names, do not work as a rehabilitative tools. As a punishment mechanism, there is little question but that they do fulfill the role, sometimes to excess. How well they serve to protect society by containing the so-called undesirable is another question. We have, then, given preliminary definition to the three basic purposes of penal institutions.

1. To punish the offender.
2. To bring about his rehabilitation.
3. To protect the public by removing the offender from the mainstream of society.

The premise, as defined above, although acknowledged to reflect the personal bias of this author, will be examined in the balance of this chapter. It is hoped that the contents will either support or destroy this premise. Support merely confirms the author's ability to diagnosis, whereas refuting or rejecting the premise indicates a prognosis that is more favorable than acknowledged; a fact that would be welcomed.

HISTORICAL BACKGROUND OF PUNISHMENT AND INCARCERATION

Punishment—or whatever hoped-for product is desired—through incarceration in state-administered institutions may facetiously be labeled as another product of American ingenuity. The Elmira Reformatory and the Auburn Prison System of New York State, if not the first on the American scene, are certainly the most famous examples of the forerunners of today's edifices of stone walls, guard towers, and steel cages. Europe patterned their systems after America's, one of the few reversals of unique note in the exchange of correctional and justice concepts that the two continents have shared over the years.

Early Forms of Punishment

Although punishment was not unknown in European countries, the methods differed from those of today, and justice—if that is the correct word—was quick to be imposed once guilt was established. In Anglo-Saxon England the administering of punishment took one of three forms: death, mutilation, or slavery. Incarceration was neither considered nor provided for. The public execution of offenders, as well as their mutilation was a form of "in kind" punishment (*lex talionis*) based on the severity of the crime. If death was the offense, then death was the form of punishment imposed. Execution, although certain, was not humane. It could take a variety of forms such as beheading, hanging, burning, drowning, or stoning. Mutilation meant branding or having a hand amputated.[1] Common criminals

---

[1] Leonard Orland, *Prisons: Houses of Darkness* (New York: The Free Press, 1975), Chap. 2.

were forced into slavery, or servitude as described in an earlier chapter, both in England proper as well as in her Majesty's colonies. Penal servitude was a most common practice under the rule of Elizabeth I in the early seventeenth century.

These forms of punishment, short of servitude, which formed an element of colonial labor but which used English rather than colonial offenders, were quickly adopted in the new country called America. Although some of the more severe offenses were initially "rewarded" with equally severe forms of punishment, there gradually came a trend toward some types of more humane acts. Public humiliation became known through the use of the stock and the pillory. Nathaniel Hawthorne's classical novel *The Scarlet Letter* is typical of the changing concepts of that time. The subject of Hawthorne's work, one Hester Prynne, became the mother of a child not of the seed of her lawful husband. Because of her sinful behavior, Hester was forced to wear the large letter *A* on her breast to proclaim the fact that she had committed the act of adultery. Although physical pain is observable, mental pain is not. It can only be assumed that Hester suffered greatly from the public humiliation of taunts, being spit upon, and other such social niceties, all part of the punishment for her act.

Another form of banishment is that portrayed in western novels and other forms of media about our frontier days, when the town lawman demanded that a renegade be gone by sundown. In the 1930s, railroad bulls as well as municipal law enforcement officers treated transients in much the same manner. The United States Department of Justice has also deported many "undesirables" such as suspected Mafia leaders. And it is not uncommon for lower level courts to grant a "float" to unwanted individuals to assure that they leave the jurisdiction. The point to be made here is that many so-called renegades were individuals who were ejected voluntarily from their communities. The use of the word *voluntary* implies a matter of one's own choosing, but the "choice" is predicated on either leaving under one's own power or having to face some type of action or punishment of a more punitive nature.

Three Theories of Correction

Three theories of punishment and related demands from correctional history have returned to haunt us on several contemporary concerns.

Retribution   English criminal law, back in the twelfth century, sought that the offender make retribution to his victim. Some sort of payment—then called a *bot*—was to be extracted as a means of "setting right" the damages done. Today, this aspect of correctional policy is being hailed as a contemporary breakthrough and is contemplated as being a new milestone in holding offenders accountable for their acts, especially to their victims.

Humiliation   This chapter has discussed humiliation as a form of public punishment and the mental discomfort that being put on display might bring. A variation of this was when the dispositions of court dockets were published in local newspapers. Exempt from such public acclamation in our more modern times were the names of juveniles. However, in the last fifteen to twenty years, one Judge Lester H. Loble of Helena, Montana, decided that public humiliation of juvenile offenders might be an effective deterrent. The apparent thinking was that the parents of the juveniles whose names were made public would be sufficiently embarrassed so that they would exercise more control over their children. It was also hoped that the public—and especially other juveniles—would take note of the fact that punishment was being administered. Therefore, Judge Loble authorized the publication of the names of juvenile offenders as a part of what must be assumed to be a humiliation process.

Incarceration as a Holding Process   A lot of discussion has currently centered around the injustice of holding individuals for trial. The consensus seems to be that there are as many—if not more—accused in jails awaiting trial than there are offenders in jail doing their time as a result of a conviction. Yet one of the primary functions of early prisons and detention facilities was to hold and to detain individuals awaiting trial.

Based on these three points, it might be assumed that (1) history does, in fact, repeat itself, and that (2) little new or innovative has taken place in the field of penology specifically and corrections in general over the years.

English Types of Incarceration

England probably unwittingly provided the foundation for prisons as we know them today. Sometime in the early sixteenth century that country gave birth to what were called *gaols*. As nearly as can be interpreted, the term *jail* by both name and function evolved from its English counterpart. These gaols were places were punishments such as floggings could be administered. They were detention-type facilities, ensuring that the offender could not escape punishment before it was imposed and providing a shield from the eyes of the public. Then, just before the turn of the seventeenth century, Parliament authorized the building of houses of correction. History provides us with the information that these institutions were not segregated cells as we commonly conceive of prisons, but dormitories where offenders lived together.

PRISONS AS PUNISHMENT

Punishment, like criticism, should be both constructive and meaningful if it is to have any positive outcome. Unfortunately, parents frequently punish their children more out of anger than because of any objective rationale. Indeed, it might be questionable whether spankings are ever predicated on an objective premise, although there are obviously some beneficial aspects in associating the painful effects of spanking with wrongdoing. Furthermore, we as parents often punish childish exuberance when our own frustrations are so great that we can neither assimilate nor tolerate such behavior. Punishment administered without objectivity can best be said to be of lesser benefit, although there exists a lesson in association between the pain inflicted and the act committed.

As a parent, a mother is often guilty of rebuking a child for unacceptable behavior or acts by saying, "Wait until your father gets home. Boy, will you get it then!" This is fair to no one. It implies that the child may be the victim of double jeopardy—first Mother cuffs him, then he remains in a state of uneasiness waiting for his father to get home, and finally Dad lays it on him one more time. Such justice is neither quick nor meaningful. Even if the child is cognizant of his error, is appropriately repentant, and is resigned to taking his punishment, he still should not be punished twice for the same thing.

Basic Ingredients of Punishment

Although this was not intended to be a discourse on child psychology, the psychological aspects of punishment are indeed pertinent and worthy of discussion. Punishment, if it is to serve any pertinent function, must contain several basic ingredients.

I. Is it meaningful? Meaningful and appropriateness appear to be what are called "wastebasket words," i.e., their true content is obscured by a degree of abstractness. Meaningful is used specifically here in an attempt to measure effect. Consider the following factors.

    A. *Is its message explicit?* Our concern should be whether or not the punishment has any deterrent effect. It is senseless to punish a child by sending him to his room if he is provided there with a TV set, cookies hidden in his bottom dresser drawer, and a bottle of soda pop in his hand. No deprivation and little deterrent effect, under those circumstances, can be expected.

    B. *Does an understanding exist as to why the punishment is being imposed?* A relatively harmless and equally nebulous put-down we have used as adolescents was, "Don't look at me, I don't want to see you." Now what does that mean? Certainly it is a verbal put-down, but it was also devoid of any message. No one is sure what is implied. Punishment, then, should be explicitly understood as the *ultimate* consequence of a *specific* act, a cause and effect chain of events.

II. Is it appropriate? Model sentencing acts have tried to tailor the sentence to meet the crime. But it is apparent that a lot more needs to be done to effect a proper matching process. For example, mention has been made earlier in this book of what are known as victimless crimes as opposed to crimes against individuals or property. Sentencing should thus be adapted to the victim as well as to the crime. Therefore, when one considers appropriateness of punishment, one facet of the topic might be, *Is it flexible in nature?*

III. Is it impartial? It is believed to have been St. Augustine who once said, "An unjust law is no law at all." Unfortunately, judges are often inconsistent. The author has worked in more than one court system where the ultimate disposition of a case was not based on either legal facts or precedents as much as it was on the individual idiosyncracies of the judge. The dispositions were so diverse that offenders were continually attempting to manipulate their docket time and date so that they might be rescheduled in front of a judge who was more lenient than another.

IV. Is it administered quickly? More than one instance has existed of accused offenders spending more time in custody awaiting trial than they probably would have to serve once convicted. Attempts to quell prison riots are done immediately. Why should individual rebellious behavior not be dealt with just as quickly and immediately? Threats do not constitute punishment; they only represent a promise of possible deterrent actions. They only become voices in the wind that are quickly blown away and forgotten. Younger children, especially, cannot grasp the association process between a prior act and a prolonged period before punishment. Quite frankly, we as parents are not doing our job if we expect threats to sustain and deter any undesirable behavior.

V. Is it done objectively? Punishment, to be effective, need not be vindictive. No child believes the parental statement made at the time a spanking is administered that "this hurts me more than it hurts you." The imposition of any kind of punishment should be done in a matter-of-fact manner. "A soft answer turneth away wrath, but grievous words stir up anger."[2] Hostile attitudes breed hostile reactions, and another vicious circle is perpetrated. Furthermore, group punishment seems senseless. For example, teachers who punish a whole class by keeping everyone after school for the acts of a few are not being objective in management practices. Punishment, then, should be individual rather than collective, unless there is reason to believe that many are equally involved.

Physical and Psychological Retribution

A preliminary conclusion to be made is that the primary function of most penal institutions is that of punishment. Any correctional facility is structurally designed to enhance punishment. This purpose is apparent by the

[2]Prov. 15:1.

staffing ratio of professional (treatment) to maintenance (security) personnel. Also the nature of institutional programs does not enhance the concept of rehabilitation. This is not a mere and casual observation. Norman Carlson, Director of the U.S. Bureau of Prisons, recently was quoted as saying, "To me, retribution is not a negative word. It's implicit in our criminal justice system. Rehabilitation has been oversold as a concept."[3]

Punishment generally is administered within penal institutions either as physical or psychological retribution. Although the trend is away from the brutal, inhumane, and vicious acts of the sixteenth century and before,[4,5,6] inflicted pain is still a part of the present prison system. The racks, the whip, and the stretching table may occupy little more than bitter memories in penal history, but there are still instances of physical punishment being administered, instances that may or may not go unnoticed and uncorrected by penal administrators. Guards, like many other institutional custodial persons, have long been underpaid positions, and as such they still attract a less than competent group of individuals to serve in that capacity. For example, the opportunity to dominate but the inability to convey and to enforce orders without physical force is all too common. One of the even less desirable methods of administering physical punishment is to allow inmate peers to "correct bad behavior" of another inmate. The usual practice is to allow several prisoners, usually the ones who bear a grudge against the nonconformist, into the cell of the latter and to then go away and return in a few minutes after "corrective measures" have been taken.

It is difficult to determine how much and what kind of pain certain forms of psychological punishment provide. Although the hurt imposed may be more mental than physical, it does not make it any less easy for the inmate to bear. The most common and consistent form used is the dehumanization process that begins at the time of admission. First the offender is stripped of any outward forms of identification, such as clothing and effects. He is then subjected to the personal humiliation of a thorough physical search that leaves no body cavity unprobed. He becomes a number rather than a name. If he should thereafter be addressed by his surname, he rarely will be accorded the privilege of having it prefaced with the use of Mister, Miss, or Ms. To do so would be to acknowledge some form of rank in the social world, and the prison is a world of its own, clearly separated from outside customs and privileges. The prisoner will probably lose any identification of a personal physical characteristic by having a prison haircut or a beard

[3]Norman Carlson, "An Address to the American Correctional Association," Denver, Colorado, August 23, 1976.

[4]Hugo A. Bedau and Chester M. Pierce, eds., *Capital Punishment in the United States* (New York: AMS, Inc., 1976).

[5]William Andrews, *Old Time Punishments* (Detroit: Singing Tree Press, 1970).

[6]John Laurence, *A History of Capital Punishment* (London: Kennikat Press, 1971).

shaved off. Although such acts are administered under the guise of health and sometimes security measures, the newly arrived inmate is immediately reduced to a nobody by such acts. He or she immediately becomes a nonentity who, short of size and perhaps color, is now virtually indistinguishable from any of the other new arrivals.

Many of the other forms of punishment to be endured are more subtle in nature. The loss of civil rights, the regimentation, the menial work assignments, the deprivation of certain social amenities of individual choice such as might involve personal hygiene, the loss of social and physical contact with loved ones—all are unmeasurable forms of punishment that will deliver varying degrees of physical and psychological pain. Punishment for the inmate is a constant reminder that he is a second-class citizen because of his conviction and sentencing to a penal institution.

Gresham Sykes picks up on an age-old theme in his classic book about captives when he questions whether prisons are designed *for* punishment or *as* punishment.[7] Sykes seems to feel that punishment is demanded but not at the level where it becomes obviously open and brutal in content. The rationalization is that imprisonment is punishment unto itself as is demanded by society. How overt the punishment becomes behind the walls is somehow a secondary concern to society unless there exists a strong social conscience. Punishment, then, has become more indirect and diffused and, hence, more difficult to define.

System of Rewards and Punishment

Regardless of what it may be called, the underlying premise for the management of prison inmates is based on a system of rewards and punishments. Although the rewards may be few in nature, they are conceived to be in the form of some type of an early out or less restrictive activities being imposed within. Many authorities feel that there exists no rewards per se for inmates since the assigned menial work tasks seem to go ad infinitum. They argue that there is no chance for any promotion, and were there such, any elevation of status might well be cause for peer concern that the individual might be a "snitch" and getting too close to the staff for peer comfort.

The author would take some issue here by stating that although "doing their time" is important, the opportunity to speed up that time must be conceived of as a reward to the inmate population. The issue is not whether a reward exists; rather it becomes a matter of how long must the individual wait before the reward is realized. Therefore, inmates will continue to "play the role" and hope that some recognition of conformity is recognized even though that form of conformity is distasteful to them at a personal level.

[7]Gresham M. Sykes, *The Society of Captives* (Princeton, N.J.: Princeton University Press, 1958), pp. 31–34.

PRISON AS A FORM OF REHABILITATION

Definitions and Implications

Rehabilitation, if it is to be effected as a result of incarceration, represents a byproduct at best. Two facts should be apparent. First, it can be assumed that the rehabilitation process is an internal matter, which results as a counterreaction to an unpleasant threat—a threat of continued commitment to the penal system. The use of the word *internal* carries the intended implication that behavioral change is an individual and singular decision that cannot be effected by anyone other than the offender. Although outside (external) pressures may condition and promote change, the decision to change must remain a personal choice. Unfortunately, the attempt or desire to display constructive change more often than not is a product of limited choice, that is, choosing the less painful of two painful alternatives.

The second part is that rehabilitation is an intangible as well as an abstract quality. It is not perceivable, and it cannot be tested for purposes of drawing conclusions while the individual remains within the artificial environment of the prison system. There can be no doubt that peer violence exists in prisons. It remains equally difficult to discern how much activity of this nature is committed out of free will and how much of it is a conditioned response resulting from the value system of the inmate structure and an attempt to cope with same.

The author must agree with the earlier quoted statement of the director of the U.S. Bureau of Prisons (see p. 167). The word *rehabilitation* is both an overworked and a misunderstood concept. Despite the fact that this word is used habitually in conjunction with penal and correctional concepts, the author contends that rehabilitation is not a meaningful and appropriate term. The point of argument can be based on its conceptual definition. If *rehabilitation* means "to restore"—certainly a classical usage—then we are faced with some very philosophical arguments that relate to the cause and effect of criminal behavior. Whether or not valid arguments can be predicated on implications is a matter to be dwelt on here, even if a true revelation cannot be determined through the process of documentation.

The implication of the restoration aspect of the word *rehabilitation* is that some unknown agent has triggered a form of social pathology that is evidenced in criminal-type activities on the part of the afflicted. Along these lines, it might be suggested that criminal behavior is degenerate behavior and as such may not be within the mental/social ability of the individual to control. Quite obviously, this is an incorrect assumption based on definitional oversimplification. The thesis of degenerate behavior *could* imply that any individual possessed of certain character defects can be expected to be endowed with criminal tendencies that will surface sooner or later; but rehabilitation would, then, focus on the correction of those defects and would be complete when the offender was "restored."

Rehabilitate derives from the word *habilitate,* a word that is itself fraught with different connotations, some implications of which could lead us, in wild moments, to believe that criminal behavior is congenital in nature. Such an argument, although obviously extreme, has semantic origins. *Habilitate,* in turn, comes to us from the Latin word habilitatus, referring to the "ability" or "tendency" of someone or something. When imaginatively applied, this could support an argument for criminal probability. It takes no more imagination to reject the oversimplification of this argument than it does to discard *any* compact and simplified explanation of criminal behavior.

We have come a long and devious way from our original discussion of rehabilitation. In the course of our detour, we are trying to make the perhaps exaggerated point that rehabilitation is not the proper word to be used in conjunction with corrections—despite its popularity. Perhaps an example will serve to bring more enlightened confusion to the subject, and that is to state that change effected by demand or occurring under duress is not expected to have much longevity or to contain much subjectivity. If rehabilitation were, in fact, subjective in nature, then it could logically be argued that the individual would constructively change his life style without the need for an intervening agency such as the court or prison. All the offender would have to do is to say, "Hey, this isn't what I want out of life. I better look around a little." His desire to change would be sufficient to allow him to do so. Prisons, then, apparently exist because the individual took too much time while looking around!

What Are The Functional Values Of Imprisonment, If Any?

Objectivity demands that both sides of an argument be presented before a judgment is rendered. What is being asked is, "Do prisons serve any functional value toward the rehabilitation of the offender? If so, what are those features and how durable are their contributions?" Although perhaps misplaced contextually, punishment can contribute to the rehabilitative process, but only, it appears, in a limited number of ways. We have already acknowledged the fact that human nature dictates that we avoid what is painful and seek what brings pleasure. The argument then is, if prisons are conceived of as places of punishment, and if punishment is a deterrent to further punishable behavior, then prisons should serve to rehabilitate offenders.

Rehabilitation, as used here, takes on a new form and meaning. It is now being used to indicate a process that makes reoffending undesirable. We speak, then, of rehabilitation becoming an understandable concept, one that conveys a change of behavior brought about on the premise of association. If such a thought process holds any merit at all, then prisons should be extremely effective in rehabilitating the young and impressionable offender. This could, however, preclude the use of probation to be used as an extensive tool. It might well call for an early and brief exposure to prisons, even at the point of the first or second offense. The lack of logic in this argument is apparent in the inability to determine the thin line between being impressed and having become hardened or sophisticated. When has there been sufficient exposure? When is the apple sufficiently ripe to pick?

The Questionable Value of Therapeutic Intervention.   If we operate on the premise that offenders, even a proportionate number within the inmate population, are "sick" individuals, then rehabilitation should consist of some type of therapeutic intervention. The ratio as reported by the President's Task Force on Crime (1965), that there is one professional (clinical) staff person for every 179 inmates,[8] makes such a treatment task impossible. The reader will undoubtedly be skeptical that all offenders are "sick" people, and this theory would certainly be refuted by most prison inmates. Rehabilitation through therapeutic intervention at the prison level will rarely be effective for several reasons.

An insufficient number of clinically trained personnel. Most prison psychologists are limited in their duties. There is no practical way, by virtue of the inmate-clinician ratio, that all prisoners can be involved in therapy. Most clinicians within the prison system will find themselves giving most of their time and knowledge to roles involving classification and preparole interviews and testing, along with some crisis-intervention tasks.

Inmate distrust of clinical personnel. Most inmates will view the clinician as one of the men with keys. In short, professional therapists are part of the staff and are not to be trusted; they are merely to be tolerated as another form of harassment. They are seen as belonging to the establishment, and are possible bearers of tales that might be used against the individual offender who seeks their help. To avail and to align himself with any member of the administration would place the status of an inmate under suspicion with his fellow peers.

Certain offenders function well in prison settings. It is impossible to establish an arithmetical mean relative to "sick" offenders within the walls of a prison. For example, the homosexual may be better protected and cherished inside the walls than he will ever be on the outside. Certain psychopaths—as they were once commonly called—who show no visible evidence of any social conscience may likewise adapt readily to the prison

[8]"Task Force Report," *The President's Commission on Law Enforcement and the Administration of Justice* (Washington, D.C.: U.S. Government Printing Office, 1967).

environment. Their greatest punishment is only the lack of opportunity to pursue their skills.

The stress of prison obscures character disorders. Areas of dysfunctioning on the outside may be repressed by new areas of malfunctioning once a commitment is effected. New and peculiar concerns related to prison demands and their accompanying value structure may repress and obscure the true pathology of the offender. His normal means of coping may suddenly and dramatically be replaced by new mechanisms designed specifically to cope with the new situations encountered in prison life.

A lack of appropriate clinical tools. There are to be found within the prison culture the chronic and violent offender as well as the clinically "sick" offender, but there is no legal way of establishing (see Chapter Seven) whether any of these individuals were that way either at the time the offense was committed or during the course of the trial and the subsequent commitment to the penal system. Although the stress of the commitment and the demands of the day-to-day regime may bring out stress factors that may contribute to a psychotic state (prison fever), it is generally assumed than an individual is either clinically diagnosed as ill or that he is just a rotten, antisocial, indifferent, and uncaring individual. These are two separate elements in which there is very little overlap as portrayed here (see Figure 8-1). The science of treatment in the sense of therapeutic intervention may be geared to treat one or the other, but we lack the universal finesse to treat both at the same time.

If the concern of the prison process is rehabilitation (defined to mean the restoration to a form of wholeness where conformity is assumed) of the offender through a program of therapy, then again prison is not the answer, because there are not adequate means of therapeutic intervention within the prison walls. If our hope is for a miracle under the guise of treatment, then we should acknowledge that there are other forms and sources for treatment purposes within the community, and the prison should not even be remotely considered as having the ability to serve this function. It can be argued that

Figure 8.1   Diagram of two types of offenders.

an element of treatment is confrontation. It certainly is obvious that being locked up is a method of gaining attention, but that the rest of the ingredients in the therapeutic recipe seem to be missing.

The Questionable Value of Prison Training Programs. One of the common arguments heard today in an attempt to account for the growth of crime is to state that it is a product of social and economic deprivation. It also is advanced that the prison population is made up of predominantly Negro and other nonwhite minorities because they have had fewer training and advancement opportunities than their white counterparts. If this were the only valid reason for the ethnic ratio, the prison training programs would have to be considered as inadequate to provide this form of rehabilitation. For example, what employment opportunities are going to be available to the black man going back to the ghetto heart of a metropolitan city who has learned to milk cows as part of his prison assignment? Or how many private firms can you name that specialize in the production of car license plates? How many ads have you seen recently in the classified section of your local newspaper for broom makers? Sykes lists some 35 job assignments within the New Jersey State Prison to which an inmate might be assigned.[9] There is no doubt in our minds but that this is representative of most prisons in terms of possible work placements. What is more significant is that less than one-third of the duties indicated have any training value for possible work placement upon release from prison. Again an exercise in futility is apparent.

The principal value of prison industries is that they help defray the cost of operational overhead and have unlimited uses as a managment tool. Prisons cannot function without an inmate labor force. The correctional budget is routinely the lowest on the allocation ladder. One wonders if greater deprivation punishes better, or are men less apt to give their keepers difficulty and to plot escapes when they are physically depleted?

Prison labor is not totally necessary nor was it so intended. Labor is to occupy time that otherwise might be used for adverse purposes.

The Future Goal of Vocational Training

If rehabilitation is to consist, in part, of vocational training, then the use of inmate labor will have to be determined and predicated on some form of meaningful endeavor. Quite frankly, this is not an easy transition to make. Many prisoners are deficient in even the most basic of remedial skills, which should, by necessity, demand attention before any actual vocational skills can be provided them. The projected fear of the author would be that certain levels of the inmate population are going to be deprived of any vocational training opportunities. There will always continue to be custodial

[9]Sykes, *The Society of Captives,* pp. 26–27.

duties that are going to require inmate labor. It is therefore assumed that the less educated and the culturally or socially deprived inmates will be those who perform these duties instead of receiving needed remedial training. If this hunch is correct, then rehabilitation will fall far short of its desired goals, and the frustrating circle of a lack of meaningful program involvement would continue to be perpetuated.

Training Programs of the Federal Prison System

The numerous state prisons around the country should borrow a page from the training programs of the various prisons under the federal system. Although most state prisons are found in rural settings, more and more of the federal facilities are being constructed in urban areas. State prisons were originally located in remote areas, somewhat like Indian reservations, and were founded on land that was practically useless for any other purpose. The theory was that this remote location would make it easier to track down escapees, that it symbolically removed the offender farther from the mainstream of society, and that much outside "busy work" could be created without posing any threat to skilled labor forces in the area.

The U.S. Bureau of Prisons has shown a great deal of innovativeness in the placement of their new institutions. Their location in, or adjacent to, urban areas makes rehabilitation as a vocational training goal much more practical for a variety of reasons.

1. It has allowed for the use of community resources as an integral part of the training program. Both staff and facilities have been utilized within the community for such a training approach.
2. It has permitted the utilization of work-training programs whereby qualified and deserving inmates are allowed to leave during the day for this purpose and spend only their nights and weekends in custody.
3. It has allowed businesses to gauge the potential of inmates as possible future employees upon their release. In short, the difficult process of job hunting from behind the walls has been greatly reduced.
4. It has allowed the institution to keep a finger on the pulse of the labor market. In this manner, new or changing employment trends can be recognized, and program changes made to deal with that need.

Penitence: A Poor Measuring Stick

Rehabilitation has been conceived of by some as being fulfilled once the offender has reached a state of penitence. This was the theory of the Philadelphia Quakers in their dealings with offenders housed in the Walnut Street Jail. However, based on high recidivism rates among parolees, it is reasonably safe to assume that few inmates reflect much more on their criminal ways other than regretfulness for being caught and some honest concern for the welfare of their families. In short, the direction of their concerns is both misplaced and misdirected. The chronic offender will devote his meditation to three given areas: (1) a refinement of his criminal skills to avoid future apprehension, (2) how to best do his sentence in the shortest period of time possible, and (3) how to survive and maintain himself in the prison subculture during that time.

Sykes makes reference to one of the argot roles of the inmates as that of the "real man."[10] This individual is described as the offender who rarely rocks the boat and who maintains habitual control of himself despite most circumstances confronting him. Sykes goes on to state that this role is one that gains the grudging respect from a majority of the inmate population. What Sykes does not enlarge upon is the fact that such aloofness is a characteristic that makes it difficult to judge just where, on the rehabilitation continuum, that particular inmate should be rated. It might be that he is stoically accepting his punishment even while maintaining an equal distance between the other inmates and staff alike. Yet, it is probable that such inmates have become somewhat like shadows whose true likeness and intent cannot be readily gauged and recorded.

Thus the various roles that inmates assume, either by choice or necessity, within the prison culture may prohibit true rehabilitation. The unctuous conformist may make points with the staff but loses them in the eyes of his peers. As such, he may find himself having a far more difficult row to hoe because some of the basic needs that can only be supplied to him by other inmates are denied him by virtue of his chosen associations. Neither can penitence be weighed since the natural abyss between inmate and staff does not allow for a free exchange of honest feelings. Prisons exist and will exist as an armed camp of sorts where neither side trusts the other and where it is virtually impossible to engage and to indulge in a satisfactory and mutual relationship.

Penitence is an outmoded concept. The true test, as practiced in corrections, of rehabilitation is not intent but deed. Many offenders are so sophisticated that they are equally adept at assuming any role demanded of them just as long as there is some reason for their doing so. Since prisons are an artificial environment, it is not possible to test the true behavior of an inmate. Choice is limited, and temptation is removed, so that no pseudo-scientific method exists, other than conformity to the prison rules and roles, to determine how inmates will act when given freedom of movement and choice.

[10]Ibid., p. 102.

PRISONS AS A FORM OF SOCIAL PROTECTION
AND INTERVENTION

Our somewhat cloudy crystal ball indicates that prison reform measures and penology innovativeness are going to be achieved only through a form of better criminal classification and mandatory sentencing acts. Despite whatever scientific and legal methods are used to consider and evaluate the necessary changes in corrections, a sizeable segment of society will certainly object to such alterations. Public attitudes toward crime are and will continue to be predicated on a variety of orientations, beliefs, and superstitions ranging from what might be called a Puritanical extreme to a demand for physical retaliation. Prisons will, by public demand, continue to house offenders who are guilty by virtue of offenses that are classically known either as *malum prohibitum* (legal wrongs) or *malum in se* (moral wrongs).

Society has every right to be protected and to have the courts and other criminal justice agencies intervene on its behalf. Certainly there is justification for its concern. It has been calculated that over 90 percent of the major crimes reported to the FBI involve the taking of someone's money or property. Some of these offenses may likewise involve the taking of a life as part of the criminal act. Generally speaking, however, murders and other crimes of violence do not seem to arise out of any tangible need for the possessions of others. Statistically, then, prisons are primarily justified as a means of isolating individuals who contribute to the high number of offenses committed against others.

Daniel Glaser suggests the appropriateness of the theory that if such a large number of crimes are committed against property, then there may be reason to examine if crime is a supplement or a substitute to gainful employment as a means of attaining income.[11] This is an age-old controversy, which, if it documents anything, does point toward the fact that hindsight is better than foresight. If there is merit to Glaser's suggestion—and there are certainly very plausible grounds to accept it at face value—there are also grounds for the argument that a certain element of offenders prefer criminal involvement despite and in opposition to subsidizing themselves at a comparable monetary level through normal and gainful means. The study of the psychology of such individuals would represent a book unto itself.

Rather than attack this isolated statement of Glaser's, we would like to point out one of the paradoxes of society. That is, we still relate to the old level of the Horatio Alger books and advocate that "anyone can make good if he wants to." Therefore, instead of corrections working hand in glove with other social movements, it—especially in the area of penology—has become little more than a reservoir for society's failures. When we spoke

---

[11]Daniel Glaser, *The Effectiveness of a Prison and Parole System* (Indianapolis, Ind.: The Bobbs-Merrill Co., Inc., 1969), p. 160.

earlier of hindsight, we were contending that corrections as a profession has failed to act as a social prophylactic to ease its own predicament. Perhaps society should assume some of the mutual blame. One of the saddest commentaries of today is the ratio of negative to positive behavior responses. We react, although not always quickly and appropriately, to negative behavior when it is exhibited. We do not, however, do other than to assume and to expect positive behavior. We neither reward nor recognize it; we merely take it for granted. Our assumption is that this is what should be, and we relegate it to a position of conformity. The penal system may be doing nothing more, then, than resigning itself to the role that society has projected upon it as its most true and noble function.

If we were able to make the assumption that the criminal justice system has the function of protecting society against criminal behavior, the crux of the matter still remains as to the indecisiveness of what is really being demanded. In a recent panel, as part of the 106th Congress of the American Correctional Association, the participants attempted to face this very issue.[12] Although the discussion was both animated and thorough, no common solution was reached. The contents covered the general confusion of the public, of the courts, and of the legislature as to common expectations. Suffice it to say, the only common denominator was that the area of corrections and the needs of the public in relation to corrections were both little more than a plethora of uncertainty.

Perhaps one of the more contemporary issues relates to the use of capital punishment as a deterrent to crime. The last one and one-half decades have seen history repeating itself by virtue of a circuitous route whereby correctional practices have returned to their point of origin. For a period of time, punishment by execution was not being practiced in the United States. In addition to some legal precedents for this state of acquiescence,[13] this period of dormancy was supported by social thought that executions were a meaningless gesture. There is little significant documentation that the death penalty and its subsequent implementation have served as a deterrent to criminal behavior; these measures only served to deter the continuing involvement of the offender who dies as the culmination of his sentence. Yet, at the very time of this writing, there is considerable evidence that the execution of criminals may again become commonplace. The current issue merely seems to revolve around a series of questions as to just exactly what crimes are applicable, by what means, and when such a practice will reconvene.

It would appear that it is time that the total criminal justice system should begin to lead rather than being content to be led. Certainly there would seem to exist somewhere some yet undiscovered means of potential

[12]American Correctional Association Panel, Denver, Colorado, August 24, 1976.

[13]Furnam v. Georgia, 408 US 238, 33 L E 2 345, 92 S Ct 2726.

criminal detection methods to be used as a diversionary procedure. And although social and economic deprivation may be contributing factors to a life style of criminal behavior, this does not in any way account for the rapid growth of white-collar and political crimes involving offenders who are certainly not of the lower socio-economic class. It would appear that the public can and should be served and protected. It also is apparent that the public is not knowledgeable enough to dictate what should be attempted as a means of overcoming a rather stagnant and unproductive approach to punishment and rehabilitation. If there ever existed a dichotomy involving the radical and the realistic in a singular grouping, this is one of those times.

Preprison Classification

A probable beginning point in intervening on behalf of the public's welfare would entail a form of preprison classification. Again we find it necessary to return to the concept of disparity in sentencing. Although it is impossible to ignore the legal ramifications of the crime, the need exists to divorce the social from the legal implications in an effort to establish some type of criminal prognosis. The public has collectively balked at the decriminalization of certain acts. Even with the recent removal of public intoxication from the ranks of having legal implications, there are various other offenses that deserve similar scrutiny, such as the use of drugs, gambling, and certain sexual offenses. Athough it is recognized that there are grounds to perhaps suspect that certain consequences of these acts may contribute to eventual criminal behavior or that they may be fostered and promoted by individuals or groups active in criminal circles, all acts that are socially incongruous with our moral structure should not be automatically seized upon as grounds for legal banishment.

There would appear to be a need for an interim step that seems to now be used primarily in juvenile diversionary programs. Some sort of a receiving center for diagnostic/classification purposes prior to the ultimate placement in an institution should be considered. Not only should the findings of such a center be socially and legally pertinent, but the center itself should have the legal option of overriding the sentencing of the court and to return inappropriately sentenced offenders to the community. This, of course, should be considered only after an adequate alternative has been agreed upon, one that holds more merit than previously attempted plans. There are, of course, many arguments, both pro and con, to be considered before initiating such a program.

What are the advantages? There are two actual premises upon which a sentence to a penal institution is predicated: (1) the legal classification of the offense and (2) the discretionary opinion of the judge as to what constitutes an appropriate sentence. If the judge is going strictly by the book, so to speak, then it is conceivable that certain commitments are not necessarily in the best interests of the offender. A very real social example is the waiving of juveniles to adult courts and their subsequent commitments to an adult institution. The fourteen-year-old who commits an act of murder and is handled by an adult court will probably end up in the most severe and punishing of adult penal institutions, the penitentiary. Yet, despite the viciousness of his act, the chances of his being rehabilitated might be greater at the reformatory level where a diversity of programs might be more in keeping with his particular social needs. The inability of the court to match program and offender is often a result of sheer ignorance of institutional program content.

We think nothing of providing the offender of questionable mental capabilities or suspected mental problems the opportunity of some form of a diagnosis prior to making a disposition. As indicated in Chapter Seven, such cases are almost routinely sent to some psychiatric facility to ascertain their basic needs. A comparable idea is advocated here, then, for the normal offender. If we entertain any hopes for rehabilitation, the appropriate form of treatment/placement must be determined through other than a mere legal process. Such a process would, perhaps, satisfy the public demand for selectivity of placement and to better guarantee that certain offenders are not going to fall through the cracks and return to be a destructive force again in the community. It is suspected that much of the public demand made of corrections is for some assurance that its fears will be appeased and its safety assured. Crime is one of the few social evils that strikes without warning as well as without any discrimination as to whom it touches. Most preventive measures at the community level do not work. Law enforcement personnel have their hands full merely trying to solve offenses. Smaller communities without the benefit of intensive probationary services or community-centered programs for assistance often see little alternative but to effect a commitment for a lack of any other choice. Even courts with adequate probationary personnel are so overwhelmed with sheer numbers that they cannot effectively put their skills and manpower to work to any appreciable advantage. Sentencing appropriateness must also include some judicial discrimination as to who should be granted probation.

A further conceived benefit of such a program would be the opportunity to establish and pursue some forms of research pertinent to criminal behavior. At this time, neither the courts nor the penal institutions can participate in any in-depth type of research. Much of the research now being done, and it is limited, is the product of outside agencies who make up for a lack of firsthand knowledge by spasmodic contacts with the system. Their role is a part-time venture at best. If the reader but compares the cost of crime to the cost of other social maladies such as mental illness and various forms of socially disabling conditions, it becomes readily apparent that time and money are not allocated proportionately on the basis of what impact these factors are having on our life styles and what the costs may be to provide counteractive measures.

What are the disadvantages?   The perceived disadvantages of such a program are at least three in number: (1) a possible duplication of services, · (2) alienation of certain members of society and the judiciary, and (3) an inability to implement the findings of such an agency at the practical level.

First, if the ultimate decision of such a board as conceived is for the commitment of the offender to a prison/reformatory, any attempt to evaluate the needs and perceived problems of that individual would be futile. There may exist the investment of time and expertise which will undoubtedly be duplicated and enlarged upon, and a different opinion of that offender may be formed by the prison classification board at the time of commitment. In effect, there exists strong potential for what appears to be wasted time and effort without any dividends from the investment. Such a community board is presupposed to have as its main function seeking alternatives, but there will also exist some offenders whose behavior defies any other alternative than to be placed in an institution.

Second, the tradition as well as the ego of the courts is such that any attempt at questioning the judgment of the system (other than by a higher/appellate judicial body) would quickly draw criticism. It is envisioned that the effect would be mockery of the judicial system and, further, that it is being usurped of its power and function. There exist enough voices now which claim that the courts are too lenient in the punishment of offenders. It would be expected that few judges would be content to stand idly by and watch their powers dwindle.

Finally, the application of effecting such recommendations by a board could be totally impractical to the facilities of the community. If the defined needs of the offender cannot be met, we would have accomplished little else than to perpetuate a futile act and gesture. Few communities can justify the establishment and maintenance of part-time agencies. While a metropolitan area might be able to absorb and utilize specialized agencies for other purposes, small communities cannot financially justify them in the first place.

The difficult part of social change is to convince the public—and often certain public officials—that any premeditated change is in its best interests. Perhaps we have gotten callous from hearing too many campaign promises and listening to too many hopefuls who have little more to offer than a good imagination and sufficient lung power to deliver their dreams to an unsuspecting public. We are becoming a world of good investors and even better skeptics who want to know the amount of the return for our initial investment. Neither can we expect efficiency if we seemingly usurp deliberately the power of the judiciary when saying, in essence, that they made a mistake by virtue of an institutional commitment and they can expect that this error will be rectified by returning the offender to the community.

OLD CONCEPTS AND NEW FACES

One of the most obvious changes to have taken place in the penal system in the last 25 years has had nothing whatsoever to do with correctional program content. Rather, what has been conspicuous is the advent of a new type of prisoner in the cell block. Although robbers, rapists, and various criminal con men will always be present, a safe assumption would be that there has been an increasing upswing in the number of white-collar and political prisoners committed in this time frame as opposed to any other measurable time element in penal history.

A further criticism of the corrective system is that the prisons generally have failed to adapt to the changing needs of the times. Such theories as relate to social and economic deprivation simply are not applicable as contributing factors to the new breed who are now mingling with the general prison population. Adding to the confusion is the fact that many prisoners are no longer content to sit back and take their medicine; they are seeking more than casual legal means to advance their respective, if not collective, causes.

It remains difficult to say why, from a sociological or any other point of view, such a change has evolved. Some citizens might suggest that the very moral fiber of society has deteriorated and that our Christian ethic has been suppressed. In short, it is being implied that some sort of moral-social degeneration process is permeating our moral structure. Many might point to the level and quality of leadership as evidenced in the Watergate matter. Those who hold this viewpoint to be true would probably base their feelings on the premise that there are few honest politicians and that their mortality rate is high. Various racist and subversive groups might contend that our capricious attitudes regarding civil liberties are now returning to haunt us. From the standpoint and perspective of this book, the cause(s) is/are immaterial. What is being stated is that suddenly we find ourselves confronted with a new and different type of criminal element—at least by virtue of the number being adjudicated and imprisoned—with no new and unique manner of dealing with the influx.

Although the author will not make even a feeble attempt to enlighten the reader as to the causes of the new criminality, an attempt will be made to examine the aftereffects. It then becomes relatively easy to correlate these factors with some of the internal problems of penology and the related administrative headaches now being experienced. Perhaps a less poetic and pleasing method of stating the quandary would be to say that the present shortcomings may well be some of the primary factors in keeping prisons at their ineffectual level of operation. In short, corrections in general and penology in particular have not changed to meet the challenge of the new breed of criminals, especially the white collar and the political offenders who are becoming more commonplace.

One of the important factors that certainly is a contributing element to prison unrest is the double standard that obviously exists as found when comparing the regulations of federal and state penal institutions. Recently, when the former Attorney General of the United States John N. Mitchell entered a federal penal facility, the media were flooded with pictures as well as written accounts of the nature of that particular institution. Some of the services that were indicated to be available to Mr. Mitchell included fishing and golf, and these activities were said to be used at his leisure. The point to be made is that if punishment is to be effective, isn't it also correct to conclude that it should be appropriate for all offenders? Disparity of justice may well be equally as bad as no justice at all.

Although it is possible to differentiate between Mr. Mitchell, who might be conceived of as a political prisoner of sorts, and an unnamed black in the Colorado State Penitentiary in Canon City doing time for armed robbery, there are other examples that demand an even greater distinction. The standards of some of the prisons found in the southern United States, the overall lack of programs in state prisons nationally, and over-crowding are specific examples of double standards that defy logical explanation for their existence. It is also safe to assume that the facilities, services, and privileges at the federal minimum security prison at Maxwell Air Force Base that housed Mr. Mitchell are far more extensive than those at the federal facility at Ft. Leavenworth, Kansas, which also contains what could rightfully be called an element of political prisoners.

The issue may be the classification of prisoners at the time of their incarceration, but perhaps the issue goes back farther in time than that, to the courts and the judicial statutes that define the nature of offenses and the sentence allowed for a given offense. Prisons are called upon to contain a divergence of offender types without respect to the polarity of offenses. The grass-root-level prison system does not, and perhaps cannot, differentiate between the political versus the nonpolitical, the vicious versus the nonvicious, the professional versus the nonprofessional offender. The unpublished rule of thumb is to base intraprison placements on the degree of manageability of the offender rather than on any other known factor. Although it must be recognized that the prison subculture will develop its own in-groups, the inmate categorization of peers is based on a variety of factors not officially included in the prison classification manual.

Certainly it must be acknowledged that the Federal Bureau of Prisons is better funded than most state systems to facilitate its progressive image. Yet the convicted felon who resides at the lower level of the spectrum will not reconcile himself to the fact that the greater the crime, as to jurisdiction, the better the services at the institutional level. It is suspected that the social scientists who study the contributing factors to prison riots and upheavals fail to take into account political factors. It may very well be that one of the primary and causative agents has to do with unseen political implications that go undetected and unrecognized by those who search for the reason why.

Most political prisoners—draft dodgers, conscientious objectors, politicians who acted improperly—are nonviolent prisoners. Perhaps this should be qualified to read that the offense that resulted in their conviction and subsequent imprisonment was not a particularly vicious act, although such offenses have a tendency to rub society's conscience raw. The degree of conformity of the political prisoner may differ little from that of his prison peers except that there exists the tendency of such prisoners to form their own in-group and have little association beyond what is necessary with the balance of the population. For a revealing insight into this perspective, the reader should acquaint himself with the book by Howard Levy and David Miller.[14]

Based on the prison caste system, political prisoners have little in common with other offenders beyond the dislike of the system and their perception of the inequality of justice in general. It is believed by this author that their value system and self-applied standards may differ widely from their peers, although there is little by way of published research to either support or to refute such a theory. Few such offenders could be characterized as anything other than passive resistors or passive manipulators who have adhered to a set of values that have, unfortunately for them, been out of step with the expectations demanded by society and their mother country. The balance of political prisoners seems to be comprised of a group of scoundrels who saw fit to abuse the privileges of public office and position in which they served. Philosophically speaking, is it any greater or less of an offense to bilk the public in an open manner than to offend behind the guise of obscurity and stealth? If to no one else other than the convicted, the difference is somehow significant.

A further theory of political prisoners is advanced by Robert Chrisman in a 1971 issue of *The Black Scholar*.[15] Chrisman suggests that black prisoners may conceive of themselves as discriminated against on the premise that their condition is an outgrowth of the political inequality of the black people in America. Although this author makes no attempt to refute

---

[14]Howard Levy and David Miller, *Going to Jail: The Political Prisoners* (New York: Grove Press, Inc., n.d.).

[15]Robert Chrisman, "Black Prisoners, White Law," *The Black Scholar* (April-May 1971), pp. 44–46.

this thesis of Mr. Chrisman, it is, at this point in time, difficult to ascertain to just what degree these feelings have been internalized by blacks, whether in custody or within society. Although there is no doubt that blacks as well as other minority groups have found many doors of progress and opportunity closed to them, it is difficult to accept the blanket implication that deprivation of many blacks should account for social retaliation by a few blacks.

It seems probable that the fear of mob violence may be a partial answer to prison administrators' restrictions of any prison movements or the formulation of groups focusing on ethnic identity. If correctional officials are fearful of negative inmate behavior, it can be understood why total dehumanization of the prison population continues. While acts of defiance against the staff and prison administration will continue, such behavior can better be contained if it is not allowed to be practiced by collective groups. Such action is sufficient grounds in the eyes of prison administrative personnel for penal suppression of any inmate organization.

A final characteristic of the new breed of prisoners is the fact that they are often better educated and perhaps possessed of a greater native intelligence than their predecessors. The implications related to this revelation are several in nature. First of all, the prison program of work of a drudgery nature is no longer sufficient to sustain and control the new breed. A weary body does not necessarily imply a mind that has been dulled by rote tasks. If rehabilitation means training, then these inmates are wasting their time as well as that of the prison staff by being subjected to the meager menu offered under the guise of institutional training and education. It is not unusual for some inmates to be possessed of the ability to devise and teach classes of equal if not more meaningful content than those devised by the staff.

Second, if rehabilitation is treatment-oriented, how does a therapist deal and perhaps prepare an inmate for release when the latter will in all probability go out into a position with qualifications and monetary expectations that the therapist will never achieve? The author cannot conceive of many instances where true help can be offered, let alone be needed under such circumstances as these. Certain offenders have had sufficient prior-to-commitment connections that will enable them to go directly into job situations without ever having to drink from the bitter cup of unemployment. Neither has their imprisonment been that difficult to tolerate beyond a mere annoyance such as a horse might experience from a swarm of flies. Their basic problem has been one of lost time and opportunities, but because of outside influence or associations, these losses are a relatively easy matter to overcome upon release.

Third, the prisoners of today are finding new ways to combat and challenge the system. Instead of a lone inmate against the world, there have been attempts among prisoners to organize themselves into unions. This is no small task to be expected of a dull and burned-out con who has never known how to organize himself, let alone others. The new breed seems better equipped emotionally and intellectually to find a variety of ethical and legal methods for testing their restraints. Organizations such as the American Civil Liberties Union (A.C.L.U.), as well as a variety of court precedents that have served to further the cause, have provided greater opportunities to prison inmates to not only cope with but to overcome the hardships of penal servitude.

Penal administrators who have noticed the variation among the new prisoners apparently have chosen to ignore such changes in the hope that such behavior will simply go away. They continue to indiscriminately lump inmates together without much rationale for their random placements. Too many administrators continue to cling to the old penal concept of dehumanization and erroneously hope that time, concrete walls, and steel bars will enhance conformity and anonymity within the prison population. It is suggested that such administrative behavioral traits may be a contributing cause to prison riots. Yet we must admit that the increasing commitment rate of offenders to penal institutions may be offered as a partial excuse for the failure to classify and place the new inmate appropriately within the system.

Prison riots are often attributed to several key factors: inequalities beyond reason, basic deprivation of human rights, inadequate facilities and programs, and unfair administrative practices, including the lack of opportunity for parole. Time and space do not allow for a thorough discussion of prisoner behavior violently directed against the system as well as against peers—behavior based on sheer frustration, frustration arising out of a seemingly hopeless situation and general public apathy. One cause has been repeatedly referred to in this section, the failure of prisons to be able to provide an amalgamation of elements of security and *amelioration* (our suggestion as an alternative to the word *rehabilitation*) on one hand and meaningful and productive use of time being served devoid of basic deprivations on the other.

Another cause of riots is that model sentencing acts have little, if anything, to do with the inequalities of different prison systems. Despite attempts to police and enforce penal standards, inequalities will continue to exist if for no other reason than that the internal dynamics of the prison structure are hidden from the public eye as well as from other agencies who should have some knowledge as to what transpires within. Likewise, the grass will always look—and may sometimes be—greener on the other side of not only the immediate wall, but within the walls of other institutions, from the inmate's perspective. Until there is equality of standards for comparable crimes and offenders, unrest and violence may have a common cause to exist. Obviously the change made or need fulfilled will never fully serve to appease offenders in custody, for to acquiesce would be viewed as "giving in" to the system.

In summary, it must be acknowledged that penal institutions exist for two basic reasons—punishment of the offender and the protection of society. From a rather callous standpoint, whatever else may occur—job training, therapy, etc., within the time span of the sentence and the walls and cell blocks—may be conceived of as a bonus of sorts. Although it never should be suggested that this is the way it ought to be, this is too often the way it has been. We can conclude this chapter by saying if there are more meaningful alternatives, then we owe it not only to the offender but to society to explore them.

SUGGESTED READINGS

ACTON H. B. et al., *Punishment: For and Against*. New York: Hart Publishing Company, Inc., 1971.

BLACK, CHARLES L., JR., *Capital Punishment: The Inevitability of Caprice and Mistake*. New York: W. W. Norton & Co., Inc., 1974.

CARTER ROBERT M., DANIEL GLASER, AND LESLIE T. WILKINS, *Correctional Institutions*. Philadelphia: J. B. Lippincott Company, 1972.

CLEMMER, DONALD, *The Prison Community*. New York: Holt, Rinehart & Winston, 1958.

GOLDFARB, RONALD L. *Jails: The Ultimate Ghetto of the Criminal Justice System*. Garden City, N.Y.: Anchor Books/Doubleday Co., Inc., 1975.

————, AND LINDA R. SINGER, *After Conviction*. New York: Simon & Shuster/Gulf & Western Corp., 1973.

GRUPP, STANLEY E. ed., *Theories of Punishment,* Bloomington, Ind.: Indiana University Press, 1971.

HARDY, RICHARD, AND JOHN G. CULL, *Introduction to Correctional Rehabilitation*. Springfield, Ill.: Charles C Thomas, Publisher, 1973.

HARRIS, JANET, *Crises in Corrections: The Prison Problem*. McGraw-Hill Book Company, 1973.

HAWKINS, GORDON, *The Prison: Policy and Practice*. Chicago: University of Chicago Press, 1976.

HEFFERNAN, ESTER, *Making It in Prison*. New York: John Wiley & Sons, Inc., 1972.

KEVE, PAUL, *Prison Life and Human Worth*. Minneapolis, Minn.: University of Minnesota Press, 1974.

OHLIN, LLOYD E. ed., *Prisoners in America.* Englewood Cliffs, N.J.: Prentice-Hall, Inc., 1973.

ROBERTS, ALBERT ed., *Correctional Treatment of the Offender.* Springfield, Ill.: Charles C Thomas, Publisher, 1974.

SCOTT, EDWARD M. *Criminal Rehabilitation. . .Within and Without the Walls.* Springfield, Ill.: Charles C Thomas, Publisher, 1973.

VON DER HAAG, EDWARD, *Punishing Criminals.* New York: Basic Books, Inc., Publishers, 1975.

VEDDER, CLYDE B., AND BARBARA A. KAY, eds., *Penology: A Realistic Approach.* Springfield, Ill.: Charles C Thomas, Publisher, 1964.

WALKER, PETER N., *Punishment: An Illustrated History.* New York: Arco Publishing Co., Inc., 1973.

9

Supervising the Offender

One of the basic premises that permeates this text is the theory that criminal behavior may be attributed, in part, to what is felt to be irresponsibility and a closely-related indifference to the rights of others by the offender. The counter-measures designed to restructure and redevelop the value system of the offender are called the "accountability factor."

Perhaps one of the most pertinent examples of the lack of accountability has often been heard to be expressed by a parent(s) of juveniles, whose children have come to the attention of the courts due to their delinquent activities. Many a parent has expressed that their child does not have any common interests in the family value system and often expresses outright defiance to normal demands. It is not unusual for these parents to admit they know nothing of their child's interests, friends, activities and, often times, even their whereabouts. A failure to maintain such knowledge is to foster irresponsibility.

It might be speculated that this breakdown is of longstanding nature and could perhaps be related to the failure to establish and/or to transmit a value system with established expectations between family members. More likely is the fact that there probably has long existed a failure within the family to confront nonconformity. A lack of overall accountability for deviant behavior and a general irresponsibility on the part of the offender toward an established value system (that continues to be ignored until no longer retractable) are two of the more common contributors to delinquent and criminal behavior.

Accountability is a major factor in the supervision of offenders. Such a reconditioning process must be honed to a fine edge if any sort of rehabilitation—as it is popularly conceived of—is to be attempted. Not only are there intersecting lines of mutual responsibility between the offender and his supervising probation/parole officer, there are varying levels of intensity based on motivational factors, expectation, and the personalities of the parties involved in this relationship.

THE LEGAL SIGNIFICANCE FOR SUPERVISION

It must remain foremost in the minds of our readers that supervision of the offender has its origins within the framework of the law. Certainly this bit of information has not been lost on the offender! The correctional system has developed into a structure that absorbs the initial thrust or crime of the offender and then processes that violator through a series of functional levels designed to deter further such behavior. Only the names, faces, judicial levels, and degrees of intensity differ within the system. Although supervision must be sufficiently flexible, based on the perceived needs of the offender, the constant and unchanging factor is that of the purpose of supervision to foster accountability. The law provides for the general format and terms of supervision, for the time element or duration, and for the mechanical processes providing for termination and revocation. It also provides a blank check of sorts, so that program adaptation can be tailored to meet the needs of the offender, the staff, and the agency of service.

At this point we would like to emphasize again that probation and parole are privileges, *not* rights. The judicial process giveth and the judicial process taketh away. Although "blessed" may not be its name, necessity and unequivocalness are its functions. We have stated that the law does not provide the opportunity of probation and parole for all offenders. The primary deciding factor as to who shall be privileged depends on two kinds of traits— social and legal. This does not represent a conflict because we have never rationally and practically been able to distinguish between the legal and social factors of the law. History and Chapter Three of this book should have made this clear, and perhaps such bedfellows should never be separated.

One of the dilemmas of the judicial process is the inability to strike an impartial pose between legal and social obligations when considering an offender for a status of being either supervised or incarcerated. The ineffectiveness of corrections in general and of supervision in particular represents both an inability and a lack of opportunity to achieve a balance between the legal and social factors. Therefore, the close association between these twin aspects may be viewed as both a curse and a blessing. Certainly there exist some serious offenders not legally eligible for probation who, from a psychosocial standpoint, might respond better to supervision than lesser offenders whose prognoses for change are far more dismal and who are unlikely to benefit from probation or parole supervision.

The hope for legislative change in the area of probation/parole eligibility seems to be diminishing in the swing away from even considering any alteration of the laws relative to eligibility. Perhaps we have become embittered by recidivism rates and built-in weaknesses of the system. We have noted the trend to try and sentence certain juveniles as adults based on the viciousness of their delinquent acts. We have also uncovered the habitual criminal sentence. The state of Colorado, for example, recently put into practice a law whereby habitual traffic offenders may be sentenced to the state reformatory.[1] All signs are pointing in the direction of more punitive legal action rather than a modification of the existing system by reviewing the rehabilitation potential of "first-time" offenders who have been committed on the basis of a Class I, II, or III felony.

Legal accountability during the supervision process is the construction of a paper prison. One might facetiously wonder how loud the disgruntled taxpayers of this nation would wail if they knew how much our various levels of government were spending on carbon paper and typewriter ribbons during any given fiscal year. Quite probably, more time is spent by probation and parole officers writing up reports and contact recordings than is ever consumed in a one-to-one, primary face-to-face relationship with the offender/client.

Much supervision of the offender is on paper; the offender is carried "administratively" in a case folder. Part of the fault for the origin of this practice is the lack of measuring tools to determine success. In Chapter 13 we will treat this subject in greater detail. Were half the battles, in actuality, won, budgets balanced, and offenders rehabilitated as are conceived of on paper, the world would be a most beautiful and comfortable place in which to live. The point is that supervision accountability suffers from the need for legal documentation and case recording, occupations that demand a minimum of 60% of the probation/parole officer's time. Transference rarely takes place between a case folder and a client alone.

Although we may have difficulty in divorcing social and legal responsibility, for the sake of understanding our discussion demands we try. Most authorities in the field of corrections have, sooner or later, narrowed the primary duties of supervision in probation and parole down to two major functions: (1) surveillance and (2) rehabilitation. If there is indeed any feasible way of separating legal and social functions, surveillance and rehabilitation provides a probable distinction.

[1]Part Two of Article Two of Title 42, C.R.S., 1973, "Habitual Offenders."

Surveillance

Surveillance bears negative connotations; at least it has the implication of the need to keep one's guard up against evil or threatening forces. Within the context of this book, surveillance must comprise the head of the legal thrust of supervision. Certainly it seems semantically appropriate if nothing else. Legally, you cannot order an individual to be good, for the legislation of morals has been proven to be ineffective. Standards may be set in the form of laws, and adherence to them upheld legally, but this is about the extent that one can hope for.

One of the major issues is whether surveillance (discipline/control) and rehabilitation (treatment/helping services) are able to function along side one another in a state of harmony. It is contended that these are divergent factors that detract from each other, thereby undermining supervision effectiveness. The argument continues to rage. On one hand, Norman Fenton cites the experiences in various California institutions that the roles of counselor and authoritarian do not conflict to the point of any diminishing effectiveness.[2] On the other hand, Louis Tomaino, writing in a recent issue of *Federal Probation*, claims that openness and firmness can be achieved but that usually one or the other will be utilized almost to the mutual exclusion of the other.[3] And Vernon Fox maintains that the most important aspect of supervision is help, not control.[4]

The author, although admitting the temptation to hide behind the comprehensiveness of the eclectic viewpoint, maintains that effectiveness in supervision depends on two techniques: (1) to tailor the approach on a need basis and (2) to be able to structure the relationship from the very beginning, so that there is a mutual understanding of relationships and respective roles. If there is general agreement and understanding of the functional relationship, some of the rough edges can be immediately smoothed down.

We recognized early in this book that probation/parole officers must wear a variety of hats. In all probability, it may be more uncomfortable for them to do so than it is for the offender to accept this as a fact. I can recall more than one instance when, as a residential counselor and member of the discipline committee, I had to punish delinquent adolescents for behavior that the subjects had earlier said was going to happen. The philosophical question remains as to whether or not this constitutes a betrayal of trust. In

[2]Norman Fenton, *An Introduction to Group Counseling in Correctional Service* (College Park, Md.: American Correctional Association, 1957), p. 127.

[3]Louis Tomaino, "The Five Faces of Probation," *Federal Probation,* 39, no. 4 (December 1975), 42–45.

[4]Vernon Fox, *Introduction to Corrections* (Englewood Cliffs, N.J.: Prentice-Hall, Inc., 1972), p. 111.

my opinion, it does not. If the probation/parole officer has carefully structured the role relationship in advance, the betrayal, if any, is that of the offender's own choosing.

Certainly we, as parents, love our children. It would be foolish, however, to assume that we would lose our children's love and respect if we corrected them when corretion was needed. Certainly children know when they have been wrong, and they fully expect consequences for their act if caught. Obviously the offender is well aware of the freedom of choice and also expects the reward and punishment system that results from his choice of behavior.

Punishment, like criticism, should have a constructive quality inherent in its makeup. In probation/parole, the supervising agent must make an individual decision as to how he wishes to handle corrective action. He may decide that the behavior of the client can only be rectified by gestures of force and threats, thereby putting the sole responsibility for change on the shoulders of the offender. Or he may choose the alternative of a more positive nature whereby weaknesses and shortcomings are pointed out and alternatives are discussed. This is the positive thrust of supervision, a mutual attempt to alter behavior. There is always the possibility of an honest mistake, and the test to determine whether an error was deliberate or unintentional may be made by evaluating the offender's ability to profit and to learn from experience.

The concept of surveillance may have negative connotations to those under supervision. To the embittered parolee, it may carry the implication that he cannot be trusted. He has the feeling that he has paid his debts and his social credit rating should now be restored. To have to continue under the baleful and perhaps untrusting gaze of another individual does little for his own image. The parolee may feel himself to be less of a man, that he is still under the gun. Legally, he still is to be held accountable, for he is merely serving out the balance of his sentence within the community, and he must understand this as a fact of life.

The first job of the parole officer is to convey the significance of purpose and relationship. Most offenders coming out of a penal institution are conditioned to distrust authority figures. Therefore, the only way a helping relationship can be positive and beneficial, regardless of the context, is through the immediate establishment of a common bond and a mutual interest or concern. When all the cards are placed on the table, there is less need to wonder and suspect what your opponent may have hidden up his sleeve.

Perhaps surveillance could be the role of the police and other law enforcement personnel. This makes sense on the premise that this is a role that law enforcement personnel are equipped to handle. The issue, however, is what the local police might construe to be surveillance. If they approach the situation from the standpoint of flaunting authority, they may be harassing more than they are helping. There may be little trust between the offender and law enforcement personnel. To "bird-dog" the offender unnecessarily may only serve to precipitate the internalization process and to make the offender less susceptible to treatment and rehabilitation services.

Ideally, police may report to the probation/parole officer their knowledge of the activities of the offender, especially when his behavior is either inappropriate or undesirable. The ultimate coup de grace, however, should be the duty of the specific agency designed for this purpose. The police or other local law enforcement officers should function primarily as informants rather than prosecutors. This is a sometimes difficult, but essential, balance to achieve. If the offender is to learn to respect the written law, he must also learn to respect the symbolism representing that law, i.e., police-type personnel.

Surveillance also contains some legal connotations that may go unnoticed by the average lay person. We speak specifically of the obligation the probation/parole officer has to the public. The reader as well as the professional would do well to acquaint himself with a recent article by Judd D. Kutcher.[5] The gist of Mr. Kutcher's commentary is that probation/parole officers are liable to, and are open for, legal action if they conceal certain characteristics of offenders from the public. Two areas are of special significance—the need to provide stringent supervision with potentially dangerous offenders, and the need to share with potential employers the risks involved in hiring those offenders. No conscientious supervisor of probationers or parolees is knowingly going to place a sexual offender, for example, in a position working with infirm geriatric patients. To do so would leave him (the supervisor) open for legal repercussions under general tort law. The implication is that intense supervision must be applied when dealing with offenders who have shown either the propensity for, or have been convicted of, certain acts that could jeopardize the safety of others with whom they might have some form of social intercourse.

There is a very strong divergence of opinion as to exactly what information about the offenders should be revealed and to whom. Perhaps this represents more of a moral than a legal issue, but it nevertheless seems appropriate to be brought to the reader's attention at this point in time. It might be presumed that the mutual sharing of information about offenders on probation or parole might be part of the supervision function. However, there seems to be no clear-cut and consistent approach. Certainly there is no known legal precedent requiring the exchange of such information other than as already noted. Apparently this function is left to the discretion of the individual supervisor and/or agency policy. From the practical stand-

⁵Judd D. Kutcher, "The Legal Responsibility of Probation Officers in Supervision," *Federal Probation,* 31, no. 1 (March 1977), 35–38.

point, the rule-of-thumb appears to be that only that information is shared that will allow agencies or individuals the knowledge needed to participate in the surveillance or treatment function. An example is given below.

The parent agency of the author tries to restrict prostitutes from frequenting certain areas or bars. In attempting to enforce this restriction, the police department is asked to maintain surveillance to determine the presence of probationers frequenting the marketplace where such wares as they have to offer are commonly for sale. This surveillance is not conceived of as harassment, certainly not when a specific condition of probation forbids their presence in these areas. It is my belief that if the prostitutes want to break away from the subsystem and the pimps who control it, they have a far better chance to do so if they can change environments and behavioral patterns. Such surveillance by the police also helps probation officers gauge their clients' level of motivation and conformity for purposes of evaluating change.

One further facet of supervision has legal origins, that is, the degree of intensity of surveillance. Parole departments have well-established legal precedents and nomenclature for levels of supervision. These levels range from intense to moderate to minimal in nature. Quite often, the level of supervision for a given offender coming out of prison may be decided on by the parole board prior to his release. William Hogan emphasized the need for certain forms of intense surveillance with organized crime figures as an example.[6] The supervising agency generally has the option, however, to increase or to decrease the level of supervision demanded, based on the adjustment or the lack of conformity of the offender.

Rehabilitation

The previous section discussed surveillance, or control, as one major function of supervision. In this section we will discuss rehabilitation, the other major function of supervision. The rehabilitation function of supervision is the helping process, sometimes conceived of as being at the opposite end of the continuum from control. However, this is an erroneous assumption, and before going any further in our discussion, the idea of incompatibility between the two functions of control and rehabilitation should be dispelled. There is no reason to accept the thinking that these two components cannot mesh and work together for the benefit of the offender.

Let us consider the plight of the irresponsible offender. Irresponsibility is not synonymous with pathology in the sense of being "sick." The characteristic of irresponsibility may well be the end product of a cultural conditioning process to which the offender has been subjected since birth. For example, perhaps the father of the offender rarely worked and preferred to

[6]William T. Hogan, "Sentencing and Supervision of Organized Crime Figures," *Federal Probation*, 40, no. 1 (March 1976), 21–24.

subsist on unemployment or public assistance, and the mother never did the dishes until there were no more clean ones left. The family dictum was, "Slide by and get away with all you can." Such an upbringing would certainly condition a client to irresponsibility. Control is an excellent counteragent to irresponsibility and it is a treatment tool worthy of consideration. The mere forcing of the irresponsible offender to meet certain probation/parole obligations is teaching him a form of accountability. Thus, responsibility and accountability are compatible concepts.

Alcoholics Anonymous is a second example peculiar to this situation. It achieves much of its effectiveness through group control. When a member feels the need to drink, he needs only to call a fellow member who will talk him through his crisis. By exercising self-control and by constantly confronting one's self with the fact that one is powerless over alcohol, members are able to retain their sobriety. Control from without, as given in both of these examples, fosters the growth of control from within.

The issue to be discussed here revolves around what constitutes rehabilitation. Is it treatment? Is it crisis intervention? Or is it an attempt to meet the perceived needs of the client/offender? Frankly, it is all of these and much more. Earlier in this chapter we spoke of the need to structure the supervisor/offender relationship at the onset. Once common understandings are communicated and roles are defined, there is less need for distrust to exist. The most essential ingredient in the helping profession is not a defined need but a mutual trust. This is one of the responsibilities the probation/parole officer has to his clients, to establish a feeling of mutual trust.

Although there continues to exist the need for directive counseling under certain limited circumstances, the rehabilitation process can never be dictatorial in nature if it is to be effective. To demand may ensure a degree of conformity, but it allows no contemplation for insight purposes. There is no mutual interaction; there is no attempt to help, only to demand. We could call this, with gratitude to Al Capp and Li'l Abner, the General Bullmoose syndrome. Bullmoose's stand was that what was good for General Bullmoose was good for the world. When the probation/parole supervisor takes this sort of stand, communication and interaction are thwarted, "I say you are sick and I know you are sick because I am your supervisor and you are nothing but an offender." Although never stated quite this way, the implications are there and certainly the resentments. What happened to the needed element of trust? It just rolled over and died a painful death.

We must, at this point, return again to giving consideration to what constitutes the rehabilitation process. In doing research for this book and in giving considerable thought as to what messages are important, I repeatedly ran across the assumption that supervision has to have a treatment component; that is, to help the offender to become a worthwhile citizen, he must have insight into his problems and the resultant effect on his behavior. I rebel at this. The basic fact is that the offender got caught and convicted, and he is now on a status of supervision. Why belabor the point? The intellectual battle of searching for dynamic and illustrative factors to justify *why* is akin to a car stuck in the sand. The faster the motor is gunned, the deeper the car digs in.

The whole point of the helping process in supervision is to simply isolate basic needs for a common purpose and mobilize the maximum extent of resources required to assist in alleviating the points of concern and achieving the goals that have been mutually identified and agreed upon.

In the elusive search for causative factors of criminal behavior, one fact seems to stand out; that is, to the question *Why*, the stupidity of choice and of action of the offender is the most consistent and prevailing answer. From this statement we can intellectualize and easily deduce that this is oversimplification in its simplest form. Yet it may be a realistic point at which to begin. In fifteen or more years in this business I have yet to meet a probation or parole officer who was qualified to enter into a psychoanalytical search for factors in the unconsciousness of offenders, factors that have been repressed for twenty years. Neither have I met an officer who had the time, let alone the ability, to begin the march on latent trauma. Furthermore, most of the offenders I have dealt with have been so culturally deprived that they are totally unable to mobilize sufficient understanding to help in such a search.

The discussion of treatment modalities and related theories can only be pertinent as they are reality-oriented. Idealism and reality in probation/parole services are often far apart, and the greatest part of this gap exists in the area of intensive treatment services. Idealism suggests some form of casework/counseling services on a one-to-one relationship as a crucial factor in the offender rehabilitation process. It has been suggested that the maximum number of clients that should be carried by any individual officer should not exceed 35 cases.[7] This is an idealistic number; in reality many officers have a caseload of two, three, and sometimes four times that number. Intake and administrative duties can stretch the demands even further and limit the level of services even more.

Plan of Action for Probation/Parole Intervention

What follows is a chronology of sorts establishing a feasible and workable plan that has merit based on experience and necessity.

Clarification of Roles: The offender should be assisted in understanding what is expected of him. One way of doing this is the mutual discussion

[7]Report by the President's Commission on Law Enforcement and Administration of Justice, *The Challenge of Crime in a Free Society* (New York: E.P. Dutton, 1968), p. 402.

of the rules and stipulations of the probation orders or parole agreement. It is a good idea for the supervisor to elicit responses from the offender as to the latter's general reaction to those demands and especially whether or not he feels he may have problems or difficulties meeting those obligations. We refer here specifically to the somewhat routine and common contingencies that most orders contain. Included are requirements such as no law violations, reporting changes of address/telephone/employment, not leaving the jurisdiction without permission, maintaining good character, and so forth.

As an outgrowth of this discussion, two important factors have been established. First, there is the implication that the relationship can be both a give-and-take process. The attempt to evoke the thoughts of the offender at the very beginning of the interview should imply that his feelings and reactions are both important and acceptable. It deliberately conveys the desired impression that the thoughts of the offender are not to be restricted; rather they are an important part of the supervision process.

Second, there is the implication that the supervisor is willing to offer comments and explanations as well as to accept them. If handled properly, this should be a prelude to conveying the idea that probation/parole officers are willing to help if and when assistance is desired. Perhaps a hidden purpose also exists, the fact that the relationship is starting off without a display of power and authority. In short, conditions are being considered and evaluated, not merely demanded. Again the trust fact is being cultivated.

Definition of Relationships: The definition of relationships gives understanding to the mutual roles in the supervision alliance. In many ways, it becomes a matter of setting limits, limits that may, but need not, have some initial negative connotations. To avoid unpleasantries, the content of the interview might be structured along the lines of the supervisor discussing accountability. He should temper this by expressing the fact that he wants to be reasonable as well as helpful, but that he is not going to tolerate excessive abuses on the premise that he is a "nice guy." The legal ramifications of supervision would be an appropriate item to discuss, such as the rights of the offender, the obligations of the supervisor, and the positive as well as negative consequences of compliance or noncompliance with the condition of probation or parole.

It has been found from experience that much of what the offender thinks he knows about his newly acquired status has been acquired through street conversations. He may be filled with doubts as well as myths as to what he can or cannot do. Many such uncertainties center around the offender's civil rights, and it therefore behooves the supervisor to be knowledgeable in this area. If issues arise for which the supervisor has no immediate answer, no harm is done by saying, "I don't know, but I'll sure find out." The very admission that we are not perfect will foster better rapport with the offender.

Setting the Contract: One of the key factors in the supervision relationship is the establishment of a contract by which the probation/parole officer and the offender will work. Its very importance is exemplified by the variety of elements that it contains, some of which are only implied.

A. *It establishes a gentlemen's agreement.* The specifics of the relationship are documented and are usually acknowledged by affixing the signatures of both parties to the document. To keep the relationship honest, no changes can be made without the knowledge or the presence of the other and only with an explanation being made for these changes.

B. *It defines special conditions.* Contracts should be individualized as much as possible. If it is determined that the offender has some needs that are peculiar to his situation and that cannot be met or serviced by the supervisor, then this aspect of the program should be defined and designated within the contract.

C. *It allows for mutual goal setting.* Edith Ankersmit states that one of the chief assets in a probation/parole contract is that it exemplifies "the adult-to-adult relationship."[8] The key ingredient is the implication of a "mutual agreement." Unless there is mutual agreement, the chaotic state of a power struggle will readily become apparent. The more the supervisor tries to impose, the greater the offender may try to resist.

Mutuality of purpose is the critical point in the supervision relationship. More cases are lost at this stage than at any other. If there is disagreement, several approaches should be considered.

1. The rationale for the questionable contingency should be discussed in depth.
2. Alternatives should be suggested and explored.
3. The contingency should be tried on an experimental basis for a specified period of time, a period that is normally shorter in duration than the full contract. Further, there should be a mutual review of the results at the completion of the time element.
4. A behavior modification approach should be considered with a reward given for trying. (See next section.) An appropriate type of a reward might be the lessening of the intensity of supervision.
5. An objective third party should be allowed to mediate and weigh the evidence before arriving at a decision. This must be done carefully so as not to undermine the authority of the supervisor nor allow the offender to manipulate the relationship.

Establishing Offender Motivation: Many offenders are guilty of "playing the role" in an attempt to get by. They report when they are supposed to, they provide the necessary facts as demanded, and they disguise their

---

[8]Edith Ankersmit, "Setting the Contract in Probation," *Federal Probation,* 40, no. 2 (June 1976), 30.

hostility and contempt quite effectively. In so doing, they thereby manage to go through their period of supervision untouched and unaltered.

Behavior Modification

The theory behind a program of behavior modification is producing a reward in exchange for a behavioral response. It is a method that has proven somewhat more palatable to certain resistive offenders than most other methods tried. Exhibit I is a form of behavior modification which was built around a contract devised by our court consultant and this author to stimulate motivation of the offender as well as to manipulate (an evil but necessary concept) the offender into programs that were designed to enhance his level of functioning.

One introductory remark should be noted. As a municipal probation department, the maximum period of time an offender can be on probation with the author's agency is one year. Therefore, our computations are tailored around this time element. Further, all of the probationers who agreed to this program did so on a voluntary basis.

We conceived that probation of a year's duration was worth 120 points. For routine reporting (see "black points" in Exhibit II), the probationer was credited at the rate of 10 points a month. This meant that unless the probationer got involved in some mutual goal setting and/or programs, he/she was facing a full year of supervision without any special consideration. The incentive was to seek a way of speeding up the process. The "black points" comprised the first category of point assessment.

The second category of point assessment—negotiated goals—was referred to as the "blue point" area. Each probationer negotiated with us for a meaningful program. The range of goals was virtually unlimited, but each goal had to be declared as possessing a meaningful element. For some, it was a classical therapy, for others it was a project of community service, and for others it meant going back to school or seeking some job skills. For each month of involvement, 10 blue points were given. The desired goal was to shorten a year's probation to a six-month period. This could be achieved by adding 10 blue points and 10 black points for each of six months, totaling the 120 points needed.

We incorporated one other dimension to our program, that of red or minus points. These were deducted on the basis of a predeclared value from the total points, standing for obligations unmet or for new offenses. Once a known deficit level was reached, one of two decisions had to be made: a renegotiation of the contract, or a possible revocation hearing.

The unfortunate part of the project was an inability to research the results. It can be said, however, that only one in the initial group of ten volunteers failed to shorten his probationary period.

Supervision of the offender is somewhat like teaching; you cannot expect

```
┌─────────────────────────────────────────────────────────────────┐
│                          Exhibit 1                               │
│                     Probationary Contract                        │
│ Probationer_____ Court Date_____ Case Number____│
│ That on the date indicated above, the named individual was       │
│ granted probation per order of this Court for a period up to but │
│ not to exceed _____ months. Said period of probation can only be │
│ extended by further formal order of the Court.                   │
│ That the period of probation may be shortened and an early       │
│ release granted on the basis of the fulfillment of negotiated    │
│ goals as stated.                                                 │
│ That points given for either credit or debit purposes will be    │
│ entered on a regular basis and to be computed/entered only in    │
│ the presence of both parties of this contract.                   │
│ That both parties shall acknowledge the assessment of points by  │
│ affixing their initials beside each entry and to do so in the    │
│ presence of each other.                                          │
│ By signing below, each party agrees to the contract and its      │
│ conditions as stated. Further, that no action of any legal       │
│ nature will be initiated unless the Probationer fails to fulfill │
│ either his obligations or unless he is involved in a new offense │
│ sufficiently severe to void his probationary status.             │
│ Signed and agreed to on this the ____ day of _____, 19__│
│                                                                  │
│ _____          _____             │
│ Probation Officer                           Probationer          │
└─────────────────────────────────────────────────────────────────┘
```

any real results unless there is mutual interest, meaningful goals, and interested participation. Behavior modification cannot work for all offenders, any more than can any single program be applied to everyone.

ADDITIONAL ASPECTS OF SUPERVISION

It cannot be expected that the majority of offenders will make it on their own. Some, under the guise of conformity, would have their supervisors believe that everything is satisfactory and that they are experiencing no problems in their adjustment process. Although this is difficult to accept, there is futility in "creating problem areas" in order to offer help. In relation to this, Lawrence Brammer raises a very interesting question when he asks, "Who is the help for—the person or society?"[9]

Our discussion calls for a response to this question, but we will do so with another question of our own. Do we owe allegiance to society in terms of protection or in terms of enlightenment? Many authorities have made reference to the fact that the welfare of society must be considered as an aspect of supervision. Although I am willing to concede this point, I feel that we may be building a road that abruptly ends at a brick wall. Like supervision, the reintegration of the offender back into society demands some mutual concessions on the part of both factions.

Society may have the right to rest comfortably, but it is perhaps too much to expect that probation and parole personnel can guarantee this com-

[9]Lawrence M. Brammer, *The Helping Relationship: Process and Skills* (Englewood Cliffs, N.J.: Prentice-Hall, Inc., 1974), p. 4.

Exhibit II Probationary Contractual Tabulation Sheet								
Routine Reporting (black points)			Negotiated Goals (blue points)			Deficient Area (red points)		
Date Posted	Points Given	Initialed	Goals Declared	Points Given	Initialed	Date Posted	Points Given	Initialed

fort. Neither of these two agencies has any control over intake and caseload. Nor can it be expected that the fleeting minutes that constitute reporting time will ever serve to totally prevent recidivism. There is no easy answer for the correctional system. One end to the other is bursting at the seams in an effort to curtail and deter the offender from reoffending, and preventive medicine has had to take a back seat to more demanding tasks.

Public Relations

Probation and parole may have to take a more comprehensive look at their obligations, especially to the public, and to concentrate some of their efforts on perhaps one of the most pertinent—but far from the easiest—of tasks, public relations. Society must recognize that the offender will eventually return to its midst. Society should also realize that it may have been a contributing factor to the cause of crime, as well as the fact that it has a crucial role to play in offering some meaningful ways of working toward the rehabilitation of the offender. It may be part of the role of probation/parole personnel to have to challenge society on this very matter. If society will not offer the offender a job—not just because he is unqualified, but because he is an offender—then what recourse does the offender have but to strike out against his tormentors again?

Public relations may seem to be somewhat removed from supervision. Yet public relations may help the offender find a job, it may help him secure academic or vocational training, and it might help utilize and foster that essential quality that has been repeatedly referred to as the main ingredient in any wholesome relationship—trust. The issue is not who shall bell the cat or who should make the initial overture, but rather who shall make the needed contribution and provide the grounds for a mutual working relationship. Although law enforcement personnel may be able to enlighten the citizenry in how to deter crime, the specific education of how to live with the offender in their midst is a perceived function of probation/parole personnel.

Crisis Intervention

One of the most positive contributions that parole and/or probation can provide is crisis intervention. A characteristic of many criminals is loss of control in stress situations. The offender who becomes a thief in order to provide for his family in a time of dire need is no less guilty in the eyes of the law. He also is deficit in social skills that might assist him in choosing more appropriate alternatives in coping with that immediate stress.

Fox is of the opinion that most probation/parole officers have little time for much else in their supervision process than for crisis intervention.[10] Gloria Cunningham, writing in *Federal Probation,* echoes this thinking.[11] In the cycle of processing the offender, there may be three distinct times that a crisis occurs: (1) at the time of arrest/detention, (2) during the presentence investigation, and (3) at the time of sentencing—the latter dependent, of course, on the nature of the disposition. This cyclic process is peculiar to probationers at all stages, although not all offenders granted probation are made the subject of a PSI. The parolees' periods of crisis would be similar, but would include two other stages: (1) the time of their commitment to a penal institution and (2) the time of their release on parole.

It is recognized that intervention by probation/parole personnel is not practical at all levels. However, because of the easy accessibility to the city jail, this author was often called in for screening purposes when prisoners were reacting adversely to stress. Most probation officers do not assume this responsibility on an official basis, but this seemed to be a rather appropriate function for this officer at his operational level. Confinement is certainly a stress-producing factor, one that has the tendency to bring out the flaws that exist in certain individuals. Although I was careful never to put myself in a position of acting as an advocate for the offender, I am certain that my presence and my taking the time to talk with the prisoners not only added a new dimension to the management of the jail but also helped alleviate some of the expressed concerns of those being held.

The PSI interview as a screening tool holds a lot of merit and uniqueness. The offender is concerned about what is going to happen to him, and he often is eager to speak about his feelings and problems. This opportunity

[10]Fox, *Introduction to Corrections,* p. 112.

[11]Gloria Cunningham, "Crises Intervention in a Probation Setting," *Federal Probation,* 37, no. 4 (December 1973), 16–25.

represents an ideal time to catch the offender with his guard down. As the anxiety level climbs, the level of inhibition seems to comparatively drop. Much of what is discussed during the interview can be effectively used as a motivational factor, and the stress/inhibition pendulum begins to swing in the other direction. If, for example, the offender makes a remark that every time he gets into difficulty, he can attribute it to drinking, then the interviewing officer has a key that may be used to unlock part of the offender's problem. Drawing out the feelings and concerns of the offender at this time also serves to project the desired helping image.

For example, although the offender may have intended to use alcohol as an excuse for his difficulties, the interviewer has failed in his obligations if he does not follow up on certain specifics, as suggested in the following list of questions.

1. How often do you drink and how long has alcohol been a part of your life?
2. Have you ever been told what you are like or how you act when you have been drinking? Do you become a lover, a fighter, etc.?
3. How does your spouse/parent feel about the trouble you are now in and the eventual court decision?
4. What do you think your spouse's/parent's biggest criticism of you would be?
5. What have you been arrested for before that was either a direct or indirect result of your drinking?
6. Has anyone ever suggested to you that you might have a drinking problem?
7. Have you ever been treated for alcoholism?

The trick is to seize upon those factors that appear to be realistic and that have the tendency to be identified by the offender during this time when his inhibitions are lowered. Sometimes, the interview provides a long-needed chance for the offender to talk about his fears, as he has lacked the initiative to seek help on his own prior to this time. The crisis, then, is the vehicle that helps in getting many of these feelings out in the open, where they can be dealt with for what they are and how they contribute to the dysfunctioning of the offender.

Such information provides meaningful ammunition for program planning. Some basic homework and collateral contacts, especially with the family and others who know the offender, may be sufficient to document the fact that this offender has a probable drinking problem. The author has used such information in a variety of ways to confront the offender.

1. "You are telling me that you aren't really sure if you have a drinking problem. Yet, as a result of too much booze, you have been convicted of

this offense and it is possible that you may end up in jail. Isn't that a problem for you? Can't you see what this drunkenness has done for you and where it puts you? Will you lose your job if you go to jail?''

2.   "You say you don't believe that you are an alcoholic. You tell me you only drink about once a month. If you think that alcoholics are only individuals who drink all the time, you are sadly mistaken about some of the facts of alcoholism. I think if you are any kind of a responsible person, that you owe it to yourself and to your family to find out more about your problem.''

There are many variations to this approach. The object of such comments is to get the offender to admit his concern and then use it as a part of the treatment plan to be sanctioned by the court at the time of disposition.

There is another crucial point when the offender's resistance is sufficiently lowered to make him receptive to program planning. This is at the moment immediately following the disposition and sentencing process. Many offenders will be so grateful and elated over the fact that they were not incarcerated that they are again in a temporarily vulnerable state. The name of the game is to capitalize on this moment of weakness to reinforce the offender's desire to conform and to become involved in a program of rehabilitation. Although such an approach may seem unfair and inhumane, it should be recognized that many offenders are equally manipulative of others when the opportunity presents itself. If they have offended previously but were never apprehended, we can accept the fact that they have been manipulating the property, the person, or the rights of another for their own personal gain. The supervisor is merely fighting fire with fire when he utilizes the crisis state for this purpose.

Many offenders will spend their period of supervision mute in regard to personal problems. They may, however, utilize their supervisor when it is least expected. I once had a mildly mentally retarded young offender on probation whose problems were compounded by the fact that he was a vulnerable homosexual. The problems he presented *au naturel* were generally beyond our immediate reach to alleviate. The only apparent interaction of meaning that took place during the course of supervision was that he seemed to relate to the fact that I was accepting of him despite his shortcomings. In an approximate seven-month period following the termination of his probation, he ushered into my office no less than three different friends who, he said, wanted to commit suicide. All three were sufficiently depressed that their hospitalization was necessary. Although this is not the type of crisis intervention we have been discussing, my former probationer had learned how and when to use help in an appropriate way.

It may be difficult for those of us who have never been "out of circulation" to view parole as a crisis; we would inadvertently look at it as a triumph for the individual. Yet the offender who is coming out of prison after years of incarceration faces two major problems: (1) learning to make routine, independent decisions, and (2) assuming responsibility for himself and his family. Prison has deprived him of the need to do little more than assure self-preservation. His decision making has entailed how to get through the day immediately at hand. And concrete planning represented only wishful thinking about the future. Like death, even knowing that it will eventually get here, preparation for parole can never be completed until the moment of reality is at hand.

To attempt to assess supervision relationships and to be able to evaluate how effectively probationers use this relationship as compared to parolees is a futile gesture. Although the parolee may have less trust for authority, his demands may be greater if he can admit to this. The parolee must start a new life in a new world, whereas the probationer has been able to cling to and retain much of his normal and natural relationships. The tools of shaping the product are essentially the same; only the clay to be used is of a different texture.

TECHNIQUES OF SUPERVISION

While the reporting process is the most commonly utilized technique in supervision of offenders, it is probably the most misused of interviews taking place between clients/offenders and those individuals responsible for conducting these meetings. The following paragraphs will attempt not only to point out some of these abuses and inadequacies but to indicate some of the deficiencies leading to general unproductiveness.

Lack of Purpose and Preparedness

Aside from the time element, which is often inadequate, many probation/ parole officers are both ill-equipped and ill-prepared to use their meetings with their clients effectively. Too often, little transpires because no common bonds or mutual goals have been established. Deprived of such a common denominator, the interview is rarely structured, and respective obligations are undefined. As such, two byproducts are probable: (1) the diminishing level of efficiency of the supervisor and (2) the growing contempt of the offender for the futility and meaninglessness of the system.

A poor client interview may be one opened with an exchange of acknowledgments that are shallow and too often given to covering up basic anxieties and a lack of preparedness. The supervisor probably perpetuates the interview with a sterile statement such as, "Well, what's been happening?" If the offender answers, "Nothing," a stalemate exists. The ineffectual supervisor is immediately deprived of conversation content because he has been solely dependent on the client to provide him with the subject matter to be discussed. Unless the supervisor can overcome this void, there will be a steady deterioration of the interview from that point onward.

Rationalizations for Supervision Inadequacies

Certain supervisors will rationalize about the ineffectiveness of such an exchange by claiming that it is the responsibility of the offender to "unload" and will criticize his general unwillingness to participate. The client, in turn, sees the role of the supervisor as being that of offering guidance or a counseling process, and he therefore sits uncomfortably silent awaiting the words of wisdom and the classical advice that he expects, sooner or later, to be forthcoming. Both parties are thereby mutely blaming the other for a lack of a meaningful relationship, and more nails are driven into the supervision coffin.

Chapter Ten will focus on devices that offenders use to manipulate the supervision relationship. In this chapter we present the problem from the administrative viewpoint. Supervisors, lacking either in skills or foresight, play games too. To justify their contacts with the client, they may resort to a variety of empty and ineffectual techniques during the interview. They may ask a series of rote questions that demand little more than a negative or affirmative response. For example:

1. Are you still living at home?
2. Do you still work for Jones Roofing?
3. What were your school grades like on your last report card?
4. Have you cut down on your drinking?
5. Do you have any problems?

Usually the offender's answers are short, one-syllable responses without elaboration or insight and are uttered with some slight alterations or even distortions so as to avoid any confrontation and or displeasure of the supervisor.

Most probation/parole supervisors are not supporters of the axiom, "Silence is golden." They fail to appreciate their own inadequacies and often interpret the muteness of the offender to be either passive resistance or indifference to responsibility. It must be acknowledged that there are instances where such a response—or a lack of it—may be so diagnosed. It is imperative, however, that probation/parole personnel maintain some cognizance of what they bring to or detract from the supervision/interview process.

Client Domination

There are several common approaches that some of the more inadequate of probation and parole officers use to hide their shortcomings. One of these approaches is client domination, often hidden behind the pretense of "directive counseling." The supervisor operates on the premise that the offender can only be "kept in line" through subjection and fear. The offender must, by this theory, be constantly reminded that he has violated the standards and laws of society, and he is therefore not only to be considered but to be treated as a less-than-responsible person. The fallacy of this approach is obvious.

Client domination will further contribute to the offender's lack of trust in the corrections system. The supervisor must acknowledge that the judgment factor is the primary responsibility of the courts or of a comparable administrative agency for parole authority. Although the supervisor may have doubts about the conformity of the offender, he can only facilitate the return of the offender for revocation consideration; the ultimate authority for judgment lies elsewhere within the legal system. Not all offenders become recidivists because of a lack of trust for the system. However, a suppression of interaction due to a lack of mutual input certainly may overbalance the scales in turning the offender away from a belief in the system of justice.

When there is client domination, whether of an overt or covert source, the offender will be conditioned to suppress his feelings rather than to reveal them. Such a discouragement of his thoughts will serve to dissuade him from revealing problems that need to be resolved. Such offenders will probably never emulate young George Washington who supposedly told his father that he would rather speak the truth at the risk of punishment than to tell a lie. Suppressing truth and one's feelings may be conceived by the offender to cause less trauma than would be the case if such feelings were exposed.

Lastly, domination is often used as a self-protection device. It makes the supervisor look good in the eyes of the public if he has the reputation of a "no-nonsense" type of person. However, what it really means is that the supervisor has been unable to effect a compromise in his priority system. He is uncomfortable unless he can control the supervision process, and he may well feel that such control is threatened if the offender is allowed to openly express his hostilities. Such a supervisor is far more concerned with the reflection of his own public image than he is able to function at the level of service his position demands.

Manipulation

Another important method of supervision is manipulation. Whether this is a negative or positive factor will depend on what and who is being manipulated as well as on the purpose of the manipulation. If the alteration process is being used to belittle or in some other way to demean the offender, then such an attempt is unethical. As a positive approach, we do endeavor, sometimes on a regular basis, to manipulate the offender in an effort to facilitate motivation. Using a variety of tools or a punishment/

reward system, we may entice an offender into a therapy program to which he has had some initial resistance. The hope would be that once he has been in treatment, he will see some benefits from the program and will have a self-imposed desire to continue.

Also, quite often we indirectly manipulate the offender by altering or structuring his immediate environment. Supervisors might attempt to subtly plant seeds of suggestion in receptive and influential ears of those primary associates who share mutual hopes for the offender. Once more, using the example of therapeutic intervention, the spouse might become the ally of the supervisor by suggesting that he or she would feel better about some common problems if he or she could talk to a mental health/marriage/pastoral counselor. Additionally the spouse might suggest that his/her better half go along for support as well as for understanding.

An employer may tell the probation/parole supervisor that an offender/client is a very productive and conscientious worker if he can leave alcohol alone. If the consumption of alcohol was a contributing factor to the offense, then there is a common cause and need between the supervisor and the employer. Entering into an alliance, the employer may indicate to his employee offender that he can only allow the latter to stay on the payroll if he will get some help in the battle against booze. The probation/parole supervisor, in turn, effects a program referral, and a truce of sorts is worked out. The employer has a more consistent worker; the supervisor retains hope that the chances of his client reoffending may be diminished; and the offender discovers the peace of sobriety, as well as having at least two authority persons in his life off his back. Manipulation can therefore be justified if the end does appear to support the means.

Screening/Diagnosis

Supervision also contains a screening/diagnostic dimension. The conscientious probation/parole officer is constantly alert to known or latent problems that might contribute to the dysfunctioning of the offender or that may constitute a roadblock to his rehabilitation. Hindsight, being what it is, would indicate that realistically such a function may be requested of probation personnel, for example, even before a formal supervision status is accorded the offender. Probation officers especially may often be pressed into service at the court's request to make a prefunctory diagnosis of an offender where clinical services are not immediately available. This is not the routine screening/diagnostic function, however, to which we would address our discussion here.

The probation department of the author's court is represented by only one professional staff member. To compensate, we purchase professional counseling and evaluatory services from a local mental health center to complement and supplement department skills. Because of its minimal size, our department has found it necessary to function primarily as a screening and referral service. In light of intake and various administrative duties and other related functions, it is impractical to work directly with a caseload of any consequence. Yet it has become a primary function of this officer to offer certain socio-psychological determinations in order to determine which offenders need more intensive services and what kinds of services might be appropriate to their needs.

The very heart of the matter is reduced to attempting to determine what offenders—in any probation/parole officer's caseload—should be matched with specific services and using selectivity in making appropriate treatment plans. Below is a list of suggested categories.

1. The offender who requires the maximum amount of control and supervision.
2. The offender who requires the minimum amount of supervision.
3. The offender who is attempting to alter his social/legal image for unknown reasons.
4. The offender who needs a program of therapeutic intervention.
5. The offender who could better benefit from one or more educational/remedial programs not characterized as of the clinical variety.
6. The offender who needs a great deal of motivation and support.
7. The offender who requires immediate and drastic crisis intervention.
8. The offender who might work well with a volunteer counselor.
9. The offender who requires physiological treatment as opposed to psychological assistance.
10. The offender who would possibly function better under the supervision of a different officer, i.e., one of a different orientation, ethnic group, or sex.

The maximum level of supervision effectiveness lies in the individual supervisor's ability to recognize his own limitations and how they affect his relationship with his clients. However, most probation/parole officers have little choice in controlling either the size of or the nature of the offenders in their caseload.

The nature of the supervisor's professional training and his ability to transmit and to use it should be determining factors in case assignment. The strength of the agency staff quite probably should be at the intake level. When we speak of intake, we are generally making reference to the subdivision of the agency where the initial screening process takes place, where the presentence investigation is conducted, and where staff assignments are made. In smaller agencies, this may often be the task of an administrative individual, although it cannot be assumed that management and intake/diagnostic skills are synonymous in functional expectations.

Criteria for Case Assignment. Case assignments should be predicated on several key criteria.

1. The perceived or expressed primary needs of the offender.
2. His prognosis for treatment and/or a meaningful relationship.
3. His level of motivation and capacity to respond.
4. The intensity level of supervision required.
5. His degree of pathology if this can be determined.

A second level of criteria might be in order to assist in finalizing the case assignment process.

1. What services are apparently needed that cannot be supplied from within the agency context?
2. Are such perceived services available at the community level and would their use constitute an appropriate referral?
3. Is a clinical diagnostic work-up needed prior to finalizing a treatment program?
4. Is the time element of supervision/presentence investigation adequate to facilitate the program needed?
5. What alternatives exist to meet the recognized inadequacies of the supervision/diagnostic program?

Each of the criteria mentioned above requires some minor explanation to allow for understanding both the purpose and differentiation of material and emphasis.

Perceived or expressed needs: The criterion of perceived needs represents a tentative diagnosis based on either observed, known, or vocalized areas of concern. We speak here specifically not of severe pathology, but rather of specific problem areas such as drugs or alcohol and perhaps less defined areas such as problems in interpersonal relationships.

Prognosis for treatment and/or meaningful relationship: The prognosis is primarily a social barometer for measuring the hostilities and defense mechanisms of the offender. It might be used also to determine the degree of intensity of supervision required to ensure his conformity.

Level of Motivation and Capacity of Response: Although this criterion may appear to differ little from the one immediately preceding it, this one particularly attempts to measure a more subtle process, the level of objectivity of the offender. Also pertinent is the offender's self-perception of his own role in the supervision process.

The Intensity of Supervision Required: The criterion of intensity needed in supervision is a projection of the probability of the offender to respond, but more important, it is a classification of sorts to be used in determining what kind or even which supervisor is most capable of exercising the control required to contain the offender.

Degree of Pathology: Although *pathology* is a rather poor and ill-defined term, the diagnosis here to be made is whether there exist problems peculiar to the client that must be given a high priority and that may or may not be contributing factors to his antisocial behavior.

Definition of Services Needed: The criterion of services needed is a more definitive diagnosis of the specific needs of the offender such as for specialized therapy, specialized processing such as would be pertinent to the mentally retarded, medical problems, etc.

Service Delivery: Are there existent services to meet the identified needs of the client? These might include placement in a foster/group care facility, neurological work-up, and specialized surgical/medical care. Also of concern would be the cost factor and the subsidization for the provision of these services.

Diagnostic Work-Up: The diagnostic work-up means a comprehensive evaluation to include psychological testing and perhaps a psychiatric opinion of the client to allow for an understanding of his needs and behavior.

The last two criteria (numbers 4 and 5 in list of secondary criteria above) would appear to be self-explanatory. Their primary purpose would be the attempt to begin to blend the elements of concern into a package or outline to be proposed either to the court for disposition purposes or to be used as a guideline by the individual probation/parole officer who will be assuming the case.

Staff/Client Relationships: The multifarious qualities of the staff will be a determining factor in case assignment. A good administrator will assign cases on the basis of staff characteristics and abilities.

1. Who is comfortable in the use of authority?
2. Who is treatment-oriented?
3. Who represents a surrogate figure?
4. Who has a better public image/relations approach?
5. Who may better identify from an ethnic/cultural approach?
6. Who is most adept at the mediation process?
7. Who can make an authoritarian approach palatable?

The last category specifically includes those staff members who see the reasons the client rejected former authority figures and who can utilize authority in a subtle new, and acceptable way.

The probation/parole version of the counter adversary function is designed to manipulate the offender into a state of conformity. If, for example, the initial officer handling the case had little success with an offender, a change of supervisors might be considered. The new officer will then tell the client that he (the client) was just about on his way "up/back" to the penitentiary. The only reason this client didn't get sent up is because the new supervisor had been watching him for some time and had positive feelings about him. Rather than see him "busted," the new officer decided to ask for the chance to intercede.

The attempt of the counteradversary drama is to impress upon the client: (1) how negatively his response to supervision has been viewed, (2) the inevitable consequences of such behavior, and (3) that he should show his pleasure at being rescued by conforming on behalf of his newly found savior and friend.

Probation/parole personnel must be aware of their feelings and how clients or circumstances may short-circuit their mutual relationships. We are referring here to two basic elements: (1) the recognition of negative/positive stimuli and (2) the ability to recognize the point at which the officer will either lose his effectiveness or is apt to get in over his head in his ability to manage and work with a given case.

Negative/positive stimuli may be defined as the nature of the response a supervisor has to different offenders. Either extreme may alter the officer/client relationship and minimize its effectiveness. The use of these terms here is to emphasize the dangers inherent in overreacting to the client, for either extreme can be negative as well as positive in nature.

As there are some marriages that are supposedly conceived in heaven, there are a like number that have their origin elsewhere. So it is with the roles and relationships between supervisors and clients. Rare is the probation/parole officer who will react equally and equitably to all clients. Part of his reaction may be conditioned by personal experiences or beliefs, and these will color his responses to the client. Such personal factors include the officer's moral convictions, his cultural background, his ethnic or nationality status, and even his socio-economic state of affairs.

I have known many fellow-officers, for example, who cannot tolerate the sight and behavior of homosexuals, bisexuals, or the transvestite. The reaction of these individuals toward this general sexual class is one of repulsiveness and hostility. If an officer is affected by such feelings, this reaction is bound to permeate the client relationship sooner or later and will quickly be recognized by the offender as a form of rejection and dislike. Several such mismatches are common and might include the moralist and the prostitute or the abstainer and the alcoholic among others. The officer's attempt to suppress such feelings cannot be successful for any prolonged period of time. Sooner or later, the offender will show his recognition for the feelings of his supervisor by acting out in some way designed to hurt or anger the supervisor as a means of retaliation. How tolerable this relationship can be or whether it will develop into a state of open hostility is never fully known in advance, but some trouble can certainly be anticipated. The officer possessed of such a client reaction would do well to endeavor to have the case transferred to another coworker. And even after such a transfer has been effected, the officer should continue to examine his feelings and their source in an attempt to gain some insight into, and control of, his reactions.

There also may be negative overtones in a positive relationship. Every once in awhile a probation/parole officer will receive a case for purposes of supervision that will cause wonderment as to the classification of the client. The client seems too good to be true. He is seemingly motivated, verbal, and extremely conscientious. The desire is to ask, "What is a nice person like you doing in a place like this?" In dealing with this type of client, there may be a tendency to attempt to forget accountability in the process. Although it is impossible to make an all-encompassing observation of such cases, it should be recognized that some offenders use compliance as an excellent defense mechanism.

Such a client as this may require more than the usual amount of working within the contract-setting situation. Too much leniency not only accounts for a lack of insight into his motivation, but it also may be just and sufficient grounds for mutiny among other clients. This is especially true in certain instances such as in group reporting where the offenders have had a chance to compare notes, reactions, and obligations. It is possible that the individual officer will be more upset about his inequalities in handling cases than are the clients. And well he should be, for he is placing himself in a position of manipulation and one that can only complicate supervision standards. Appropriateness of affect in the supervision relationship is a factor that is pertinent to the officer as well as to the client.

Probation/parole officers must constantly be on the alert for cases that are beyond their means to control and work with. We speak of individuals who need some type of crisis intervention. The longer the officer dawdles with the case, the more likelihood of permanent or chronic harm to the client. Resistance is not always what it appears to be. If the offender lacks the ability to respond and appears to be deteriorating by his actions, it may not imply that he does not care. What is likely is that he simply is so besieged by his problems that he cannot view them objectively, let alone be able to mobilize himself to attack them.

Inadequacy of Court Intervention In closing our discussion about supervision, we need to touch on a facet of inadequacy that is directly related to the monitoring process, especially at the level of probation. That is, it is a well-known fact that a high proportion of misdemeanant courts offer no formal probation opportunities and/or no supervision when probation is granted. Although supervision is a legal tool, it becomes useless unless it can be implemented and be made effective at all levels of jurisdiction. Probation may be seen as even more influential at the lower court level because of the emphasis on initial intervention. There is undoubtedly more merit in trying to intervene with offenders at the lower court level than attempting to effect change once a felony offense has been committed.

Supervision is not the sole responsibility of the probation/parole officer. The courts should never choose to ignore the value of supervision merely because of a lack of staff or services within their immediate context. There will always be appropriate programs and concerned individuals within the community who are willing to invest their time and talents to this end. The matter is not who should have the opportunity as much as the fact that intervention must be attempted if there is to be any hoped-for success factor.

SUGGESTED READINGS

ARCAYA, JOSE "The Multiple Realities Inherent in Probation Counseling," Federal Probation, 37, no. 4 (December 1973), 58-63.

CARKHUFF, ROBERT R. *The Art of Helping: An Introduction to Life Styles.* Amherst, Mass.: Human Resource Development Press, 1973.

COMBS, ARTHUR W. DONALD L. AVILA, AND WILLIAM W. PURKEY, *Helping Relationships: Basic Concepts for the Helping Professions.* Boston: Allyn & Bacon, Inc., 1976.

DIANA, L. "What Is Probation?" *Journal of Criminal Law, Criminology, and Police Science,* (1960), pp. 189-204.

FISCHER, C. T. "Rapport as Mutual Respect," *Personnel and Guidance Journal* (1969), pp. 201-204.

GASAWAY, DONALD D. "The Probation Officer as Employment Counselor," *Federal Probation,* 41, no. 2 (June 1977), 43-44.

PEARMAN, JEAN R., *Social Science and Social Work: Application of Social Science in the Helping Profession.* Metuchen, N.J.: The Scarecrow Press, 1973.

YELAHA, SHANKAR A. ed., *Authority and Social Work: Concept & Use.* Toronto: University of Toronto Press, 1971.

10

Games Offenders Play

BEHAVIORAL MOTIVATION

Any effort to guide and direct others in effecting positive change requires some fundamental knowledge of the dynamics of behavioral motivation. It is suggested here that the motivational process has four distinct stages, and when even one is discounted, this weakens the process structure sufficiently to ensure its ineffectiveness. These four stages are described in the following paragraph.

First, motivation must be built on a foundation of a recognized need(s) or on a perceived discomfort that demands alteration. These needs can be classified as being either physiological or psychological in nature, although there is sufficient overlap to make one sometimes indistinguishable from the other. Second, this need or discomfort must create a sufficient amount of tension. The creation of tension serves as the catalyst in the development of a desire to change, i.e., a motivational force. Third, there must be a mobilization of activity to enhance movement toward goal realization. Fourth, there must be goal satisfaction based on achievement or the reduction of the need/discomfort and its subsequent-producing tension.

When attempting to effect a change within the offender, an extra ingredient of manipulation must often be utilized. Probation and parole officers may find that their clients are motivated to change—or to show evidence of attempted change—only as a way of portraying conformity. Therefore, the discomfort the offender is experiencing may become recognizable only as a result of the superimpositions of demands that his supervisor has imposed on him.

THE CONCEPT OF RESISTANCE

The word *resistance* has many meanings, most of which have negative connotations. Were we to conduct a word-association test, some responses to resistance might include *defiance, militancy, opposition,* and *physical contempt.* Such specific responses, however, are reflected only in the social context of the word, and other semantical dimensions should be considered. At least two other qualities must be woven into the definitional fabric—*instinctual responses* and *psychic conditioning.*

Since our definition of resistance as it pertains to this discussion and its eventual integration into the mainstream of the book encompasses various aspects and meanings, we would defer formalizing it for the moment. First, it seems pertinent to examine the social, instinctual, and psychic ingredients that contribute to its overall meaning.

Instinct is difficult to define by itself, for there are both human and animal derivatives that are not cross-accountable. For example, birds migrate and later return to their point of origin. Their routine is so regular at times that some communities can account for their arrival by calendar dates. Salmon fight their way, at the possible loss of life and fin, upstream to spawn at the location of their own conception. These birds and fish are incapable of relating to their behavior on an intellectual level; they are merely responding to some primitive instinct that defies origin. Although their purpose is apparent, the route, time, and knowledge of their destination are generally secreted in biological obscurity.

As a higher order, we, as human beings, react instinctively to the responses of our five senses. For example, we flinch or blink if an unexpected movement in our direction threatens us. We become nauseous when certain odors or flavors offend our senses of smell and taste. We do not consciously repel; we react to an unconscious reflex. Our sensory system trips a silent mental alarm, which then triggers a response to counteract the offensive stimuli. With our reasoning process, we can project that we are reacting to an elementary pleasure/pain process. The concept of pleasure is, in a sense, the avoidance of pain. This functions as a physiological/mechanical process not predicated on a preconscious level of thinking. W.B. Cannon refers to this response as the principle of homeostasis.[1] His theory is that there is the desire on the part of all living matter to attempt, when disturbed, to return to a resting state. All creatures long for and seek a restoration of their initial state of equilibrium.

[1] W. B. Cannon, *The Wisdom of the Body* (New York: W. W. Norton & Co., Inc., 1939).

The common spider is a prime example of this need to return to an initial state of equilibrium. Our furry little friend spends hours creating a web of an intricate design. Then, if one of us human creatures brushes this web, even inadvertently, the delicate fabric is structurally damaged, and the small world's equilibrium is upset from the spider's perspective. The spider will immediately begin to restore its nest to its original and detailed shape, sparing no detail in the process. Just so, will all creatures great and small react to ensure their own equilibrium and the preservation of their respective vested interests.

Psychic factors and our adapted responses to those factors allow us to play all sorts of games with ourselves as well as with others. We deliberately and perhaps regularly take ourselves on little ego trips to heighten our own images. We arise in the morning and behind the locked bathroom door stand somewhat scandalously in front of our mirror, preparing ourselves for the day ahead with some beautification process. As we view ourselves in our respective mirrors, the image that returns our gaze transports us into a microcosm fantasy world. We suck in our guts or fluff our coiffure and become Cinderella in reverse, transformed into creatures of youth, beauty, and virility. We preen like an adolescent getting ready for his or her first serious date, and then we are suddenly retransformed to our old selves when the myth is shattered by another member of the family demanding to know if we intend to make our stay within an all-day affair.

Little harm is done except to those who wait outside our bathroom door. It is when we role play continuously and when we have internalized as well as externalized those roles that the danger flag begins to climb up its flagpole. Good mental hygiene is the ability to adjust to ourselves and to our environment. The inability of some individuals to accept themselves as they are, forces them into making a mental transformation to a fantasy self and a world that they cannot relinquish. These are our mentally ill.

Most of us have escaped the clutches of mental illness and fortunate we are to have done so. Yet we all have our little hang-ups that may periodically result in our being labeled as odd, weird, peculiar, or eccentric. As long as we can slip in and out of these roles like clean underwear, making the required changes as necessary, we shall probably survive.

Resistance arises out of psychic phenomena, when we selectively become dependent on certain forms of defense mechanisms to block out or to reject reality, which—for some reason—we prefer to avoid. All of us rely on certain forms of defense mechanisms on a periodic basis. The fallacy of their use is determined by whether we crawl inside them and hide instead of only utilizing them on a temporary basis for remobilization and regrouping purposes. They become dangerous instruments if we are conditioned to use them instinctively without cognizance of our doing so. To be dependent on them means that we have internalized such mechanisms and have become subordinate to their being able to counteract threatening stimuli. We have therefore repressed normal counteractive methods of coping and have substituted a psychological crutch to bear the weight of our personal trauma.

Social responses to resistance are directly related to our value structure and perhaps to our cultural/ethnic conditioning. Studies of mob psychology, for example, reveal that individuals identify with the mood and the immediate values of the group in responding to stimuli. Although the underlying nature of the challenge to the group may be recognized by a few of its members, most of the group will probably react collectively to the challenge, having temporarily adopted the immediate value structure through a process of association and identification.

Our society currently is showing concern and is appalled about the upheaval of traditional values. There are contemporary reactions to time-honored values and institutions that have us shaking our heads in disgust and frustration. Yet nothing is infinite nor permanent. Change is routine and continuous and only becomes threatening when it begins to impose on customary structures and institutions that we have come to accept as being commonplace within our lives. Neither is resistance a contemporary phenomenon. Each new generation brings new concerns to the older generation as well as evoking new value structures and methods of response.

Resistance has become a cultural commonality. We are facing—and certainly we have faced similar situations in the past—an epidemic of sorts that we will call *cultural paranoia*. This social phenomenon is prevalent among ethnic groups that have found it necessary to counteract inequalities superimposed on them over the years. The idea of "the white man's law" is a counterreaction that attempts not only to strike back but to unify. Cultural paranoia may be conceived of as a form of resistance through the attempt to retain individual cultural/ethnic identities rather than being assimilated into anonymity. We have, then, a cultural/ethnic-originated defense mechanism, one designed to resist further domination by a perceived alien system. The use of "paranoia" in conjunction with such a theory seems properly conceived. Various injustices, domination, and deprivation have caused such groups to fear and distrust any outside influences—irrespective of intent—as a further tool to suppress them, a social form of taxation without representation.

The white/Anglo authority figure who must deal with various ethnic group members will, sooner or later, face this sort of resistance. When he "comes on strong," he exemplifies the culturally inherited belief that such domination is to be expected from the system. If he takes a "soft sell" approach he is conceived of as attempting to manipulate. Such reactions are deliberately labeled as *cultural paranoia* by this author because the revulsion is an instinctive, ingrained, and conditioned response, one that has become—in a manner of speaking—second nature to the individual or groups who feel threatened.

Resistance may be defined, then, as an instinctive, conditioned, or internalized response used to repel what is either unpleasant or threatening from a physical, cultural, or social standpoint to the individual and his life style.

RESISTANCE DURING SUPERVISION

Resistance during the supervision process is an expected fact of life. There may be as many types and reasons for its existence as there are offenders. Each offender may have different methods of coping and dealing with stress. Certainly supervision is a stressful situation for many. Their fear of failure and its possible consequences is a threat, their feeling of helplessness against being manipulated in the supervision process is distasteful, and the supervisor's lack of trust that is either acknowledged or perceived does little to enhance their own feelings of worth.

The resistive offender will always be present in the probation/parole caseload. This premise retains a degree of logic if for no other reason than the offender has already exhibited traits of nonconformity by virtue of having offended. There is every reason to expect some degree of defiance on a one-to-one level of interaction if defiance has been repeatedly shown for the law and the rights of others. After years of interviewing offenders, it has become obvious to the author that a high percentage of clients have difficulty in controlling their anger when speaking of the criminal justice system. Few components escape their criticism, from the law enforcement officer who arrested them down through the courts and the balance of the system. A high proportion of the offender's time and energy is spent expounding on the general injustices of the world and especially on the inadequacies of the law.

Certain offenders never will acknowledge their own involvement in the world of crime. It becomes not a matter of implicating themselves to others as much as it is traumatic to have to accept themselves as being an offender. Self-admission is the final acceptance that their world isn't just a bad dream that will dissipate in the early morning vapors of reality. Likewise, many offenders practice a form of self-denial by not admitting their arrest and conviction to their immediate family. Although some may refrain for fear that the knowledge of disclosure will increase domestic friction, others abstain to enhance their practice of denial. One further fact that may support the use of this particular type of defense mechanism is the possibility of the legal ramifications of a public confession. If appeals of the conviction are projected or pending, the offender may be instructed by his attorney to say nothing that could be used against him.

The moment of truth is not so much determining that there is resistance; rather it lies in the method of helping the offender to deal with it. All resistance is not out in the open and displayed for everyone to see. Quite often the hostility is hidden and it becomes apparent only through a passive form of resistance that may be misconstrued as fear, nervousness, or mere uncomfortableness in the presence of an authority figure. There are mixed emotions as to which form of resistance is most uncomfortable for probation/parole personnel to deal with. On the one side of the ledger, it is not a very desirable situation to have to deal with a person so full of hate and anger that he has lost all traces of objectivity. On the other hand, the supervisor may realize that there is something bothering the too-quiet client, although the nature of the issue is not open for examination, only for speculation.

Much time is wasted by supervisors in their relationships with clients while this initial sparring takes place. One cannot deal with an angry and resistive client until he has gotten rid of all his anger and has spent his energy doing so. The passive/aggressive offender engages the supervisor in a symbolic game of hide-and-go-seek by not revealing any facet of his feelings that can be seized upon and worked with. Depending on which client type the supervisor is dealing with, the supervisor might as well force the issue of feelings initially and get the facts out in the open. The obviously angry offender can be dealt with by merely saying, "You are as hostile and mad as anyone I have ever seen. Tell me why?" We stress this to be the easy way of opening the conversation, but the more difficult part lies in attempting to help the offender regroup his thoughts, so that he can examine the various aspects of his feelings. Anger is not comprised of one single item, but of many. In dealing with open feelings of anger, there are many points along the way where it is necessary to stop and deal with the immediate anger, then start again with the next point of friction on the temper agenda. Most anger is hidden with only the surface visible to the eye.

The passive/aggressive client represents a greater challenge in eliciting his true feelings. He will endeavor to maintain control and composure in the hope that his true feelings will not be discovered. The anger that lies just below the surface cannot be dealt with either by the supervisor or by the offender as long as it remains hidden. There are two basic ways of drawing this anger out in the open. One is to lull the client along paths of noncontroversial discussion in the effort to convey to him your acceptance of him. Then, when it seems most feasible, challenge him and say that you feel he may be holding his true feelings back. A very direct approach is appropriate in keeping with an honest relationship. "John, I am getting the feeling that there are things you would like to say, but which you haven't been able to get out. Why are you holding them back? Are you afraid if you say what you feel that I will not be accepting of them?"

A second, but less diplomatic method, is to deliberately touch, and touch hard, on sensitive areas of the client. In effect, you are challenging him to a showdown of sorts. "John, you have denied to me several times that you have been messing with drugs. So far, I have not challenged you on this, but I feel you are lying not only to me but to yourself and to others. Why do you want to play these games?" Although not an artful approach, the direct confrontation sometimes will work. There is one further step that might be considered, especially if the response falters or is noncommittal. "How do you feel about me calling you a liar, for really that is what I am doing?"

This second, less diplomatic method is not an orthodox treatment approach, and many clinical practitioners would undoubtedly frown on such tactics. However, not many clinicians have had much success in working with the therapy resistive client. Treatment, but more important, communication, cannot be effected as long as there is no reality factor present. If you cannot get the offender to enter into a reciprocal therapeutic relationship, then there is nothing wrong with a direct challenge in a language and manner that leaves no doubt as to what is expected. Whatever kind of a response can be elicited should be dealt with, even if it is a matter of challenging the offender of being a phony and guilty of "copping out" in his responses.

Little seems to exist either in correctional material or in clinical literature about handling the resistive client, especially the one who is in therapy by necessity rather than by choice. Many mental health centers and even psychiatric care institutions fall flat on their respective faces in this respect. One of the major gaps between corrections and the use of mental health services as a treatment resource has been that the latter may make the necessary and initial therapeutic overtures and when no response can be elicited, give up. The offender is labeled either as untreatable or as unmotivated and is then unceremoniously dumped back in the lap of his correctional supervisor.

Many university professors involved in social work programs feel that probation and parole are social work in a correctional atmosphere. These same authorities feel that the primary role of correctional personnel in treatment is to point out to the offender those flaws in his character that can and have contributed to his antisocial behavior. This is fine and appropriate but only under the following conditions:

1. If the offender is mentally competent to enter into and benefit from therapy sessions.
2. If the supervisor is diagnostically certain of his role and the approach that he is taking in dealing with the offender.
3. If the environment and the opportunities to effect change can be manipulated to act as a resource.
4. If there is sufficient treatment time and skills to work on behavioral changes.
5. If the offender is not resistive to treatment.

All of the first four conditions listed above are useless if the fifth condition is apparent. Although the premise of those authorities who advocate treatment is correct as far as it goes, there remain too many offsetting variables to allow such an approach to be a common factor in the supervision process. For example, treatment with resistive offenders is not apt to be productive within the normal caseload and time factor of most probation/ parole officers. Realistically, the supervisors of such cases may have to content themselves with accountability and merely trying to hold such offenders responsible for the bare necessities of their reporting and supervision obligations. What might be useful in these rehabilitative attempts and efforts is dealt with in Chapter 11. We are merely alluding here to some very basic possibilities in an effort to whet the appetites of the reader for a more comprehensive look later on.

THE CLASSICAL DEFENSE MECHANISMS

Many offenders resist treatment/supervision somewhat unknowingly. Over a prolonged period of time, they have developed an excellent network of defense mechanisms that unconsciously provides a buffer against many reality situations. These defense mechanisms may have become so integrated into the offender's personality and unconscious level of coping that he may be unaware of their existence as well as how, and perhaps even when, they are being used.

It might be theorized here that offenders who chronically reoffend are possessed of an overabundance of defense mechanisms, most of which are in good working order. Quite often we make reference to a habitual criminal as being a sociopathic individual or having a sociopathic personality. The characteristics attributed to this type of an individual include: (1) the lack of any kind of social conscience (a greatly diminished lack of any anxiety or guilt feelings), (2) one who manipulates interpersonal relationships without any desire to enter into a meaningful relationship, and (3) a definite lack of any social maturity. Probably more significant but less recognized is the characteristic of a distortion of reality in order to subconsciously justify one's behavior. What is being implied is that the sociopathic individual is nonadaptive to the general value system of society. He is able to insulate himself by adopting and utilizing a variety of defense mechanisms that allow him to internalize his deviant behavior. For example, such individuals might justify thievery by rationalizing that the victim was "asking for it," or "had so much that he wouldn't miss or be hurt by what was taken," or "had acquired it in an unscrupulous manner at the expense of others." A well-functioning defense mechanism will allow the offender, for example, to deny to himself that he is acting in an unscrupulous manner in his efforts to reacquire said property. An offender so conditioned might well perceive himself as a Robin Hood of sorts; the only difference might be that the goods acquired will never part from his own hands unless he can profit from their exchange.

Perhaps the label *sociopathic* is poor in taste and meaning. It is believed that this social diagnosis reflects and is used in conjunction with a stereotyping of individuals whose behavior represents any lack of social feeling for others. The origin of the word *sociopathic* escapes this author, but a breakdown of the syllables gives us some insight into its interpretation. Very roughly, it means inappropriate behavior (*pathic* derived from pathology), which is directed against society (from the abbreviated use indicated by *socio*). Yet, what lies within a name? Not all sociopathic individuals are criminal; neither are all criminals sociopathic. It might be assumed, however, that the individual who lacks any social conscience may have some latent sociopathic tendencies. If he or she sees an opportunity to profit at the expense of others, through his own rationalization process, for example, he may attempt to resort to such behavior, and it will be recognized as criminal in nature.

There is the need to reemphasize a premise attributed to many correctional authorities, that criminal behavior and the criminal mind are related to an inadequate personality structure.[2] Since the use of defense mechanisms is a psychological device that may either shape or be indicative of an inadequate personality, it behooves us at this point to review some of the theories of Freud about the mental structure of the personality.

Freud conceived of the structure of the personality as being divided into three parts—the id, the ego, and the superego. The id is the seat of all basic instinctual drives. Supposedly, it is the first and the oldest of all of the three divisions and is present at the time of the birth of an individual. The ego is the seat of consciousness and the "tester" of reality. Its primary function is to act as a buffer of sorts between the id and the outerworld, a unit of control that regulates or denies the gratifications or the urges/instinctual drives and demands emanating from the id. The superego represents a censorship functionary, which has as its duty the regulation of right and wrong, good and bad. For purposes of clarity, we might call it our conscience, although this is but a rough comparison of psychic components.[3]

We often speak of "ego strengths" and "ego ideals." Such a reference connotes the ability to integrate meaningful social values, and as Pinocchio's little friend Jiminy Cricket would say, "Always let your conscience be your guide." The offender may, then, from a psychoanalytical perspective, have his ego bombarded by adverse stimuli or factors due to the in-

[2]Georg K. Stiirup, "Treating 'Untreatable' Criminals," *Federal Probation*, 36, no. 3 (September 1972), 22-24.

[3]A. A. Brill, ed., *The Basic Writings of Sigmund Freud* (New York: The Modern Library, 1938).

tegration of a perverted set of values. Unless there are sufficient ego strengths, or if the ego functioning breaks down, basic instincts may be gratified without regard to their origin of satisfaction. If hungry, for example, you take what will appease that hunger irrespective of whom you take it from or how. In an effort to further reinforce its role, the ego builds up a series of defense mechanisms to thwart the achievement of gratification through unacceptable methods.

Freud introduced the concept of ego defense in 1894 when he unveiled the idea of repression.[4] He suggested that the initial defense by the ego was in response to instinctual pressures demanding gratification. Although all defense mechanisms are of an unconscious nature, the overindulgence of their use becomes a visible, and therefore conscious, phenomenon to the practiced clinical eye. Defense mechanisms, then, may have a symbiotic quality, meaning that they can become incorporated into the ego and are assimilated to the point of becoming a distinct part of the individual's personality. Rather than remaining at an unconscious level to be used only at appropriate times of ego stress, they become apparent at a conscious level due to their prolonged and repeated use.

It is appropriate at this point to review the classical defense mechanisms as we know them. Each will be described below. There is no doubt that certain forms of these mechanisms are more characteristically used by offenders than others. Our initial purpose here, however, is to reacquaint the reader with their use and to provide a better understanding of how they may be abused to justify certain forms of behavior including criminal activity.

Sublimation

Most clinicians would acknowledge that sublimation is the most appropriate of all defense mechanisms for use in an honest purpose. This defense is a substitute device of sorts that attempts to channel less desirable instinctual drives into a more socially acceptable and approved method of gratification. Rather than a blocking effect with no alternatives, sublimation seeks other appropriate outlets that can be equally well utilized.

Since criminal behavior is, in a sense, pathological behavior, it would be expected that this defense mechanism is not a commonly used psychological tool. The offender can easily be conceived of as desiring immediate gratification. Instead of finding a legitimate way of financing a car he wants and being able to wait to obtain it by a sanctioned method, he gives in to his instinctual drives and achieves immediate gratification by stealing a vehicle. He might, however, substitute an alternative such as the theft of other articles that can be used in bartering for the car. The assumption may be

---

[4]Sigmund Freud, "The Defense in Neuropsychoses," from *Selected Papers on Hysteria, Nervous and Mental Disease Monograph Series,* No. 4, 1894.

drawn that if this is the most "normal" and "healthy" of defense mechanisms, although one not used readily by offenders under normal conditions, then criminal behavior is not healthy psychological behavior.

Repression

Repression is purposeful forgetting that occurs at the unconscious level. Usually such a defense is erected to shut out either internal drives or external circumstances that, if and when recognized, could cause pain and/or discomfort to the individual. It is difficult to relate this particular defense mechanism as being a contributing factor or a commonly used defense device in conjunction with the offender. It may be, however, that what is being repressed is the socially accepted value structure of society. By repressing such standards, the offender can symbolically divorce himself from being governed by or having some declared allegiance to, social norms. He thereby can avoid any possible feelings of guilt for opposing expectations predicated on those norms.

Denial

Denial, simply stated, is the ignoring or denial of reality factors. The individual who practices denial may have convinced himself that reality factors are totally nonexistent in nature.

We have also referred to the fact that the sociopathic personality has this tendency to deny certain aspects of reality. Perhaps a significant characteristic of the sociopathic offender would be the development of his or her own standards and then adhering rigidly to them. The fact that these standards are predicated strictly on selfish motives and do not represent the interests of the whole (society) but just a segment of that whole (self-interest) is immaterial in the value structure of that offender.

Although a sensitive subject for discussion, class and ethnic conflicts often are considered to be related to this particular defense mechanism. The socially acceptable method of disguising such a theory is to classically label it the battle of the "have" and "have-nots." This author chooses not to support this concept other than to note that such an explanation represents an oversimplification of the facts in arriving at a conclusion about this being one of the contributing factors to criminal behavior.

Projection

Projection is a form of denial. The individual who makes use of this mechanism refuses to accept the unacceptable things or qualities within himself and relegates them to others.

In our brief discussion of the sociopathic personality earlier in this chapter, we spoke of his self-justification for acts of thievery and used the example of the offender not feeling uncomfortable in any way about taking from others under most circumstances. Certainly this concept is related to the projection mechanism wherein a thief or robber is able to satisfy himself that his act was not one of creating deprivation to his victim, but that the latter takes from others under the guise of legal manipulation or profiting from the disadvantaged who are not responsible for the socio-economic status.

Introjection

Introjection is a mechanism by which an individual incorporates into himself certain characteristics, traits, or forces. The incorporation process may be done either to use or to destroy the trait that is assimilated.

With caution and perhaps at the risk of treading on some Freudian toes, we might conceive of some of these traits as being either cultural or representative of the value system of the immediate environment. If the individual assimilates traits that are viewed as being against the social norms, or if these traits are illegal in nature, then it is probable that the assimilator may—sooner or later—run afoul of the law because of his participation in this behavioral pattern. For example, the child who is reared in a neighborhood where drugs, alcohol, and prostitution are commonplace may learn to practice or participate in these acts merely by the process of physical association.

Reaction Formation

Reaction formation means the setting up of traits that will prevent the emergence of undesirable attitudes or characteristics, usually traits that are of an opposite type to the undesirable ones.

Probation/parole officers may often note such behavior in offenders under their supervision. Such clients would just smile and agree even if they were being rudely castigated during a reporting session. Their "too nice and sweet" attitude represents an attempt to hide their real feelings of anger and hostility toward their supervisor, feelings that cannot be revealed because of the risk of possible retaliation.

Undoing

Undoing may be best described as an unfounded belief that one can undo or nullify previous actions that have resulted in guilt feelings. In effect, the attempt is to neutralize previous behavior rather than learning to understand and to cope with the resultant feelings.

This is one of the more difficult defense mechanisms to recognize since there exist no overt indicators that can be detected. The author has a hunch—and it must be stated that there is no documentation for this hunch— that certain shoplifters may utilize this particular type of a defense. My suspicion is that the attempt to justify the act of taking things which results in guilt feelings, could trigger such a response and could contribute to reliance on such a defense mechanism as this one. The offender, then, may end up robbing Peter to pay Paul in the circular process of trying to rectify his act.

Isolation

Isolation is a mechanism whereby the original memory and its affect are separated. The affect remains at an unconscious level, whereas the memory is allowed admission to the conscious level.

We too frequently hear accounts of a youth or young adult who methodically killed his mother, father, and all of his siblings. He then contacts the local law-enforcement agency and advises them of his act. The investigation would probably indicate that he discussed the details in a rather casual but explicit manner, showing no emotion whatsoever. The oft-used term of "cold-blooded killer" could apply to this type of defense mechanism.

Regression

The concept behind regression has to do with a sliding backward or a psychic retreat to a level—one usually conceived of as more infantile than not—where the individual seeks security denied him at his present psychosocial state. Although there may be a variety of reasons for regression, deprivation is certainly one of the most common and popular premises for this type of behavior. Regression might well be noted within the offender's use of defense mechanisms as a means of seeking immediate gratification of his needs, and the attempt would be to alleviate his instinctual drives by becoming involved in an act that would produce satisfaction or alleviation of his perceived need.

Rationalization

We have made reference numerous times to the fact that many offenders fail to acknowledge their criminal behavior or do so without embellishing the circumstances in an effort not to look so bad. It can be assumed, then, that rationalization is one of the more commonly practiced of the defense mechanisms. It involves the substituting of an acceptable reason or explanation for an unacceptable one. Rationalization is the process of justifying or explaining a given attitude or action.

Rationalization represents both a psychic and a social cop-out; it is nothing more than an excuse for its user to justify involving himself in an act he knows he should not be participating in. For example, we all can conceive of a variety of reasons for obtaining an article we desire even if we really don't need it and don't have a legitimate means of acquisition. Similarly, the offender is able to justify and convince himself that it is all right to engage in a criminal act.

Displacement

Displacement is the transferring and directing of a feeling or reaction from the original set of stimuli to another. Displacement involves the misdirection of feelings and the use of a more vulnerable and less threatening target for our hostile and angry feelings. There is another thin line existing here between rationalization and displacement. Perhaps we can clarify it in this manner. Let us say an individual feels he has been discriminated against in some way by society and he strikes back through a criminal act. If he attempted to set up this behavior through a premeditated or planning process, it would be rationalization. If he struck back blindly against an unknown victim, in an effort to release his feelings, this would be a displacement process.

Rationale for Defense Mechanisms

Defense mechanisms undoubtedly exist on the basis of the pleasure/pain principle. As the reader will note, the attempt of most of these defense mechanisms is to protect the user from psychic pain or discomfort. It is rather meaningless that although the act itself or the manifestation of the mechanism occurs at a conscious and visible level, its justification is at a subconscious or unconscious state of being. Consciously and unconsciously, the individual's first and primary concern is the protection of himself, the avoidance of pain, and the enhancement of pleasure or comfortableness of being.

It is commonly recognized that all individuals have certain needs which include the need for recognition and self-fulfillment. The individual who is mentally healthy needs only to use defense mechanisms sparingly to achieve these needs. Psychoanalysts would tell us that the mature (meaning mentally healthy) individual has a well-developed ego, one that is not threatened constantly, because the needs of that individual have been met during his various psycho-social stages of development, i.e., oral, anal, etc. Self-contentment through self-fulfillment reduces the need for defense against unknown factors and for engaging in certain fantasies.

Continuing to pursue these lines of reasoning, there may be some basis to consider the relationship between insecure/defensive individuals and criminal behavior. The need to strike out or back, the feeling of rejection or deprivation may be difficult to understand and to isolate any origin for such behavior. In fact, its source may be so far removed from the present that any attempts to seek its origin within the individual will be futile. If there is, actually, such a social condition as cultural paranoia, then such behavioral patterns as noted here may be further obscured as to origin, and the individual may be reacting to a process of cultural conditioning from without rather than from within. The Negro, the American Indian, etc., may be reacting to social suppression that has its roots in events taken decades ago and which are reflected, not originating, in contemporary times. Values, methods of coping, and other such responses may be historically and socially instinctual through an association and assimilation process. Our search, then, for the understanding of criminal behavior origins may demand more examination than we can possibly give.

NEO-DEFENSE MECHANISMS

Probation and parole officers are only too well aware that the use of defense mechanisms is a routine wall that the offender uses in the supervision process. Many offenders will build new defenses on the foundation of the classical ones, and these will produce some unique as well as some frustrating confrontations. We direct this particular section to some of the different forms used that seem peculiar to the professions of probation and parole.

We may accept and even expect certain psychological shortcomings in others. These occur at an unconscious level, and many people may be unaware of using them. We have accepted, also, sin as being an existing factor that all of us are saddled with. For example, most of us try to avoid overindulgence, although there are a few who gorge themselves. We cannot, however, accept severe legal disobedience in ourselves, especially if we are caught and confronted, for we recognize that such behavior is largely a matter of free choice. To be or not to be, that continues to be the question with which we are faced. It is nobler in the minds of men to accept their criminal fate, but far more difficult to live with themselves upon their admission of it.

It is for this reason that offenders play games. A weakness succumbed to that could have been avoided through self-control is difficult to accept. It is also difficult for the offender to accept the consequences. The chronic offender may chalk it up to a personal profit and loss ledger, but even in an authority relationship, he feels it necessary to play his peculiar role. Perhaps the resistance is not always directed at the supervising probation/parole officer as much as it is directed by the offender toward himself for his own benefit. "If I don't let myself be confronted by it, maybe it will go away." The balance of this discussion in this section of the chapter will focus on some of these methods of avoiding responsibility. Such tactics are used by the offender in an attempt not only to deceive the supervisor but also to deceive himself.

We call these tactics neo-defense mechanisms since they are neither apparent nor well-known other than to those who use them and to us who sometimes feel we are abused by them. They are ranked neither by priority nor by repetition, but each one will be recognized by officers in the probation and parole professions.

The Semantic Syndrome

The semantic syndrome is a sensitive area requiring diplomacy of fore-thought. It is not intended here to direct any assaultive thoughts or to con-tain any negative reflections of a deliberate nature on any group, religious sect, or cultural commonality.

One example of this tactic that was experienced by the author involved an Oriental female who had been arrested innumerable times for a variety of sexually related offenses. My interview with her remained relatively routine when we were discussing subject matters that could be described as statis-tical fact gathering. During this part of the interview, she responded readily and with some degree of honesty. However, at the point in time where answers were sought relative to her sexual behavior, her probable relation-ship to a pimp, and her feelings about her level of involvement, she suddenly and conveniently lost her ability to both understand and to express herself in the English language.

The Tear Trauma

Historically, crying is supposed to be a woman's weapon. The theory is that most women can turn tears off and on like an electric light when it behooves them to do so. Neither the output nor the cutoff seems to cause them any undue labor. Although I occasionally have had men try a similar tactic, it seems to be a woman's weapon.

There is little question as to the therapeutic value of the purging of emo-tions. Tears are often used as a quasi-honest form of relief and may well mask the ability to look at the feelings that they symbolically represent. The astute therapist must learn to gauge the validity of those feelings as to whether such behavior is a method of dealing with stress/anxiety or whether the client is attempting to elicit sympathy. For example, the author knew of one woman who, when she wanted to evoke tears, concealed a small piece of onion in her handkerchief.

In the tear trauma, the female offender who chooses not to have to discuss her offense may suddenly succumb to a barrage of tears. Her game seems to be to gain control by symbolically losing in the hope that the super-visor—especially if the supervisor is male—will (1) become bored and tired of waiting for an answer, (2) become sympathetic, (3) feel guilty, (4) run out of tissue, or (5) have no more time to wait because of other commitments. The purpose is, of course, to put the supervisor off balance and keep him there.

The Sexual Game

The sexual game, surprisingly so, is not the sole property of the female offender. Many female officers can relate incidents where male offenders under their supervision have attempted to utilize verbal sexual behavior and mannerisms in order to win favors or leniency. Provocative gestures, mannerisms of dress, double-meaning statements, all are fairly common weapons utilized to throw the supervisor off guard and to perhaps keep him/her in suspense about the atmosphere of the relationship with his or her client.

Certain female offenders may deliberately use sex to entice for purposes of blackmail against the supervisor who foolishly decides to treat it as a fringe benefit of the job. It is sometimes for this reason that mixed caseloads are discouraged. It is damaging to the manipulative offender if the office door remains open or if a third party is present. Quite frankly, the individual officer who is swayed to actively respond is devoid of ethics and should be immediately divorced from his role and profession.

Religious Revelations

Like motherhood, country, and apple pie, we tend to accept religion as a way of life in our country. Because it is sacred we do not criticize it openly even though certain of us fall into the category of nonbelievers. However, because of its exalted position, religion is sometimes used in an inappropriate manner. The author has no intention here of belittling religion, only to chastise those who abuse that for what it stands. Consider the following example.

During my career in the mental health profession, I was a caseworker in a large state hospital. One of the patients in my caseload always seemed to regress following a visit from her minister. My concern for her behavior was such that I finally had to eavesdrop—which I'm certain was neither ethical nor in good clinical taste—when her minister made his next visit. One of the first things he accosted my patient with was, "Well, Mary, have you been able to figure out what sin you must have committed for God to have punished you so?" Predicated on the fact that much therapy time had to be given Mary in an effort to alleviate the anxiety and depressive states these accusations created, we found it necessary to deny any further such visitation privileges. Her minister was convinced mental illness was a divinely imposed punishment, and he would not relent in expressing his belief either to us or to her.

Since being a probation officer I have met many offenders who have been arrested for sexual offenses. A high percentage of these arrests were for public indecency or indecent exposure. Many of these offenders were highly religious individuals, some were theology students, and at least one or two claimed to be ordained ministers. Consistently they fought therapy. Each felt he had neglected his obligations to God and had failed to pray as diligently as he should have done. All felt that prayer alone would solve their problems.

The author's conception of a Divine Being—you may call Him whatever is appropriate to your belief—is of a Being who favors the man or woman who wants to help himself/herself to a better way of life. However, man must apply some individual efforts rather than throwing himself at the feet and mercy of that in which he believes. God is assumed to work through man, but He cannot be visualized as wanting man to be a puppet who can neither think nor do anything for himself.

The Apostle Paul taught that man should not marry nor lie with a woman unless he could control his urges.[5] Only then should he marry (if he could not practice celibacy). I am convinced that those male offenders of whom I speak failed to realize that their own religious beliefs and practices were not sufficient to overcome their basic biological urges. If, for example, they were religiously conditioned to believe that sex should only be engaged in for procreation purposes, they would feel guilty when their normal sexual drives were awakened. The female, whose sexual feelings were perhaps more easily controlled, would refuse to engage in sexual activity with her spouse because of psychological, physiological, or social—to include religious—reasons. The frustrated male, whose religious convictions were not sufficient to overcome his basic urges, would then resort to acts that contributed to his own guilt, such as forms of sexual self-abuse or making verbal or physical sexual overtures to unknown females.

The Whipping Boy

Various individuals who have close relationships to the offender under supervision often attempt to use the probation/parole officer to achieve their own expectations of the offender. For example, parents who have lost control over their delinquent child, which may account for the child's antisocial behavior, fully believe that the supervisor not only can but should restore a desired value system to the child and to the family as well. Subconsciously, those parents are asking for a miracle to overcome some of their guilt feelings. Quite often, however, their demands are for the enforcement of some simple (and sometimes selfish) forms of conformity. The nature of these requests may be hard for the lay person to even believe, let alone accept as factual, and are even more difficult for the supervisor to relate to and to deal with. A few can be noted here to include some that are routine, some far from being so.

1. I want you to tell Johnny/Jane that I want him/her to be in the house by 9:00 P.M. and in bed by 10:00 P.M.
2. I want Johnny/Jane to get all A's this year in school. Tell him/her you expect the same thing.
3. Johnny/Jane thinks he/she needs only one bath a week. He/she won't mind me when I tell him/her to take at least two baths a week. Please tell him/her to take more baths.

[5]1 Cor: 7:1–9.

4. I wish you would make Johnny/Jane find a job so we can have more money.
5. Johnny/Jane (who is now ten years old) thinks he/she is big enough to not mind me. Please make him/her respect what I ask of him/her.

Wives and other adult females are equally as demanding about enforcing rules for their spouses or lovers. Only the nature of the demand changes, not the reality aspect.

1. Will you please make Fred get a job. We're behind on our payments on our combination color TV/stereo set as well as on our new car.
2. Sam spends all his time and most of his money at a bar; he won't even take me with him.
3. I think Bill has a girl friend. Can you find out and tell him he should leave her alone and spend more time at home with his family.
4. George just will not go to church with me. Don't you think he should and can you make him go?
5. Pete cusses at me all the time. Make him stop.

There is a third type that will periodically make certain demands of the supervising probation/parole officer, the self-proclaimed vigilante. This role is characterized by the individual who feels his primary function is to bird-dog the use of the taxpayer's monies and to demand more and closer supervision of the offender. Such individuals must have a magical means of existence, for they seem to have nothing else to do for 24 hours a day but to spy, report, and to demand. An example, perhaps slightly removed from context, is one individual in our city who follows the parking enforcement personnel around constantly. He is concerned that no favoritism is granted and no expired meters are missed. If one of my probationers went to the dog races, bet $5, and drank a beer while there, there are several such citizens who will surely have the voluntary obligation to let me know the very next morning; they greet me outside my office door before I can even unlock it.

The Perpetual Loser

Two situations I have repeatedly faced in this business never cease to amaze me—how a person can become intoxicated having never consumed more than "a couple of drinks," and how many people can get into trouble who are victims of circumstances or just plain unlucky. I recently was asked by the court to interview a defendant who has received fourteen traffic offenses in an eight-month period of time. His initial explanation was that he was unlucky in life in general and in his driving habits specifically. When I assured him that I could not buy that excuse, he then attempted to justify his record by the excuse of the law of averages, meaning that he drove a lot more miles per day than the average citizen and his chances for violations were therefore greater.

The ultimate in uniqueness must go to another traffic offender who should have gotten an "A" for effort if nothing else. In reviewing his traffic offense record, I paused at each entry for an explanation. When we got to one that indicated he was driving with no inspection sticker—which should have been firmly affixed to the inside of his windshield—he had a most exotic reason for this situation. His explanation was that he had been driving with his window rolled down and the wind blew it off! Anyone who has ever tried to scrape an expired sticker from its glued position will have serious doubts about the validity of this explanation.

The Victim of an Unjust Legal System

Closely related to the above syndrome are those who feel they have been victimized by law enforcement personnel or the courts. Many offenders seem to view themselves as sacrificial lambs who were conceived only for the purpose of appeasing the gods of the criminal justice system. Unable to cope with their own life style, which has brought them repeatedly to the attention of the system, such persons feel they are repeatedly and unjustly being picked on.

Although some such offenders are chronic recidivists, others are acting in a defiant, semimilitant manner to challenge those injustices they believe are superimposed upon them. Like the old gunfighter in the television plot, their reputation has preceded them, and they have become entangled and entrapped in a web of their own making. They cannot or will not look at the cause/reaction, act/consequence life style that surrounds them and dogmatically resist viewing their role in the chain of effects.

The Bandwagon Dweller

Many offenders have reached the status and plateau of being violators of the law by virtue of association and conformity to the immediate and primary group of identity. According to this theory, if it feels good, do it, and if everyone is doing what feels good, perhaps there will be both security and anonymity within the mass. Yet the herd of sheep, following their leader over the cliff, suffers as much collectively as each sheep does individually.

Many offenders are under the impression that an unfair law can be nullified by overwhelming it through sheer numbers. Recently, in the city of the author, a group has formed with the sole purpose of inundating the courts by never pleading guilty and demanding a jury trial for each and every offense. Their contention appears to be that most traffic laws are insignificant, that a ticket quota system must be met by the police, and that the courts will either by forced to plea bargain away or dismiss most cases if such a deluge hits. The results are unknown at the time of this writing since the organizing for this specific purpose has just now begun.

It is suggested that there are many other examples that could be given and expounded upon. Perhaps those given here do not really represent new defense mechanisms per se as much as they are indicative of old defenses in new disguises. It might be appropriate to note that any method of coping will be conditioned and colored by the user and will be specifically adapted to the circumstances as well as to the context of the stimuli that appear to threaten or offend. Yet any probation/parole officer who has been in the profession for a period of time can or will—sooner or later—identify with the defense mechanisms described above.

THE RESPONSIBLE OFFENDER

Perhaps this heading should be posed as a question, i.e., "How responsible is the individual who offends?" The perceptive reader should be well aware by now that the author's contention is that offenders are as much irresponsible as they are possessed of any other given characteristics or qualities. Whether a discussion of this "affliction" is appropriate in this chapter or would better be discussed in the chapter to follow is debatable. We will, however, speak of irresponsibility as it relates to crime in both chapters, using it here as a summary of sorts, as it correlates with the contents of this chapter, and we will discuss it as a treatment tool in the chapter that follows.

When we speak of responsibility, we address our statements to a dual target area: first, responsibility to one's self and to one's immediate or primary obligations, and, second, responsibility as a function to be assumed for the promotion of the well-being and overall harmony of society as a whole. It is the author's contention that chronic offenders—irrespective of the jurisdictional level at which they offend—are individuals who either cannot or will not assume any responsibility for their own behavior. Therefore, there may be no such creature as a responsible offender who continues to engage in criminal behavior.

This chapter has dealt with two basic concepts, resistance and the use of defense mechanisms, as common reactions to the unpleasantries of the probation/parole contract. We contend that such dynamics are relatively routine methods used by offenders to subtly express their negative reactions to the supervision process. Open defiance is unacceptable and dangerous to the offender's status quo, for he fears that the expression of his hostilities will be an avenue for his supervisor to use legal retaliation. The use of defense mechanisms—new or old—justifies two needed elements: (1) gratification of the offender's need to strike back and/or to resist, and (2) avoidance of having to confront reality situations that may be uncomfortable for him to face.

The inability to face reality is a basic characteristic of the irresponsible person. Socially defined, irresponsibility refers to the putting off or the avoidance of reality and perhaps the altering of reality situations to enhance pleasantness and/or to avoid pain. There seems to be no basis for differentiating between mental and physical forms of confrontation; the totally irresponsible individual will block out either or both with little effort, as long as it serves his immediate needs. This may be a partial explanation for the use of the social diagnosis of sociopathic as applied to certain offenders. The apparent lack of any social conscience does not allow for much anxiety, a state that forces most of us to act in a responsible manner. Most of us would prefer to face stressful situations head-on rather than deal with the anxiety of the unknown.

The irresponsible offender refuses to acknowledge any accountability for his criminal behavior. He may conceive of himself as a political or cultural prisoner and therefore may alter or enlarge upon social factors/pressure to justify his behavior. Although a few individuals may have every right to believe they have been denied a "fair shake" in society based on their cultural heritage, color, or religion, these few, reacting without any sense of responsibility, have served to taint the many by their unfair use of such facts to justify their criminal behavior.

Other offenders cannot find any rationalization process about social deprivation upon which to build their defense mechanisms. They simply practice abstinence from responsibility on the grounds that self-accountability alters their projected image of themselves. To admit to a weakness is to deny being "cool" or is indicative of a lack of sophistication. The acceptance of reality forces us to destroy our fantasy conceptions that we have surrounded ourselves with. The irresponsible person cannot do this. He avoids obligations to himself as well as to others. He especially avoids the self-acceptance of blame; and his major regret, if he is apprehended or confronted, is that he lacked the skills to "pull it off" without endangering himself in the process. It makes no appreciable difference what kind of act is involved—whether it is robbery, racing a car down Main Street, or reneging on social obligations. The attitude of the irresponsible offender is still the same—he accepts no blame.

Most criminal acts represent some form of a direct attack on other individuals, their property, or their rights. And because of this abuse, new laws have come into being to protect society. I constantly hear offenders complaining about meaningless laws that appear to be designed as a form of harassment without any legal precedent. However, there is no justified basis for disobedience to the law merely because it restricts one's life style.

The chronic offender is overly selfish. He demands and acts to achieve immediate gratification of his perceived needs. Unfortunately for society, he feels no compunction to restrict the gratifying of those needs and will readily do so at the direct or threatened expense of others. He is responsible to himself only, if that. Yet no man lives alone. A society without social and legal structure is like an orchestra whose members play the music as they see fit and avoid the score as having no purpose. Probation/parole officers have the obligation of trying to integrate the offender into a harmonious role within society, to join together opposites to create a whole. Just as the physician seeks to treat before contemplating surgery, so must corrections seek to change the offender before cutting him out from the body of society. We have recognized some of the symptoms of the sick and diseased; now let us examine the tools of treatment to promote the recovery of the offenders.

SUGGESTED READINGS

COHEN, ALBERT K. *Delinquent Boys—The Culture of the Gang.* New York: The Free Press, 1955.

ENGLISH, SPURGEON O. AND STUART M. FINCH, *Introduction to Psychiatry.* New York: W.W. Norton & Co., Inc., 1957.

HENSHEL, RICHARD L. AND ROBERT A. SILVERMAN, eds., *Perception in Criminology.* New York: Columbia University Press, 1975.

MACNAMARA, DONAL E. J. AND EDWARD SAGARIN, eds., *Perspectives on Corrections.* New York: Thomas Y. Crowell Company, 1971.

PARLOUR, RICHARD R. "Behavioral Techniques for Sociopathic Clients," *Federal Probation,* 39, no. 1 (March 1975), 3-11.

RAPPEPORT, JONAS R. ed., *The Clinical Evaluation of the Dangerousness of the Mentally Ill.* Springfield, Ill.: Charles C Thomas, Publisher, 1967.

STRATTON, JOHN "Correctional Workers: Counseling Con Men," *Federal Probation,* 37, no. 3 (September 1973), 14-17.

WICKS, ROBERT J. *Correctional Psychology: Themes and Problems in Correcting the Offender.* San Francisco: Canfield Press, 1974.

WOODWARD HARRY H. JR. AND FREDERICK M. CHIVERS, "Teaching Motivation to Inmates," *Federal Probation,* 40, no. 1 (March 1976), 41-48.

11

Measuring Effectiveness in Probation and Parole

It is difficult, if not impossible, to formulate standards of consistency regarding a universal definition of success in the field of human services. We can readily isolate trends, but we cannot measure wholeness. In the helping professions, we find so many variances, so many variables in behavior patterns, that often we have to establish our own criteria that we use as personal measuring sticks. Success and failure are difficult factors to isolate and identify, especially in the field of corrections. What constitutes an achievement for some individuals is representative of only mediocrity for others. Therefore, the author's concept of success will not necessarily agree with the concepts of all other professionals in this field. No one side is right, nor by the same token is everyone wrong in his respective approach. We must adapt to our own skills and ideals as well as to the needs of the offenders with whom we must deal. Hopefully, a point can be reached where there is a meshing of ideas and concepts that can be fruitfully applied by all probation/parole officers in dealing with their clients.

Many of us in the corrections field have learned to survive by reacting to intangibles or to instinctual feelings, rather than by applying theories. This is a most difficult concept to portray. I shall always remember our field work students who, almost to a person, began much like young children approaching the philosophy and functions of our agency with the ever-present question of "Why?" Although this was not necessarily a negative reaction on their part, it was difficult for me to convey my instinctual responses that many times affected my approach to a specific offender. Hunches and instinctual reactions are seen by the dogmatic as being nonclinical tools, but their worth is invaluable when coupled with experience.

It is not easy to give satisfying answers to eager but unknowledgeable students. Furthermore, the true function of the educational process is the opportunity to examine and challenge rather than to merely accept everything at face value. It is unfortunate that some educators think this to be blasphemy. They become threatened, as if their students were challenging elders rather than ideas, and treat each such assault as a personal affront. The social sciences cannot truly be called a specific or an exact science as compared to the physical sciences. Experiments with live subjects must be humanely limited in nature. We cannot dissect and study our peers, then restore them after our learning process is complete. Cadavers reveal no perceptible social facts other than that a cirrhotic liver may give some indication that the deceased was a social creature who may have felt alcohol helped in his interpersonal relationships, at best a limited social index.

Psycho-social theories can only represent learned and sophisticated forms of speculation. The practiced eye and ear can readily discern extreme cases of pathology as noted with the mentally ill. But the author cannot support, nor should the reader accept, any theory that chronic offenders are mental "basket cases." Most offenders—as socially maladjusted individuals—rarely fit into the neat pigeon holes provided by various psychometric tools.[1] In a broad and generalized sense, we should be less concerned about the diagnosis of an offender than we are about his prognosis. Although there may be grounds to doubt that you can't have one without the other, it is the assumption here that, with proper intervention, criminal behavioral patterns can be diminished, if not halted. The issue remains of defining the most feasible way of altering the trend.

The primary function of this chapter is to examine what works and whether or not it is possible to develop a method of measuring success in probation/parole services. To attempt to do this is comparable to skating on thin ice. There exist so many combinations and complexities within human behavior that the reader must be forewarned that no concrete conclusions can be reached.

HOW TO MEASURE SUCCESS

Our first roadblock presents itself quickly. If we can't define success, how can we measure it? How can we be certain that probation/parole efforts are of any lasting value? The initial and logical assumption to be made would be that if the offender refrains from further criminal or illegal

---

[1]Lloyd E. Ohlin, ed., *Prisons in America* (Englewood Cliffs, N.J.: Prentice-Hall, Inc., 1973).

behavior, then the "treatment" has been a success. Were it that simple, however, we could readily terminate our discussion at this very point. The major issue is complicated by the various levels of expectations—from the supervisor, from the offender, and from society in general. To further muddle the picture, we should point out that overt behavior may be replaced by surreptitious acts that go undetected or unreported, and thus the subsequent statistical representation becomes immediately invalid.

Success, according to neophyte probation/parole officers, is attainable only when there are no compromising features. Such professionals might not, for example, accept a heroin addict going on methadone or an alcoholic staying sober through the use of Antabuse as indicators of success. Such an unrealistic approach may well alter the recidivism rate and paint a portrait of failure that should not exist. We have previously made mention of the fallacy of unfair standards being superimposed on offenders, thereby dooming some to almost immediate failure. Probation/parole demands and contracts must offer the offender some degree of flexibility and the opportunity of alternatives other than remaining free versus being incarcerated.

Offenders may be so deeply conditioned to life styles that they cannot be changed merely by threats or demands made by the supervisor who has a "blank check" to structure the probation/parole contract as he sees fit. Such contracts must contain stipulations that are not only reasonable from a legal/social standpoint; but they must be equally reasonable for the client to adjust to and to eventually meet. The demanding of an abrupt and immediate about-face is easier said than done.

Success is somewhat of an optical illusion. For example, we may view an acquaintance's style of living with awe and envy and think how fortunate he is, whereas, in fact he may be deeply in debt in order to maintain the illusion he wishes to convey. What price has he paid for victory, if indeed this is a triumph? Similarly, success with an offender cannot be judged solely by his conforming to the demands of probation and parole. Except in those cases that are considered hopeless, the responsibility for effective change must be a mutual investment by both the offender and the supervising officer.

Another factor that can affect the definition of success or failure is when success is confused with progress. There is no reason to believe that human behavioral changes should be instantaneous in nature and content. Perhaps we dwell under another illusion that the individual's own recognition of his deficient behavior should be sufficient grounds to allow him to effect change.

In working with offenders, it is necessary to attempt to replace one form of behavior with another that is more personally gratifying as well as being more socially acceptable. The failure to be able to instantly substitute one cornerstone with another may cause an individual to crumble unless a lot of outside support can be given. The replacement process is almost never an immediate act. For example, success cannot be expected of an individual who has the tendency to offend while under the influence of alcohol as long as he continues to drink. Progress in this case may mean gradually weaning him away from drinking, even though the transition to total sobriety may take a prolonged period of time. The impatient supervisor will never experience success if he is unable to cope with any behavior except on a "now" level.

Offenders need meaningful gratification as well. To attempt to convince a ghetto offender that his life style is inadequate as well as inappropriate is meaningless if we cannot help him replace the void with either an equal or a more gratifying substitute. One of the weakest links in probation/parole services is the inability to convey to offenders the true reason for alternate forms of behavior. For example, regardless of the inadequacies of the father or the mother, irrespective of how much negative manipulation they bring to bear on their children, most juveniles will continue to identify with their families even at the cost of possible legal and social difficulties for such allegiance. Therefore, any attempts to counteract the subversive acts of parents of juvenile delinquents may be futile.

The use of the word *meaningful* is highly appropriate when speaking of the need to substitute alternate forms of behavior in an attempt to counteract criminal forms of behavior. Unless there exists sufficient personal gratification in the alternate role, the chance to effect change is useless and unworthy of the time spent in the attempt. The basic needs of the individual must be assured under the different life style, and his identity must be retained before he will even contemplate trying to change. Conformity is often evidenced by offenders who have yielded to the clout of the legal system, but conformity and change are not to be viewed as having the same meaning. Instead, we may be confronted with the individual who "plays the role" for purposes of expediency. The name of this game is to convince others he has changed by substituting a new outward image while retaining the old image either internally or where its appearance will not be harmful.

There are countless reasons why probation/parole services fall short of their purpose and why the client reoffends. First of all, caseloads may be too large. Although the suggested effective caseload, as earlier stated, of 35 is a reasonable and idealistic figure,[2] it is not uncommon for two and sometimes three times that number to be carried by a single officer. Obviously the level of service delivery is limited as well as the degree of success or failure, when a larger caseload is carried.

Another reason for the lack of success in client treatment is the inability of probation/parole personnel to intervene as needed and to manipulate

[2]See Chapter One.

those elements needing to be changed to move toward a better level of service. If the offender cannot find training and work, if he must be retained in the same physical/social environment that fosters and, in some cases, sanctions antisocial and criminal behavior, rehabilitation efforts will be thwarted. The inability to find and obtain subsidization for the juvenile offender's placement or to effect other beneficial changes may be impractical, and the pattern of criminal involvement may well be perpetuated.

Another obstacle to client success may be the fact that the supervisor cannot establish a feeling of mutual trust with the offender. Some supervisors, like nagging fishwives, constantly remind the offender of past behavior, and this technique may do more harm than good because it tends to convey general distrust on the part of the supervisor. Although prior offenses may well be pertinent in the rehabilitation/treatment process, constant reference to them will not alter the fact that they happened; the point is to attempt to discourage future occurrences. Constant reference to past crimes is akin to the psychoanalytical approach in therapy whereby past factors are pertinent in changing present ones. However, such a Freudian type of reverting back is not valuable to the point of excluding other methods of approach and treatment. Some offenders may feel appropriately guilty, and the attempt to dwell exclusively on past behavior may be sufficient to allow an internalization process to be assumed, but this approach is not beneficial to all offenders. Unless used with skill upon which to build and change, practitioners of such an approach serve to do little more than to flog a dying horse.

What we advocate here is a simple matter of beginning where the offender is and establishing realistic goals around his immediate area of hurt. Although references to his past are not out of order, they should be used primarily for identification purposes in the act-consequence relationship to the offender's level of dysfunctioning. Many offenders cannot use their past behavior in any effectual way.

Positive results—if we choose to portray this as success—emit from a positive relationship between the "treater" and the "treated." In this profession, we should not discard the past history of the offender, but we should certainly be content to shelve it until it can be viewed mutually in an objective manner rather than using it against the client. If there are any dynamic thoughts and words of wisdom to be conveyed by this book, it simply is that goal-setting should be started at that point where the offender is *now* and *immediately*.

If your client is hostile and bitter, deal with that situation first. You will not enlist his help in an objective planning process until he can be objective himself. Hostility will cloud and obscure his ability to think effectively. Much can be said of the same nature about anxiety, another common characteristic. What is the source of his anxiety? Perhaps he is fearful of the supervisor's role and power; perhaps he is a defeatist based on past inabilities to "make it"; maybe he doesn't even know what he is anxious about. The ability of the supervisor to express and to transmit his concern about the client's stress is a positive gesture of help.

There are countless other examples that serve to establish the beginning of the supervisor/client relationship at the "now" point. Employment might be a factor, but this goal is not attainable without going through some intermediate steps. Maybe remedial skills are needed; maybe the GED (General Education Development) should be worked for; perhaps vocational training or some type of an apprentice program should be considered. Can an immediate living as well as training for the future be satisfied at the same time? These are primary considerations that must be dealt with if an effective relationship is to be fostered.

Considerations of this type are the very heart and soul of the functions of probation and parole. Yet as Chapter Thirteen will point out, many referrals made by the courts, especially at the probationary level, are inappropriate and futile as meaningful alternatives to incarceration.

TRACKING THE OFFENDER

Perhaps a different factor in determining the success or failure of probation/parole services is the inability to track the offender adequately. Two issues seem pertinent: (1) the legal/philosophical question and (2) the inability to monitor the progress or the lack of same of the client.

The Legal/Philosophical Question

The author, in retrospect, realizes that he may well be posing more questions than he is answering. We have spoken of attempts at success without a definition of it. Now we perhaps unfairly must speak of failure without a definition of it as well. It seems very probable that the elusiveness of the definitions of these concepts exists primarily because we, as probation and parole officers, tend to base the success or failure of our clients on the view from our perspective rather than from theirs. Although success and failure can elementarily be defined as not reoffending or reoffending, respectively, this is rather an insufficient distinction. The reader's indulgence is asked here, since it is hoped that our continuing discussion in this chapter will enable us to recognize qualities that frequently defy description.

Legal and philosophical concepts may initially seem to be antithetical terms, for the former portrays exact and precedented facts as compared to the latter, which is more diffuse—a rifle in opposition to a shotgun, so to speak. However, in light of our discussion here, these two concepts are not at all in contradiction to each other. Most probation and parole agencies, despite their existence being predicated on a legal precedent, choose to interpret certain legal facts based on the treatment philosophy of their respective agency. Let me cite a specific example for the sake of discussion. Most probation and parole orders specify that the offender should not violate any laws of the city, state, etc. Laws are specific instruments and are therefore relatively easy to define, but circumstances can alter the fact of criminal intent. For example, would you revoke the probation of an offender who receives a traffic ticket or shoplifts an item of rather insignificant monetary value? Perhaps not, but would it alter the fact if that probationer was under supervision for those specific acts to begin with?

It is at this point that philosophical/legal conflicts can occur. It is not sufficient to pass judgment without giving consideration to the overall adjustment and level of progress of the offender while under supervision. Yet, what other alternatives are there other than to legally punish or to mildly rebuke? "How many trees make a forest?" This is obviously a philosophical question. A second question that contains a legal element as well as a philosophical one is, "How many failures constitute a basis for revocation?"

Inability to Track Offenders Adequately

When we speak of tracking the offender, we mean the probation/parole officer's ability to maintain a sufficient degree of supervision so that the whereabouts and the activities of the client can be accounted for. This is very difficult, and as a result the monitoring of the behavior of the client is often inadequate. Furthermore, the ability to present a comprehensive statistical accounting of success and failure/recidivism is equally difficult. Several reasons for this problem exist. First, many minor offenses go unreported and statistically are unaccounted for in terminal record-keeping centers. Smaller law enforcement agencies, lacking sophisticated equipment, may do little more than make a local contact entry.

Second, many acts that could constitute a probable consideration of having violated the terms of the probation/parole contract may not be bona fide violations of the law. Because such behavior does not constitute required intervention at the level of law enforcement agencies, it goes unnoted and is not reported.

Third, the mobility of our society allows for freedom of travel, and the offender may often do so unsanctioned and undetected. Offenses occurring outside the immediate area of jurisdiction as well as out of the sight and knowledge of the probation/parole supervisor will therefore go unnoticed.

Finally, unless there is a known need for intense surveillance and unless outside assistance from law enforcement personnel can be utilized, the hope for total accountability of the offender and his behavior is most unlikely.

If, then, the tracking of the offender and continued surveillance of his activities is this difficult to maintain, then it remains that any attempt to define success and failure in probation and parole will be equally difficult.

Recidivism, even when unknown and undetected, will have a specific impact on society. Crime always has a victim of some sort. The victim may be an individual who is directly affected by the act such as the immediate and direct victim. Or the victim may be an indirect one, such as a member of the offender's primary relationship group—usually a member of the immediate family—and/or the community in which the offense takes place. Lastly, it is the offender himself who is the victim as he has somehow lost or failed to even grasp the principle of self-control and responsibility to himself as well as to others.

INHERENT WEAKNESSES IN THE SUPERVISION PROCESS

From the preceding discussion, two elementary conclusions can be realized in conjunction with the supervision process. First, more effective screening of potential candidates for these privileges by the courts and parole boards would quite probably eliminate some of the problems encountered in supervision. Technically, this should not even be necessary if the respective screening agents—the courts and parole boards—were more selective in making those administrative decisions as to which offenders represent good risks for these privileges. What is being specifically implied is that certain offenders are poor supervision risks and should probably never be accorded this privilege unless some form of intensive supervision can be assured.

The second conclusion, and even more pertinent to our discussion here, is the obvious fact that the offender is either insufficiently motivated to succeed or there are too many mitigating circumstances in his immediate environment that prevent him from making an adequate adjustment. Although many offenders have good intentions, they either lack the resources to uphold their end of the bargain or they refuse to avail themselves of formal programs of assistance to overcome their own weaknesses.

There are two probable reasons why offenders refuse to utilize services in an appropriate manner. First, it is suspected that they feel that becoming dependent on or yielding to their supervisor and his demands means a loss of their own identity. Part of the unwritten code of offenders is that they must play the role and pay the price by themselves if they are convicted of an offense. This is especially true of those who are incarcerated. Two good books that exist on this subject are *The Effectiveness of a Prison and Parole System*[3] and *Paroled But Not Free*[4]. Offenders feel they must make it on their

[3]Daniel Glaser, *The Effectiveness of a Prison and Parole System* (New York: The Bobbs-Merrill Co. Inc., 1969), p. 76.

[4]Rosemary Erickson, et al., *Paroled But Not Free* (New York: Behavioral Publications, 1973), pp. 87–95.

own. To adhere to the system would certainly cause speculation about them among their peers who share the same custodial penal setting. The unwritten code of criminals works somewhat along the same principle as that used for offenders retained within the community who may be accused of becoming "Uncle Toms" or similar name/roles, implying a deliberate overthrowing of their cultural/social roots and loyalties. It would appear that the thinking of most offenders is that success or failure to adjust and to conform is a self-imposed decision. Likewise, to take such a stand is a conscious step in rejecting the impositions made by the system, a system that many offenders are convinced is as much to blame for their legal predicament as is any other factor. Such a stand allows for the retention of their own identity, the only chance some offenders feel they have after the dehumanization process imposed at the various levels of the correctional and criminal justice system.

The second reason why offenders refuse to utilize services is because involvement in therapy/treatment has negative connotations for them. The offender may be possessed of the belief that his supervisor feels him to be mentally incompetent in some way if therapy is demanded of him. Fearful of the unknown as well as conditioned by his own response to distorted implications, he will resist any and all attempts to involve him in any kind of a therapeutic relationship. He may make his required appearances under duress, but he will use every means available to avoid being drawn into the treatment process.

Success with offenders will also depend on their ability to find substitute roles and better methods of coping with stress, and the tendency to reoffend will correspondingly diminish. Thus, success in the area of the helping professions is the ability to help the client to find more appropriate and socially acceptable ways of dealing and functioning in response to the demands of everyday living.

Failure on the part of the offender should be understood to be not so much a form of social malfunctioning as a lack of desire by the offender to learn to deal and cope with those elements that cause dysfunctioning. Although the offender may well have been aware of the act(s) that precipitated the consequence(s), he should also be recognized as an unfortunate who lacked internal and external assistance to intercede at an earlier point in time. Most such dysfunctional disasters—be they physical, mental, or social in nature—can be recognized early enough in their progressive state that prevention can be attempted.

BEHAVIOR ALTERATION AND TREATMENT TOOLS

The ultimate function of treatment is to assist the offender in the attainment of greater control over his feelings and therefore, and subsequently, to alter his patterns of behavior. In probation/parole services, we may approach treatment from two basic standpoints—which may be defined as being either direct or indirect in nature. The indirect approach is concerned with the alteration of the environment of the offender through certain forms of interposition and manipulation. This might include working with employers, family, teachers, and other such individuals who indirectly can provide supportive services to the individual but not in the same vein as would be found in a clinical relationship. Such relationships certainly have therapeutic value, but in this section we are principally concerned with curative/treatment (primary) approaches to rehabilitation, and we shall discuss here the various forms of therapeutic/clinical intervention that constitute direct treatment.

The theories of offender behavior and the tools used to alter and change such behavior are countless. The author, although laying no personal claim to any particular treatment modality, can recall the efforts of many well-intending individuals who have offered various means and sometimes perhaps dubious skills in attempts to help. I have been besieged, at one time or another, by citizens advocating the use of graphology, astrology, and even biological intervention as possible methods of either understanding or deterring criminal behavior. The past decade has seen a variety of new concepts of self-understanding as well as new treatment tools making their debut. Biofeedback,[5] socio-biology,[6] and bio-rhythm,[7] for example, are contemporary theories that are gaining a lot of attention and whose values have yet to be thoroughly researched and determined. Like diets, there continually appears to be a new item or theory regularly pushing itself into the fore amidst fanfare and hopeful sounds.

Despite touches of sarcasm here, no theory or program of help should be discarded as a perceived form of quackery or sorcery. Neither should practitioners of the helping professions attempt to try to hammer the square pegs of offenders routinely into the round holes of any given program without some foresight, especially as regards the planning and melding of the needs of the individual and the skills of the therapist/supervisor. The general rule of thumb must be that particular tools of therapy must be those that are equally comfortable to both the supervisor and the offender. This statement must be qualified, however, to suggest that programs should quickly be shelved and a new approach attempted when it becomes apparent that the treatment tool in question does not allow for a sense of satisfaction and progressive gratification in the achievement of the needs of the offender.

The level of effectiveness of a given method will be determined by how

[5]Barbara B. Brown, *New Mind, New Body: BioFeedback: New Directions for the Mind* (New York: Harper & Row, Publishers, Inc., 1974).

[6]"Why We Do What We Do," *Reader's Digest,* (condensed from *Time*) 111, no. 668 (December 1977), 183–190.

[7]Jennifer Balch, "BioRhythms: A Key to Your Ups and Downs," *Reader's Digest,* 111, no. 665 (September 1977), 63–67.

successful it is with the particular offender. Throughout this book, it has been suggested that treatment need not be limited to the antiseptic qualities of a strict clinical approach. The reality confrontation of incarceration is not conceived of as a clinical approach. Nor is the responsibility of the offender being demanded to regularly report to the probation/parole supervisor considered a clinical approach. Both tools have their place and are effective with certain types of offenders.

The formalized training of the probation/parole officer and his exposure to educational/treatment theories will largely determine his techniques of supervision and his choice of methods of coping. However, the theories of professional training and the reality demands of the position will not always be found to be compatible, because of the diversities of the demands of probation/parole work and because of the size of the caseload of each individual officer. It is at this point of recognition that the nature of the probation/parole contract should be determined.

The probation/parole contract should be kept as simple and as uncluttered as possible. One of the complexities involved in trying to maintain this approach is the necessity of having to renegotiate forms of behavior and to be able to do so with the offender objectively. It is almost impossible to plan effectively for *all* future alternatives at the time the contract is conceived and developed. Some type of control and check system must be adopted that allows for holding offenders responsible for their behavior while under supervision, but it should be flexible in design and stop short of revoking their probation/parole for minor infractions.

It may be that the goals of some cases can be worked on mutually with a minimum of time and a maximum of results, but there are other cases that demand intensive care and will not be as easily absorbed. Under such circumstances, a specialized caseload may be assigned to an officer more skilled in treatment techniques, or if non exist within the agency, a referral may be made to an outside treatment agency for this purpose.

Determining the Best Treatment Approach

Let us assume that we, as probation/parole officers, are shopping for consultant services for those offenders who need intensive therapeutic intervention. How, like Simple Simon in the nursery rhyme, can we sample the wares and gauge the quality of the product? There may be no relatively easy answer, but we can try. First, one must measure the ability of the offender to utilize therapy in a meaningful way and to be able to grasp the significance of the issues raised within therapy sessions. In short, does he have the intellectual capacity to relate to possible psychological/sociological sources relative to his criminal behavior as well as to the theory of treatment? Specifically, certain forms of therapy would be meaningless to an offender of less than average intelligence.

Second, how motivated and how much personal insight is the offender possessed of? Does he have sufficient cognizance of his own personal psycho-socio dilemma—aside from the legal ramifications—that he sees a need for some sort of therapeutic intervention? In conjunction with this, the probation/parole officer must be able to assess the degree of hurt the offender feels, his level of uncomfortableness. A determination must be made as to whether or not the offender is sufficiently psychologically uneasy with himself that he really wants therapeutic intervention and is willing to work toward the alleviation of his discomfort.

Third, can the offender utilize the insight he may gain from a therapy experience? One of the most frustrating experiences in life is to be able to recognize our various shortcomings but not to be able to learn to accept, to cope, or to overcome them. For example, the young adult who may develop some self-awareness into the nature of his behavior as being related to a conditioning factor superimposed upon him by his parents may well have difficulty in coping if he continues to live with those parents. The conflicts that can arise may have as much negative qualities as if he did not have any insight whatsoever.

Fourth, does the therapeutic approach correlate with the needs of the offender? In short, can he relate the process and theory of treatment with where he sees himself to be? It might be that certain minority and/or oppressed group members may rightfully feel that the system is a primary cause of their difficulties. It is most likely, under these circumstances, that their relating to therapy—or lack of relating—may be because they feel that such therapy is totally irrelevant to a better level of functioning. The author is well acquainted with criticism about the probable invalidity of norms based on cultural factors in certain psychometric tools. However, I am unaware of any comprehensive studies that deal with therapy norms/approaches as to possible cultural biases and subsequent loss of effectiveness. As a matter of fact in certain self-help groups such as AA, it has been the practice to develop specific chapters around ethnic memberships and to note a higher level of overall involvement because of this factor.

Last of all is the time element. Certain schools of therapeutic theory are not intended for short-term sessions or even for crisis intervention. Some of these approaches may involve ongoing treatment encompassing several years in time. Unless the offender is extremely motivated and is desirous of continuing in a program of therapy beyond his legally imposed time frame, programs that are "now" oriented and less demanding as to a time factor may be far more appropriate and therefore more beneficial to agency use.

The cost factor, whether born by the agency or the offender, also must be considered.

Treatment Modalities

It is difficult, and perhaps it is somewhat unnecessary, to attempt to categorize treatment modalities and orientation. Two good books that exist on this subject are *Inside Psychotherapy*[8] and *Basic Approaches to Group Psychotherapy and Group Counseling*[9], and one of the best such analyses is one by C. H. Patterson.[10] Individuals who are contemplating an entry into the helping services might well acquaint themselves with such works as these for future reference and possible planning for formalized training. It is for this reason that a brief discussion of treatment modalities and their orientation is included in this book.

There are probably five basic categories of treatment theories, although Patterson lists more. Rather than bog the reader down in a formalized and detailed discussion, we will make but a brief presentation here of the natural divisions as seen by this author.

Psychoanalytical   The psychoanalytical approach, popularly attributed to Freud, focuses on the various levels of personality development and structure from the early period of life onward.

Phenomenological   Generally speaking, phenomenological therapy focuses on self-perceptions of the individual as well as on his conceptions within relationships/interaction processes. Gestalt psychology is one of the more popular and hallowed theories within this category.

Behavioral   The behavioral therapy approach operates on the premise that all forms of behavior are learned through life experiences. What you are is merely a result of what you have been conditioned to believe. The treatment principle concentrates, then, on the unlearning process.

Rational   The rational approach is sometimes referred to as empirical or emotive psychotherapy. It functions on the premise that faulty logical conclusions and assumptions contribute to the individual's irrationality and subsequently to his dysfunctional level of behavior.

Transactional   The transactional approach may be defined as one which places emphasis on levels of interaction and communication both within the individual and among individuals as well. The emphasis is less on a

[8]Adelaide Bry, *Inside Psychotherapy* (New York: Basic Books, Inc., Publishers, 1972).

[9]George M. Gazda, ed., *Basic Approaches to Group Psychotherapy and Group Counseling* (Springfield, Ill.: Charles C Thomas, Publisher, 1968.

[10]C.H. Patterson, *Theories of Counseling and Psychotherapy* (New York: Harper & Row, Publishers, Inc., 1973).

systematic approach to problem solving than on communicative patterns of examination.

Eclectic Form of Therapy   One further theoretical approach deserves some mention here, one that is often referred to as the *eclectic form of therapy*. Although sometimes viewed as a "potluck" approach, encompassing theories from many of the other forms of treatment disciplines, its functional approach is said to be along inductive lines of fact-gathering and analysis with a theory to be arrived at only when the exploratory work has been completed.

There are, of course, countless variations and integrations of any and all of these theories used in treatment that cannot readily be identified as either fish or fowl as to their conception, categorization, and content. Our brevity of their treatment here is based on a lack of space, pertinence, and author expertise. The suggested reading list at the end of this chapter may serve to satisfy the more discriminating reader for further resources and explanations.

Casework Approach

Many authorities, on treating the offender, view the work of the probation/parole officer as a casework approach. Further, they insist that the method of treatment differs little, only the context or the circumstances under which it is applied are altered. In a technical sense, casework is a form of generic social work along with group work and community organization. We are suggesting here that probation/parole services might be more aptly referred to as a form of social work, with casework being but a specialized tool within that discipline. Even so, casework services may include certain disciplinary approaches in the treatment process, depending largely on the philosophy of the academic institution attended.

A discussion of treatment disciplines puts us in a very vulnerable position immediately. The use of the word *vulnerable* seems most appropriate here because the forms that counseling takes are representative of the academic disciplines from which they originated. The author is well aware that many educators are sensitive to such a discussion, even to the point of being overly defensive. I am fearful that I may be a bit callous about such feelings and may, out of sheer ignorance and a lack of research, label such feeling as vested interest nit-picking. I shall immediately defend my position against the criticism and reaction that I know will result.

Let us assume I am seriously injured in an automobile accident. So extensive and severe are my injuries that I am whisked away by ambulance to the nearest hospital emergency room. I seriously doubt that those who are concerned about my welfare will quibble about the fact that I might be attended by a doctor of osteopathic medicine rather than a medical doctor. By this same analogy, I doubt that the individual who is suffering from a severe depression and who might even be contemplating suicide could care less whether he is treated by a "shrink" who is a Rogerian by theory and training or not. In a time of hurt, it becomes a case of "D___ the credentials, full speed ahead." Further, I believe most of the public—unless because of some sort of a prejudice or vested interest—could care less about the background of the practitioner as long as the latter can do the job and meet their needs. We react positively to those whom we are comfortable with and feel we can trust; we ignore those who are not within our positive sphere and relationship.

In the helping professions, clients tend to lean on what is available to them and what meets their immediate needs. Practitioners of these arts, in turn, utilize the approach they know best. Yet one may be no more valuable or effective than another. Although it may be true that certain disciplines may be more effective with one specific case over another, nothing is sacred in the approach taken along treatment lines other than the ethics of the practitioner. It is therefore doubtful in the mind of this author that the casework approach is, in any way, any more profitable or meaningful to use than the talents of a psychologist. The only realistic and empirical judgment to be made is that there appear to be more caseworkers practicing their skills and therefore more available to the public than there are psychologists.

When we attempt to project the clinical disciplinary approach into the realm of corrections, little seems to differ. Most penal institutions have at least one psychologist on their staff and often the services of a consulting psychiatrist. As we have referred to earlier, the psychologist, in this capacity, often serves a dual function of a diagnostic/classification officer and usually will also function as the treatment team leader. Although the psychologist may do some counseling, the brunt of treatment will be the responsibility of the caseworker/counselor.

In probation/parole services, casework may be a luxury if for no other reason than that the casework approach usually implies a one-to-one relationship. Few agencies, based on caseload volume, can justify a primary relationship except on a crisis-intervention, intensive-treatment approach. After countless references throughout this book being made to oversized caseloads, the reader may detect some traces of bitterness by the author. However, if it be bitterness, it is also reality. Private practitioners can limit their intake (patient/client load) and therefore can regulate their scheduling procedure. In the public realm—where probation and parole fall—there is no opportunity to limit the workload except through the use of diversionary programs. It is for this specific reason that corrections has found it difficult to cope with the demands that are being made of it.

There are questions raised periodically as to the effects of counseling in the rehabilitation process of the offender and how meaningful such practices are. It already has been recognized elsewhere in this book that all the clinical tools, all the facilitating by the probation/parole officer, are only going to be as meaningful and pertinent as is the level of the offender's motivation to seek and to effect change. Daniel Glaser suggests that there may be an even better and more meaningful relationship between inmates and their work supervisors than exists between the inmate and his caseworker/counselor.[11] The general consensus of Glaser's statement is that there is more prolonged contact and more of a reality value within this relationship, that the work supervisor is easier to relate to because he is not so differentiated from the inmate by an educational gap, and that caseworkers are generally more concerned with administrative tasks and do not have a firsthand, primary knowledge of the prison atmosphere and inmate experiences/needs, as viewed from the offender's perspective.

A similar observation might be made of the relationship of offenders to their probation/parole officer. All offenders are immediately aware of the power their supervisor holds over them. There are probably more instances than one cares to acknowledge where offenders have violated the conditions of their contract, and they might have sufficient guilt about these acts so that they would like to discuss them; but they may be realistically fearful about doing so because of the risks involved and the possibility of punitive action being taken against them. Although the fault for nonacceptance may be the failure of the supervisor to communicate his flexibility, some offenders are frankly conditioned not to trust *any* authority figure.

In conjunction with this, many offenders will relate to a volunteer and will reveal much more to him than they ever will be able to do with their supervisor. Many offenders genuinely feel that the probation/parole officer is only pretending to care as a part of his job function. The volunteer, on the other hand, receives no monetary compensation for his efforts, and therefore he must be honestly concerned about the offender assigned to him. Many offenders find it difficult to believe that anyone would give his own time without compensation in return for his efforts.

Ineffectiveness of Treatment

In his book *Prison Treatment: An Empirical Assessment,* Gene Kassebaum suggests that there seems to be no appreciable difference between the success of offenders out on parole who participated in therapy and their peers who did not.[12] The authors contend that the corrections system (and its manner of dealing with inmates) has to be viewed as inadequate in its at-

---

[11]Glaser, *The Effectiveness of a Prison and Parole System,* pp. 85–92.

[12]Gene Kassebaum, David A. Ward, and Daniel Wilner, *Prison Treatment: An Empirical Assessment* (New York: John Wiley & Sons, Inc., 1971), p. 242.

tempt to rehabilitate. Other authorities seem to reflect the same feeling.[13,14] The hypothesis for and against treatment as being an effective tool for rehabilitation purposes is a difficult one to advance, let alone to research. Therefore, any and all conclusions should be taken with a grain of salt and with an eye out for better tools for evaluation purposes. If the premise of Gene Kassebaum, as an example, is correct, we would argue along the lines that it is highly probable that a certain percentage of parolees would reoffend whether subjected to treatment while in custody or not. The issue, then, appears to us to be that treatment alone is insufficient to counteract certain negative factors such as unemployment, the influence of criminal social elements, and other such deterrents to a successful adjustment upon parole/release.

THREE MOST EFFECTIVE TREATMENT METHODS

After many years in probation, which does not make me an authority as much as it attests to my endurance, three treatment modalities stand out in my mind as having been the most practical for my purposes as well as for those of the clients I have dealt with. Let us, then, for the balance of this chapter, look at these three tools—behavior modification, group therapy, and group reporting.

Behavior Modification

Behavior mod, as it is popularly called, has come into its own in perhaps the last ten to fifteen years. It represents a variation and updated twist on the old Pavlovian theory of rewarding appropriate responses and ignoring (a nonreward response) anything else. Although there are several variations of this tool, the basic premise behind it is a conditioning process based on appropriate responses in answer to certain stimuli. Used properly, behavior mod can be a very effective tool with offenders *if* the bureaucratic red tape surrounding their legal status can be circumvented.

The author, in conjunction with our court consultant, used behavior mod as a means of reducing the probationary period of offenders by putting into effect a contract where extra credit or good time was given for outstanding efforts and meaningful extracurricular activities. What was being attempted was to enlarge on the goal-setting within the contract and to reward our offenders for attempting to work toward their goals. Not only did it

[13]Robert Fishman, "An Evaluation of the Effect on Criminal Recidivism of New York City Projects Providing Rehabilitation and Diversion Services," mimeographed (The Research Foundation and the Graduate School and University Center, The City University of New York, 1975).

[14]Judith Wilks and Robert Martinson, "Is the Treatment of Criminal Offenders Really Necessary?" *Federal Probation,* 40, no. 1 (March 1976), 3–9.

allow for a greater degree of participation, but the reward became a twofold object—the achievement of a goal and a reduced period of supervision.

Following along these lines, such a behavioral approach gives the offender greater self-control over his own destiny, an opportunity too often either misused or totally deprived in corrections. Too frequently we expect, demand, and attempt to enforce conformity rather than seek to achieve it through a cooperative relationship. Greater depth and meaning are added to this approach when nonrewards/punishments for failing to achieve are partially self-imposed by the offender rather than being administered solely by the supervisor. A program that operates along these lines gives the offender/participant a greater voice and role with regard to his own status and program.

To be objective about this treatment tool, the reader should be aware that it not only can but has been misused. In 1974, the Senate Constitutional Rights Committee, under the leadership of Chairman Sam J. Ervin, Jr., became concerned about reported abuses of the behavior modification theory. Certain institutions, especially mental hospitals and prisons, were alleged to be using such things as mind-altering drugs and electroshock therapy to stimulate—literally and figuratively—appropriate responses from inmates of those institutions. Such programs were labeled "aversion therapy" and represent a throwback in the progress of humane treatment and concern for humanity. The author can vividly remember patients in a mental hospital who had been given lobotomies or ECT (electro-convulsive therapy) as a means of ensuring their manageability.

The selection of the assets and liabilities of any program or of any treatment tool must be predicated on several things. First, it must include the voluntary submission of the client to participate as well as to withdraw without punishment on the basis of good and just reasons. Second, the program should be shown to be of greater benefit to the client than to those who are entrusted with his management. Third, there should exist no negative residues from treatment that will affect the functioning level—either physically or mentally—of the client following termination of his treatment.

Group Therapy

Group therapy is largely a clinical tool—although not limited to clinicians—used effectively as a treatment modality. Although often referred to as a specialized form of social work, group therapy is practiced by several disciplines and does not constitute the sole property of any one school of thought. Sometimes referred to as *group counseling*, group therapy ranks high with many probation/parole officers because it allows for more intensive treatment efforts and thereby more effective utilization of counseling time. Ideally, the group approach in treatment can encompass the involvement of up to about twelve to fourteen offenders at one time and can do so without much discomfort or loss of effectiveness. The probation/parole officer who prefers to utilize the one-to-one approach would find it necessary to use many more hours to give equal therapy time with the same number of offenders. Furthermore, as this discussion evolves, it will be noted that groups offer certain elements that are not found within the casework approach.

One of the more effective uses of group therapy lies in the confrontation process. Many offenders will only reluctantly react to a verbal confrontation in a primary relationship with their supervisor—if they will react at all. Even when interacting, it is safe to assume that they will be quite guarded in their responses. In contrast to this, groups seem to provide for a sense of anonymity, so that the members will sooner or later find it easier to voice their thoughts. Although the anonymity theory is only an illusion, reluctant members seem to draw strength from others sharing the same fate. It also becomes apparent in this approach that group members will more readily accept advice and judgments from their peers than from an authority figure such as the group leader or their probation/parole officer.

The confrontation process may have still another dimension; that is, group members may feel somewhat more secure due to the mutual support as well as a common cause, and therefore may be more comfortable in confronting authority figures. Quite often group members have similar concerns, but individually they are fearful of attempting to "bell the cat." Sometimes the issue of being able to confront the authority figure/group leader may be unfounded or without any logical basis. Nevertheless, the substitute polemics allows members to test the nature of both the issue and the supervisor/leader at the same time. Our experience with juvenile delinquents in groups invariably witnessed some examples of baiting or shock word content used by the offenders to determine our acceptance of them.

Groups also offer some hope for meaningful decision making by offenders. If a group is to move in a positive direction, the tone or atmosphere must be conducive for member participation. This necessitates a relatively permissive climate, one that assures there will be no retaliation, no unjust criticisms, and no manipulation brought against members for free expression of thoughts. If an issue is determined by the group to have discussion merit, then woe be unto the leader who attempts to suppress it as being mundane. Nothing will serve to disrupt group morale and structure quicker than will the leader's domination of the group members.

Another important asset of group involvement is that it may provide some opportunity for peer acceptance. The inability of offenders, especially parolees, to find acceptance except among their own kind can only serve to handicap assimilation into the community. If offenders can, in a group process, relate to each other in a positive manner, some gratification and identity retention may be enhanced. The need to belong may have to be given some priority over negative associations and relationships.

Finally, groups assist in the reenforcement of positive values. When a group achieves an identity, it follows that some form of group value is being established. Properly structured and with a definitive purpose in mind, groups can develop and instill an appropriate role fulfillment within their membership. Many offenders are solitary individuals who have never learned the positive factors of a meaningful relationship. The value of learning to help and to make positive use of others for socially acceptable results contains much in the way of social merit. If our premise that many offenders are irresponsible individuals is logical, then relating to others and seeing their concern(s) may also represent a chance for a unique transformation. The group can foster such positive learning experiences.

To this point, our discussion of group therapy has focused on its positive features. This is perhaps unfair, for there are many case histories that show the near impossibility of creating a functioning group that has an identity and an understanding of meaning and purpose. The difficulty of establishing this group purpose is one of the biggest criticisms of this particular treatment approach, including the time it takes to establish the proper atmosphere, common purpose, and working method. The crucial point in group work is the ability of the therapist to be able to set up a therapeutic milieu where meaningful communication and interaction can flow without the presence of a dominating figure. If the therapist controls too much, group spontaneity is depressed, and a group dependency on leadership is established.

Many therapists attempt to deal with this problem by maintaining silence once the climate and purpose has been established. The theory is to deliberately create an element of silent uncomfortableness, which will eventually be broken by an overanxious member reacting negatively to the silent treatment. Unfortunately, this may allow for too much silence and unproductive time, often alienating the members in the process who will claim that nothing is to be gained by attending.

Groups are one of the primary treatment vehicles in penal institutions; yet they often fail in their purpose for several reasons as listed below.

1. Many offenders are self-oriented and are worried only about themselves, rather than feeling any concern about others. When the focus is on one individual demanding answers only about himself, such as his chances of parole, there is the tendency to lose contact with the balance of the group members.
2. The "con" value system often restricts subject matter. The possibility is always present that the too-verbal inmate may reveal information that is not intended for other than a select few. His verbosity may endanger other inmates and thereby endanger himself in the process.

3. The need for the inmate to role-play always exists. The personal value structure demands that he respond to gain administrative points on his own behalf. He therefore enters into a discussion but deliberately limits the content so that he is not revealing anything that might be used to his disadvantage.

4. The institutional pecking order may allow for the domination of the inmate group by a few. The lower part of the order only responds in support for the "main man," and attempts to keep the attention on him for ego purposes in keeping with his perceived if not established role within that order.

5. The reality of staff time and expertise may often restrict the use of groups on a regular and meaningful basis. Therefore not only is the nature and content of the group often limited, but the selection process may also be inadequate as to inmates selected for group purposes.

Group Reporting

Group reporting is largely peculiar to probation/parole services and represents a less formalized approach in dealing with offender problems. Group reporting is a semistructured process of supervision as to content, form, and purpose. Because of its practical relationship to corrections, it is not a widely known concept, and its merits are therefore frequently misunderstood.

Group reporting occupies a position some place between group therapy and the standard form of reporting to the supervisor on a regular basis. As stated, this is an unstructured approach, and the content varies in nature. We have, in our use of this tool, allowed an informal agenda to exist for several reasons. First, it promotes a relaxed atmosphere conducive to interaction among members. Discussion content is usually nonthreatening and nontraumatic because it is structured by the participants. Second, the discussion is under group control, so the choice of subject matter will be theirs to make. Except for those instances where members come while experiencing a major crisis, the atmosphere operates along democratic lines as to subject matter. Third, group reporting seems to be a major resource for personal experiences rather than a more dogmatic approach, one that periodically results in classical group therapy.

Discussion topics, although diverse, are characterized by mutual information sharing either from within or through the utilization of an "outside" resource person/service. When discussions of specific matters have proved unfruitful, the group would seek expertise from a knowledgeable person who would be invited to the following meeting for this purpose. An example was when the group needed information on the management of their personal finances. Their idea was to seek counsel for the group as a whole, and a banker was invited to share his knowledge with them. Exchanges of information also centered around employment. Issues would include where to get job leads, what companies might be hiring at the time, and how to handle the pressure of the companies' reactions to the offenders' legal status/arrest record. On occasions, our consulting psychologist was invited to discuss matters such as handling anger and frustration.

Rarely did this program bog down. When it did, we merely adjourned early instead of dragging out the hour set aside for this purpose. Sometimes the group voted to substitute other activities for the regular reporting sessions. During the summer, it might be a cookout or a picnic, and one winter there were enough active and interested members to field a team in a bowling league.

In addition to providing the necessary accountability of the offender, group reporting met several basic needs. First, it provided meaningful experiences through a variety of learning experiences that were often both formal (structured by the group) and informal (group sharing of knowledge). Second, the informality allowed for input and feedback from the group members based on their immediate needs and concerns. Third, it developed a group identity readily, perhaps because its contents were less threatening, more immediately gratifying, and it contained an element of "fun" activities not usually associated with probation/parole obligations. Those enjoyable activities also served to keep offenders off the streets by stimulating them to involve themselves in meaningful and acceptable social interests. The time management factor, always an issue, was a further benefit because group reporting provided better utilization of time (than the casework one-to-one approach).

THE *NOW* PROCESS—SUCCESS REDEFINED

In summary, success and failure in probation and parole still remain elusive and shadowed figures that defy a concrete definition. Effectiveness of treatment approaches is equally nebulous if we are concerned about giving priority to one modality over another. Perhaps we are attempting to make too big an issue of such matters and should content ourselves with what we have referred to in this chapter as the "now" process. Most important, students or practitioners of probation/parole services should restrict themselves from getting too far ahead of both themselves and their clients in goal setting. In an earlier chapter, a source was quoted as maintaining that the most crucial point in the treatment of the offender occurs at one of two stages, either at the time of the presentence investigation or at the time of sentencing.

The "now" process simply means handling first things first. Goal setting must be comprised of two components, short-range and long-range. In "now" therapy, if we may coin that phrase, it is necessary to deal with any offender at the point of his greatest and most immediate area of discomfort. With some such clients, there never will be a point where long-range goals can be realized, for there are too many immediate crises that will demand immediate attention. We must assist the offender to be able to walk before we entice him into running. By the same token, we must react to goal setting and treatment approaches in much the same manner. "Now" therapy will convey to the offender that we are concerned about his total readjustment and that we wish to work with him at that point where stress exists. Success is, in this sense, dealing with the offender at the immediate and realistic point of his friction, for it is in this way that a foundation is laid for future goal setting, and treatment planning if the latter is in order.

Success in probation and parole must focus on the social as well as on the legal problems that beset the offender. We have attempted to convey this as being a crucial function of the court at the time of sentencing; it is an equal crucial point in supervision. Furthermore, success in probation/parole services, if it is to exist at all, must convey to the offender that he has the opportunity to utilize these services, not merely as an act of conformity, but as an opportunity to better himself and alleviate some of his personal problems. For example, I have a case that was discharged from probation six years ago. This client was repeatedly in trouble for her failure to exercise control over her emotions, and someone was usually the victim of her displaced hostility. Although she has not gotten into any difficulties of similar nature since, she will frequently return to vent her hostility and frustration in the privacy of my office where it can be absorbed, rather than directing it toward society and the first available scapegoat that presents itself.

Thus, although success means keeping the offender from reoffending, it also means the ability to convey to the offender that probation/parole services are willing to help him absorb and deal with those frustrations that exist within and around him. Simply speaking, if we can assist in helping the offender handle those feelings that he is besieged with, it follows that we probably will not have to concern ourselves about other forms of behavior, for one may well assist to resolve the other.

SUGGESTED READINGS

BAILEY, ROY AND MIKE BRAKE, *Radical Social Work*. New York: Pantheon Books, Inc., 1975.

BERNE, ERIC, *Games People Play*. New York: Ballantine Books, 1964.

BRIAR, SCOTT AND HENRY MILLER, *Problems and Issues in Social Casework*. New York: Columbia University Press, 1971.

CAMPOS, LEONARD AND PAUL McCORMICK, *Introduce Yourself to Transactional Analysis*. Stockton, Calif.: San Joaquin T.A. Institute, 1974.

DICKMAN, IRVING R. *Behavior Modification,* Public Affairs Pamphlet #540, New York: Public Affairs Committee, Inc., 1976.

FRIEDLANDER, WALTER A. ed., *Concepts and Methods of Social Work.* Englewood Cliffs, N.J.: Prentice-Hall, Inc., 1958.

GLASSER, WILLIAM, *Positive Addiction.* New York: Harper & Row, Publishers, Inc., 1976.

GLASSER, WILLIAM, *Reality Therapy.* New York: Harper & Row, Publishers, Inc., 1965.

HAMILTON, GORDON, *Theory and Practice of Social Case Work.* New York: Columbia University Press, 1956.

HILTS, PHILIP J., *Behavior Mod.* New York: Harper's Magazine Press, 1974.

KENNEDY, DANIEL B. AND AUGUST KERBER, *Resocialization: An American Experiment.* New York: Behavioral Publications, Inc., 1973.

LOZARUS, ARNOLD A. *Behavior Therapy and Beyond.* New York: McGraw-Hill Book Company, 1971.

MILLER, SHEROD, ELAM W. NUNNALLY, AND DANIEL B. WACKMAN, *Alive and Aware: Improving Communication in Relationships.* Minneapolis, Minn.: Interpersonal Communication Programs, Inc., 1975.

MOBERG, DAVID O. AND RICHARD C. ERICKSON, "A New Recidivism Outcome Index," *Federal Probation,* 36, no. 2 (June 1972), 50–57.

NATIONAL INSTITUTE OF MENTAL HEALTH, *Behavior Modification: Perspective on a Current Issue.* U.S. Department of Health, Education, and Welfare, Publication No. (ADM) 75-202, Washington, D.C.: U.S. Government Printing Office, 1975.

PARLOUR, RICHARD, "Training Manual for Responsibility Therapy." Loma Linda University School of Medicine and Riverside Day Treatment Program, 1976.

PECK, HARRIS B. AND VIRGINIA BELLSMITH, *Treatment of the Delinquent Adolescent.* New York: Family Service Association of America, 1954.

REID, WILLIAM J. AND ANN W. WHYNE, *Brief and Extended Casework.* New York: Columbia University Press, 1969.

ROBERTS, ROBERT W. AND ROBERT H. NEE, *Theories of Social Casework.* Chicago: University of Chicago Press, 1970.

ROBISON, J. AND G. SMITH, "The Effectiveness of Correctional Programs," *Crime and Delinquency* (January 1971), pp. 67–80.

SCARPETTI, FRANK AND R. M. STEPHENSON, "A Study of Probation Effectiveness," *Journal of Criminal Law, Criminology and Police Science* (1968), pp. 361–369.

STEPHENSON, RICHARD M. AND FRANK R. SCARPETTI, *Group Interaction as Therapy: The Use of Small Groups in Corrections.* Westport, Conn.: Greenwood Press, Inc., 1974.

STUDT, ELLIOTT, "Casework in the Correctional Field," *Federal Probation,* 18, no. 3 (September 1954), 19–26.

VOGT, HERBERT, "An Invitation to Group Counseling," *Federal Probation,* 35, no. 3 (September 1971), 30–32.

WRIGHT, JACK JR. AND RALPH JAMES, JR., *A Behavioral Approach to Preventing Delinquency.* Springfield, Ill.: Charles C Thomas, Publisher, 1974.

YOUNG, HOWARD S., *A Rational Counseling Primer.* New York: Institute of Rational Living, Inc., 1974.

12

Probation, Parole, and Community Relationships

The majority of correctional literature has, for some unknown reason, failed to treat the respective roles of probation and parole as members of the family of social services. The rationale for this omission is unclear. It is unfortunate and perhaps somewhat ironic that such a void exists because it only serves to widen the existing gap between the field of corrections and the community functions to which corrections is obligated. By this omission, probation and parole services are relegated to a lesser position in the social service structure than they probably deserve. There may be several reasons for this state of affairs and the matter will be dealt with in depth as this chapter progresses. The irony of the situation is that those who tend to characterize probation/parole as a form of casework within the correctional context criticize the attempt to integrate the classical casework method of treatment within the penal institution itself.

The initial assumption to be made is that corrections has become a sort of social leper, encompassing not only the offender but also those who deal with him as well. Perhaps this is an exaggerated assumption. Yet there are some very real concepts and theories that may account for this illusion, if an illusion it may be. The purpose of this chapter is to attempt to determine if and why there exists any distinction in the level of service expected as opposed to the actual amount delivered.

CRIME AND THE SOCIAL ALIENATION CONCEPT

"Alienation is a phenomenon concerned with man's estrangement from the society in which he lives or his estrangement from himself. This may be either a social or a psychological state of affairs and usually implies deviancy."[1] Although this concept is a contemporary one, the most publicized— if not one of the most original—concepts of social alienation goes back in sociological theory to the writings of Karl Marx. We can only speculate as to whether or not there was any loss of concepts in the translation of his writings, but it would appear that his original use of the term was applicable within the context of his economic/political thinking. Marx first used this term in discussing the state of alienation of workers from the means of production.[2]

The point to be made here is that where Marx appeared to establish social alienation as being a rather natural process, Emilio Viano and Alvin Cohn place it within another dimension with the specific inclusion of criminal behavior.[3] Further, the "unnaturalness" of crime causes Viano and Cohn to characterize such behavior as being deviant in nature and content. Without devoting a chapter or more to sociological theory, it is impossible to include even an adequate cross-reference of theories dealing with confluent concepts, yet a short discussion is important here. Social alienation is a superimposed fact that serves to color and to condition the perceived role of the offender as well as the status of the system designed to work with him.

Crime may be defined as a legal interpretation of a social act. Deviancy, then, is determined by a sanctioning process that is the presumed right of certain agencies of authority designed for this specific purpose. Thus, alienation in the contemporary sense of the word has lost some of its meaning, which initially was associated with a sense of purposefulness. We have regressed somewhat from the original ideas presented in various sociological theories by having inadvertently associated alienation with nonconformity. Especially in conjunction with criminology, we label offenders collectively as being "deviants," a rather gross misrepresentation when applied as a blanket statement/description. Richard Quinney states that "criminal definitions describe behaviors that conflict with the interests of the segments of society that have the power to shape public policy."[4]

The first conclusion that can be deduced from the above definitions is the

---

[1]Emilio Viano and Alvin Cohn, *Social Problems and Criminal Justice* (Chicago: Nelson-Hall Publishers, 1975), p. 25.

[2]T. B. Bottomore and Maximilian Ruben, *Karl Marx, Selected Writings in Sociology and Social Philosophy* (London: Watts and Company, 1956), pp. 167–177.

[3]Viano and Cohn, *Social Problems and Criminal Justice,* p. 25.

[4]Richard Quinney *The Social Reality of Crime,* (Boston: Little, Brown & Company, 1970), p. 15.

fact that (1) criminal behavior is conceived of as deviant behavior, and (2) such deviant behavior is not desirably assimilated within the normal channels of social intercourse.

The alienation process has become somewhat of an ambiguous and ill-defined two-way street. We may concur on the assumption that certain elements/subgroups react in a deviant (criminal) manner because they have been alienated from the system via various forms of social injustices, both real and imagined. On the other side of the ledger, society becomes alienated against senseless acts perpetrated against it and symbolically rejects the offender from the immediate social structure of the community proper. Whether the alienation process is super- or self-imposed remains somewhat secondary. The fact exists that the social/legal displacement process creates a subculture predicated on a diagnosis of deviant behavior.

Deviancy is fraught with negative connotations, but so, for that matter, is criminal behavior. It is highly probable that one term is most readily associated with the other because of the still-reigning concept that criminal acts are a result of a behavior involving a free or personal choice, one entered into without any form of mitigation or social duress. Suffice it to say, what may be a mitigating fact to one offender is not necessarily so to another. As long as we accept the concept that social control means the maintenance of order in society, anything that upsets the social equilibrium will be conceived of as a form of deviancy.

The concepts of at least two other social theorists seem appropriate to be examined in conjunction with our discussion here, those of Emile Durkheim[5] and Robert Merton.[6] These two sociologists are singled out here for their respective thoughts on deviant behavior and the contributions of the school of functional thought on the study of social phenomena. Both concepts seem pertinent to the issues at hand.

Durkheim adhered to the premise that deviant behavior is related to the group process that elicits or attempts to elicit social conformity. Although he treated this subject primarily in his study on suicide,[7] his thrust or premise dealt with the importance and influence of the group and the level of the individual's integration within the group. He saw the group as being a "regulator" of individual action and behavior. It may also be suggested that one of Durkheim's major contributions to the theoretical development of sociology was his emphasis on the role of social pressure and the general limitations on the personal freedom of the individual.

Equally pertinent to our discussion is Durkheim's related thinking about

---

[5]Emile Durkheim, *Suicide: A Study in Sociology,* trans. John A. Spaulding and George Simpson (New York: The Free Press, 1951); and *The Division of Labor in Society,* trans. George Simpson (New York: The Free Press, 1947).

[6]Robert K. Merton, *Social Theory and Social Structure* (New York: The Free Press, 1957).

[7]Durkheim, *Suicide: A Study in Sociology,* pp. 241–76.

the law in general and criminal/deviant behavior specifically. Undoubtedly he was one of the first theorists to point out that crime may be distinguished from other forms of deviance by its illegal nature. He did not, however, go as far as to state that all forms of socially disapproved behavior were necessarily bad. Neither did he feel that society would or could exist without some form of criminal behavior, and he indicated that such behavior has a very necessary role within the social structure. His concept of what is popularly conceived of as repressive and restitutive forms of law also concerns itself with deviance in an indirect fashion, and Durkheim enlarges upon deviant behavior as being against the "social solidarity" of society.[8] The theory of social solidarity is conceived by many scholars to be a dichotomy between a degree of expected deviance and that which becomes totally unacceptable in nature.

A second authority, Robert Merton, is probably best known for his anomie theory of deviant behavior. It is especially appropriate for consideration in this section of the chapter, for it has been referred to by many as one of the primary sociological explanations for criminal behavior. In essence, this supposition states that there is a definite strain that is generated when individuals are socially encouraged to structure their aspirations around a set of cultural goals but are constantly and even habitually denied access to a means of satisfaction through attainment of those goals.[9]

In our initial reference to Merton, mention was made of the fact that he ascribes to a theory of functionalism. Like Durkheim, he speaks of functional theory as having both manifest and latent consequences. The resemblance between Durkheim and Merton is to be noted in the latter's concept of a choice of consequences or "functional alternatives." He goes on to label the lack of social integration between society and culture as being *dysfunctional.*[10]

The pertinence of this discussion leads us to a second conclusion wherein we may attempt to relate deviancy to alienation. The dysfunctional concepts of Merton[11] and Durkheim[12] relative to deviancy stress the fact that the inability of certain individuals to integrate the cultural values into their frame of social reference does represent an alienation process imposed both from without as well as from within.

We have admittedly gone a long and tedious route to substantiate our point, that criminal behavior results in social segregation and the subsequent development of a subculture by those individuals who pursue this particular type of activity. Those professionals who choose to attempt to

[8]Durkheim, *The Division of Labor in Society,* p. 109.

[9]Merton, *Social Theory and Social Structure,* pp. 131–60.

[10]Ibid., pp. 33–36.

[11]Ibid.

[12]Durkheim, *The Division of Labor in Society,* pp. 70–110.

reestablish and to reintegrate this type of deviant into the social order—and we speak specifically here of probation/parole personnel—are somehow socially tainted by their relationship to the deviant. Society has never really relinquished the concept of *lex talionis*. We are willing to give the shirts from our backs to those whose deviancy is acknowledged to be beyond their control and perhaps their comprehension, but are only content to give the back of our hands to those who are deviants or assume a pattern of deviant behavior as a seeming matter of choice.

Probation/parole officers are sometimes viewed as being guilty of mollycoddling offenders, which certainly is in social contradiction to what the public believes should be the common practice. These professions are conceived by some narrow and misunderstanding minds to be supporters of deliberate losers. If there is any logic to this premise, it is that there may be alienation toward these services because of the stigma of criminality. It is not difficult to have some level of compassion for most individuals who are in need of and attempt to avail themselves of rehabilitative efforts, regardless of what name you label the process for attempting to evoke change. The chronic users of alcohol and drugs are sooner or later labeled "addicted" because they made the choice to indulge initially through a free will process of sorts. Yet we never speak of the *addicted* offender, only the chronic one. Even from a semantical standpoint, there exists an alienation process that becomes quite obvious.

We might conclude, then, that probation and parole services provided to the offender may be viewed by the public with a jaundiced eye. Society does not care to view the rehabilitation process of the offender along lines of classical treatment; it prefers a punishment approach, and counseling is not conceived of as a way of making the offender pay for his behavior. It is suspected that if a public poll was taken as to what vital obligation probation/parole should have, the answer would be heavily slanted in favor of surveillance.

We have noted that most penal institutions, with a few notable exceptions, are both geographically and symbolically situated far outside the mainstream of society. Many medium-size American communities are known as prison towns, for it is not unusual to have a high percentage of the employment in such cities prison-related. There is reason to believe that this separation of the prison population from society is a deliberate decision. First, it serves to isolate a high percentage of the inmate population from their place of residency and families. Second, such isolation in remote areas gives a semblance of greater security. The ability to escape successfully usually involves a trek by the inmate through a desolate area where he may be more easily detected. Third, it provides a symbolic appeasement for any social guilt the public might have on the premise that being out of sight is also out of mind.

Parole officers find themselves splitting their duty hours between their

home office, the residential community of the offender, and the penal institution itself. Unlike the probation officer—unless the latter serves a large
geographical area made up of small and rural communities—parole personnel may spend less than half of their time directly involved within the
primary community they serve, which is their agency home. They, therefore, will have less personal interaction with local community agencies except on a referral and follow-up basis. As such, it might be expected that
professional relationships among parole officers and other community
agencies may be more active in larger metropolitan areas than in less
populated parts of the nation.

We may, then, draw a summary conclusion of sorts that the alienation
process extends to the entire correctional complex. Whether crime is on the
upswing or not is a statistical crossword puzzle. Suffice it to say, there continues to exist great consternation about the fact that nothing seems to
deter, let alone prevent, the avalanche of crime. The public generally reacts
to five elements of the criminal justice system for blame placement in the
failure of prevention: (1) law enforcement, (2) the courts, (3) probation, (4)
the penal institution, and (5) parole. Although law enforcement personnel
receive their share of unjust criticism, society is generally ready to
acknowledge that the police have done their job once the offender is apprehended. Also the penal institution is a remote and misunderstood agency
that is viewed as serving a purpose even though that purpose may be little
more than to contain the offender.

The brunt of public criticism is therefore directed at the courts and at the
supervisory agencies of probation and parole. The courts and the proba-
tion/parole services are exposed to criticism for perceived as well as real inadequacies since they are readily within the view of the public and, to some
degree, within the clamor of public demands. The recidivist, then, is attributed to an inadequate and ineffective system according to the common
social viewpoint. Without objective insight, the repeat offender is conceived
of as being the byproduct of inadequate public agencies entrusted with his
care and restoration. As such, the alienation process is fostered, since it is
impossible to fight and to defy an unseen enemy. Because the community
elements of the correctional system are visible, they have become the focus
of criticism for their failure to restrain, to correct, and to redirect.

CASEWORK CONFLICT IN PROBATION AND PAROLE

Each and every one of us must serve a variety of masters during the
course of our lifetime. Therefore, there are times when we find ourselves in
the unenviable position of having to serve more than one taskmaster at the
same time while attempting to please all and slighting none. No place does this
become more apparent than in the public sector of service. Governmental

agencies must build their purpose and set their directives partly in response to the pressures and counterpressures of the general public's expectations of their service. When conflicts result, primary service deliveries may have to take a temporary back seat, and priorities may have to be altered for the sake of good public relations.

Corrections is no exception to such demands in the normal course of its operation. Because of public indignation and alienation to criminal behavior, corrections constantly finds itself in an ever-vulnerable state. Crime certainly affects the public as much as any other social malady. It is big business and one of the most costly operations in the world, employing more of the taxpayer's dollar than any other public undertaking. Although the author knows of no specific statistics, it is a reasonable assumption to state that the dollars spent at all levels of jurisdiction for the courts, law enforcement officers, operations of penal institutions, probation and parole services, costs to the victim, etc., will far exceed the money that is spent for purposes of national defense.

Probation and parole officers will often find themselves in a quandary of varying dimensions. Although their first obligation may seem to be to the client/offender, we have already specified that the public feels that it too must be served. Thus it becomes necessary here to enlarge on the issue of many masters, all of whom must be served in the fulfillment of the specific duties of the corrections profession. Certainly the pressure of diverse obligations—both recognized and perceived—is going to affect and dictate the policy of probation/parole agencies as well as alter the specific methods of working with offenders. Because of this problem of many masters, the individual probation/parole officer's obligations may be affected. Not only must he serve the public, but he also must learn to live with himself as a professional person, as a member of his agency, and, of course, as a private individual.

Several factors are suggested here as pertinent to the subject matter of this chapter. First, it must be recognized that the professional training concepts that the individual officer has used to prepare himself for this position may not be pertinent to the job demands. Second, conflicting roles and demands tend to isolate the probation and parole professions from other social service agencies and functions. Third, it may be assumed that probation and parole are in a position of uniqueness that defies a "natural" association with other social agencies based on the nature and the needs of the clients served. Since the trend among many authorities is to treat probation/parole as being aligned more toward a casework approach than any other discipline, let us use casework here as our guinea pig of sorts and attempt to relate the predisclosed pressures to this particular discipline and position.

Casework is, first of all, geared for treatment purposes as a way of effecting behavioral change. Although this would presuppose that "treatment," in turn, implies a level of dysfunctioning that needs attention, casework as a method does not appear to be at its highest level of effectiveness in dealing with individuals who may be cognizant of their social shortcomings but are not necessarily desirous of changing. Many chronic/habitual offenders will, by necessity, have to be classified as belonging in this category. Whether generic social work in general and casework specifically are prepared to cope with this type of client is debatable. As we shall discuss, it is contrary to the understood principles of any form of counseling to exclude casework services.

We generally conceive of casework techniques as working along with the client in an attempt to effect problem solving. This is in direct opposition to directive therapy or what might be conceived of as a "lecture/educational" discourse on the noted, perceived, and suspected problems of the individual in an effort to direct change. Directive therapy is often the form that corrections takes. It cuts out the clinical, facile, and subtle approach and substitutes a very concrete and emphatic demand based on the fact that the client is subject to such directives on the basis of his legal status and character. Preconclusions are more generally made by probation/parole officers, with accompanying instructions for their implementation, than a caseworker in any other agency context could ethically and professionally tolerate.

The mention of professional tolerationism brings into focus the need for a discussion of the transition from professional training to practice. Lloyd Ohlin, Herman Piven, and Donnell Pappenfort suggest that two basic issues are involved in this process.[13]

1. Those charged with the responsibility for professional education must maintain close integration between preparation and practice.
2. Educators and practitioners alike must create conditions in the field which will make professional behavior possible.

For whatever reasons, the professionally trained caseworker or the student/trainee has not always found this principle of professional toleration practiced in the area of corrections. For example, prisons have not readily opened their doors—primarily at the state levels—to having female counselors working with male offenders or the reverse situation of male workers dealing with female offenders. Although there are chinks developing in the traditional staff-inmate sexual ratio, these are only appearing with caution so as to prevent public overreaction. Therefore realistic training op-

[13]Lloyd E. Ohlin, Herman Piven, and Donnell Pappenfort, "Major Dilemmas of the Social Worker in Probation and Parole," from *Social Perspectives on Behavior,* Herman D. Stein and Richard A. Cloward, eds. (New York: The Free Press, 1958), p. 251.

portunities may not be available or may only be available on a piecemeal level of experience.

Much conflict may be found to exist between professional ideals of casework and agency and public expectations of services. The individual who becomes entangled within this web must, sooner or later, succumb and declare his allegiance to one vested interest or the other. Although it may be possible to meet all expectations and to still maintain a degree of effectiveness, the individual strain of such a tenuous position may lead to a high increase in staff turnover. We have not yet reached that point in time where most probation/parole administrators are treatment-oriented. Rather, they appear to be selected on their ability to run a tight and somewhat tough ship. This may be necessary if for no other reason than to satisfy the perceived conception of the service required.

The inability of the new professional to utilize his casework principles can create an identity crisis. If the new caseworker attempts to make waves, he is apt to receive a negative reception unless he is unduly skillful beyond normal comprehension. He may be repressed, ignored, and/or criticized for his efforts. If he chooses to stay and to therefore probably succumb to the system, he may well lose his professional status among other fellow caseworkers who are employed with more traditional agencies of service and identity. Neither will he have much chance to upgrade his skills since these are now becoming somewhat alien and nonprofitable for his immediate purpose and assignment. He, then, becomes alienated from his profession as a victim of association and necessity based on the dictates of his parent agency.

Such an alienation process does little to cement relationships between probation and parole and social service agencies. The problems, the clients, even the language and customs of probation and parole become an alien form of behavior to other agency employees. It is at this point in time that the caseworker probation/parole must assess his own position and feelings and research any identity crises he may have. No worker on the labor market, whether a professional or not, can function at an effective level if he is unhappy or cannot identify with the purpose and philosophy of his immediate organization. If he cannot effect change without a loss of purpose and fulfillment of agency obligations, he must make an immediate choice for the sake of himself, his employer, and his clients.

In circumstances other than probation and parole, it can be assumed that there are several rather basic facts peculiar to the client who seeks casework services. First, it can be assumed that the noncriminal client has some self-awareness of a crisis/problem that is causing him discomfort and therefore personally seeks to alter this condition. Second, this client is able to shop for an agency that will provide him with a service that will hopefully alleviate his problem. Third, this client is able to sell himself for casework services by actively describing areas of discomfort and perhaps can even set some tentative, realistic goals. Lastly, this client is motivated and probably possessed of the capacity to make changes with the assistance of some professional help.

The offender that the caseworker must deal with within a probation or parole agency is almost in a position of direct opposition to what has been described above as basic and elementary facets of a casework model. First, the offender probably has no self-direction or purpose in being within this type of a relationship other than the fact that it is a demand made based on his legal status. Second, it is highly unlikely that he would seek services on a voluntary basis from an agency, even if he were allowed this choice. Third, he will volunteer nothing because he cannot relate to the process. Lastly, his only motive for even showing up for such services is predicated on his chance to make points rather than progress, for he is presently under duress.

Such an approach (of the offender) is in contradiction to most principles of good mental health procedures. Although any good caseworker or therapist must be able to deal with hostility in clients, offenders present a different form of hostility. The caseworker who must deal with this hostility may find at least three specific forms of resistance that are not usually found in noncriminal clients who come for services on a voluntary basis. First, there is the offender who shows up because of the pressure placed on him but who will not participate in therapy. Second, there is the offender who talks constantly and is conditioned to give the correct responses. Lastly, there is the offender who views the consultant/caseworker as a member of the system who cannot be trusted with any revealing information.

Caseworkers in probation and parole who find that they must deal with this type of a resistive client certainly must experience a further conflict that would be "abnormal" to the social work profession, that of the possibility of having to assume a punitive and authoritarian role within the relationship. Caseworkers who serve traditional agencies need only close a frustrating case under the label of client unresponsiveness or lack of motivation, whereas the probation/parole caseworker must continue to supervise unresponsive clients since the latter's being untreatable is hardly sufficient grounds in itself for consideration of a revocation hearing.

Although the trend is slowly changing, there still exist many probation and parole officers who distrust the casework approach. Perhaps because of an identified or perceived association with law enforcement agencies, they often feel that their primary obligations are surveillance and investigation. Part of this feeling about their functions is in response to what they perceive to be the demands of the community. Also, because of vested interests, a lack of treatment orientation, or a callousness conceived and designed for self-protective purposes, the old guard probation/parole officer feels the offender is capable of change of his own volition. By keeping the offender in line, by forcing him to be accountable, conformity will be effected.

Such an approach is alien to the professionally trained caseworker. He (or she) will possess no such formal skills as might be related to law enforcement techniques. He has been trained to work with clients to effect change rather than to work in an undercover capacity. Although in larger probation/parole agencies the trained caseworker may find some duties commensurate with his skills and professional training, such as intake or treatment, a placement in a smaller agency where he must assume all duties is not within his bag of skills and sometimes not even within his immediate comprehension.

The conclusion to be drawn here is that professional casework training has many advantages, and theoretically it is one of the better professional assets to bring to probation and parole work. However, the general philosophy of the parole or probation agency and the standard operating procedures of these professions may well be such as to suppress the use of normal casework skills. The only common relationship between probation and parole and other social service agencies is that all are dealing with people who have problems and that they are in the common position to try and to effect change for better social forms of behavior.

THE NEED FOR COMMUNITY RELATIONSHIPS

It is rare to find any probation/parole agency that can function independently without the assistance of other agencies. Those probation or parole agencies that can function independently must fall into one of two categories: (1) either they are fortunate enough to have a staff that is plenteous and qualified, or (2) they are blind and insensitive to the function and purpose of the rehabilitation process and its requirements. Certainly there must be some such agencies so well-endowed as in the former category, but it is felt that these are in the minority. But again, these cannot be mere agencies to function so independently; they must be facetiously classified as empires.

Relationships with Local Police

Little has been said about the relationship of probation/parole agencies and other law enforcement bodies, especially the police at the local level. Certainly if ever a primary and meaningful relationship should be cultivated, it would be so recommended at this particular level. The stereotyped approach by many law enforcement bodies is to view probation/parole as being a singular creature designed, with the blessing of the courts and penal authorities, to turn loose a multitude of offenders back out on the streets without much second thought.[14] It is because of such a general attitude that good working relationships have failed to grow between probation/parole and local police departments.

Two very basic factors will determine the extent or limitation of these relationships. The first factor is the operational philosophy of the police model. Earlier in this book we mentioned the article by Daniel Glaser about the changing concepts in dealing with crime. In that essay, Glaser made mention of the service model approach.[15] One of the implications is that the normal and routine legal method for solving certain problems that have a social basis for their existence is to utilize social agencies whenever possible for appropriate services.

Obviously the only routine legal dispositions that can alleviate, for example, domestic problems requiring police intercession might be the issuance of restraining orders or the granting of divorces by the courts. If the police are oriented to the fact that probation can function as a diversionary unit, it is probable that a bond can be established that may work to the mutual benefit of all systems and all parties concerned. Probation departments that have good primary, face-to-face working relationships with the police or who can instill some mutual intimacy based on firsthand knowledge or geographical associations through areas of duty responsibility can enhance the work of the police.

The second basic factor for determining interface relationships is that probation/parole agencies should be willing to do some public relations work with local law enforcement departments. Such efforts can fulfill a variety of purposes; as listed below.

1. Public relations can assist in demolishing barriers of misunderstanding based on a lack of any functional knowledge of duties and purpose.

2. It may help in gaining the assistance of law enforcement personnel in providing surveillance functions of probationers and parolees who may be apt to reoffend.

3. It may reduce the amount of "harassment" from police that known offenders are sometimes subject to. If the police are relatively convinced that the probation/parole supervisor is able to perform a vital function, then the absence of their (the police's) bird-dogging tactics may result in less offender hostility toward the system.

4. Under certain circumstances, probation/parole officers may be able to avail themselves of law enforcement facilities for resource and for training /learning purposes.

[14]"Statement of Director J. Edgar Hoover," *FBI Law Enforcement Bulletin,* 27 (November 1958), 1–2.

[15]Daniel Glaser, "From Revenge to Resocialization: Changing Perspectives in Combating Crime," *The American Scholar,* 40, no. 4 (Autumn 1971), 60.

5. A united front allows for greater effectiveness in the completion of the immediate tasks at hand, i.e., more and better concerned law enforcement.

Relationships With Other Community Agencies

If we assume that the roots of crime lie within society as much as within the individual offender, and if the causes of crime are many and varied in nature, then we should be presupposing that a multiapproach is needed to alter these postulations. A multiapproach implies the need for a variety of involved and available community services. With no disrespect intended, this author has known many probation/parole officers who have deliberately avoided not only the use of community agencies but the idea of even communicating the fact that a mutual client was under some form of legal supervision. It can be assumed that there are a variety of reasons—some good, some questionable—for such an attitude.

It is possible that some probation/parole officers are attempting to prevent community or specific agency alienation when they fail to divulge the status of offenders. The seeming rule of thumb seems to be that the less that is known about the offender, the better chance he may have to function in a normal manner. The author can relate from firsthand experience the opposition encountered from various schools when approached relative to readmitting juveniles who had previously been a problem to those schools. The school authorities did not mourn the initial departure of such juveniles, and they were now only concerned that the reentry of such individuals would complicate or reactivate dormant problems.

Many a probationer or parolee has expressed genuine concern about being prejudged by prospective employers, school officials, and other members of community agencies when his or her legal status or past record is discovered. Many hours have also been spent by this author in an intervention process and counseling clients about issues concerning job applications. The main concern has generally been that of past arrests, public interpretation of the stigma of charges, institutional history, etc. Offenders are fearful of being denied opportunities if they are honest in their responses and equally concerned about being "discovered" if they falsify this information. The "damned if they do and damned if they don't" syndrome causes a lot of conflicts and subsequent offender alienation toward the system. It may even be sufficient in degree to thwart the rehabilitation process.

Two ethical issues are apparent. The first issue centers around our immediate discussion above as to just how much the offender should reveal about himself and his past. The second issue is the problem of ethics that the supervisor must face relative to client confidentiality and what may be required by the law relative to his status. (The reader is referred back to the discussion on this point in Chapter Seven.) There is no easy answer, especially when the offender's past record—particularly that of adults—is a matter of public record and therefore readily available to community agencies.

Part of the answer for deciding on the extent of factual presentation about the offender is going to have to be determined by the philosophy of the respective probation/parole agency. Such policy may be dictated both by the agency supervisor and by the law. Much depends on agency public relations and commitments to other agencies in the "sharing process." For example, the officer who avoids dealing with or confronting the juvenile offender who is acting out in school is avoiding his obligations for client accountability. The attitude often taken that school behavior is strictly a school problem can only result in negative cooperation from that respective agency.

Most offenders are multi-problem individuals. It is foolhardy to expect that any one probation/parole agency can hope to recognize, let alone combat, anything other than the most elementary of these problems and to operate other than in a crisis-intervention role. If there is no single factor that may be isolated as a causative force for criminal behavior, likewise there is no single cure. Criminal behavior is an outgrowth and culmination of a multitude of social factors, factors that cannot be segregated and isolated through a scientific, comprehensive, and totally conclusive method of social research. Although this does not preclude the need to try, our biggest enemy is oversimplification of facts.

Offenders may often need the benefit of a variety of services to assure the possibility of effecting change. No simple panacea exists. Total mobilization is required, and the ability to pursue interagency relationships for this purpose becomes necessary. Probation/parole departments are not subsidized to become all things to all offenders, nor should this be their primary function. Primary roles may vary, but certainly a key and most essential role is to be able to effectively assess the basic needs of the client and to plan for the supplementation of those needs. This will often require the use of other agencies, skills, and services.

Client Needs   It seems appropriate to make some passing reference here to client needs, not only to isolate how the offender perceives himself but also to note the diversity of content. Table 12-1 represents a ranking of parolee responses to a list determined, in part, from a composite of offender studies.[16]

[16]Rosemary J. Erickson et al., *Paroled But Not Free* (New York: Behavioral Publications, 1973), p. 68.

Table 12-1 *Rank Order of Needs and Adequacy of Need Fulfillment as Indicated by the Parolees (N = 60)*

Needs*	Rank-Order			Adequacy		
	Original Sample	New Parolees	Overall Total	Below Average	Average	Above Average
				%	%	%
Education	1	1	1	15	63	22
Money	2	2	2	53**	37	10
Job	4	3	3	37	40	23
Job training	3	4	4	33	35	32
Circle of friends	6	5	5	25	58	17
Home/shelter	7	7	6	10	55	35
Medical care	10	8	7	23	50	27
Recreational activities	5	10	8	25	52	23
Legal assistance	9	11	9	50**	42	8
Sexual life	12	6	10	20	53	27
Dental care	8	12	11	25	55	20
Marriage/home life	11	9	12	13	60	27

*Not listed in the order that they appeared on the interview schedule.
**Modal response is "below average" on these only. All other modal responses are average.

It should be recognized that the priorities given in this table will differ between probationers and parolees. This happens if for no other reason than because of the prolonged absence of the parolees from the community due to their incarceration. This tabulation stresses the point that the basic needs of offenders require more services than can be provided for by the supervising agency and its related services. This just reemphasizes the fact that probation/parole personnel are limited in the nature of their functions and, to be effective, must learn to operate along the lines of screening and referral services.

Changes Needed in Correctional Agencies' Relationships with the Community

Probation and parole services need to reintegrate themselves within the community social service structure. Although there will be some opposition from "old school" officers who do not care to be labeled as pseudo social workers, the fact is that conformity acquired through supervision/surveillance alone is always going to be insufficient to accomplish more than maintaining control and certainly will not meet needs other than the legal expectations of the particular agency.

If there exists a gap between corrections and other social service agencies, then much of the blame must be placed on the shoulders of the correctional system itself. The propagation of the image is somewhat self-imposed and therefore is restrictive by nature. Any basic change that can be accounted for in the last fifty years lies not in the alteration of the system as much as it lies in the nature and type of the offender coming through the system. The failure of probation and parole to occupy a meaningful niche in the social service structure, not just in the criminal justice and correctional system, tends to point out a professional lag in progress.

It must be recognized that this approach of total involvement is not going to be effective at all levels and with all offenders. We know that there will always be a percentage of criminals who must be either physically contained within an institution or symbolically contained through tough supervisory practices while remaining within the community. For those individuals, little more than surveillance can be offered. But, as we will see within the final chapter of this book, the trend points toward greater community involvement and more retention of offenders within the community. If this is the case and the shape of things to come, then images, roles, and relationships as they now appear to exist must begin to change.

SUGGESTED READINGS

CHAMBERS, CHARLES A., *Seedtime of Reform: American Social Service and Social Action 1918–1933*. Minneapolis, Minn.: University of Minnesota Press, 1963.

CHAMBLISS, ROLLIN, *Social Thought*. New York: Holt, Rinehart and Winston, 1954.

COHEN, NATHAN E., *Social Work in the American Tradition*. New York: Holt, Rinehart and Winston, 1958.

DEMONE, HAROLD W. JR. AND DWIGHT HASHBARGER, *The Planning and Administration of Human Services*. New York: Behavioral Publications, 1973.

DRESSLER, DAVID, ed., *Readings in Criminology and Penology*. New York: Columbia University Press, 1972.

KEITH-LUCAS, ALAN, *Giving and Taking Help*. Chapel Hill, N.C.: University of North Carolina Press, 1972.

KNUDTSEN, RICHARD D., ed., *Crime, Criminology and Contemporary Society*. Homewood, Ill.: Dorsey Press, 1970.

POLLAK, OTTO, *Human Behavior and the Helping Professions*. Jamaica, N.Y. Spectrum Publications, Inc., 1976.

SUTHERLAND, EDWIN H. *On Analyzing Crime*. Chicago: University of Chicago Press, 1973.

SUTHERLAND, EDWIN H. AND DONALD R. CRESSEY, *Principles of Criminology,* 7th ed. Philadelphia: J.B. Lippincott Company, 1966.

TAYLOR, IAN, PAUL WALTON, AND JOCK YOUNG, *The New Criminology: A Social Theory of Deviance.* London: Routledge & Kegan Paul Ltd., 1973.

TIMASHEFF, NICHOLAS S. *Sociological Theory: Its Nature and Growth.* New York: Random House, Inc., 1967.

VINE, MARGARET WILSON, *An Introduction to Sociological Theory.* London: Longmans, Green & Company, Ltd., 1959.

WOLFGANG, MARVIN E., LEONARD SAVITZ, AND NORMAN JOHNSTON, *The Sociology of Crime and Delinquency.* New York: John Wiley & Sons, Inc., 1962.

13

Problems in Probation and Parole Administration

Any organizational structure of consequential size can be characterized by at least two basic divisions of labor and respective functions: (1) the line personnel and (2) the administrative/supervisory hierarchy. Although some degree of overlap in duties may be noted, directives and policy decisions normally extend from the top level downward rather than appearing in the reverse order. Much time has been devoted to the duties of line officers in probation/parole during the course of this book. We now wish to turn our attention to management problems peculiar to the discharge of agency duties and roles.

In any organization, there exist complementary roles of line personnel and office management. The degree of effectiveness of the line personnel enhances the agency image and speaks of good management skills. The administrators, in turn, must set precedents and provide leadership as well as be able to transmit these qualities if the line personnel are to reflect and actively seek to effect agency purposes and goals. Management wholeness, then, requires the ability to coordinate these complementary roles so that they can function as a team.

Management skills and techniques vary little from one agency to another. Those deviations that do exist may generally be accounted for by the fact that there are always new methods or skills arising, and these skills/methods may be changed or adapted to fit a given situation.

There are certain unique characteristics to be found in the management of probation and parole work. The reader will remember from the previous chapter that there apparently exists a degree of stigma related to corrections. Coupled with this are peculiarities of management techniques relative to governmental organizations in contrast to the private sector. Thus, certain unique qualities in administrative approach can be expected.

Still some of the administrative headaches are as old as time itself. Purpose, goals, and self-evaluations are milestones along the paths of any successful venture. The recruitment, the training, and the retention of staff personnel are equally applicable in any endeavor. What, then, is unique enough about the administrative processes of probation/parole agencies to merit special consideration in a chapter unto itself? The uniqueness simply is the raw material ingested by the agency and the hoped-for product that it is supposed to expel. No process can mold and stamp out desired human behavior consistently and uniformly as might be done in a production line where inanimate products such as cars or TV sets are produced. Despite agency efforts to provide better services, corrections has been unable to meet the expectations of the general public. This is one of our concerns to be discussed here.

AGENCY PHILOSOPHY AND POLICY

In spite of the standards and policies imposed by the laws and governing bodies of the respective probation and parole agencies, the individual tone of an agency will be strongly influenced by the personal biases of that agency's own administrator. Subsequently, it can be expected that the orientation of the chief agency officer will reflect on the type of staff he gathers about him, the approach to the offender, the public image the agency has, and, perhaps even its level of success or failure in the fulfillment of its overall functions. Mediocre administrative practices may be able to meet minimum standards but generally will restrict flexibility in adapting a program of supervision to the specific needs of the client.

Similarly, the management's operating philosophy will influence the type of agency program. For example, it might be anticipated that a supervisor with considerable tenure and who may have worked his way up through the ranks to the top will take a tough, no-nonsense approach; whereas an agency head who is treatment-oriented and who selects his staff accordingly may create the image of being more flexible and perhaps even more permissive than his counterpart.

Shaped by personal vested interests as well as by the directives provided by legislative acts that establish a formal milieu, the external expectations of the agency are also known to be a guiding force in its approach to the offender. Reinhard Bendix offers a model of sorts when he notes the following:

> Democratic administration is defined as the art of compromise through which divergent and contradictory social forces modify one another and reach a final expression simultaneously reflecting the wishes of all but those of no group completely.[1]

In contrast to Bendix's model, probation/parole agencies, aware of a multitude of pressures both internal and external, often tend to "lump it" alone, pretending to owe allegiance to no one other than their clients, their immediate and affiliated agencies, and themselves. It becomes a case of choosing to ignore the horseflies of pressure and swishing them away without being deterred by their presence. It would appear that an operating principle exists to the effect that the end justifies the means.

It seems rather senseless that, despite the stress factors suggested, a platform of sorts composed of treatment and rehabilitation principles must be declared. Yet we have somehow backed ourselves into a figurative corner where we find that we (probation and parole) must give an accounting to the public for our services. In the private sector, we would no more demand to know the treatment program of a neighbor who is seeing a private practitioner than we would attempt to fly free-style, but agency practice must be open to public inspection. This does not mean throwing the door so wide open that all who pass may see within, but it does symbolically portray the fact that our agencies do have some obligations above and beyond their immediate context and clientele.

Corrections has long been a sacrificial lamb used extensively, and often unfairly, by political aspirants as a step from which to begin their upward climb to personal glory. It has also been stressed that this particular area has been a ping-pong ball batted back and forth between power factions either for personal gain or because this area has become a time-honored whipping boy. As stated by Lloyd Ohlin and co-authors,

> Elected judges, legislators, and other public officials have a vested interest in being on the popular side of a crisis, and occupational groups whose interests are inherently in opposition to client-centered probation and parole supervision are able to use periods of public excitement to further their own purposes. Consequently the administrator is under pressure to anticipate possible criticism and to organize the agency and its policies in self-protection.[2]

[1]Reinhard Bendix, "Bureaucracy: The Problem and Its Setting," *American Sociological Review,* October 1947.

[2]Lloyd E. Ohlin, Herman Piver, and Donnell M. Pappenfort, "Major Dilemmas of the Social Worker in Probation and Parole," in *Social Perspectives on Behavior,* ed. Herman D. Stein and Richard A. Cloward. Reprinted from *The National Probation and Parole Association Journal,* July 1956, pp. 211-25.

The probation/parole administrator may then find it necessary to react in certain ways to deal with this common intrusion. The housewife whose husband is leaning across her shoulder while she attempts to prepare dinner or the checker player whose moves are commented upon by a nearby kibitzer can well appreciate this position. The administrator recognizes the presence of his critics and their disruptive tactics and prepares a defense accordingly. He will find, however, that the more he resists outside interferences, the more the onlookers are convinced that he has something he is trying to hide.

The reader may wonder if client-centered services can be provided for by probation/parole agencies under such conditions and circumstances and just how effective they can be. This is one of the crucial factors that agency administrators must deal with. It is essential that the administrator become the buffer, and he must insulate his agency against outside pressures. Only by his doing so can the agency personnel focus on the immediate jobs at hand—the client and his problems.

The nature of the client served often dictates agency policy, although there is some question as to how far this policy should go. Juvenile probation departments, for example, often seek younger officers to facilitate communication with the adolescent client. In keeping with this approach, agency officers have adopted "cool" or "mod" mannerisms of dress and even evidence "macho-type" activities to lessen the apparent age gap. The assumption has long existed—and has been predicated in part on the age-of-reason theory—that juvenile offenders generally do not need classical forms of treatment as much as they need identity, acceptance, and understanding.

It is questionable whether such affectations will make any appreciable difference in client relationships if they are only used to cover up an otherwise routine task and are devoid of any genuine interest in the client. Sophisticated delinquents can spot a "phoney" a mile and a half away and will react accordingly in their relationship to that individual. Yet some agencies seek such unique approaches to try and fathom or penetrate the culture of the delinquent and to thereby understand what makes him operate in such a manner as he exhibits. One might call this "agency color" but the hues and roles are nothing more than a reflection of a specific agency policy.

Gimmickry is nothing more than innovativeness that sounds and appears too improbable to measure its possible degree of effectiveness. Although new approaches must be tried, it is relatively impossible to "con a con." Effectiveness in relationships should not be obscured by false impressions and loud but meaningless noises. The test of true counseling skills centers around the ability of the counselor to convey concern and a *genuine* attitude to work with the client rather than to entertain him. The probation or parole officer cannot expect to hide his intentions behind anything without fostering somewhat of a reciprocal reaction from his client.

Agency policy and philosophy must follow some very basic guidelines.

1. Policy and philosophy must be in keeping with the professional purpose of the individual agency.
2. The agency must convey dignity to itself by its actions, but more important, it must enhance the dignity of the client it serves.
3. The agency must set specific goals for its own growth and delivery of service as well as constantly evaluating its purpose and level of efficiency.
4. The agency must recognize its specific role(s) within the criminal justice system and must limit its activities, within its ethical standards, to those defined tasks at hand.
5. The agency must assist in conveying its true and explicit function as a community agency by fostering complementary working relationships with other services in the fulfillment of its primary obligations.

STAFF PROCUREMENT AND RECRUITING

A war cannot be won by the general alone who conceives of and formulates the battle plan; he must have the support of the low-ranking soldiers to fight the battle. Likewise, the ability of the probation/parole agency to meet and to improve on its primary obligations will depend on both the plan of action by management and the implementation of this plan by the line personnel. It is the line officer who enhances the agency, but it is the role of the administrator to plow, to cultivate, and to seed the fertile ground for such growth to take place.

Some discussion has centered around the subject—and some delicate toes were probably trod upon in the process—of the inconsistency of educational and employment standards and opportunities for individuals desirous of a career in probation and parole service. We recognize that most B.A. (bachelor) programs are not able to focus extensively on the subject of corrections so as to provide appropriate training for probation and parole. Thus, one of the primary problems that an administrator must face is the recruitment and procurement of personnel who can be made to fit in with agency needs and policies. Specifically, there are three suggested major areas of concern that administrators must deal with.

1. How to recruit effectively.
2. What academic disciplines to recruit from.
3. The matching of employee potentials with agency philosophies and goals.

The effectiveness of agency recruitment—the first major concern—is based on the product the agency has to sell and the quality of public relations used to portray its merits or services. Recruiting for governmental positions does, however, pose different problems from those found in the private sector. The government supposedly is a nonprofit organization and therefore cannot offer prize packages such as monetary-type incentives, profit-sharing, or stock awards to its employees. Neither can it mobilize and subsidize large-scale recruitment programs such as can be done by private industry. It is also common practice for the government to recruit, whenever possible, from within its ranks rather than to advertise "outside," except in cases where most other means have been exhausted.

Most governmental agencies have little to offer as an inducement other than the "opportunity to serve" approach. Furthermore, political affiliations can make or break certain agency positions where tenure is ensured only as long as the incumbent party can maintain its public status and position. Governmental service discreetly offers incentive programs for the good of the agency rather than for the individual's satisfaction. What we want to say is that personnel assignments within an agency are not necessarily individual achievements and accomplishments.

Probation and parole services are difficult to recruit for. The poor image of corrections is too often substantiated by reality. How does the administrator overcome the facts of unwilling clients, oversized caseloads, and inadequate budgets in his attempt to secure adequate personnel for adequate services? How can one make cod liver oil palatable, or trips to the dentist enjoyable? A comprehensive answer does not appear to be readily available.

The second major area of concern relates to the selective wooing of specific academic disciplines for agency personnel. Because of limited direct recruiting from college campuses, many probation/parole agencies may be guilty of lowering or altering their personnel expectations so as to adapt their recruiting policies to academic availability. For example, if correctional concern is a strong point of the sociology department of a nearby college, then local administrators will seek sociology graduates. The selection process is based more on availability and interest than on functional skills within the needed area of service. It is obvious that probation/parole administrators would like to have graduates with specific expertise such as casework or criminal justice training to select from, but it may well be that the chosen substitute is a viable alternative seized upon out of necessity, expediency, and availability.

Most areas of disciplinary desirability such as social work and criminal justice are only available at the graduate level of study. However, graduate-level students from such programs may not realize any appreciably larger monetary consideration than the undergraduate plebe when both enter the governmental field fresh from school at the same time. Unless, for example, the state system is highly progressive, most such governmental levels fail to differentiate on the basis of degrees unless it is for an administrative position. Furthermore, such a position will be offered the existing staff first before outside recruiting will be resorted to. Although this is fair to the incumbents within the agency, it does not allow for the infusion of new ideas and concepts that might be representative of an "outsider" who has not become stereotyped within the system.

It is also a brutal but frank fact that the civil service systems as we recognize them within our bureaucratic structure do not go out of their way to promote incentives or to reward staff readily by upgrading positions based on such factors as an advanced degree acquired during the course of employment. Probation/parole administrators may, then, settle for less, and be less selective in staff recruitment, because most academic levels will probably start as equals within the system.

Gad J. Bensinger of the Criminal Justice Program at Loyola University of Chicago recently conducted a study of a training program for criminal justice personnel in Cook County, Illinois. Under funding from the Law Enforcement Assistance Administration, a program was established to try and upgrade the skills of various levels of staff, both professional and semiskilled. One of the secondary conclusions made as a result of the effects of this program was the need for a reward system.

> A correlation between training and promotion, salary increments, job assignments, and other relevant factors should be established. The lack of such a reward system in Cook County is one of the major weaknesses of the training effort.[3]

This problem seems typical of many agencies throughout the country. It can be concluded that all men are created equal in both the eyes of God and the civil service system! Because of this built-in handicap, probation/parole administrators are not as selective as would be desirable in staff procurement. It becomes a simple case of manning all posts with what is available. Thus the selection process becomes somewhat methodical with few exceptions.

One of these exceptions is predicated on the basic philosophy of the agency and represents the third area of concern that some administrators feel the need to give priority to, that is the integrating of employees who are going to be compatible with the agency philosophy and goals. For example, if a probation/parole agency sees its primary role to be that of providing surveillance, then it may be less discriminatory when considering the skills and training of potential employees. On the other hand, the agency that is more clinical and treatment-oriented will attempt to recruit individuals who have specific interests and skills to effect this purpose. Or again, it might be

---

[3]Gad J. Bensinger, "Training for Criminal Justice Personnel: A Case Study," *Federal Probation,* 31, no. 3 (September 1977), 36.

ideal to seek a jack-of-all-trades to fill the position of a one-person office; yet to do so, may dull his primary skills because the pressure and total demands of the agency functioning level will only allow him to use such skills on a spasmodic basis.

One only foolishly uses a table knife as a substitute for a screwdriver. Similarly, the inept administrator is one who fails to utilize individual staff potential or places employees in roles that are incompatible with their basic skills or orientation. Not only are the general abilities of the staff of importance, their individual idiosyncrasies must likewise be accounted for in the placement of their respective roles and obligations. This, in turn, brings us to a discussion of staff utilization, a subject demanding more than a few passing comments.

EFFECTIVE STAFF UTILIZATION

The good administrator, the effective one, has the ability to recognize the strengths and weaknesses of his staff and thereby will actively seek ongoing methods of enhancing and/or overcoming those respective qualities. It is quite probable that individual assets and liabilities may not readily be detected until the staff members actually begin to assume the responsibilities of their new positions. The investment in procurement and the time spent in establishing new personnel within the system demand that every attempt be made to train and to utilize them in the role of their strongest capacity whenever it is possible to do so.

Aside from administrative positions, most probation/parole agencies of any consequential size contain several definable agency roles. One of the key positions that certainly demands expertise is that of the intake diagnostician who must process new cases, try to assess client needs and other related problem areas, and perhaps assume responsibility for case assignments to specific officers. All agency roles, however, should be complementary roles such as evidenced in the "hard-nosed" and the "maternal /paternal" figures that most agencies have. Cases assigned to officers are usually predicated on the perceived needs of the offender and the ability of the officer to best meet those needs. In this context, we are speaking of probation departments more specifically, although there are comparable roles within parole as well. There are also specialized duties among the employees of both types of agencies, including field investigators, treatment personnel, sometimes group or street workers, and minority/ethnic group specialists.

With perhaps the exception of treatment/diagnostic skills, few academic programs prepare students for the variety of roles, or, for that matter, even for the specific roles they may need to assume at the agency level. Edwin Sutherland and Donald Cressey note three role levels (which within the context of their book they direct specifically at parole)—the parole board, the case investigator, and the parole supervisor—where they feel that "training facilities are very inadequate, largely because no significant body of knowledge which can be directly applied in such training has been developed."[4] Where adequate training exists pertinent to line officers, it is suspected that such academic exposure merely serves to polish latent qualities that can later be more effectively defined and perhaps put to use. Tolerance of a job such as in the human services is rare; most potential staff members either quickly adapt or quickly leave, for it takes very little practical exposure to determine their capacity for these positions.

Thus, probation/parole administrators are placed in a position of attempting to assess the potential of new personnel, seeking to try and match roles with abilities, and trying to provide the exposure of responsibility without the risk of overexposure. The human services professions face unique problems in the sense that their clients and their needs and levels of motivation are, at best, difficult to readily ascertain. The complexities of the human personality does not readily adapt itself for easy matching of new clients and new staff members despite outstanding credentials of new personnel. The sophistication and prolonged exposure of the chronic offender to the system have given him a distinct advantage over the new officer in the battle to manipulate him (the offender) to effect change.

Two answers exist to the dilemma of staff growth and development of expertise. The first of these is effective supervision and the second is ongoing training. Ongoing training might be conceived of as an extension of routine supervision, but we would recommend that the training programs should be under the guidance/auspices of a specialist.

Yona Cohen indicates that staff supervision should encompass three basic functions:[5]

1. To ensure a minimum level of professional performance.
2. To promote the professional maturation of the individual officers.
3. To ensure that the administrative policy is carried out.

Supervision may be conceived of as sharing experiences and information that are new to the incoming personnel as regards their exposure to the field, the agency, or the type of a client. The primary function of supervision is orientation, initially for the incoming staff and then to continue along lines of information dissemination relative to policy and procedure. Most supervisors train and impart knowledge that is based on their own ex-

[4]Edwin H. Sutherland and Donald R. Cressey, *Principles of Criminology* (Philadelphia: J.B. Lippincott Company, 1966), 661.

[5]Yona Cohen, "Staff Supervision in Probation," *Federal Probation*, 40, no. 3 (September 1976), 17.

periences in their years of service. Although this may cover some of the basic staff needs, the supervisor may not be able to build on and add to this wealth of information simply because he lacks the opportunity for new personal experiences and further professional training. Therefore, outside specialists should be called in to impart additional needed training.

It is often necessary in smaller agencies for supervisors to carry some cases of a selected nature. This burden, coupled with administrative duties, may restrict the supervisor from acquiring new experiences and from learning new training methods. Alan Leavitt suggests that probation administrators should concern themselves with "learning outcomes rather than teaching processes."[6] The implication is a meritorious one, for it allows the administration to focus on defined problems rather than on anticipated ones.

A realistic danger in supervision is the tendency to restrict the creativity of agency personnel without awareness of such behavior. It cannot be expected that all agency members can be molded into a unified approach to their clients, and neither is this desirable. Although it should be expected that agency personnel will support the agency purpose, both the needs of the clients and the skills of the employees will be neglected if flexibility of treatment methods is discouraged just because these methods are not in step with the philosophy of the administration. We speak here of the need to allow "blank checks," within reason, for treatment approaches on the client's behalf. Most probation/parole officers are not devoid of motivation, or they would not be in such a profession in the first place. However, an apparent lack of motivation may be indicative of an officer "burning out." If such a characteristic is noted among more than one officer, it could well reflect a need for an evaluation of agency practices, which might be a contributing factor to such a noted effect.

Staff training is often more theorized than it is practiced in probation/parole agencies. We recognize that limited funding and resources, as well as the routine demands of the workload, are contributing factors that detract from this need being readily met. Several suggestions are made below for solving this problem of staff training.

First of all, training of the individual officer may be utilized as a staff function. Many social service agencies are able to meet dual obligations by a popular process called client "staffing" or "case critiquing." This is a process of group learning as well as individual help to the officer who presents the case for consideration. Introductory information usually contains a brief social history, an accounting of the offender's antisocial behavior, in-

[6]Alan Leavitt, "The High Art of Staff Leadership," *Federal Probation,* 38, no. 3 (September 1974), 31.

stitutional history if any, mitigating factors, and level of dysfunctioning. The staff is then presented with the immediate problems of concern the officer is experiencing in his client relationship, what attempts he has made to cope with it, and the general results. The staff as a whole then attempts to suggest alternatives and to evaluate the potential of new treatment/coping methods.

Such an approach not only offers fresh thoughts on behalf of the immediate case, but it may create an identification situation for other officers who are experiencing similar problems with cases of their own. The total input of the staff not only allows for a sharing of concepts but it serves to foster staff unity and mutual concern. This is obviously of as much value as are the supervision/treatment concepts that are discovered in the course of the staffing process.

A second suggestion for staff training might be the exploration of community resources and services. The purposes and skills of other agencies that might be utilized by the probation/parole staff could be detailed along with the necessary explanatory material as to intake or referral procedures, eligibility factors, cost, etc. It is further suggested that such information be subsequently retained in a written form and be maintained in a resource manual of sorts for future reference by the staff when needed.

Another suggestion for staff training pertains to time management. There are instances when so much time is devoted to staff meetings that it becomes almost impossible for the staff to meet the primary needs of the agency.

This author vividly remembers a training program he once was required to attend on "The Management of Time." The program was scheduled to last for a one-hour period, but it extended to almost two and one-half hours before it finally terminated. Supervisors must remain cognizant of the commitments of staff and how an overabundance of training can alter their morale as well as affect primary agency commitments. Bensinger stresses that there is one fundamental principle relative to training that should never be compromised, "Training must always be conducted on agency time rather than on the trainee's own time. Repeated efforts. . .to experiment with alternative approaches, especially in correctional settings, have failed miserably."[7]

Probation/parole administrators must learn ways of implementing agency deficiencies for staff as well as for client purposes. Consultant services may offer an alternative, but this is often expensive and is often not included within the agency budget. The agency of the author has attempted to circumvent this problem by attempting to utilize our consultant in a dual role. His primary function is client evaluations and treatment, but we have utilized

[7]Bensinger, "Training for Criminal Justice Personnel," 35.

his "idle time" by placing him in a position of staff trouble-shooter. Such things as interviewing techniques, methods of dealing with resistance and defense mechanisms, the feasibility of certain clients as treatment candidates, or alternate methods of exploration of client problems such as might fall into medical categories have become his secondary function. Although we are fortunate to be able to budget for him, we are continuing to protect our dollar's worth by having him serve in a variety of capacities.

Agencies who cannot monetarily retain consultants might do well to consider the use of advisory boards comprised of voluntary members. Some probation/parole administrators may revolt against such a suggestion, and we can only attribute this to their assumed role of agency self-containment.

Our agency, which boasted a bigger advisory board than it did a professional staff, used such a group in a presentencing, staffing manner. We attempted to include a cross section of community resources, which comprised our consultant, a lawyer, a minister, a nurse, a member of the division of vocational rehabilitation, a representative of the state employment office, an AA member, a staff member from the Salvation Army, our volunteer coordinator, and a representative of the public school system. On certain instances, where juvenile offenders were involved, adolescent peers were selected to serve as part of the board. Recommendations were made after an interview with the offender and were presented to the court at the time of disposition for consideration. These recommendations also served as guidelines for the supervising line officer to use when probation was formally granted by the court.

The utilization of such a board as this served to meet a variety of needs.

1. It brought together a variety of orientations and perspectives on behalf of the client and the court.
2. It established a resource person(s) within an agency who had prior knowledge of the case, and sometimes a rapport with the offender, who could be utilized if a referral to that particular agency was made.
3. It provided some expertise both to the client and to the agency without cost.
4. It changed the concept of the offender about the corrections system from that of being only punitive to that of having some social concern.
5. It enlisted community support and concern from the representatives on the board for the role and problems of the court as well as a better understanding of its function.

PROBLEMS FACED BY AGENCY ADMINISTRATORS

Probation/parole administrators often find their respective agency's effectiveness diminished because of a variety of factors that might be attributed to "natural" distractions. Although many indirect as well as direct references have been alluded to throughout this book, our discussion priorities here will be focused on the lack of controlled intake and the inappropriateness of agency use by referring services.

Probation services are the recipients of referrals from the court, whereas parole agencies are the beneficiaries of recipients from the penal institutions. There are certain exceptions to this format, but these variations comprise a small percentage of the overall agency intake. For example, some of these exceptions for probation may include referrals from the school system, cases involving children who are required by law to attend school on the basis of age but who fail to be in attendance as expected. Child welfare departments also may find it necessary to utilize juvenile courts and their probation departments in certain cases involving custody and supervision of minors. And parents in many jurisdictions may file a formal petition with the court on behalf of their children who are alleged to be beyond parental control and in need of supervision. But the total number of such referrals is small in proportion to total court referrals.

Parole agencies may also have the responsibility of supervising cases—including probationers—from other states on the basis of what is known as interstate "compact referrals." A change of residence, for example, of a probationer from one state to another could legally place him under the guidance and surveillance of the parole officer from another state. Parole departments would also supervise offenders who are on some sort of a furlough or leave from out-of-state penal institutions and who are within the community for a short period of time on a trial basis.

Referrals of this nature are not at all uncommon and may account in part for some of the oversize caseloads that inundate most probation and parole agencies. All of this is in contrast to the ethical standards and professional concepts that regulate most other social agencies (or professionals) in their control of intake. For example, your doctor or dentist may not be able to see you for a week unless it is an absolute emergency that prompts your request. Mental health centers also put clients in holding patterns when staff time is overcrowded, and they ethically feel that it would be unfair to the client to try and work with him on a spasmodic bases. But whoever heard of a waiting list for probation or parole?! Since probation and parole are legal statuses provided for and accorded by an act of law, the agency as well as the offender is bound by such directives.

Such an influx of cases certainly taxes the abilities of any administrator in these fields. Because the client is virtually unknown and because there is no way of knowing in advance the time demands that will be required of the supervising officer in conjunction with a case, it is impossible to budget staff time accurately. Further, even when experienced officers can predict the periods of time when intake will be heavier than normal, this knowledge will not necessarily solve the problem of adequate staffing.

It may be anticipated that there will be peaks and valleys in the work load, although the valleys are never appreciably frequent enough to allow for much more than the opportunity to gain a deep breath. Administrators cannot staff agencies accordingly and hire extra hands just for the harvest season. Somehow they must develop techniques for handling the over-flow when it occurs and to do so within the context of existing staff and time.

Not only is the size of intake overwhelming, the nature of many of the cases referred is equally disconcerting to agency administrators. Referrals are often of an inappropriate nature and can therefore subject the officer as well as the offender to probable failure. Both the client and the officer may recognize the futility of the situation and symbolically concede defeat without much more than a faint effort at altering the perceived situation.

One reason for such failure is that the judicial prerogative of granting probation may often be abused.

> A pre-probation investigation is mandatory in only a few states. Even in these states, many judges do not wait for an investigation; instead they base their decisions on the offender's statement about himself, the nature of the offense, or the recommendations of persons outside the probation department. These are likely to be decidedly inadequate as a basis for policies. It is largely because of this inadequacy that probation has been brought into ill repute.[8]

It is possible that some of the judiciary may be under the impression that an intake interview will automatically be conducted by the probation department for purposes of program determination. As such, the thinking may be that it doesn't matter whether the interview takes place before or after the fact of granting probation. Such circumstances haunt many proba-tion administrators because some judges apparently are under the impres-sion that they have sufficient judicial sense to compensate for a lack of awareness of the offender's prognosis, and thus many offenders who should be incarcerated are released to the probation department. Judicial unawareness of the potential of probationary services is not an uncommon situation.

Many judges are not only uncertain about how to effectively use proba-tion services but are also reluctant to find out. The assumption that a proba-tion department too often serves as a sort of judicial garbage can is a relatively honest one. If nothing else has worked from past judicial disposi-tions and nothing either innovative or effective permeates the judicial mind, it may be commonplace to grant probation outright without the benefit of any investigation whatsoever. Probation should not be promiscuously granted without the knowledge in advance of some basic facts.

[8]Sutherland and Cressey, *Principles of Criminology,* p. 485.

1. Is the probation department capable of providing the nature of services required to rehabilitate the offender?
2. Is the offender motivated to change and to utilize help, or is he offering a facade to the court in the hope of leniency?
3. Has the offender been under supervision before, and if so, how did he respond to those services at that time?
4. Is there any reason to believe that the offender may reoffend, or is he facing other charges that may alter his status for probation consideration if convicted on those pending charges?
5. Is the offender cognizant of probation and what expectations may be demanded of him if he is accorded this privilege?

Probation administrators will, sooner or later, acquire a primary concern about selectivity of clients. To have the court unload unlikely, unwilling, and undesirable cases on the agency is to create a variety of problems. First, it diminishes staff effectiveness, which will be compounded by accompanying problems of morale. Second, it results in inadequate services to deter recidivism and therby fosters the image that probation does not work. Third, it serves to deter professional growth and agency status, a self-reflecting concept that also tarnishes the image of the court based on ineffectiveness, inappropriateness, and a lack of communication from within. Fourth, it creates a level of contempt among offenders for the system and enlarges on the imagined inadequacies of that system. Lastly, it serves as a deterrent to the expansion of probationary services into more meaningful areas of work, and it limits the opportunity to focus intensively on clients who can and are willing to respond to the services that would be available to them.

Parole agencies face similar problems. The overcrowding of our prison systems is resulting in the infamous revolving door policy whereby it becomes almost necessary to release one offender in order to admit another. Like probation, parole cannot control the amount and nature of its referrals, for it has no control over in-take. Even though the facts that might be contained within the preparole report are of a negative nature and even though planning for the release of the offender has been unproductive, the release may still be granted because of space necessities.

Prediction scales that attempt to measure the probability of success or failure of parolees are merely indicators of trends and variables that may enhance or restrict adequate adjustments. The ability to gauge the reaction of individuals or groups to adjust to one environment while being retained and conditioned to another is not a practical determiner of anything other than the establishment of a probability factor. Therefore, parole administrators must concern themselves with even a greater unknown factor than faces probationary agencies and their staffs.

If we knew just how crowded our penal institutions are, we would recognize that talk of a revolving door policy is more than facetious banter. It may well be that many individuals are being paroled not because they are ready, but because of a need for more inmate space within the walls and cellblocks. The offender who has "looked good" may get an early out because he *appears* to be a fair risk to make it. Parole administrators are only too well aware that prisoners are being "shoved out" periodically without the benefit of adequate community planning for their release. Parole boards are not notorious for their utilization of scientific methods of determining offender release readiness and therefore are operating primarily on a calculated risk basis.

Parole agencies have little control over the degree of supervision demanded of their officers. Probation departments are largely self-determining as to the intensity of client accountability, and they have somewhat of a free rein in defining the degree of supervision required, but it is not unusual for the parole board to specify the level of supervision demanded of the officer and agency in respect to a parolee. Therefore, time allocation of staff is predetermined and is taken out of the hands of the administrator as well as of the individual parole officer.

RESEARCHING FOR EFFECTIVENESS

Aside from the individual as well as some of the collective problems of probation/parole agencies, one common area of concern is determining a method of judging agency effectiveness. Whether you label such a task as an evaluation process or program monitoring or agency accountability is of no real importance. Good management practices demand that there exists the need to regularly back off to attempt to determine the correlation between predetermined objectives and the agencies' abilities to meet those established goals.

Probation/parole administrators have the tendency to gauge agency effectiveness on a crude criterion that looks at little else other than the recidivism/revocation factor. Under this standard, there is the fallacy perpetrated of trying to relate the number of failures to the number of cases the agency is responsible for. This has become somewhat of a necessary evil since this particular statistic is a reality factor that is easier to account for than the abstract qualities of success. Success is viewed collectively, and erroneously, as an absence of new offenses or revocation proceedings. The premise is a correctional variation on the axiom that no news is good news.

The fallacy of this approach is that we are attempting to predict success or failure largely on the behavior of clients rather than examining offender behavior in light of staff effectiveness and efficiency. Furthermore, it is highly probable that there exist no standard criteria that can be used for general program assessments in probation/parole services. The variables involved are too many and perhaps too complex in nature to be readily resolved. Let us attempt to elaborate on these points for reasons of clarity.

Offenders who are granted probation or parole *should* be screened candidates who are capable of and are motivated to alter their behavioral patterns. What our research plans cannot measure is if the offender would make it without any supervision whatsoever. In other words, are certain offenders under the legal status and guidance of probation or parole going to "make it" anyway? The author contends that present research methods are still dealing with a biased deck of cards since members of both the control and experimental groups *are still offenders.* A better method of researching staff and agency effectiveness would be for the staff to practice their skills on one group that is composed of nonoffenders to determine if this particular grouping would respond to the method rather than the context. However, this obviously is not a practical method.

The second factor that hinders research methodology is that it is relatively impossible to determine the "assisting" nature of other influences on offenders such as family and what we could call "important others" with whom there are positive associations. Again, what cannot be measured is the amount of negative and positive influence on the offender and to what degree these associations have been pertinent to the adjustment level of the offender.

A third factor is the possibility that the supervisor may have to be changed because he is not achieving positive client response. Probation/parole agencies that are not treatment-oriented may not evaluate the relationship of the client/supervisor in the light of what characteristics the officer brings to this relationship, characteristics that can contribute to a negative client response such as acting-out behavior that might include future lawless acts. Although the playing of a variation of musical chairs with the offender and the supervisor is to be discouraged both from a management and from a philosophical standpoint, some change in supervisor may be required. Too often, failure to achieve a positive response or conformity is attributed to the client rather than attempting to examine the supervisor's approach to that client and understanding his role within the relationship. Such changes of supervising personnel will of course cause havoc with any research techniques.

Fourth, the variations in offenders, the different sizes and qualifications of the agencies, and the diverse staff skills all present too many variables to effect a common research method to be used collectively. Thus, if the offender's needs cannot be met by his immediate supervisor, this should not imply that the deviant behavior of the client is irrevocable.

The prior experience and the degree of legal involvement of the offender previous to the time of attempted research are some of the many variables to be considered. An offender who is placed under supervision on the first offense in contrast to an offender who has been arrested many times before being granted probation will require different techniques and will show different results for research purposes. Still, both individuals will be treated on the basis of having a common denominator, that of having offended and having been convicted.

Our bureaucratic methods tend to seek out cold statistics rather than to measure social factors, but administrators have no clear-cut standardized yardsticks that can be definitively used, other than personal criteria, to measure success. The agency administrator must also necessarily act in response to established accountability factors as imposed and demanded by his parent body of authority. Thus the reader must accept the fact that certain problems facing probation and parole agencies are self-imposed or self-perpetuating. Other problems are related to the fact that certain expectations are of legal and bureaucratic origin and are used more on behalf of such matters as budgeting and fiscal accountability rather than being client-centered. Furthermore, as discussed above, we are still unable to isolate the many social variables that exist in the human services professions, and the blame for this should be selectively placed where it belongs—on society, on every one of us—not just on probation and parole.

SUGGESTED READINGS

DRUCKER, PETER F., *The Practice of Management.* New York: Harper & Row, Publishers, Inc., 1954.

FRIESEN, ERNEST C., EDWARD C. GALLAS, NESTU M. GALLAS, *Managing the Courts.* Indianapolis, Ind.: The Bobbs-Merrill Co., Inc., 1971.

HEMPLE, WILLIAM E. AND WILLIAM H. WEBB, JR., "Researching Prediction Scales for Probation," *Federal Probation,* 40, no. 2 (June 1976), 33–37.

HOREJSE, CHARLES R., "Training for the Direct-Service Volunteer in Probation," *Federal Probation,* 37, no. 3 (September 1973), 38–41.

KLEBER, T. P., "The Six Hardest Areas to Manage by Objectives," *Personnel Journal* (August 1972).

MALI, P., *Managing by Objectives.* New York: John Wiley & Sons, Inc., 1972.

MCCONKEY, DALE D., "Applying Management by Objectives to Non-Profit Organizations," *S. A. M. Advanced Management Journal* (January 1973).

MCGREGOR, DOUGLAS, *The Human Side of Enterprise.* New York: McGraw-Hill Book Company, 1961.

MURPHY, PATRICK J., "The Team Concept," *Federal Probation,* 39, no. 4 (December 1975), 30–34.

MYREN, RICHARD A., "Education for Correctional Careers," *Federal Probation,* 39, no. 2 (June 1975), 51–58.

SECHREST, DALE K., "The Accreditation Movement in Corrections," *Federal Probation,* 40, no. 4 (December 1976), 15–19.

STRAUSS, GEORGE AND LEONARD R. SAYLES, *Personnel: The Human Problems of Management.* Englewood Cliffs, N.J.: Prentice-Hall, Inc., 1967.

WALDO, GORDON P., "Research and Training in Corrections: The Role of the University," *Federal Probation,* 35, no. 2 (June 1971), 57–62.

WALDON, RONALD J., "Correctional Administration: Employee Promotions *Federal Probation,* 41, no. 1 (March 1977), 49–54.

WICKS, ROBERT J., *Applied Psychology for Law Enforcement and Correction Officers.* New York: McGraw-Hill Book Company, 1974. Chapter 14.

14

Future Trends in Probation and Parole

It is easy, in most subjects to put together an article that deals with future trends. If the author who makes such an attempt even comes close in his prognostications, he is hailed as being of great insight. Should he miss the boat completely, he can rationalize his inaccuracies by saying that when guessing games are played. the participants must be well aware of the odds and that the odds were not in his favor when the cards failed to come up right for him. The field of corrections, however, may present special problems in forecasting future trends.

Perhaps it should be relatively easy to produce some reasonably accurate predictions in corrections based on its lack of a radical and convincing track record over the years. Facetiously, one might state that any new and unique changes in the field may be considered to be radical in nature. Notwithstanding, some trends are becoming apparent; although for every two steps forward, many such alterations and changes have been characterized by one step backward. This chapter will examine several "hunches" of the author about the future of corrections. We will also look at the concept of community corrections in depth, including a variety of local-centered programs, and will review some of the changing roles in probation and parole, and finally, we will make some wild guesses about the future of the penal system.

COMMUNITY-BASED CORRECTIONS

The idea of community-based corrections is a generic concept that encompasses a diversity of programs. There is only one distinction to be made in regard to incarceration—an offender is either "in" or he is "out." The fact that the prison that contains him is located in the city where he has lived most of his life does not serve to make his "time" any more tolerable than that of the man in the cell next to him. When we speak of community-based corrections, we may be referring to regional penal settings, halfway houses, work-release programs, and prerelease parole centers—among the more common of such facilities and programs. Within these, there may exist some variations of purpose and operational procedures; but probation and parole will have certain specified roles, although it may be anticipated that the nature of these roles will be increased or altered in time to come.

Vernon Fox speaks of community services as a means of utilizing non-traditional roles that exist to supplement and complement the rehabilitation process of the offender.[1] Our Chapter Twelve reflects Fox's in-depth thinking that the role of ancillary services that exist—but that exist independently of correctional services within the community—must be mobilized and utilized to effect the redirection process of the offender. This is one of the trends that is projected to expand and to be enlarged on in the years ahead, that is, the greater recruitment and/or purchasing of outside services to enhance the correctional processes in an attempt to return the offenders/clients to the community with a greater hope for their ability to adjust and therefore to be less apt to reoffend.

Corrections has not always been the function of governmental agencies. We are aware of the role of the church and especially of the Quakers in the correctional movements of this country. Furthermore, until just over twenty years ago, at least one state still lacked a specialized program for the administration of its prison system. It was not until 1957 that the State of North Carolina removed the administration of the state prisons from under the state highway commission, where inmates were used as a labor force on the road networks there.

History records that some of the first halfway houses were in use in the late 1700s in England and were used extensively for juvenile offenders. A comparable program in the United States—and one of the first on this continent—was founded in New York about 1845. This program was privately administered and was under the auspices of the Quakers. This effort was followed about twenty years later when a private group in Boston opened a residential center for females coming out of prisons and out of other correctional/penal institutions.

Although these events are recorded here in a matter-of-fact manner, their inception, as well as the inception of similar offender-housing programs that soon followed, was not without incident. Accounts in correctional history indicate a great deal of public hostility to the presence of such dwellings within the community. Ronald Goldfarb and Linda Singer note that public indignation was not limited to the citizenry alone. Those authors

---

[1]Vernon Fox, *Introduction to Corrections,* 2nd ed. (Englewood Cliffs, N.J.: Prentice-Hall, Inc., 1977), p. 257.

relate that the police reaction shortly before the turn of the twentieth century was so great that it took the official intervention of New York City's police commissioner, Theodore Roosevelt, to put a stop to such practices.[2]

Society has always had, and will always have, a distinct role in the correctional master plan. It has been society that has nurtured and fostered, in part, certain types of criminal behavior, and it is society that must ultimately absorb the offender following the disposition of his case. The community presents a kaleidoscoping of roles, including rejection and demands on one extreme, and assistance, concern, and professional mobilization of services on the other. The unalterable fact remains that society cannot escape its social responsibility to the offender; it can only attempt to avoid the immediacy of confrontations that will, sooner or later, be inevitable.

Our projections suggest several trends that will become increasingly apparent in community corrections.

1. The greater use of split sentences by the courts.
2. An increase in regional detention facilities.
3. The advent of community court-level classification systems.
4. An increase in diversionary programs within the community.
5. A growth of specialized services within existing, but nontraditional, agencies to deal specifically with clients from the correctional systems.
6. The increase of self-help groups within the community by and for ex-offenders.
7. An expansion of purchased services from private agencies.
8. The remodeling and restructuring of the courts to allow greater effectiveness in the sentencing procedure.
9. Greater use of work-release programs for offenders.
10. An increase of lay groups to deal with problems of offenders, with such programs to be spearheaded by volunteers.

These projections will initially be discussed in the general sense of their conception. Then, in keeping with the theme of this book, the specific roles of probation and parole will be examined in relation to such suggested areas.

THE SPLIT SENTENCE

The origin of the split sentence escapes this author, although the underlying philosophy and method of use are well known. This particular judicial tool involves a sentence with a specified period of incarceration, but suspension may be made on the basis of contingencies observed. It is customary to suspend a high percentage of the sentence, and the offender therefore does but a short period of time imposed before being released. Hence the term *split sentence.*

[2]Ronald L. Goldfarb and Linda R. Singer, *After Conviction* (New York: Simon & Schuster, 1973), p. 553.

The purpose and philosophy of this technique are based on two factors: one is the shock effect, and the second is the secondary nature of punishment via-à-vis more important and meaningful alternatives that should be considered on behalf of the offender.

The shock factor is simply an attention-getting mechanism imposing a reality status on the offender. He is subjected to incarceration to instill within his thinking that if he has one more conviction, he can expect a prolonged and uninterrupted stay at the point of his next sentence. In effect, he is being asked to evaluate for himself if this is what he wants out of life and to gently remind him that he controls his own destiny in this respect. Initial impressions are vital and can be a deciding factor to the younger and more impressionable offender when confronted with an immediate exposure to this way of life.

The second factor relates to contingencies imposed at the time of sentencing. The split sentence implies that either the court doubts the need for such a heavy sentence to be served in full, based on either a lack of chronic criminal behavior, or that there exist other needs that cannot be met in this particular manner. Certain mitigating or contributing factors may be primary as to treatment needs, and punishment may therefore be conceived of as somewhat secondary in nature. The split sentence is, then, predicated on the meeting of certain imposed contingencies in exchange for the partially suspended sentence. The most common such contingency would be that there are no new violations of the law, although there may be other demands, usually for some involvement in a specified program.

Although split sentencing is most common in conjunction with local detention facilities, i.e., the jail, it may not be uncommon in the future to see an extension of its use into a reformatory-level placement. There are, of course, decided disadvantages to using such facilities since they do not allow for classification and effective programming, they are expensive beyond current comprehension, and they only serve to compound the revolving-door concept by placing administrators of the institutions in roles of inn-keepers. We therefore would not anticipate this particular placement being used extensively, although it can be predicted that more than a common amount of thought will be directed toward consideration of using reformatories in this manner.

REGIONAL JAILS

Jails at the local level—both municipal and county—have long been the backbone of community corrections, and have often been the only intermediate step that many courts have available to them. Unfortunately, they are usually found to be in poor physical condition as evidenced by many required closures, they are staffed only on a need basis, and they are largely devoid of programs. Many of them are expensive white elephants that exist only because of a legislative mandate and therefore lack any humane features whatsoever.

It is anticipated that rural areas or areas made up of small county seats will eventually form a program of regional services that will include a correctional facility serving a broad geographical area. Local jails will serve as a substitute for detoxification/detention facilities for short-term inhabitants such as the drunk driver. They also will continue to function as temporary facilities for offenders at the time of trial, for those awaiting bond, and for those waiting to be transferred to another facility.

Regional jails could serve as many as four or five smaller counties on a shared budget. They are foreseen to operate under a combined regional council of governments where per diem rates would be assessed and where a variety of services and programs could be centrally utilized. To ensure correctional effectiveness and to meet the needs of the inmates, it is suggested that all occupants should be those who have been sentenced rather than those who are awaiting trial. There may, by necessity, be a few offenders who are awaiting trial, but these should be segregated from the population mainstream.

Local jails cannot provide rehabilitation programs and can only offer custodial care. Neither can most small communities afford the luxury of budgeting for any more than the basic needs of the inmates. This economic factor becomes even more of a reality when there may be prolonged periods without any occupants in the local facilities other than perhaps the town drunk sleeping it off. Sheriffs of smaller counties are faced with a "family-run" operation of local jails and thereby may be distracted from other needed duties such as investigation and apprehension, which should be their primary functions.

Regional jails can possibly provide meaningful time utilization of the offender, can provide physical and mental health services as needed, can establish and maintain better inmate control, and can do all this at a reduced cost when predicated on a sharing basis. Therefore, cost effectiveness and program diversity are products to be considered in addition to the impact of mere punishment of the offender. Because judges fail to effectively "punish" due to a lack of meaningful alternatives, the courts openly become targets of criticism for being ineffective in the processing of many cases and thereby not fulfilling a deterrent role. Regional jails would allow the courts better utilization of meaningful alternatives at the time of the sentencing of offenders.

DIVERSIONARY PROGRAMS

Almost any act that attempts to throw up a roadblock could qualify as a diversionary gesture. However, when we address diversionary programs in the area of corrections, we speak specifically of meaningful alternatives to legal action such as an arrest and a court appearance. We project that such programs will not only increase in the future but will become more diversified.

Most diversionary programs, as they now exist, are directed toward juvenile offenders. Few such programs are in existence along the same functioning lines for adults, with the probable exception of those for certain substance abusers in a detoxification gesture. In matters such as the latter, many cities either have in existence or have access to "drying-out centers" where those persons can be placed rather than being jailed.

The author believes that such a diversionary program could be expanded to include at least one other area, that centering around domestic affairs. We recognize that a high percentage of law enforcement calls pertain to family disturbances and neighborhood issues. It is also recognized that this is one of the most dangerous situations for the law enforcement officer to enter. It has been repeatedly documented in law enforcement literature that more police are physically beset upon in responding to this specific type of call than any other. Therefore, although it seems likely that the law enforcement officer will still have to put out the initial fires of conflict and assume a continuing role in family mediation, it is suggested that he should be able to utilize specific services of a domestic/human relations agency for assistance on a referral basis. It does not make sense that law enforcement personnel should continue to play a peacemaker role repeatedly on behalf on one family and to do so over and over again without any measurable success.

Like many diversionary programs, there will be certain limitations to overcome. Most existing family-type services are limited to large urban areas and are limited as to operational hours. It does appear, however, that there may be an increase in the type of services provided that will serve as a more meaningful alternative than taking such cases to court and thereby compounding the size of the court dockets. With the assistance of such agencies, the police will be able to exercise greater judgment for purposes of determining arrests as opposed to referrals for services, for example, to some type of diversionary program.

This suggested diversionary program, on a broad and perhaps idealistic scope, would encompass several different types of cases.

1. Domestic problems on a family level.
2. Neighborhood issues that currently are resulting in complaint/counter-complaint matters.
3. Certain incidents where the sources of conflict arise out of discriminatory acts between ethnic/minority groups, primarily due to racially centered confrontations.

WORK-RELEASE PROGRAMS

There will certainly be an increase in the number and type of work-release programs within corrections. Such an increase will arise out of sheer economic necessity related both to the cost of incarceration and to the need to defray subsidization necessary to provide for the family of an offender during the period of time the offender is in custody.

Such work-release programs may take one of two possible forms. One form would see the offender released from jail within the community to go to his regular job and to return into custody upon completion of his normal day's work. A period of extra time might be granted to allow him to take care of necessary family business in addition to his working hours.

The second form of work-release programs would utilize work crews for offenders who are not gainfully employed at the time they are placed in custody. We refer specifically here to meaningful forms of work in exchange for a minimum wage. By meaningful tasks, we are trying to avoid what could be termed "busy work"—for the sake of management or to merely occupy time. Certain seasonal jobs could be considered, such as snow-removal tasks or beautification/maintenance projects within city parks. It might even be possible to offer some type of community service projects such as providing assistance to other institutions, including such activities as menial but essential tasks for schools for the handicapped—if the offender has specific skills that could be utilized without depriving regular employees of the opportunity for a full-time job. The author can recall the use of juvenile offenders making lapboards for a local hospital with the hospital providing the material and the juveniles the labor; both benefited from the project.

A byproduct might be that outstanding attitudes and work skills could result in eventual full-time jobs for certain offenders. Although this relates to the work-ethic principle, our attempt here is not to imply that labor is sufficient to overcome criminal tendencies. We are attempting to convey the fact that it is possible to accomplish several objectives through such acts.

1. Services are rendered that are meaningful from the standpoint of having a monetary measurement at the completion of the service or an aesthetic quality that is both pleasing and functional to recipients of that act.
2. The offender indirectly is supporting his family by such an activity.
3. The concept of punishment as demanded for the criminal act is also being honored.

We project that this form of service will also go a long way toward the provision of certain management tools for jail administrators, even though this should not be the primary purpose. Although it is an empty exercise to correlate jail and prison riots with a lack of mere meaningful programs alone, the probable cause of such uprisings can be related to penal vacuums where there is nothing else to do but to think, to hate, and to react. Thus, even though work-release programs anticipated at the local jail level will probably not be the sole answer, the opportunity to function from 8 A.M. to 5 P.M. certainly breaks up the monotony of 24 hours of nothingness.

COMMUNITY CLASSIFICATION OF OFFENDERS

It may be conceivable that the classification of criminal offenders may eventually come to be a community function. We are not seeking a method of label pasting, which has been wrongfully construed to be an integral part of a diagnostic process; but we do feel that there is room for growth and alteration to be initiated either at the community or regional level. The need is for a comprehensive look at certain offenders prior to a final disposition and/or sentencing once guilt has been established.

Although the above recommendation is in keeping with some of the recommendations of the National Advisory Commission on Criminal Justice Standards and Goals,[3] there are certain variations that could enlarge upon such an approach as we foresee it. The dangers in the adjusted approach are great, and such a project should only be considered with a great deal of advance planning. One such danger is the usurping—sometimes real, sometimes imagined—of the powers of the court. If we are to deprive our judicial system of its rights of judgment and legal skills, we will have sold it down the proverbial river and created, in its place, a figurehead of sorts devoid of power and of authority. On this basis and this basis alone, many members of the judiciary would oppose such a proposal.

We do *not* envision this community classification scheme as a citizens' committee that would assume the role of directing the courts as to a disposition. The selection of key community resources that would work with the courts to explore alternatives in a presentence investigation of sorts is anticipated as being worthy of consideration and merit. We are advocating and projecting a resource jury of sorts, not to determine guilt, but to determine and advise the court on possible sentencing alternatives.

This remains a rather cumbersome concept. Its awkwardness extends to attempting to maintain a level of case selectivity for its use. It cannot be applied except to a minority of cases and would therefore demand some in-depth planning as to when and how it could best be utilized. Representation by agencies and services would be based on the fact that these same resources may be asked to provide a similar, if not singular, form of assistance at that point in time when the offender returns to the community

[3]National Advisory Commission on Criminal Justice Standards and Goals, *Corrections* (Washington, D.C.: U.S. Government Printing Office, 1973), pp. 215-18.

on parole or discharge from prison. It is anticipated that the motivational level of the offender will be greater and better capitalized upon prior to sentencing than after he has "done his time."

In addition to these local advisory groups composed of noncorrectional personnel, it is suggested, if not anticipated, that regional community receiving centers will be eventually established that are geographically removed from the prison proper. These will act on and evaluate cases that might be committed on an indeterminate-type sentence without specific placements by the courts. Such centers would work in conjunction with the court and penal systems in attempting to evaluate and effect the most meaningful placement possible on the basis of their knowledge of the offender and his needs. Sentencing, then, would be based on the ultimate decision and joint venture of the evaluation center and the judge responsible for the case.

SPECIALIZED SERVICES TO OFFENDERS

Two types of services can be expected to expand greatly in the future to assist in corrections: (1) the greater use of specialized service and (2) the growth of volunteers, especially at the institutional level. It might be expected that the future will see some intensive training of offenders in some of the skill occupations. It is safe to assume that many professionals presently have no firsthand knowledge acquired through their professional/academic training of the specific needs and problems presented by offenders. They therefore tend to meet those needs in a head-on fashion through a process of trial and error methodology. Thus, such professionals need in-service preparation to be able to train the offenders in the various skilled occupations.

While remaining in the distant future, it can be expected that there will be a realignment of eligibility factors to allow certain agencies to provide services for the offender. A possible example of such projected services might be the division of vocational rehabilitation accepting parolees based on prison classification profiles and related social prognosis.

Special-interest groups designed to help the offender will grow both in number and in their degree of effectiveness and service level. Agencies such as Synanon and Bill Sand's Seven Step Program[4] will be but forerunners of new programs to come. Although self-help groups will flourish, progress will only come slowly in other areas. Some new efforts will continue to be noted. We speak here of citizenry groups wanting to bring more programs into the world of prisons as has been evidenced in institutions such as mental hospitals.

[4]Bill Sands, *My Shadow Ran Fast* (Englewood Cliffs, N.J.: Prentice-Hall, Inc., 1964), p. 205.

Probably the biggest influx will be seen in the area of volunteers working at the prison level. Although volunteers have long been active at the level of probation, and in some cases parole, it can be expected that a push will be made to create volunteer sponsors for offenders coming out of prisons. These volunteers will endeavor to assist offenders by paving the way through providing personal contacts and opportunities for jobs, temporary housing, and even temporary financial assistance until the offender can sustain himself.

CHANGES IN THE COURT SYSTEM

Our court systems are due for a major overhaul, and the time is rapidly approaching when this will become a reality. The supposition is not that the structure is rotten and decaying, but that there is a consistency defect based on the multilevels of jurisdiction. This problem, coupled with the expectations of the law by society, has reduced the court's effectiveness, especially regarding levels of jurisdiction.

Quite obviously, this is not a limited opinion. Harold Vetter and Clifford Simonsen, for example, in a study of the criminal justice system, address at length the disparity not only of the double system of the courts—federal and state—but also note that the lower courts of limited and special jurisdiction only add to the state of confusion.[5] What might be an addendum to this is that the more systems that exist, the more standards that will be applied. Charles Sheldon notes, "It is not the distinctiveness of the policies emanating from the courts that sets them apart, but the characteristic manner in which these policies are arrived at and the unique nature of the authority accompanying the decisions.[6]

Another criticism is that the concept of the power of the law has been twisted and altered over the years.[7] The legal system now is conceived to be a panacea to a variety of problems, encompassing criminal, civil, and social areas. In the alteration process, it has become difficult to remember the basic premise upon which our legal system was founded and the purpose it was meant to serve. We do not mean to say that the courts should not be restricted in their function, but the forest has now become obscured by the trees. The term of *parens patriae* is no longer limited to association with the juvenile court system alone. We have become conditioned to thinking of the court as a legal father figure for all social ills that should be remedied.

Some place in the future, the court system will be revitalized and perhaps

[5]Harold J. Vetter and Clifford E. Simonsen, *Criminal Justice in America: The System, The Process, The People* (Philadelphia: W.B. Saunders Company, 1976), Chap. 7, pp. 155–180.

[6]Charles H. Sheldon, *The American Judicial System* (New York: Dodd, Mead & Company, 1974), p. 1.

[7]Lois G. Forer, *The Death of the Law* (New York: David McKay Co., Inc., 1975), pp. 183–97.

specialized. Some of the lower levels of courts will eventually come under the legislative wing of the state courts, to better ensure conformity of legal approach. It might be expected that the specialization of courts would include a delineation along particular lines of jurisdiction differing from existing models. Certainly this would allow for specialized ancillary services that are especially pertinent to correctional services such as probation. Although we can become overspecialized and engage in a form of bureaucratic scintillation, the present overload both of cases and expectations can only serve to sidetrack the judicial system from its designed purpose, as well as create increased dissatisfaction with the level of justice administered.

We have seen the growth of three such specialized courts over the years—juvenile, domestic relations, and small claims courts. The feeling of this author is that this is merely the beginning. As our prisons continue to bulge, and if community classification of offenders comes to be, then it can be expected that we will eventually see a specialized criminal court dealing exclusively with criminal behavior. Our courts, as they now function, must deal with a multitude of cases and thereby do not allow for much more than summary expertise by their judges. This will change, and law schools will alter and expand their program content to meet those specific needs.

PURCHASED SERVICES

Because of an ever-increasing caseload as well as a greater diversity in the type of offenders—to include white-collar and political offenses that seem to be on the upswing—it will be less and less probable that corrections will be able to provide the comprehensive and diversified level of services needed. We therefore can anticipate a subcontracting of sorts to provide some of the services now totally lacking or lacking in sufficient number to be influential in the rehabilitative process of the offender.

It is now commonplace to purchase clinical services at the community level. Mental health services, both from public and from private practitioners, are used for evaluation, diagnosis, and treatment purposes at this time. In some instances, the offender must be self-subsidizing for certain forms of this process, usually treatment. In most instances, however, the agency of referral may pay a percentage of the treatment costs and, more often than not, will be responsible for the evaluation/diagnostic fees in full. We predict a greater use of such services, especially where the courts or other institutions are unable to mobilize their own resources and staff for this particular need.

The reader can look for an increase in the purchasing of other services for offenders as well. Although a minimal number of these projected programs might, and in a few cases have, been filled by volunteers, the impending stress on a total push will more than likely tip such programs over into the area of commercial suppliers.

Perhaps the most specific example that can be conceived of is the attempt to upgrade certain basic deficiencies that have long been associated with probable contributing causes to criminal and delinquent behavior. We address here factors such as specialized tutoring for remedial skills, certain forms of training for vocational reasons or educational-type programs for specific offenses/offenders, and the development of certain social skills that may be attributable to, for example, cultural deprivation.

It is a futile gesture to advocate that the juvenile or young adult offender try to obtain his G.E.D. or return for his high-school diploma if he does not know how to study or if he is too deficient in basic communication skills to cope. Such corrective services may be provided for either on an individual or group level by purchasing help from community resources.

What we may see in specialized areas of training to come are courses that take a semi-educational approach to areas of dysfunctioning. Chronic traffic offenders will find themselves in training programs both at the classroom and road level. Substance abusers may be subjected to a variety of rehabilitation stimuli that deal with such things as physiological results of continued abuse, and these courses would be taught by purchased medical personnel.

Cultural/social deprivations are less easy to define. Let us use a specific example from my past experience. A probationer of the author's, despite the fact that he possessed some marketable skills plus a lot of desire and a need to work, could not seem to find employment. When I checked with some prospective employers he had been referred to, I quickly discovered that he had made a rather routine and self-defeating approach in his quest for a job. His initial remark was, "I don't suppose you need any help, do you?" The negative connotations, which he didn't realize he was using, garnered an equally negative response, "No, we don't." This type of self-defeating approach can be avoided by training in basic social skills. Such courses are often provided through commercial programs that can be modified to include treating those inadequacies that exist not only out of sheer ignorance but also out of social/cultural deprivations.

Perhaps the most common area of purchased services, and one that will continue to expand, is the halfway house concept. Because of its importance and its rapidly increasing state of commonality, it deserves more than a brief examination.

HALFWAY HOUSES

Halfway houses, sometimes referred to outside the realm of corrections as "recovery placements," are where the future of corrections lies. The halfway house is usually conceived of as a placement of a transitory nature. The general tendency is to think of such a service as being provided for the individual to recover/remobilize *after* his release from an institution. This is not necessarily so in corrections since such placements can and are often utilized *prior* to the offender being committed to a correctional/detention facility. Therefore, this transitory state is applicable to both probationers and parolees, not just in lieu of incarceration, but to serve as a remobilization center of sorts.

Our discussion here of halfway houses could have figured into those categories of projection made earlier in this chapter. But because of the variety of functions this service assumes, we have decided to give it independent treatment here. We see at least three basic directions that this correctional approach may take, as discussed below.

Halfway Houses as Diversionary Programs

Halfway house placements in community-based programs have primarily been utilized for juvenile offenders. The basic purpose is, of course, to attempt community placements in lieu of a commitment to a juvenile detention facility and to focus primarily on what are commonly referred to as "status offenders." There are several offenses peculiar to juveniles that can result in their apprehension and thereby the possibility of the acquisition of a police record. These specific offenses would not constitute, in any way, an act for which an adult could be arrested. Offenses that fall into this category would be habitual truancies from school, runaways, and being beyond parental control (child in need of supervision).

Such behavioral acts in juveniles can usually be related either to some handicaps that are beyond the control of the child, such as a learning disability, or to factors in their immediate environment that contribute to such dysfunctioning, such as an alcoholic parent or a general breakdown in communication and interpersonal relationships. These offenses (as listed above) do not represent bona fide crimes since they have no comparable counterpart within the adult area of jurisdiction. Yet such chronic forms of behavior have been legally sufficient to result in the commitment of juveniles to detention facilities where there may be no physical segregation from peers detained for criminal acts. In this instance, such "status offenders" may become contaminated by virtue of association and may return to society far worse for their experiences and more sophisticated in new criminal techniques.

Halfway houses are designed to serve juveniles in one of two ways. First, they function as a crisis-intervention facility for short-term residency. The young offender receives temporary shelter until a plan of treatment can be formulated on his behalf. Second, they function as group placements for longer term care to allow juveniles to continue leading a relatively normal life through the continued utilization of community programs such as school and continued social interaction. From all outward appearances, the normal obligations of everyday living are fulfilled with the exception that the child returns to the care facility at the close of the day rather than going to his natural home.

Such diversionary programs are limited in numbers and use for adult offenders. Quite often, the focus is on specific programs related to alcohol or drug offenders, and this represents a different orientation, a treatment approach rather than a shelter/maintenance situation. Our discussion of such adult-care diversionary programs will follow under the next heading of recovery/treatment units.

Halfway Houses as Recovery/Treatment Units

The majority of private institutions that subcontract residential facilities are usually treatment-oriented in nature. There still exists some feeling that criminal behavior is pathological behavior, and therefore the level of rehabilitative success is going to have to be predicated on therapeutic intervention.

Part of this spinoff is related to the fact that recovery units were originally designed and utilized on behalf of individuals coming out of nonpenal institutions such as mental hospitals or alcohol/drug treatment programs. The theory was predicated on the possibility of a need for crisis intervention with follow-up services available to intercede in case of any relapse. The staff for the maintenance of such programs was recruited from the clinical ranks of social work, psychology, and psychiatry, continuing today from these diciplines since there exists no formalized training programs for other than adjunct roles. It has therefore been feasible to continue to staff such programs along these lines of treatment approach.

We do not favor lumping offenders together as being pathological individuals. If this were the case, most prisons could be replaced by mental hospitals, and our concerns about the future of corrections would be alleviated. We cannot, however, disregard the need to offer assistance to offenders along the lines of adjustment needs. The trend of corrections has been to contain rather than to treat, and correctional staffs in general still must remain somewhat dependent to varying degrees on other disciplines in the fulfillment of the treatment function. Other than social services agencies, there exist no other specialized services than probation/parole within the community to absorb the offender and to try to assist in effecting an adequate adjustment for that client.

Halfway Houses as Supportive Agents

The adjustment the offender must make upon his release from prison may only be exceeded in degree of difficulty by the changes necessitated at the time of his original commitment. It is not uncommon to see or hear articles in the media that deal with the long-term offender who has indicated a preference for remaining in prison rather than being discharged to a wasteland of unknowns. His family is long since lost; he is unable to work perhaps because of age, health, or a lack of skills; and he has found some security through penal regimentation. The fear of suddenly being released without any resources to use on his own behalf is overwhelming to him.

Thus, halfway houses can provide support to the parolee in many ways.

1. His immediate basic needs are met until he can become self-sustaining both emotionally and physically.
2. Parole may be denied to the marginal offender unless a workable plan can be devised on his behalf. Halfway houses may be the answer.
3. The parolee has an understanding environment that can identify with his feelings and can help him deal with them on a realistic basis.
4. His progress in the reintegration process can be adequately monitored on a regular basis, and appropriate feedback can be provided to the correctional agency responsible for the offender's accountability.
5. The halfway house may allow for the continuation of the offender's training program by allowing him ready accessibility to resources not otherwise available to him at the institutional level.
6. It allows for a feeling of trust in the offender, thereby releasing some of the emotional factors he may feel are a personal barrier to his readjustment.
7. Halfway houses can function and serve as a rallying point in the mobilization of services functional in purpose for the overall adjustment of the offender.
8. Structured environments as evidenced in most halfway house situations can be used as a testing ground for offenders on furlough in determining their readiness for parole.

Inherent Weaknesses in Halfway House Programs

Despite the fact that halfway houses represent one of the brightest hopes for the future, several obstacles must be overcome before their latent possibilities may be evidenced. At this point in time, we have only begun to be able to cope with some of the problems of growing pains relative to the expansion of halfway houses.

One major obstacle is community resentment, which continues to be a roadblock to halfway houses. The reaction of the public might well be compared to that found in the integration of neighborhoods, "I strongly support the idea, but I can't tolerate it right next door." Any attempt to place a facility within the community raises some classic complaints such as the lowering of property values, the undesirable element that it may attract, and the security factor it presents predicated on prejudgments made about the probable nature of the residents. The attempt to convey that the program is ably staffed and under the guidance of a professional person who, for example, may be a psychologist, immediately conveys the impression to the resistive neighborhood that psychologists only work with "crazy people," and the defenses quickly rise and become stronger than ever.

As a result of such public defamation, alternative placements may have to be sought, although these may not be as helpful to the offender. One of these alternatives is to seek individual residencies for offenders in rooming houses, motels, or at the local "Y." Instead of being integrated into a program and an understanding unit of assistance, the offender becomes socially isolated and thereby internalizes the bitterness of his fate. Some offender housing programs open their doors under clandestine circumstances, without either fanfare or community awareness, and thereby further arouse the wrath against corrections in general. Another device used to obtain offender housing is to seek governmental condemnation of an area, pay the owners a token price, tear down or remodel the existing structure, and set up housekeeping. Suffice it to say, rather than attempting to enlist public support, such alternative housing may cause the alienation process to grow because of these so-called underhanded methods.

A second obstacle to the expansion of halfway houses lies in a lack of any empirical evidence as to the correlation of halfway house placements and the reduction of recidivism. Again we find ourselves facing the old dilemma of what constitutes success. Different programs measure factors in different ways, and there may well be some serious questions posed as to the lack of objectivity in efforts to sell the merits of a program.

Following the publication of *Courts* by the National Advisory Commission on Criminal Justice Standards and Goals, in which it was suggested that a moratorium be declared on the building of new state institutions for juvenile offenders,[8] the State of Massachusetts quickly closed all of its state and county training schools. In an effort to evaluate the effect of such an act, the Harvard Law School Center for Criminal Justice undertook a seven-year study. At the time of this writing, the results have not been published in full. It would have been interesting to have reviewed the findings in conjunction with this part of our study.

In October of 1976, Andrew Rutherford and Osman Bengur authored a study in which they attempted to examine short-term community institutions for juveniles and to evaluate their level of effectiveness. With the prefatory warning that recidivism should not be used as the sole criteria in determining correctional policy, the general consensus seemed to be that all surveys conducted revealed that alternatives in programs have had no greater impact than programs of incarceration.[9]

[8]National Advisory Commission on Criminal Justice Standards and Goals, *Courts* (Washington, D.C.: U.S. Government Printing Office, 1973).

[9]Andrew Rutherford and Osman Bengur, *Community-Based Alternatives to Juvenile Incarceration* (National Institute of Law Enforcement and Criminal Justice, Law Enforcement Assistance Administration, U.S. Department of Justice, October 1976), pp. 29-30.

Correctional research remains weak. There are so many variables that may account for the conclusion from Rutherford and Bengur that we cannot be certain of its finality. There are many unanswered questions relating to the degree of control at the community level placement. For example, how does one establish the relationship of accessibility to crime versus the lack of opportunity of those in custody, and changes in criminal patterns relative to mode of operation and frequency level? The establishment of a valid testing model is prejudiced when comparing custodial and noncustodial groups on the simple premise that freedom to exercise judgment and response is restricted within the one group.

A third obstacle for the expanded use of halfway houses is that there exists little other than a rather nebulous form for offender selectivity for halfway house programs. John Pettibone, writing in *Federal Probation,* states that certain offenders are not suitable for community-based programs because public fear of these specific types of offenders will subsequently reflect an increase in the commitment (recommitment) rates.[10] We have become dependent on some rather routine criteria for determining the prognosis of the offender, and the process is hardly foolproof. The judge must be guided by legal precedents and/or feedback from his probation department if his court has such a service. The paroling agency must rely on the institutional track record of the offender, which may be inadequate or disguised, and on the findings of the prison classification committee. By these methods, the fate of the offender is cast.

Halfway house programs can be virtually destroyed by the inappropriate placement of certain offenders within their midst. Offenders, even when at bay, are notorious at covering their true feelings and reactions when it benefits them to do so. Most psychometric devices can do little other than measure tendencies, not absolutes. Because of the offender's desire to "fake good," it becomes more commonplace than is desirable to place square pegs in round holes. Because of the diversity of offenders, proper assignment of candidates to halfway house programs is difficult to achieve.

THE PLACE OF PROBATION
AND PAROLE IN THE FUTURE

Although the courts and the penal system may carry the most clout, probation and parole officers have certainly carried a fair share of the criminal justice load over the years. The hope for offenders has to be predicated on their ability to relate rather than to react. Their prognosis would appear to be more hopeful if they can relate to and work with their supervisor rather

---

[10]John M. Pettibone, "Community-Based Programs: Catching Up with Yesterday and Planning for Tomorrow," *Federal Probation,* 37, no. 3 (September 1973), 3.

than if they react out of fear of the system. This is not meant to be a sentimental salute by an old soldier; it is a statement of fact. Change, treatment, rehabilitation—all are products of individuals working and sharing together. It is for this reason that probation and parole services will be difficult to dislodge from the correctional system, for it is people working with people, the only profitable way to effect change.

Probation and parole are emotionally charged social issues. Although it has long been acknowledged that prisons exist as a necessary evil, the shift in critical thinking is now focusing more and more on the roles of probation and parole in an attempt to measure their respective levels of service delivery. Probation has come in for its share of criticism as being a method of sheltering offenders and generally lacking in control. Currently, parole is also under the gun with much discussion centering around the issue of whether or not it should be abolished completely. The author favors the retention of both services personally and focuses here on some probable alterations in functions that would enhance their longevity.

Probation

Several references have been made throughout this book about the stigmatism of crime based on the concept of a "free will" choice by offenders. This thinking will gradually diminish as greater emphasis is placed on crime as being generally socially determinable. The stage has already been set for this philosophy to emerge. More and more offenders are not being processed through the criminal justice system that have political and ideological causes that separate them, in many senses, from the common criminal. As such, both the courts and the correctional institutions are largely inadequate to deal with little more than the overt characteristics of such offenders.

One of the more pronounced roles that probation will eventually assume is that of a sentencing advisor to the courts. It might be said that this is one of the key purposes in the use of the presentence investigation as it is currently being used. Certainly PSIs should include some diagnostic and prognostic thoughts as to the capabilities of the accused to either respond to supervision or to continue to offend despite interventive efforts. In this respect, probation is fulfilling its part as the role of court advisor.

Probation, in the future, will eventually enlarge on this function. This author has enjoyed both the ego trip as well as the professional obligation of having certain judges indicate that they have ordered PSIs for the purpose of wanting a second opinion. There certainly is nothing wrong with such a judicial practice as this. Doctors often seek the assistance of associates even when a customary part of their professional training is the development of diagnostic skills. Why should not judges utilize similar resources? A judgeship must often be a very lonely position. The judge alone must make a social as well as a legal decision at the time guilt has been determined. He must also do this devoid of any assistance from other professionals within the courtroom since neither the prosecutor nor the defense attorney can assume an advisory role. Although legal precedents exist, the only source on the social factors of the case and offender that may be available to the judge is from the court's probation department.

The judge has no personal training beyond experience and intuition upon which to evaluate the needs and contributing social factors to the state of the offender. Law schools cannot adequately provide for this training. A statement from Frank D. Day best characterized this dilemma.

> Modern psychiatry to the contrary, the criminal law is grounded upon the theory that, in the absence of special conditions such as duress, compulsion, etc., individuals are free to exercise a choice between possible courses of conduct and hence are morally responsible. Thus it is moral guilt that the law stresses.[11]

It is, then, the expectation of this author that probation may be utilized by the courts in a confidante role more than ever before. If, in fact, crime may be socially determinable, the corollary that becomes pertinent to our discourse here is that a social solution must be from within the community context rather than from without. This should be the role of the social scientist rather than a restricted legal approach of an artificial solution through the incarceration process. The ideal probation/parole officer then might be constituted as a social scientist working within a legal context.

A closely related premise for this projection arises out of certain legal precedents that are bound to alter sentencing procedures and to thereby—either directly or indirectly—strengthen the supportive role probation must provide the courts. In 1949, the Supreme Court ruled that "retribution is no longer the dominant objective of criminal law. Reformation and rehabilitation of offenders have become the important goals of criminal jurisprudence.[12]

Of further significance and arising out of this decision is the realization that the sentencing function is anything but a simple process. The Supreme Court held that judges need as much comprehensive information as possible about the offender prior to sentencing. Certainly it is implied that probationary services are not only needed to be utilized more but also in more innovative ways.

The Federal Rule of Criminal Procedure 32 has equal implications relative to the expanding role of probation officers.[13] Among other matters, this law details the probation officers' duties relative to PSIs before the im-

[11]Institute of Contemporary Corrections and the Behavioral Sciences, "Evolutionary Implications of Legalized Punishment," *Criminal Justice Monograph,* 5, no. 3 (1974), 18.

[12]Williams v. People of New York, 337 U.S. 241, 248, S. Ct. (1949).

[13]P.L. 64-96, effected December 1, 1975.

position of sentencing and the disclosure of the contents of that report to the defendant upon request. The result is an emphasis on more professionalism *before* sentencing rather than on the cut-and-dried role of supervision and surveillance, which is often considered to be the primary function of the probation profession.

Our predicated trend in probation should be becoming apparent, that is, a greater role in activities pertinent and prior to the sentencing act. A further perceived function of probationary services will become apparent in the eventual use of community classification programs. The new pattern in corrections may be for more diversification in offender placements. This is obvious from our discussion of status offenders among juveniles and the peculiarity of their needs. It is to be anticipated that the bulk of the work in the community classification process will be absorbed by probation officers.

Two functional obligations of probation in this expanded role have been addressed but not placed into the new context as it is idealized. First of all, the concerns of the court must be conveyed—in a nonprejudicial manner—to the community classification committee to allow for an objective decision and subsequent finding. Certainly a large part of this investigation will be assigned to probationary staff. Second, as an officer of the court and confidante to the judge, probation will be responsible for the compiling of the total findings of the community classification committee and its subsequent recommendation to the court. Again, as in a presentence investigation, the inclusion of volunteer advisors as a part of the court's team will broaden the scope of probation services as they are now known.

Probation must also expand its level of services. One of the most neglected areas to date is the provision of services to courts and offenders at the misdemeanant level. Although probation has had the reputed role of intervention, the level of intervention has only rarely permeated downward to the point of dealing with lesser offenders. Probation has been ignored at this court level for a long time and for a variety of reasons.

1. Most lower-level courts in lesser populated areas are "part-time" operations, perhaps convening once a week or on an "on call/need" basis.
2. Such courts do not feel the need for probationary services due to the following:
   a. A lack of volume of cases.
   b. An equal lack of budget.
   c. A lack of judicial professionalism based on the fact that this may represent a secondary job and ranks beneath the priority of a private practice.
3. There exists little by way of research to document the needs of this type of offender. As a result, any services provided are usually the domain of nonaffiliated court/correctional agencies.

4. Little significance is attached to certain forms of behavior at the lesser court levels. For example, this author recently finished reading a study that attempted to explore the makeup of a deviant driver. The ultimate conclusion was that the more miles an individual drives, the greater are his chances of receiving a ticket. Suffice it to say, any and all courts should be concerned with intervention, and those courts who avoid this responsibility to foster change are deficient in their duties.

5. The variations in the levels of "courts," i.e., police courts, magistrate courts, justice of the peace courts, etc., do not make for any consistency of justice, let along for unification and a determination of the needs of the offender.

6. Probationary services at this level are often less glamorous as to duties, pay, and professional recognition of services both attempted as well as rendered. Therefore, it is difficult to obtain qualified agency personnel.

It is predicted that if regional jails come into existence, a probation officer will be assigned to each such institution. Not only will he be fulfilling the classical duties of his office, he may also find himself functioning as an ombudsman of sorts concerned with various needs of the offender in custody. Although many probation officers have been accused of being Pollyannas, most members of the profession are concerned about human rights and weaknesses on both sides of the social/legal fence(s). Probation officers have also—unofficially and sometimes unknowingly—functioned more as public relations personnel for the correctional system than any other position *on a continuing and routine basis,* parole excluded. Such placements as in regional jails enhances this function as a community corrections specialist of sorts.

Parole

Parole is the end link in the criminal justice chain. Because of its position, it not only represents the ultimate end in the continuum of attempted change, but it is extremely vulnerable by virtue of its placement. As a youngster, we often played a game called "crack-the-whip." I am certain that many readers are acquainted either with this game or its variations. Those who have engaged in or watched it know that the tail-end position is the most difficult to maintain and the least desirable. Parole is in this position.

In the correctional chain, parole has collected as much if not more abuse than any other of the links. The law enforcement officer has fulfilled his function at the time of apprehension and waives the offender to the court. The court, in turn, upon conviction, may waive the offender over to probation. If the offender "blows it," the probation officer obtains the necessary legal sanction and waives him over to the penal system. The penal system eventually disgorges the offender to a parole status, and like the old song about the "Farmer in the Dell," parole stands alone. The ultimate judgment made about the reformation of the offender is determined, after this lengthy process, while he is under parole supervision. His adjustment is reflected upon and the blame for failure is inappropriately placed upon the immediate agency. In the vernacular, if probation is sometimes used as the garbage can for the courts, parole might be compared to the city dump, for it collects all that are spewed out from many sources.

It is along these lines of reasoning that the contemporary discussion for the abolishment of parole has, in part, been predicated. As Maurice Sigler, ex-chairman of the U.S. Board of Parole, phrased it, "Parole has now become the scapegoat of all of corrections' ills."[14] We know that prisons are generally not reformative in philosophy except through inmate suppression. We know that the high commitment rates to penal institutions demand a certain number of administrative "outs" for some inmates because of overcrowding. We also know that the true criteria for determining parole readiness are obscured and inadequately researched. These factors alone have helped cock the weapon of destruction and pointed it at the heart of parole services. Is the death knell inevitable? The arguments rage pro and con.

Proponents of parole feel that the flaws that exist can be relatively easy to overcome. The arguments they present include inappropriateness of the numbers sentenced to prisons, inadequate penal programs, inadequate methods of evaluating inmate readiness for parole, and the inconsistency of paroling authorities. The fault of parole failure, they would say, is not necessarily the inadequacies of the line officer who supervises; rather the inadequacies lie within the system that feeds into the parole officer's caseload.

Sentencing disparity certainly has contributed to variations in parole effectiveness. For example, parole boards and penal authorities may be in common agreement that an inmate is ready for parole, but since the sentence as originally imposed regulates, in part, the time that must be served before parole can be considered, the power to release the offender is denied by legislative definition. Also, judges may commit certain offenders to prison for specific reasons other than punishment purposes, such as for treatment or training, whereas in all probability the offender could better utilize community resources because of prison program inadequacies. In summary, parole should not be blamed because of inconsistencies in the sentencing process.

Opponents of parole are recommending the determinate sentence, stating that this is more fair to the offender and will eliminate the need for parole. Two realities speak of the fallacy of this thinking. First of all, the chance for an early out via parole is an incentive for good behavior on the part of the offender. The denial of this privilege may only serve to create greater

---

[14]Maurice H. Sigler, "Abolish Parole?" *Federal Probation,* 39 no. 2 (June 1975), 42.

management problems at the prison level. Second, such thinking precludes the possibility of the self-reformation of offenders who want to conform because they feel the need to change rather than merely conforming for purposes of external rewards.

The author does not anticipate the dissolution of parole services at any time in the future. It is felt that if anything dramatic takes place, it will be to strengthen parole services, and this will occur along some of the following lines.

Changes in the Use of the Indeterminate Sentence   Perhaps unfairly, the author made the statement earlier in this book that the indeterminate sentence has been used as a form of a judicial "cop-out." This statement, in hindsight, should be clarified to say that this is only partially true. It applies only to those judges who fail—for whatever reasons—to view the social facts of the offense and the offender along with the legal implications. In effect, these judges are placing the burden of the sentence on the prison classification system and parole authority.

Although indeterminate sentencing will continue to be utilized, it is predicted that legislation eventually will make the task simpler and more refined. The courts will commit, but the time element for the commitment period will eventually be removed (by legislative action) from the hands of the courts almost entirely. Only certain offenses will remain under the governing determination of the court system. Even so, there will be provisions within the law to alter this time element when it is determined feasible on behalf of the offender to do so.

Greater Uniformity Among Paroling Authorities   There remains a great deal of inconsistency in methods of reviewing cases and making determinations for parole eligibility. Part of this may be attributed to the initial sentence as imposed by the court and sanctioned by the law. Decision making for parole remains somewhat of a guessing game, and reality testing is limited. Changes in the law will greatly assist the revisionary process.

There will come to pass a great deal of legal intervention to create and to enforce standards relating to parole authorities and the method used for determining parole eligibility. Parole board members, in some cases and areas, have become tainted because of political overtones, and it is suggested that this may be one of the primary and causative factors for the need to overhaul the system. As part of the housecleaning, it may be expected that parole board members will be required to undergo extensive training, which is virtually nonexistent at this time. It also is predicted that parole boards may be infiltrated by new members who are professionals in fields other than corrections.

An Increase in Preparole Programs   The concept of preparole programs is not new or unique. Unfortunately most such programs exist within either the walls or the shadows of the parent penal institution and represent little more than an honor ward or cellblock. Others take the form and name of honor/work camps, programs that have come in for a great deal of abuse and discussion at this time due to what appears to have been some inappropriate and untimely placements.

Preparole centers will grow, and in conjunction with their growth, there will be an increase in the tempo of furloughs. Most centers will eventually be regionalized rather than located in metropolitan centers as is customary at this time. Their programs will become more intensive, with a greater integration of specialized community, noncorrectional types of services. Quite probably, parole boards will operate out of these centers, more so than out of the prison proper, which is now the rather general rule. It would not be surprising to see these centers become conjugal in nature so the spouse can also become involved in various aspects of the program.

Correctional Unification

In order for probation and parole to get their respective acts together, they are physically going to have to come closer together in their working relationships. This may well mean an administrative consolidation of sorts. This idea is not totally new. The National Advisory Commission on Criminal Justice Standards and Goals called for this in 1973.[15] Yet, as noted by Daniel Skoler of the National Institute of Law Enforcement and Criminal Justice, in this country only seven states "can claim integrated departments which have brought together all or substantially all recognized correctional functions.[16]

There is some evidence that such a process would work. The federal system has, for example, used staff members in the simultaneous roles of probation and parole officers. But the success of this new projection is questionable since there are separate administrative governing bodies in the federal system. However, some state systems have experimented with one officer serving both capacities without any apparent loss of effectiveness.

Opposition to such a melding of correctional services offers some logical arguments. Some fear the bureaucratic snowball that gains in momentum and size as it rolls downhill. We may rightfully concern ourselves with agency management if there exists too much bulk. We may tread on some sacred toes, toes that have become sensitive at the lower jurisdictional levels such as at the municipal and county level. For example, how would a county-elected official such as a sheriff react to his jail being put under the jurisdiction of another level of government? Where, in effect, would we draw the proverbial line?

[15]National Advisory Commission on Criminal Justice Standards and Goals, *Corrections* (Washington, D.C.: U.S. Government Printing Office, 1973), Chap. 16.

[16]Daniel L. Skoler, "Correctional Unification: Rhetoric, Reality, and Potential," *Federal Probation,* 40, no. 1 (March 1976), 15.

Although the author cannot answer the question just posed, an obvious commentary is that political jealousy and failure to work together can result only in partial, fragmented, and inadequate services. Yet varying levels of jurisdiction and a general lack of communication tend to hinder continuity. If probation and parole deserve professional status, they must unite and work together to produce a more favorable direction, reduce duplication, and regroup to find solutions to mutual problems.

Until we learn to work together at *all* levels of corrections, we can anticipate problems. Probation and parole services will only be as effective or as weak as the overall system. As professionals, we have obligations to improve the system. We who are in these professions have entered them because there is a social demand for our presence, our services, and our responsibilities.

SUGGESTED READINGS

CHANELES, SOL, *The Open Prison*. New York: The Dial Press, 1973.

COATES, ROBERT B., "A Working Paper on Community-Based Corrections: Concept, Historical Development, Impact and Potential Dangers." Unpublished paper, Harvard Law School, Center for Criminal Justice, 1974.

FLEMING, MACKLIN, *The Price of Perfect Justice: The Adverse Consequences of Current Legal Doctrine on the American Courtroom*. New York: Basic Books, Inc., Publishers, 1974.

GLASER, DANIEL, "National Goals and Indicators for the Reduction of Crime and Delinquency," *Annals of the American Academy of Political and Social Science*, 371 (May 1967) 124–126.

GLICK, HENRY ROBERT AND KENNETH N. VINES, *State Court Systems*. Englewood Cliffs, N.J.: Prentice-Hall, Inc., 1973.

GRIGGS, BERTRAM S. AND GARY R. McCUNE, "Community-Based Correctional Programs: A Survey and Analysis," *Federal Probation*, 36, no. 2 (June 1972), 7–13.

HARLOW, ELEANOR, "Intensive Intervention: An Alternative to Institutionalization," *Crime and Delinquency Literature* (February 1970), pp. 272–316.

HARRIS, JANET, *Crises in Corrections: The Prison Problem*. New York: McGraw-Hill Book Company, 1973.

KELLER, OLIVER J. JR. AND BENEDICT S. ALPER, *Half-Way Houses*. Lexington, Mass.: D.C. Heath & Company, 1970.

KRISBERG, BARRY, *Crime and Privilege: Toward a New Criminology*. Englewood Cliffs, N.J.: Prentice-Hall, Inc., 1975.

LAMB, RICHARD H. AND VICTOR GOERTZEL, "A Community Alternative to County Jail: The Hopes and the Realities," *Federal Probation*, 39, no. 1 (March 1975), 33–39.

LATINA, JANE C. AND JEFFREY L. SCHEMBRA, "Volunteer Homes for Status Offenders: An Alternative to Detention," *Federal Probation,* 40, no. 4 (December 1976), 45–49.

LIPTON, DOUGLAS, ROBERT MARTINSON, AND JUDITH WILKS, *The Effectiveness of Correctional Treatment: A Survey of Treatment Studies.* New York: Praeger Publications, Inc., 1975.

MACPHERSON, DAVID P., "Corrections and the Community," *Federal Probation,* 36, no. 2 (June 1972), 3–7.

MARTINSON ROBERT AND JUDITH WILKS, "Save Parole Supervision," *Federal Probation,* 41, no. 3 (September 1977), 23–27.

MILLER, MERCEDES M., *Evaluating Community Treatment Progress: Tools, Techniques and a Case Study.* Lexington, Mass.: D.C. Heath & Company, 1975.

MITFORD, JESSICA, *Kind and Usual Punishment: The Prison Business.* New York: Alfred A. Knopf, Inc., 1973.

NATIONAL INSTITUTE OF MENTAL HEALTH, Center for Studies of Crime and Delinquency, *Community-Based Correctional Programs* (Washington, D.C.: U.S. Department of Health, Education, and Welfare, 1971).

New Directions in Probation: A Commentary on a Field in Rapid Change. Report of the Model Probationary Task Force (San Diego: 1973).

OHLIN, LLOYD E., ROBERT B. COATES, AND ALDEN D. MILLER, "Evaluating the Reform of Youth Corrections in Massachusetts," *Journal of Research in Crime and Delinquency* (January 1975), pp. 3–29.

Index